Surrounded...Run

Surrounded...Run

A Memoir: Formation
Volume Two

Donald K. Campbell, II

Copyright 2010
by Donald K. Campbell, II
All rights reserved. For permission to reprint any material
from this book, please contact the author at the address below.

Donald K. Campbell, II
510 Brookside Drive, Apt. 32
Little Rock, Arkansas 72205
501-219-6846
revdcampbe@aristotle.net

ISBN: 978-0-9845341-3-5

Editing and design: H. K. Stewart

Front cover photograph: Harkness Tower on the Yale campus in
    New Haven, Connecticut
Front cover inset photograph: Don Campbell on the day he graduated
    from Yale College in January 1949
Back cover photograph: Iona Community, Scotland

Ask Press
P.O. Box 251301
Little Rock, AR 72225

Printed in the United States of America

This book is printed on archival-quality paper that meets requirements of the
American National Standard for Information Sciences, Permanence of Paper,
Printed Library Materials, ANSI Z39.48-1984.

For Aaron, Paulina, Catherine,
Celeste, Grace, and Andrew

Therefore, since we are surrounded by so great a cloud of witnesses, let us also lay aside every weight and the sin that clings so closely, and let us run with perseverance the race that is set before us.

Hebrews 12:1

Table of Contents

Introduction 17
East Side Junior High School Years..22
   Starting at East Side 22
   Social Life in Junior High...29
   How We Dressed in Junior High 31
   School Politics 33
   Reading 35
   Trip to New York 36
   Impact of the War 39
   My Religious Life 42
Senior High School Years 45
   The Summer of '42 45
   Starting at Little Rock Senior High School................................47
   Faculty and Staff..53
   Study in High School 58
   Discipline at High School...63
   Academics in High School 65
   Cheerleading 68
   High School Politics 71
   Social Life at LRHS...75
   Some Special High School Friends 83
   Gordon Campbells 88
   The Browning Murder 89
   Class Structure in High School..92
   How Boys Dressed in High School...93
   How Girls Dressed During High School 95
   Home Situation in High School 97
   Being an Only Child 103
   Summers of '43-'45 104
   Transportation to and from LRHS..108
   1944 Flood 110
   Selection of a College 112
   High School Religious Life...115
   Race Relations in High School...118
   Black Baptizings...119

Sex Life in High School 119
Death of Franklin Delano Roosevelt 120
Graduation from High School 122
Self-Analysis in High School 124
How I Think Other People Saw Me 127
Psychological Testing 129
My Predicted Grade Level at Yale 130
Yale College Years **132**
My First Trip to Yale 132
First Sunday in New Haven 136
Second Sunday in New Haven 137
First Days at Yale 138
Introduction to Dwight Chapel 141
Noondays at Dwight Chapel 142
Battell Chapel 143
First Contact with Latourette 146
Bible Study/Cell Group 148
Pattern of My Quiet Time 149
Early Catholic Worship 150
Bursary Jobs at Yale College 151
Hiroshima 154
V-J Day 155
My Finances — Yale College 156
Traveling to and from Yale 159
Architecture of Yale College 161
Gym at Yale 164
Physical Activities at Yale 165
How Men Dressed 166
How Women Dressed 169
Laundry and Cleaning 171
Yale Football Games 172
Berkeley Players 176
Political Ethos at Yale College 177
Intellectual Expansion 178
Myself as the Last Speaker 180
T. S. Eliot 183
Charles Fielding Affair 184
My Senior Essay 186
Spring in North Court 189

My Last Semester	190
Pilgrimage on Vocation	197
Adults Who Influenced Me at Yale	200
Some Undergraduates Who Influenced Me	216
My College Summers	239
Ann and Hoyt's Wedding	242
Arkansas Interlude, 1949	**245**
New Haven to Fayetteville	245
Academics at the University of Arkansas	246
Life in Spring of 1949	247
Religious Life in Fayetteville	250
My First Church Job	254
Life in Summer of 1949	258
Art's Impending Marriage	260
Yale Divinity School Years	**262**
Returning to New Haven	262
First Days at Yale Divinity School	263
YDS Orientation	264
Start of School at YDS	267
My First Semester	269
First Year Cell Group	273
Beauty of the Fall	275
Appendectomy	275
First Year Friends	277
First Year Disillusionment	280
Glimpses into Uncle Ken	281
First Year Social Life	287
Ben Marais	289
Episcopal Bishop	290
Inter-Seminary Conference	291
First Year Spiritual Life	293
My Finances at YDS	295
Summer of 1950	297
Lizzie Nowden Bonner	301
Returning to YDS in 1950	304
Early Memories of Marnie Smith	307
Second Year Courses	308
Under Care of Presbytery	314
Trip to Buffalo	316

Holy Cross Monastery 317
Art and Florence in New York 319
Thirza Jones 321
Second Year Friends 322
Thoughts of Taking a Year Off 325
End of School, 1951 327
Intern Year **329**
Larned State Hospital 329
Credo 334
WaKeeny, Kansas 335
Grandmother's 90th Birthday 337
Boys Industrial School 339
Chuck Gerkin at Boys Industrial School 344
George Chauncey at Christmas 346
Bellevue Hospital, January-March of 1952 347
My Psyche in New York 353
Living in New York 355
Dating Ann Williamson 359
Looking for a Job in Arkansas 360
Cotton Plant, Arkansas 361
Ministry in Cotton Plant, Arkansas 367
Dating Ann in Summer of 1952 376
End of Intern Year, Return to Yale Campus **379**
Trip to New Haven, 1952 379
Returning to YDS, 1952 380
Third Year Courses 387
Some YDS Professors Who Made an Impression on Me 393
Dating Ann in Fall of 1952 398
Christmas and Ann in 1952 400
Presbyterian Progress 403
Christmas Church Life in 1952 405
Winter of 1953 407
Engagement in Spring of 1953 411
Ordination, Marriage, and My Fulbright Year **414**
Our Engagement Announcement 414
Getting Ordained 415
Ann in Summer of 1953 419
Fullerton Wedding 421
Orange Street Church, Hot Springs, Arkansas 422

Wedding Rehearsal 424
Wedding...425
Honeymoon and After..430
Crossing the Atlantic...432
London in 1953 436
London to Edinburgh 437
Robin Barbours, 1953-54...439
South Street No. 17..442
Start up at St. Mary's 447
Health Care in Scotland..451
My Finances – Fulbright Year 452
Snow in Angus..453
Thanksgiving in St. Andrews 454
Donald Baillie..456
Christmas in 1953 459
Winter Activities in 1954 464
Church Life in Scotland..467
Eating in St. Andrews...475
Friends in St. Andrews 478
My Relationship with Ann in 1953-54..................................485
Spring 1954 486
Start of Summer in 1954 493
Austria-Germany in 1954 498
Theological Students Conference..500
Geneva Waiting for Our Ship 504
On the Mauritania..506
Living While We Were Waiting 509
Epilogue: The Shifting of Gears..514

Dear Grandchildren—
Aaron, Paulina, Catherine, Celeste, Grace, and Andrew:

In volume one of my memoirs, *Surrounded ... Run: Beginnings*, I told you about the first 12 years of my life, through the end of the seventh grade. Most of those events and developments took place in Scott, Arkansas, a plantation community about 15 miles from Little Rock. "Downtown" Scott consisted of a post office, two general stores, a rarely used train station, a cotton gin and seed house, one white and one black church, and about 20 houses. "Scott" really meant an area about 15 miles north and south, and ranging from three to 12 miles east and west. There were plantations, "places," and farms ranging from 40 to 5,000 acres, and the dominant crop was cotton. There were far more black people than white living in this area.

This was the first Delta community reached when traveling from Little Rock to Memphis. The ethos was definitely "old South." In the earlier volume, I described what that was like, as I saw it, and wrote about the impact this made on my early life.

But 1940 brought a profound change in the world, and in my life. In this volume I want to tell you about my formation in the following years. Again, at your present ages you may not be interested in this story. But by the time you reach middle age, 35 to 50 years old, you'll probably want to know about your roots, including me—what the world was like, what I did, and who I became before I was your grandfather.

Introduction

World War II started when Germany invaded Poland on September 1, 1939. I did not mention it in the *Beginnings* volume because it really had no impact on my life until the very end of my seventh grade year. The war was pretty much a stalemate, except in Poland, until the spring of 1940 when Germany captured France in May, and would have destroyed the British army if it had not been rescued at Dunkirk. It was assumed Hitler would invade the British Isles. Instead, he began a massive bombing of the cities, trying to break their will to resist. You can read more details about all this in history books or see on whatever form of videos exist when you get interested. What you will not learn from those sources is the influence all this had on me for the next 14 years.

The war had been "over there" until the fall of France and the threat to Great Britain, and German submarines began sinking ships carrying supplies to the British. The big question was whether the United States would get involved. Some people felt we must go to the rescue of the free democracies (called the Allies) against the totalitarian dictatorships in Nazi Germany and Fascist Italy (called

Our house at Scott as it appeared in the 1940s.

the Axis). In that same year of 1940, the United States was involved in a Presidential election. Franklin D. Roosevelt, a Democrat, was running for an unprecedented third term. There was a real battle in the Republican nominating convention between Senator Robert Taft and a businessman named Wendell Wilkie. Although 98% of the people at Scott were Democrats, the Arthur Campbells were Republicans. Daddy wanted Senator Taft, who was something of an isolationist, to get the nomination. I was in favor of Mr. Wilkie, who was much more of an internationalist. I remember staying up until the unheard of hour of one or two a.m., listening on the radio as votes were taken. To my great joy, Mr. Wilkie won the nomination. I, still 12 years old, was vitally interested in the campaign between the two. I remember being deeply disappointed when Roosevelt won in November. All our neighbors gloated.

That year, my life changed profoundly, not only because of political and economic forces at work, but because I pushed to transfer to East Side Junior High in Little Rock. Mother had majored in Latin in college and talked about it so much I was anxious to study the language. It was offered in the eighth grade in the city. Latin was not available at Scott. There was also a negative motivation for my change. At Scott, all boys in the ninth grade had to take agriculture and manual arts. I was not good with my hands and did not want to farm, and I desperately wanted to get out of that requirement. It so happened that manual arts

Margaret Campbell, my mother, in her garden in 1939.

was a requirement in Little Rock also, but it was in the seventh grade! I'm sure I was not smart enough to realize ahead of time I was achieving a double escape by transferring in the eighth grade, but that's the way it worked out. I have an idea I would have failed at woodworking or electrical wiring or anything else. As a result, I've never been able to repair anything around the house

My brother and sister, Art and Ann, went through the ninth grade at Scott before transferring to Little Rock. Students wanting to meet the admission requirements of a really good college had to spend their senior high years in the city. But transportation from the plantation to Little Rock Senior High was difficult and expensive.

Arthur W. Campbell, Sr., my father, in the late 1930s.

When Art was in the 11th grade, he quit riding to school with the Hal Pembertons. Daddy had an old car he could use. One day a car salesman left a note on his car, parked at high school, asking how much he wanted to sell the car. Art took that information to Daddy who looked into it. They sold the old car, and on Valentine's Day 1940, Art drove home with a new 1940 two-door Ford. He drove that the remainder of that year.

But in the fall of 1940, the situation changed. That year of 1940-41, we were without a cook, for Mother had let Bea go because she was incompetent in that position. At the same time, Mother and Mrs. David Terry teamed up to enable Neoma Lyons to start Junior College. Neoma was the daughter of a sharecropper on the McLaughlin place. She was the first one in her family to graduate from high school. She had ambition and was intelligent. (She later went on to get a master's degree.) Mrs. Terry agreed to pay the cost of college and books. Mother agreed that Neoma could live with us and ride with us to town, and in exchange Neoma would help Mother in the kitchen.

Art was a senior in high school. Ann was transferring in the 10th grade from Scott to Little Rock High, which was located at 14th Street and Park. Neoma Lyons was living with us and needed to get in to Junior College, located at 14th and Chester. I was starting East Side Junior High, 14th and Scott. Truman King also wanted to transfer to East Side. I don't know if the Kings asked if she could ride with us, or Mother and Daddy made the offer. There was no way Truman could get there if we did not take her. So the years of 1940-41 began with the five of us riding in and back home again, leaving home about 7:00 a.m. and returning about 4:30 or 5:00 p.m. I think Art was out for intramural football that year, so he had to stay late some, if not all, afternoons. If he was going to be late, we would walk down to Hagerty's Drug Store at 4th and Main and wait for him there. Hagerty's was a general meeting place for folks from Scott. I do not remember much about the commuting that first year. There was no question that Art was in charge. At that point, Truman had not started smoking, so there was no issue about that.

A model of our plantation house made by my brother, Art.

In 1941-42, when I was in the ninth grade, Art had gone to college, so Ann, who was in the 11th grade at Little Rock High was due to drive. The only problem was that she had skipped a grade, and although she was a junior, she was only 15 and would not turn 16 until March 29. In Arkansas at that time, one could get a full license only after becoming 16. Fortunately, or providentially, my parents found a woman named Ann Crutchfield who lived at Scott (perhaps her husband worked for Mr. Bob Dortch) but taught at Pfeifer Elementary School in east Little Rock. In exchange for her driving us, she had use of the car, and Daddy paid for the gasoline. (At that time gasoline was about 12 cents a gallon.) That year, I believe our passenger list was Ann, Mrs. Crutchfield, Alice Coles, Truman, and me. Ann would, illegally, drive the car up to Scott, and back in the afternoon. This arrangement worked quite well. Mrs. Crutchfield was pleasant and cooperative. By this time, I believe I was giving Ann a hard time, but so long as Mrs. Crutchfield was in the car I did not bother my sister. That changed after Mrs. Crutchfield got out, and Ann, Alice, and I were the only ones left in the car.

America's entry into World War II did not come until December 7, 1941. Immediately, there was concern about a shortage of rubber, for most of America's supply came from the East Indies and the Japanese cut it off. Gasoline rationing did not come into effect until December 1942. We did not have to worry about gasoline coupons until then.

East Side Junior High School Years

Starting at East Side

All my life, I had been called "Donald." For some reason, I grew to dislike that, for it seemed cumbersome and childish. I'm not sure where the idea came from, but I decided that since I was going to a new school and would be associating with people who had never known me before, this was the time for me to change my name. I announced to the family I was going to introduce myself at East Side as "Don" and asked them to change to that. I do not remember any objection on their part. I am sure they slipped from time to time and used "Donald," and many of the people at Scott continued doing so for years. But with relative ease, I changed my name and hoped it would enable me to be a new person in a new environment.

I don't have a memory of leaving home for the first day at East Side Junior High School. It was a red brick, three-story building occupying a city block. It was built in the early part of the 20th century as Little Rock Senior High School (for whites) and served in that capacity until 1927 when the new senior high was built at 14th and Park. At that time, it was made into a junior high school. Little Rock had three junior highs (grades seven, eight, and nine) for white children. Because of geography and housing patterns, there was a definite class distinction among the three. East Side included a small section of "old Little Rock" big homes around south Broadway, but most of the students came from the east end of town where the houses were small and the socio-economics were low- to low-middle-class. West Side, about 30 to 40 blocks west on 14th Street, was pretty solidly middle class. Pulaski Heights was located in the hilly west end of the city were the upper-middle-class and wealthy people went. Some of the people who drove in from Scott chose to go to Pulaski Heights. I'm not sure why I was at East Side, except that was where I was assigned when Mother registered me, and it was the closest to Scott. Typical of the culture at that time, I was not aware if there were junior highs for black students, although I do think I was conscious of Dunbar Senior High School for blacks. It was

The East Side Junior High School building as it appears today (2010).

designed something like Little Rock Senior High, but in red brick rather than buff, and was much smaller.

While I can't pinpoint a memory of that first day at East Side, I do remember a blur of the first weeks there. At Scott, I knew everyone in the class. I had my "place" in the group of some 30 or so pupils, and I was a "somebody." At East Side, I knew no one except Truman King, Carolyn Alexander, and Buddy Craig. I have vivid memories of the lunch hour. After eating, we had free time, and people gathered with those they already knew from the seventh grade or from elementary school. I would go out on the playground and stand by myself, watching others play games or visit. I felt very lonely and knew I as a "nobody" in this big school. It was large not only in terms of numbers but also the building. There were three floors. Schedules differed from one student to the next, so I was on my own to find the right room before the bell went off. If I had missed that, I would have been tardy. I did not know what the punishment would be for arriving late, but I knew I did not want to experience it.

My memory of classes that first year is pretty hazy, except for Latin. It was quickly apparent that the students taking Latin were the brightest ones in the eighth grade. (The other students were taking manual arts or home economics.) But not all of them were in my particular class. I know there were two, and perhaps three, sections of Latin, for I was never in the one Truman attended. But when I began to put out feelers to make acquaintances, it was generally to the Latin students I saw in other classes. The "core curriculum" consisted of math, science, social studies, and English. During the eighth and ninth grades, one of those four was omitted each semester, so we got three semesters in each. In addition, I took Latin each semester, and I had art class or music in the eighth grade and special music for the whole of the ninth grade. We also had to take gym every semester.

Most of the teachers made little impression on me. I remember thinking some of them were not as good as their equivalents at Scott. That was especially true in math. I do recall the athletic coach who was in charge of the boys' gym classes. I hated that time. I was just into puberty, but was less developed than some of the boys, and I was ashamed of my body. I hated having to undress, then at the end of the hour shower in public and dress. There was very little time left for physical exercise because of all the undressing and dressing. And I did not like it even when we were supposed to be playing. I was not athletic, and the other boys soon found that out, so I would be the last one chosen to go on a team, and then would be given some insignificant position to play. There was no indoor place for gym, so when it rained, we didn't have to dress out and could study. I recall a number of mornings there would be heavy fog as we were driving in, and I would get up my hope that gym would be canceled. But I soon learned that in Arkansas a heavy fog in the early morning will lift by mid-morning and turn into a clear day—with no excuse in gym class. I also did not like the coarse language used by the coach. And he turned out to be in charge of the study hall I was assigned. This, too, was a letdown. At Scott, I was allowed to read novels I brought with me once I had done my homework. At East Side that was forbidden. I could only use my textbooks, and I quickly did my homework. As a result, I slowed down in my reading and other preparation, and never recovered my former speed until the 1970s in Atlanta.

While I did not like Mr. Scott (the coach), I did like his wife, who was the music teacher. It was clear from the start that I was not artistic. I also could not sing well, but I did enjoy music, so in the ninth grade I took special music. Part of that was singing. The whole class was made into a chorus. My voice, at this point, had not changed, and I was placed next to a girl who was the strongest alto in the class and told to sing quietly or just mouth the words. Part of the class was an exposure to classical music, some of which I had heard on the radio at home. Although we made fun of it, I did like it. So we had records played for us in class and learned something about the music and the composers. We were also introduced to opera. *The Barber of Seville* was coming to Little Rock that year with a full cast and costumes. We spent many weeks studying it. Mother and Daddy bought tickets, and I got to see and hear my first opera there. I guess it was also at that point I began listening to the Metropolitan Opera on the radio on Saturday afternoons. That class, for which I was not equipped in terms of talent, was very stimulating in my life by opening up the world of good music. I continue to be grateful for it.

Another teacher who had a profound influence on my life was Miss Corinne McMahan, the civics teacher in the ninth grade. At first I was very frightened of her. About the first day when I went into her classroom, I somehow sat on her desk. That set her off in a tirade. She had a "thing" about no one touching her desk for any reason. She had red hair and displayed the associated temper that day. However, a few days later she found that Sue Campbell was my cousin. She had taught Sue a few years before and liked her, so she turned her positive attention to me. I found the whole civics course interesting, but the section that was life-changing for me was a study of vocational choice. We were to study some of the options, then write a report on it. The summer before, we had taken a family trip to the East. In driving through Washington, we passed a building, and Mother commented that it was where people who wanted to be diplomats studied. I was not sure what a diplomat did, other than what I had picked up from news broadcasts, but in civics I did some research. I was intrigued by what I learned and announced I was going to be a diplomat when I grew up, and after that I might run to be President. I think the idea of President faded rather quickly, but the dream of being a diplomat stayed with me all through high school, guided me in my selection of college, and dictated my selection of a major in International Relations until halfway through my junior year in college.

A third teacher who made an impact on me was Mrs. Danner, the Latin teacher. As I have already written, it was my desire to learn Latin that led me to East Side. I had hardly started the course when I realized Mrs. Danner was a dud. My enthusiasm dwindled, and before long, studying Latin at night was a chore. I was fortunate in that Mother was available to help me as she dug up her long-unused knowledge of the language. I was not the only one who reacted negatively to Mrs. Danner. It was the general attitude of the class, and of all the other classes studying Latin. In Little Rock at that time, junior high students took three semesters to cover Latin I. In order to get any credit, it was necessary to take Latin II, one semester in junior high and the last half in the first semester in high school. I dreamed of the day when I would finish Latin II. Then at the end of my first semester in the ninth grade, suddenly Mrs. Danner was no longer our teacher. There was never any explanation of why. Was she fired? It was during the war. Was her husband called into service and located elsewhere? Was she pregnant? We speculated, as we celebrated, but never got an answer to our inquiries.

This led to a fourth teacher, whose impact was as positive as Mrs. Danner's had been negative. Our new Latin teacher was Mrs. B. B. Williams, the sister of my Aunt Marion McCain. I had been taught all my life to call her Aunt Frances, and I liked her very much. She had always been much fun when our families were together. Now, I was going to have to call her Mrs. Williams at school and Aunt Frances out of school. I learned later that when Mrs. Danner suddenly disappeared Mr. Matthews, the principal at East Side, was between a rock and a hard place. He had all these classes of Latin students, but no other Latin teacher available in Little Rock. I suspect the president of the Little Rock School Board told him about her next-door neighbor and good friend whose husband had gone off to war. Frances Vinsonhaler Williams was a graduate of Vassar where she had taken some Latin but had not majored in it. And she had never had a course in education. But she had a terrific personality. During the war, rules were waived, and on the first day of the second semester she appeared in our classroom. All at once, the class that had been so dull took on new life. The hour with her was exciting. My interest in Latin was revived. I learned more Latin in that last semester at East Side than I had in

A newspaper photo of when I was elected president of the National Junior Honor Society at East Side Junior High School.

the three previous ones. I later learned from Aunt Frances that she was one chapter ahead of us in the Latin textbook, winging her way as best she could.

A fifth teacher made a mild impression on me, mostly because of one examination. His name was Mr. Gold, and he taught science, not in an exciting way. Part of the curriculum for the year was to study the theory of evolution. He had told us what the textbook said. This had not bothered me in the least, for it was assumed in our household that what scientists had discovered was accurate and that this was the way God created the world. When the final examination came, it contained a question, "How was the world created?" Mr. Gold wrote the question on the blackboard, then he turned to us and said, "Of course if you write 'I believe what the Bible says,' I'll count it correct." Immediately 30 students, including me, scribbled, "I believe what the Bible says." Any respect I had for the man went out the window.

A sixth teacher had a lot of influence on me, but not in her field of study. She was Miss Davidson, but I can't remember her first name. She was the art teacher for the whole school. Everyone had to take one semester of art. I had done poorly during my required time, for my manual dexterity was as bad then as it is now. However, Miss Davidson was also the advisor to the Student Council. I'll tell later about my election as vice-president of the student body, but in that office I worked closely with Miss Davidson and we hit it off. One of the things I liked about her was that she would write me an excuse from gym when there was something I needed to do with the Student Council. I would have done anything to stay in her favor if she'd let me out of that dreaded hour. When I lost the race for president of the Student Council, I must have been elected the representative from my homeroom, for somehow I continued to be active. And even though I did not hold an office with the Council, Miss Davidson was able to find something for me to do almost every time gym class rolled around. I think in the ninth grade I dressed out for gym only three or four times.

In the seventh case, it was the class more than the teacher, Mrs. Taylor. This was introduction to typing. During my last year at Scott, I had taken a few lessons from Mr. Baker, the principal, but had injured my left middle finger and had to drop out, so this was really starting all over. It was the usual typing class, with rows of tables, each equipped with a typewriter. We started out with "f, f, f, j, j, j" and moved on. Even though my manual dexterity is very poor, I did catch on to typing and began to build up speed. I never took another course in typing, but learned enough from this one to use a little bit in high school and in my bursary job at college, to type all my papers in college and divinity school, to take my comprehensive exam at college by typewriter instead of long hand, and to type all my divinity school exams. I composed sermons that way, as well, and when I was forced into using computers, I had the typing skills required. It probably was the most practical and useful course I have ever taken.

Social Life in Junior High

I don't have a lot of memories about social life during the East Side years. My guess is our series of every other Friday night dances, growing out of dancing school, probably came to an end in 1938 or 1939 when Art and Stanley Keyes and Pud Steele went to high school and got involved in their fraternity and sorority life. But I am not sure about this.

Once I started going to East Side, I had little contact with people at Scott other than those who attended All Souls Church. Wayne Douglas and Dick McDonald were the two boys. I especially liked Wayne. Often he would help me take up the offering at church, for I was given the responsibility of seeing that this was done. After Wayne and I had carried the offering up front to the minister, we would return to the back, but instead of stopping at the back pew, we would go through the swinging doors and sit in the ladies' bible class room where we would visit and he would tell me dirty jokes during the sermon. We would always creep in to the back seat before the benediction so it would appear we had been there the whole time. Somewhere along the way, I got Buddy Craig to come to Sunday school and church. I guess it was after he turned 14 and could drive (illegally, for there would be no adult with him), for no one else in his family ever came. Perhaps Wayne Douglas moved, for the offering team became Buddy and me.

I remember one Sunday we were sitting on the back pew during the early part of the service. We began pulling our pant legs up to knee level and showing off the hair that was beginning to grow on the calves of our legs, competing to see which one had more hair. We were so entranced by this we were unaware of what else was going on. Suddenly there was a strange, and protracted, silence filling the room. I looked up to see the minister standing in the chancel with the offering plates in his hands. Obviously, he had just said, "Let us worship with the morning offering." I jabbed Buddy in the ribs with my elbow indicating with my head what was going on up front, and at the same time managed to pull my trouser leg down to my shoe. However, Bubby was so startled, he forgot to do the same. When we got up front, as the pastor was praying, I looked down and saw that the pant on Buddy's leg was gathered around the knee. I nudged him and looked down for him to see the situation, but at that point the minister said "amen" and we had to start down the aisle passing the plates. Buddy was frantically trying with his clothed leg to dislodge the other one tucked around his knee. It was all we could do to keep from laughing out loud right in the middle of church.

My "social" friends during East Side days were Truman King, Carolyn Alexander, and Buddy Craig, although we did not see much of each other at school. We did on the weekends and in the summer. There was a junior high sorority named CAT that Carolyn joined. This meant a couple of dances each year. I think Carolyn invited me as her date for one of them.

Once Buddy Craig got his driver's learner's permit, he and I began seeing a lot more of each other, for he would drive over to my house. We had a pier for swimming (the Craigs were also on Old River, on the other side, but no pier), a golf course, and the use of the Bob Alexander concrete tennis court, and Mother was always glad to have him for a meal or to spend the night. In all our years of friendship, I was never invited to the Craig house for a meal or to spend the night, although they were friendly in every other way. (I think Miss Elizabeth was ashamed of the condition of the house.) The house, which I later learned was started in 1861 and finished after the Civil War, was similar to ours in outward appearance. Buddy was a year ahead of me in school, so we were together at East Side only in my eighth grade, for then he moved on to high school. He filled a real hole in my life, the first male contemporary who was a close friend.

At East Side, other than the people who came in from Scott, I began to develop some "school friends," but I never invited any of them to visit me at Scott. I remember one boy named Jim Patterson, who was in some of my classes, invited me to spend the night with him, and I did go. But he and his mother lived in an apartment in a house that seemed to me below standard, and I never returned his hospitality. A girl in my class named Helen Nail invited me to her birthday party that was held at Mexico Chiquito at Protho Junction. It was the first time I ever tasted Mexican food. I felt her mother was "pushing" our friendship, and I never responded. I continued being the snob I had grown up to be in my years at Scott School. But these people were good "daytime" friends at East Side. I enjoyed them in class and at lunch break, and after school while I was waiting to get picked up to go home. Louis (he later changed his name to Carl) Brunck was one I especially enjoyed. Among the girls, I recall Christine Templeton (who moved to New Mexico before we got to high school) and June Henderson who was a lot of fun, but also very loud. After school, if I was going to have to wait for my ride, Truman and I would stroll down the sidewalk on Main Street to Hagerty's Drug Store. I remember how noisy we were, and how funny we found our stories and jokes. I am sure we were obnoxious to the people who had to share the sidewalk with us.

My driving experience started while I was at East Side. Daddy would have been a terrible driving instructor, for if something went wrong he would get excited and often mix up his directions by saying "Turn right" when he meant "Turn left." None of the three of us wanted him as our instructor. Fortunately, Fred "Tom Cat" Nowden was by this time our yardman. He was an excellent driver and was very calm in guiding us. I remember after he gave me basic instructions about steering and shifting gears and putting on the brakes, he would take me to the golf course where there was grass and nothing to run into except the greens, which he would avoid. He would have me start and stop, turn and back, and pretend I was parking over and over again. We spent many hours on the golf course before we got on the dirt roads of the plantation, and then finally on the paved county road leading up to Scott, five miles away. By the time I got my learner's permit, I knew how to drive, and as soon as I was 14, I had a restricted license that allowed me to drive on highways and in town, but only with an adult driver in the car. My parents were not as lenient as Buddy Craig's parents were, so I was much more restricted in my mobility. But it was the beginning of freedom from the plantation and Scott, and thus was a significant step in my formation. It was hard for people who lived within walking distance of friends in town and who had access to street cars and buses to grasp what a revolution access to a car made in someone's life.

How We Dressed in Junior High

There is not a lot I am going to be able to say about this subject, for I have a very hazy recall. I am not sure whether I was still wearing knickers when I went to East Side, but I am thinking that

I was not. That would mean I was wearing corduroy long pants by the time I was in the eighth grade. I am sure by the ninth I was in long pants. In the summer, other than for church or going in town, I wore white short pants or tennis shorts. Around the house, I would go without a shirt. Mother said that boys and men were welcomed at her table shirtless until they grew hair on their chests. That was the least of my problems in junior high school — or as far as that goes, in high school, college, and afterward. There were some advantages of being of North European heritage.

I would take a sweater with me to school in the fall and spring even though it would warm up during the middle of the day. Then I would use the sleeves to tie it around my waist and let it hang down behind. I had a heavier jacket to wear in the winter, but did not own an overcoat, or scarf or hat. Because I was riding to school in the family car, I did not have to stand out in the cold, as I had done when riding the bus in elementary school. I was always cold-natured.

The most distinctive fad in those years, for both boys and girls, was saddle shoes. These were oxfords that had brown leather in the middle of the shoe, over the instep, with white leather for the toes and heels. The soles were pink rubber. The goal was to have the toes of the shoes turn up as much as possible. This was easy for me since my toes are short and all my shoes have always tended to turn up in the front. I was "in fashion" on this point.

Another fad at that time was to have friends write their names in ink on the white part of the shoe. The more signatures one got, the more "in" one was. Because the signatures in ink would "run" if water was applied to them, these shoes were never polished and would get dirtier and dirtier as the year wore on. Fortunately, our feet were growing at that stage, so we had to get new shoes about every year and would start over on their disfigurement.

If I am unsure about how boys dressed, I am certainly vague about how girls did. I do know that girls always wore dresses to school, or skirts and blouses or sweaters. It would have been unheard of for one to wear slacks to school, unless there was a snow or an ice storm. In the summer, many girls wore shorts, although my sister Ann never did. The only time she wore pants was when she was going to ride a horse. I think at that stage, she would have worn jodhpurs rather than blue jeans.

I know by junior high school I had quit wearing wool swimming suits. As I recall, I wore suits shaped like men's jockey underwear but made out of some kind of stretchy material. At that point we were not wearing the boxer short style. We never wore tops to our suits in Arkansas, but when we went to New York, we were required to have tops at Manursing Swimming Club, so we would put on undershirts that had straps over the shoulders.

I always wore a suit to church, except during the summer when I would wear long white duck trousers. Year round I would wear a shirt that had a collar but no tie, with the collar folding back over the collar of the suit. This is the way I would dress for a dance or for Christmas or other special occasion. I always had two pairs of shoes, one for school and one for Sunday. In the winter they would be black or brown. In the summer they would be white. We did not wear tennis shoes except to play tennis. When we played golf, we often went barefoot.

School Politics

As I sit down to write the following development in my life, I have no idea how it came to be. It is still a mystery to me.

I had always been a leader at Scott, and I guess assumed it was my right to fill that role. But that was with people I had known since first grade, and most of them were from a socio-economic background I considered "beneath" me.

When I moved in to East Side, I knew no one except Carolyn, Truman, and Buddy. I do not remember if I was elected to the Student Council from my homeroom in the spring of 1941, but I don't think so. But an election was held for vice-president of the student body, to come from those who were going to be first-semester ninth graders in the fall. Knowing so few people and not coming from one of the supporting elementary schools that fed into East Side, how in the world I thought I had a chance to win this position I still can't understand. Also, Truman threw her hat into the race. So here we were, both new to the school, riding in the same car and competing for the top honor in our class. In the election, a girl named Patty Brown, a friend from Latin class, was elected. I came in second, and Truman came in fifth. We assumed that was the end of it, but Patty was the daughter of a Methodist minister, and during the summer he was appointed to another church elsewhere in Arkansas. This left the office of vice-president vacant. As a result, another election was held soon after we returned to school in the fall. Clearly I was a contender, with the person who had been third in the spring as my strongest competition. I knew the boy who had come in fourth, but only slightly. I went to him and asked him to be my campaign manager. To my surprise, he agreed. With the votes of his friends, and speeches on his part and mine as part of the campaign, I wound up being elected vice-president of the school! That got me involved in Student Council work that often had to be done during a free period. As I've already mentioned, Miss Davidson, the sponsor, would write notes for me to be excused from gym to do that work, and I loved it.

At the end of that semester there was another election, this one for president of the student body, who had to come from the second semester ninth graders. Justice got its revenge. I ran for president, but my campaign manager decided to do so also, and

> **Elected Vice President Of East Side High**
>
> **DONALD CAMPBELL.**
> Donald Campbell, the new vice-president of East Side Junior High school, is the son of Mr. and Mrs. A. W. Campbell of Scott, Arkansas. He is a member of the 9B2 home group, having entered from the Scott school in 1940. Donald is a star pupil, making an almost "Straight A" record ever since he has been here.
> Donald has made several extensive trips, having been to New York and Canada during the vacation last summer.
> He loves to swim, play tennis and drive a car. Reading, however, happens to be the most important of his hobbies.

A newspaper photo of me when I was elected vice-president of East Side Junior High.

he beat me in this election! It served me right. His name was Bill Prewit. He was an orphan who lived in an orphan's home. He was a nice guy and deserved the honor. But by this time, I had established myself as a leader in the school.

Reading

My reading career had started when I was in the fourth grade and read *Gone With The Wind*. Through my remaining years at Scott School, fourth through the seventh, I read voraciously. When I got to East Side, the quantity of my reading during the school year slowed down, for we were allowed to read only textbooks in study hall. But at night, on weekends, and during vacations, I continued to read a great deal. (I was not athletic, and I was too young to work on the plantation—and not too excited about doing it.) I can remember reading while lying on one of the gliders on the front porch with the ceiling fan on and also in the upstairs living room, looking down on the top of the mimosa tree and hearing the doves coo in the distance.

Some of the titles I recall were *Anthony Adverse*, *Of Mice and Men*, *The Good Earth*, and the Lloyd C. Douglas novels such as *Forgive Us Our Trespasses*. I read everything that was in our house, including *Compton's Encyclopedia*. I would look up some item, then get fascinated by the articles preceding and following it, and would go from item to item for hours. Also in our house, having been brought down from Jonesboro when Main moved in with us, was a series by Thomas Nelson Page about the South before the Civil War and during the reconstruction period. Later I learned that he was one of the most racist writers from and about the South, but I swallowed his whole defense of the Confederacy and his attitude toward black people. It took me years to recover from that indoctrination. There were several series of books from the library I enjoyed, such as the Maudie novels about a sophisticated girl from the Philadelphia area, several of the Booth Tarkington novels, and a series of Mark Tidd books about a boy who was very fat and stuttered but was very bright and creative. I also read the *Arkansas Gazette* each day and *Life* magazine each week, so I was aware of what was going on in the nation and the world.

In those junior high years, books were my companions. Art was in high school and college by then and had "flown the coop." Ann was around, but by then we were squabbling a good bit. There was no compatible boy on the plantation except Dick McDonald, and he had to work all the time. None of my parents' friends had sons my age except for Buddy Craig, and we could not get together easily until he could drive. I began to know people at East Side, but when the school day ended, I got in the car and disappeared at Scott until the next morning. As long as I had a book to read, however, I was quite content, most of the time. I came to think of myself as a loner.

I have heard that most people have done the bulk of their reading, and are better informed, by the end of junior high school than they will be for many years to come because they get involved in other activities, and the burden of homework at school gets heavier. That certainly was true for me.

Trip to New York

It was our family's custom to take a trip each August after the cotton crop had been "laid by," which meant there could be no more plowing or cultivating. Perhaps cotton poisoning could be done that late, but the real fate of the crop was up to weather in August, and Daddy could do nothing about that except fume. The weather could make or break the prospects for a good harvest. Our pattern was to go to Bloomington, Illinois, for several weeks to stay with Grandmother and Grandfather Campbell. In 1937, however, we drove up the East Coast as far as New York, then came back through Bloomington.

Again in 1941, we made the trip "up East." This was the last summer Art was at home before leaving for Texas A&M, and he objected strongly to going and gave our parents fits along the way in his adolescent rebellion. Daddy had him drive some of the time.

We went through Knoxville, Tennessee, to look at the University of Tennessee as a possibility for Ann. We drove through Virginia and took time to slow down or stop to read many of the historical markers placed along the highway. I was already very interested in history and had read a good bit about the Civil War. We went to Lexington, Virginia, where the widow of one of Mother's cousins, who had been Professor of English at Washington and Lee College, lived. We visited that campus, and I was very impressed. I always had an idea I might like to go to college there. Then we went to Lynchburg, Virginia, to see Randolph-Macon Women's College where Mother had graduated in 1918.

From there we went to Washington. I remember the night we drove in we had a hard time finding a place to stay. This was before the day of good motels, so people stayed in what were called "tourist homes." These were usually large old homes that were turned into rooming houses for people passing through. In Lexington, I remember we stayed in what had been the manse of the Presbyterian Church when President Woodrow Wilson's father had been pastor there (and Stated Clerk of the Presbyterian Church, U.S—or the "Southern" Presbyterian Church). But in Washington, Daddy could only locate a house out in the country. When he went in to check it, he was not pleased, but there was no alternative for that night. I remember he told us to hang our clothes from the chandelier in the middle of the room so we would not get bedbugs in them. Fortunately, the next day he found better accommodations in Washington for our several days there.

We did the usual tour of sights in Washington, but one stands out in my memory. The year before, in 1940, Congress had nationalized the National Guard because of the fall of France and the perilous situation of Great Britain, but the Guard had been called up for only one year. The United States was not at war, but there was a clear sense we were headed that way, so a bill had passed the Senate to extend the service of the National Guard for another year. While we were in Washington, the bill was before the House of Representatives, and our Congressman, Mr. David Terry, had arranged for us to get passes to the House. The debate on the National Guard issue was heated, and the galleries were jammed. I remember sitting on the steps in the gallery. There were impassioned speeches for and against the extension. Daddy was against the extension, as were most Republicans. We had to leave before the debate ended, so the next morning he rushed to buy a paper to see how the House had voted. The roll call had been taken about midnight, and the bill had passed by a one-vote margin. This was only about four months before Pearl Harbor. If it had not passed, the United States would indeed have been caught flat-footed on December 7.

On that trip we also went to Princeton University, and I found the campus to be beautiful. We also went to Princeton Theological Seminary (I'm not sure we understood the difference) where Grandfather Campbell had graduated in 1872. We did not go far enough up the East Coast to see either Yale or Harvard.

We also headed to Scarsdale, New York, where the Arthur McCains lived. Art happened to be driving when we went through the Holland Tunnel, and when he came out on the Manhattan side, he did not know which way to turn to get to Scarsdale. Daddy, as usual in crisis situations, barked orders that were the opposite of what he meant. Art came to a stop, and a policeman came up and told him he was blocking traffic and would have to move. Art still remembers the trauma of that situation. I don't know how, but we managed to get to the suburb of Scarsdale.

I don't remember all that we did in New York, but Aunt Marion was a wonderful tourist guide. We went to some kind of science display at Rockefeller Center where we saw a demonstration of television in its very rudimentary phase. We visited Radio City and saw the Rockettes. Art was probably more interested in them than I was. We also saw my first Broadway play — *Life With Father*. There were several sons in the play (including one about my age), and I remember fantasizing about what it would be like to have a part in a professional theater. We went to the Chase National Bank, where Uncle Arthur was a vice-president. We took in Coney Island (I think it was) with some friends of the McCains named Diffendorfer. They lived in a huge house and had a large number

Uncle Arthur and Aunt Marion McCain.

of children. The chauffeur brought around a Cadillac to transport some of our group to the beach. Mrs. Diffendorfer told him the Cadillac was not large enough and to bring the "big" car, instead. It turned out to be a limousine. I'd never seen one before.

Later, we drove up to Vermont to see Mr. Gray who had been president of the bank Daddy worked for until it went into FDIC receivership. I think that had already happened before the 1941 trip. I do remember he got permission for Art and me to play tennis on the University of Vermont courts. I was shocked that they were not clay or concrete, but just plain dirt.

We drove through upper New York state on our way to Buffalo, where we visited the Howard McCains. On our way, we passed through the Finger Lakes area. Mother had read about a famous restaurant called The Krebs at Skanneapolis. The cost was $5.00 per person, which was a fabulous price in 1941. We ate light for a day or two ahead of time to save up for the big splurge. It was worth it. We all still remember that meal of many courses and unlimited quantity.

I don't recall much about our stay in Snyder (a suburb of Buffalo) with Uncle Howard and Aunt Jane McCain except I did get to know Charles and David, their sons. I think that was the last time I saw them until I was in divinity school.

I know we came back through Bloomington to visit Grandmother and Grandfather Campbell. I guess he died the following winter. Alice Coles was due in Bloomington on her way to Arkansas to spend the winter. Art was eager to get home, for he was about to head off for college. It, like the 1937 trip, was a mind-expanding experience for me.

Impact of the War

Even in 1940, although the USA was not legally at war, there was no question that the sympathy in this country lay with the Allies. There was deep concern about the fall of France and the Battle of Britain.

When I was at Scott, there was no school-wide recognition of Armistice Day. This was to celebrate the cessation of fighting in Europe on November 11, 1918, to end "The War To End All Wars." But on my first Armistice Day at East Side, there was the sound of a bugle and a moment of silence throughout the school. It had an eerie feeling, with all the fighting going on in Europe. I suppose we took note of it too on November 11, 1941, for America was still technically at peace with the Axis.

Then on December 7, 1941, the Japanese bombed Pearl Harbor. Ann and Alice had gone to a Delta Beta Sigma (DBS) meeting on Sunday afternoon. Mother and I were sitting in the car as we waited for them for an hour or an hour and a half. We were reading the Sunday paper and listening to the NBC Symphony on the car radio. Suddenly, the symphony was cut off and a voice announced that the Japanese were at that moment bombing Pearl Harbor. I remember Mother asked, "Where is Pearl Harbor?" I replied, "I think it is somewhere in the Pacific." We could not believe what we were hearing. Before long the girls came pouring out of the house where the DBS was meeting, for some parent had called to tell her child to get home immediately. The country was in shock, and stayed glued to the radio. I guess it was the next day President Roosevelt made his "day that will go down in infamy" speech. Perhaps it was Tuesday before the formal act was taken declaring war on Japan and Germany.

People who did not live through World War II of course have no idea of the patriotic spirit of that era, and the various ways people tried to boost the war effort. This was seen as a crusade to stop the aggressive Axis powers and save the world for freedom. It was totally different from the Vietnam War when at least half the country thought we should not be there, and people expressed their anger toward the American troops; and the Iraq invasion, when there were serious doubts about the war, but support was given to the individuals who fought. World War II was seen as a fight for survival. People were asked to make sacrifices, and most did quite willingly.

There was the anxiety, especially in 1942, about which way the war might end. After Pearl Harbor and the conquest of the Philippines and Singapore and Burma, there was some real doubt about the outcome in the Pacific. And in Europe, we waited tensely for the D-Day invasion and then through the Battle of the Bulge in 1944.

There was the constant concern about brothers and fathers and friends who were in danger on land, sea, and in the air. We would hear of people getting injured and killed. I remember when Ralph

Pemberton went missing over the Adriatic Sea, and Billy Young was killed, and my cousin George Coles (a Canadian) was shot down while bombing the dams in Germany. But none of them were close to me. And for the boys in high school, there was the inevitable future of our going into the military ourselves. When I was in school I had never heard of pacifism and did not know there were provisions for conscientious objectors. It was a very militaristic environment. So a "cloud" hung over everyone, people of all ages.

Almost immediately there was a violent rise of nationalism. Songs sprang up like "Praise the Lord, and Pass the Ammunition" (based on the response of a chaplain at Pearl Harbor), "You're A Sap, Mister Jap, To Make A Yankee Cranky," "God Bless America," and "White Cliffs Of Dover." Because the US was cut off from the source of tin in the East Indies, we were urged to bring in our toothpaste tubes (for they were then made of tin) as soon as we finished with them. We'd also flatten and turn in used food cans. As I recall, we were encouraged to bring in paper to be re-used. Soon sugar was rationed. I had always loved iced tea, and put so much sugar in it that the bottom half-inch of the glass was white. I cut out all use of sugar—and tea never tasted as good again. By then we had got rid of our cows on the plantation and were buying butter at the grocery store. But butter was limited in supply, and we often had to settle for oleomargarine. It was white in a squeeze bag, but there were yellow coloring pills that could be massaged into the oleo. It is hard to remember when various restrictions came into play. There were war coupons for various food items such as coffee and sugar and meat. We on the plantation suffered very little because Daddy would have a steer killed and butchered and stored in a deep freeze plant in North Little Rock. Whenever Mother went grocery shopping it always included a stop at the deep freeze place. The only problem was that a steer had not only roasts and steaks and ground-meet, but also a heart and liver and neck bone, and various other parts of the animal we did not want to eat. Mother would give those to the black people on the place.

Another big effort was to sell War Bonds and War Savings Stamps. A $25 bond could be bought for $18.75, to be cashed when the war was over. Saving Stamps were for people who could not afford the $25 (or larger) bonds. We school children would by one or two stamps with pocket change. When a book was filled with stamps it could be turned in for a bond. While the ostensible reason was to raise funds to fight the war, the real reason was to siphon off excess income to head off inflation, for with the mobilization even prior to Pearl Harbor, factories were turning out supplies for the Allies as fast as they could, and wages were going up. The exodus of labor from the plantations to factories in Detroit and the West Coast began. Soon clothes were hard to buy in the stores. There were also coupons for shoes. And air raid practices started in all the schools. People in Little Rock (like most cities in the US) were convinced that ours was right at the top of cities the Japanese or Germans would want to bomb because of the air base at Jacksonville. We did not have to put blackout curtains on our windows at night, as people on the two coasts did, or turn out streetlights lest the glow provide a background by which submarines could spot freighters and torpedo them.

It was during my time in junior high that the scandalous executive order was issued by President Roosevelt to remove all people of Japanese ancestry from the West Coast and put them in concentration (called relocation) camps, two of which were in southeast Arkansas. But I did not know of their existence until I went to Yale in 1945. It was an open secret. And it is one of the blackest marks on the history of this country.

Some of my older relatives were already in military service. Tap Hornor and Gaston Williamson had both been in the National Guard and were called up into service in 1940 for a one-year term, that in 1941 was extended for another year. Art was a freshman at Texas A&M, a military school in which all students were in ROTC (Reserve Officer Training Corps). It was inevitable that he would be called up, for he had turned 18 on November 6, 1941. But by staying in school the summer of 1942, he qualified for Officer Training Camp rather than going in as an enlisted man.

However, the war was still pretty distant for me in these early years.

My Religious Life

I draw an almost total blank when I reflect back on my religious life during junior high school. I know I went to Sunday School and church every Sunday, for that's what people in our home did. This was not debatable. But I have no memory of rebelling and not wanting to go. This was when I would see my Scott friends. Much of All Souls' draw was the fellowship and social life that centered around it. This was true of my parents, but also of us three children. If, in the country, you didn't go to church, you didn't get invited to parties. These became less crucial as I began to function in Little Rock more of my life. But Scott social life was still important.

Mother had long since ended the childhood practice of my "saying my prayers" to her. I don't know when that stopped, but I would imagine in early elementary school. I am pretty sure I did not have any practice of daily Bible reading or prayer during those years. We always said the blessing at meals, except breakfast. That was often so rushed we did not have time, and the family did not all sit down at the same time. For supper, usually one of us kids would "say the blessing," each of us having one we had memorized. Ann had one that included thanking God for nature and the birds that sing. I would often say, "Mother, let Ann pray about the birds and bees."

During grades fourth through sixth, I had been in the Junior Department at All Souls Sunday School. Lucille Blann was not only the pianist there, but also the teacher. She followed the pattern Miss Gertrude Young had set—that is, learning the Books of the Bible, the Ten Commandments, the Beatitudes, and the Twelve Apostles. When I went into the seventh grade, and through the ninth, I was in the Intermediate Department. It seems to me Mr. Gordon Brown was head of that department. I know Mother taught there for years. She taught only the girls. I guess I was in the boys' class. I know Miss Lillian Brown was our teacher at one point. We gave her such a hard time she quit, and I felt guilty because I was one who had given her trouble. I have no memory of who took over to fill her place, and I do not remember anything I learned. We were using David C. Cook materials. As I later learned in Divinity School, there was not much to learn from Cook materials. I am sure we did not raise questions about the authorship of books of the Bible, but on the other hand we were not indoctrinated in a rigid fundamentalism. I came out of those years with little knowledge and less opinion.

I also went to worship every Sunday. I had quit joining my family in a pew up front, for we young people would sit on the back pew, on the right side. I think by this point I was taking up the offering—at least by ninth grade. Perhaps I started this when Art and Stanley and Ralph all went off to college. The minister during part of that time was a Mr. Hedges. He had a limited education, and a more restricted vocabulary. Two adjectives were his favorites. One was "meaningful" and the other was "inspiring." He would use one of them up to 20 times in a single sermon and the other perhaps 26 times. We on the back row would start at the beginning of the sermon and keep score. Every time he used either of them, the pew would rock as we stifled our giggles.

The next pastor, who I think came before I was out of junior high, was a Nazarene minister named Wesley Pruden. We kids did not like him, but at least he did have a larger vocabulary than Mr. Hedges had. Mr. Pruden had a radio program in Little Rock in which he pretended he was out in the country and preached in country language. At Scott, which was in the country, he preached in a much more "citified" style. I have little memory of what he preached about. Later, much later, during the 1957 school crisis in Little Rock and the South, he became "chaplain" to all the anti-integration organizations. If he taught racial prejudice in his sermons, I was not aware of it—but then at that point, neither I nor the congregation would have been aware, for we were all segregationists. Race was not an issue discussed in church.

I guess my feeling is that my religious life during junior high school was pretty much a wasteland. I was faithful in attendance. I did not object to anything. But I don't think I was learning much, and certainly was not growing. I had had no instruction when I "joined the church" at nine years of age. At the point when kids are moving into puberty and can for the first time begin to think adult thoughts, I was getting nothing except the habit of going.

Senior High School Years

The Summer of '42

The "Summer of '42" for me was not like the famous coming-of-age movie that was filmed some decades later. I was far less sophisticated.

My senior high experience began as soon as I graduated from East Side Junior High. World War II had drained into military service, or work in war factories, many of the men who had supplied the labor on the plantation. Yet farmers were urged to increase production at the same time. As a consequence, wages had gone up. A man would now earn $1.00 for a full day's work, and a woman could earn $.75. The value of cotton and beef had also gone up. The economy had been brought out of the Great Depression by the war effort. I was 14 years old that summer and had a restricted driver's license. Because I was able to drive a truck on the plantation (but not in town), I was paid $1.25.

Certainly the money was a motivation for my getting a job on the plantation, but it was also expected that the sons of planters would go to work in lowly positions in order to learn farming from the bottom up. Also, I suppose, there was the patriotic motive in the background, although it would have been phrased in terms of "shortage of labor." Art had been working on the farm for several years and loved doing it. I was expected to do the same, although I had always been more of an in-door than an out-door person.

As soon as school was out, I was needed to help in the oats harvest. We did not grow barley or wheat at that time, but oats were important as feed for the cattle and mules. Mules still supplied most of the power for farming, although Daddy did own a small number of tractors. Daddy planted oats in the fall. They covered those fields during the winter and were ready for harvest in the late spring. They were cut by a "combine," a power-driven machine that in one operation cut the stalks of the oat plants and separated the individual grains from the heads, thus giving the machine its name by combining what had previously been two labor-intensive processes. When the hopper on the combine was full, the operator would pull up to a one-and-a-half-ton truck on which sides, or walls, had been erected on the flat bed. The grain would be poured in. The truck would wait until several hopper dumps had been made, and then it would be driven to a storage bin for unloading by hand. The opening through which the oats were thrown into the storage bin was always higher than the bed of the truck, for the intent was to pile up oats on the inside to a level of about eight or ten feet. This was heavy work. It was also dirty, for the oats were always full of dust and some husks. Because I was the boss's son, my starting job was to drive the truck between the oat field and headquarters, where the grain was stored, and to unload it by hand, using large scoops, throwing it into the high opening. As hard and as filthy as the work was, though, I had a much easier job than most of the workers, for while I was waiting for the combine to make its rounds I could rest. But I earned my wages during the unloading process. We worked five full days, and half a day on Saturday.

Once the oats had been harvested, it was time for hay baling. This was important as feed for both mules and cattle. Various kinds of grasses could be cut, left on the ground long enough to dry, then collected by a tractor-pulled machine called a baler that compressed the vegetation into oblong cubes bound together by wire. (There were no large round bales as now seen on farms and often left in the fields for months.) These were dropped on the ground as the baler progressed through the field, and then picked up manually and stacked on a slow-moving truck that followed. On our place, the desired crop to bale was alfalfa because it was rich in nutrition for the animals. Also, the greener the alfalfa the more nutritious, but if the hay was too green, it was subject to internal combustion that would set the whole hay barn on fire. My job was to drive the truck as men loaded the bales on the flat bed, then drive to the hay barn. There, my helper and I would have to lift the bales, one by one, to the floor level of the barn and stack them neatly so they would not fall down. They, too, were dusty, but nothing like the oats. Each bale, depending on how "green" the content, could weigh from 60 pounds up to 90 pounds if the hay was green or wet.

I worked on the farm all that summer and in the process developed an allergic reaction to dust. My eyes and nose were streaming most of the time. It was the first real manual labor I had done. I sure liked earning wages that seemed like a lot to me after having had only an allowance before. What was spending-money for me, however, was real income for the men working alongside of me, mostly black, with which they had to support their families. The real negative was my reaction to the dust. This generated an allergy that some three years later, after World War II ended, disqualified me medically from serving in the military.

I was always filthy when I came in from the field, at noon and at night. During this time, Mother and Ann were carrying on their usual social life, often having luncheons in the dining room. In the past, I would have greeted the guests, even though I would not have sat at the table during a ladies' luncheon. But now I was ashamed to be seen and kept myself in the kitchen and ate in the breakfast room. I remember having some feeling of guilt for being so dirty, rather than pride at holding the job of a grown man.

We had Saturday afternoon and Sunday off work. I continued going to Sunday School and church, but during the two afternoons Buddy Craig would often drive over to our place where we would play golf or tennis (on the Alexanders' court) and swim and sunbathe. Toward the end of the summer, Buddy invited me to some "rush" parties for the high school PIE fraternity. I'll write later about the role of that boys' group in my life for the next three years.

Starting at Little Rock Senior High School

Even though I had attended East Side for two years, and had been to Little Rock High, starting school there was awesome. I can imagine what it must have been for Art and Ann, coming from Scott, especially Art, since he was the first one in the family to go.

The LRHS building, erected in 1927, was at the time of its construction one of the largest and most expensive high schools in the country. I can't imagine how Little Rock got the money to build it. Fortunately, it was finished two years before the 1929 Crash, or it would never have been completed. For those who have not seen it, it is two city blocks long, made of yellow-buff brick, with a reflecting pool and stage in front of two staircases that sweep up on both sides. Most of the building is three stories, but the central tower has five floors. There are statues over the main doors. The building is massive and beautiful.

Little Rock High School, now Little Rock Central High School.

At that time, there were about 3,000 students enrolled, all white. There was no residential white college in town, so the LRHS Tigers were the city's teams.

Fraternities and sororities were also operating at the school, but they were not recognized by the administration. Officially, they were discouraged, but tacitly they were condoned. The two big fraternities were PIE (for awhile called the Stag Club) and Delta Sigma. There was a smaller one named Tri-S. There were two main sororities—Delta Alpha Delta (DAD) and Delta Beta Sigma (DBS)—and a smaller one that I think was named Delta Gamma. There were also school-sponsored "clubs." Then there were official groupings, such as the Band, the A Capella Choir, the Civil Air Patrol. And each student was assigned to a homeroom. These were various ways of breaking a student body of 3,000 down into manageable groups where people could get to know one another.

At the top of the entry staircases on the main floor, there was a lobby. This was the gathering place before school, and to a lesser extent at lunch. Each fraternity or sorority had its "corner" where its members gathered.

Because Art had been a member of PIE, and because others from Scott, especially Buddy Craig, were in it, and also Edwin Stitt, I had been "rushed" as a legacy. I had not even been approached by the other two fraternities, and would not have been interested. I was invited to the parties, but there was no big effort to "win" me. On the Sunday when bids were extended, I heard nothing. I assumed that meant I had not been invited to join. Up to then, I would visit with people in the PIE section of the lobby before school. But on that Monday I felt this would not be appropriate, so I went directly to my homeroom—and felt desolate. It was a good experience for me, because it let me know (if only briefly) how the non-Greek majority of the student body must have felt. But later in the day, Edwin Stitt asked where I was, and said of course I had received a bid. I remember how I felt a cloud had lifted. This made a crucial difference in the rest of my high school career, for it provided me a nucleus of acquaintances, introduced me to the top social and economic level of students, and gave me a sense of identity. On the other hand, while I knew people who were Delts, and others who were not Greeks, in a sense I was somewhat removed from them. It was snobbish and could be brutal. I can see pluses and minuses on the high school fraternity issue.

Ann was a member of DBS, and through her, Truman King received a bid to that. It was part of the "Scott myth" that boys would be PIEs. Some girls were DBS, others DAD. This did not apply to Imogene Henry, but Peggy McNeil was in DBS even though she was so poor she had to work as a maid for a family on Edgehill.

If my memory is right, that first semester I took Latin (the second half of second year Latin—taught by Mrs. Chandler); English (taught by Miss Spear, whom I did not like—I compared her to a steel fist covered by a velvet glove); world history (Miss Hensley); and algebra I (taught by Mr. Ivy, I think). Latin was OK, but we all looked forward to the end of the semester when we would be through with Latin forever (I mistakenly thought). I liked world history. I did well in algebra, although I never understood it. I memorized it, made an A on the test, and the next day could not remember what we had covered. I think that first semester I made maybe three A's and one B. I also had to take physical education (I think it was three days a week) which I hated as much as I did at East Side, and for the same reasons—I was no good at sports, and I was embarrassed at having to undress and shower.

I was in Mr. Ivy's homeroom. We had to elect officers the first or second day. I guess he had us give a show of hands about the junior highs from which we had come. The largest contingent was from West Side. But there was a good group from East Side and another from Pulaski Heights. Having been vice-president of the student council at East Side, I regarded myself as something like the captain of the team. There was a student from Pulaski Heights named David Davies, who was to pledge PIE with me, but had not at the time of this election. He had gone to East Side before moving out to Pulaski Heights. I suggested to the East Side people that we talk with the PH boys and make a deal about dividing up offices, and thus take over from West Side. They agreed. I wanted to be Student Council representative, for that is what I had enjoyed at East Side. So I proposed that we elect Louis Brunck as president, me for Student Council, and David Davies from PH as chaplain, and I think we must have given PH the vice-presidency and secretary jobs. I can't remember if we cut out West Side completely. Maybe we gave them one office. Looking back, it was pretty "bare knuckles" politicking. We kept those offices for the three years in high school, except when I was elected president of the student council/student body I yielded my spot on the council to someone else. I was always a part of homeroom, but it was never where I got my sense of identity—because that was through PIE.

A major part of that first semester was being a pledge, or "hog," in PIE. We had to call all the members "Mr." If a member called "Hog" off the school grounds, we had to drop our books and lean over to dust our toes. Each Sunday afternoon, we went to a fraternity meeting at some member's home, and at the end of it the pledges had to line up, lean over, and the members would come down the line and hit our butts with belts. Some of them were gentle taps. Some members were sadistic, especially on a hog who had irritated them. Our friends in Delts were going through the same process—only they were called "Rats"; and the girls in the sororities had hazing, although not of the physical variety.

At the end of the semester there loomed "hell week." During it, a pledge was not to speak to anyone other than a member, except for teachers and family members. This made it difficult for those of us riding together in a car from Scott. For PIEs, this also meant roller-skating to school from home—except for people who lived out in the country. We could start at 14th and Main and skate out to high school. (This presented problems for those of us in the country who had never learned to skate for lack of sidewalks and pavement.) On the Monday of hell week, we had to go to a barber shop where our heads were shaved, so we stuck out clearly in the student body. Then at the end of the week, there was initiation on Saturday night. We started at Dawson Drug Store at 15th and Main. We were given a plug of chewing tobacco and were told not to spit. (That cured me of ever smoking, for I would gag at the smell of tobacco.) We carried two buckets filled with water, with a brick in each one. Every time a member yelled "Hog," we had to drop the buckets (and were warned not to spill the water), lean over and wipe our shoes. We had to walk all the way to Main Street Bridge. There, we were taken into cars, blindfolded, and driven to some undisclosed place (it turned out to be the barn of Coleman Dairy on what is now Asher Avenue). There, we were stripped naked (and it was cold in that barn) and smeared all over with used motor oil. We were made to eat and drink various things we could not see. I think one was a raw oyster with a string tied around it. I'd swallow it, then they would pull it back up and make me swallow again. I have forgotten all the things that were done to "humiliate" the Hog. One thing we were told was to reach into a jar, take out some ointment, and rub it well into our scrotum. This turned out to be "hot balm," which is an analgesic that when rubbed on an injured muscle is healing with a warm sensation but that causes excruciating pain when it comes in contact with the lips, eyes, or scrotum. Then there

A photo of me in 1943.

was the trick of tying one end of a string around the scrotum and the other end around a brick, then making the hog feel the string to realize it was connected; then telling him to drop the brick. This was very frightening. In the meanwhile the string was cut, and there was great relief. At this point the blindfold was removed and the initiation was over.

Usually, whoever was the pledge's friend who had helped him get a bid, would take the pledge in tow afterward. But my friend, Buddy Craig, was away at military school that year. I guess he was the one who asked Newt Vestal to take care of me. He invited Dubey Sullivan and me to spend the night at his house, but said he first would take us to the YMCA to get cleaned up. I was hurting so from the hot balm that I forgot all about modesty. Dubey and I went into the shower room and showered, then we sat on one of the lavatories filled with cold water and put our scrotums in it, then back to the shower, then back to the lavatories. I think we stayed there about two hours, leaving our filthy clothes behind and putting on fresh ones that we had brought along. I guess I stayed so long all the oil was washed out of my skin, or maybe I had been badly chilled in the cold barn. Dubey decided he would go home to spend the night, but I went to the Vestal house in Park Hill and was deeply grateful to Newt. I remember how good it was to get in a warm bed. (Newt's real name was Walter Vestal, but he was called "Newt" [meaning of the neuter gender] because he had had a tumor removed from one of the nipples on his chest.)

I don't know if it was the next day, or the second, that the glands in my neck began to swell. They got so bad I had to spend one or two days at Trinity Hospital and missed a week or more of school. I also had to miss the formal initiation ceremony, so mine was a very brief one for me alone a week or so later and never meant a lot to me.

By the end of the first semester I was a full member of PIE, and I was feeling at home at LRHS. I remember at the end of the last Latin class, we all threw our books in the air. I cannot recall what course I took in place of Latin that second semester.

This was Ann's senior year. While I despised the male phys. ed. teachers in high school as much as I had the one at East Side, the girl's phys. ed. teacher was Kay Mitchell, who had been the riding instructor at Ann's summer camp, Camp Sequoya. Kay used to come down to visit us at Scott and would ride our horses. She was the sponsor for the cheerleading team.

Faculty and Staff

The faculty and staff at Little Rock Senior High were mostly seasoned veterans of high school situations and students. Several of them had taught for a number of years when the high school was located in what I knew as East Side Junior High, then they made the transition to the new building in 1927. I arrived 15 years later in the fall of 1942. A number of these individuals had served at both school locations and were known to generations of students. John A. Larson, the principal, had been there for 31 years when I arrived; Celia Murphy, head of the English department, 25 years; Mary Murphy, the French teacher, 25 years; Essie Hill, head of Latin, 26 years; Flora Armitage, head of mathematics, 36 years; S. E. Tanner, biology, 27 years; E. F. Quigley, head football coach, 29 years. All of them, to us teenage students, seemed ancient, but all — with the possible exception of Mr. Tanner — were very sharp and "with it." There were some younger teachers, but they were under the supervision of those with experience. They were dedicated to their profession, not just "holding a job" until they could get married or find a higher paying position in some other field. Looking back on them, I think on the whole I was blessed with a very good faculty. When I arrived at Yale, I felt well prepared in every field except English literature.

I want to comment on some of these men and women, mostly women.

J. A. Larson, the long-time principal, continued on for my first two years. I had been in student council, and he was the advisor for that, so I had worked with him a good bit. Even though the school district's policy was to get rid of sororities and fraternities, Mr. Larson was very lax in enforcing it. He had been a PIE himself when he was in high school. This made those of us in the Greek groups disposed to like him. When, in the spring of my junior year, I was elected president of the student body, I looked forward to working with him. I was dismayed when, in the middle of the summer before I took office, he announced his retirement. A man from Texas, T. Q. Shrigley, took his place. He chose not to sponsor student council and turned it over to Miss Edna Middlebrooks, the number-two person in the English department. He also cracked down on fraternities and sororities.

Edna Middlebrooks had been teaching for 18 years. She and Miss Celia Murphy, head of the English department, had a feud going. Miss Middlebrooks and I clashed from the very start of my year as president of the student body. She was very firm in her ideas about how the student council and student body should be run, and pushed hard to get them carried out. She was very masculine in her appearance and had whiskers that had to be shaved. I got my back up. We sparred for the whole year. If I had known she was going to be the student council sponsor, I doubt I would have run for president. I was fortunate in that I never had her for an English class.

Miss Alma Spears taught me English in the 10th grade. She had been around for 19 years. She was very sweet and gentle on first impression, but was hard as a rock on the inside. I used to describe her as "a steel fist covered with velvet." We used to spend one half of a semester on grammar and writing, the second half on literature. Her idea of studying a play or novel or poem was to master all the details of the life of the writer. Once we got into the piece itself, we had to memorize vocabulary appearing in it, then we had to memorize certain lines or sections, including capitalization and punctuation, so what I had to drill into my head was "(Capital A) All the world's (apostrophe "s") a stage, (comma, capital A) and all the men and women merely players (colon)...." Any enjoyment of the piece of literature was squeezed out long before we got to the end of it.

Miss Edith Leidy taught me English the first half of my 11th grade year. She was a joy and the bright exception to my experience in that department. I have no memory of what we studied, but I liked her from the start. Then one day as she was philosophizing or preaching, as our English teachers were wont to do, she said, "When you are seeking to find your life's work, don't settle for anything unless you enjoy it so much you won't really mind if you never get a vacation." I sat up and took note. At the end of that semester, she resigned from teaching and went to work for the Girl Scouts. From then on, through all my vocational struggles in college, and in making job decisions since, I have kept that as a test of each possibility before me. And it has worked. For years I kept up with Miss Leidy at Christmas.

I can't remember the name of the woman who taught English in the first half of my senior year, but I do recall a major component of the content. This was the semester when all college-bound students had to engage in a debate. It was something students dreaded from the day they entered high school. The teacher paired us off as teams and chose which pairs were to debate. My partner was Patty Carson, a fellow cheerleader and a delightful person and good friend. She was very popular—but not one of the school's academic heavyweights. Our opponents were Dorothy Hammett and Virginia Dilworth, numbers two and three in the academic ranking of our class. This was in the middle of World War II, about the time of the Battle of the Bulge, when the whole nation was caught up in news from the fighting in Europe, as well as in the Pacific, and when every boy in the class knew that as soon as he turned 18, he would be drafted. The topic we were to debate was "Resolved, that universal military conscription should be required when the war is over." We were given the negative to defend! In doing research, I discovered publications I had never heard of and read about conscientious objection, an option to the draft I had not known existed. But for all my research, it was clear we were the underdogs in the debate. At the end of each debate, the class voted on who won. Patty and I decided we would turn our charm on the members of the class and try to win that way. It did not work!

In my last semester in school, I had Miss Celia Murphy, the head of the English department. She was a well-known half of the "Murphy sisters," the other being Miss Mary, the teacher of French. Miss Celia was rather tall and angular. Miss Mary was shorter and a bit plump. Stories about them would be passed down from one student generation to the next. Miss Celia had a brown dress with metal gold dangles hanging from it. I am sure the dangles were on all the material originally, but they had all been worn off on the seat. People who had had her as a teacher 10 to 15 years before, upon learning that I was in her class, would inquire about the condition of the brown dress with gold dangles. As long as I reported it was still in use, they seemed to relax and know that all was well at Little Rock High. I don't remember what we studied that final half year. I think it was the English and American Romantic poets, but I'm not sure. I still did not know we were supposed to enjoy poetry.

Miss Mary Murphy, the other half of the Murphy sisters was the only French teacher in the school. I had her for two years. She liked me and would often address me as "precious" when she was sending me on an errand to her sister's room down the hall to get "the purse." The folklore about them was that they shared in driving their car. One would steer and the other would shift the gears. I can't verify that, but I do know they shared one purse between them. There were two teachers of Spanish, but at that time in academic circles Spanish was regarded as a second-rate language, so I took French. Little Rock had also offered German until World War I when it fell victim to the war fervor and had never been restored to the curriculum. Miss Mary did a good job of teaching me grammar and vocabulary so I could read and write well. When I went to Yale in my first semester of French I got a grade of 92, and the second semester a 90. But as we got more into conversation, my grades went down. For my fourth semester at Yale, I took "Conversation and Composition" that was designed to equip people for the diplomatic corps. At the end of the semester the instructor said, "M. Campbell, I did not know one could speak French with a Southern accent, but you do. I suggest you drop French." And I did. Miss Mary came from middle Tennessee and taught generations of Little Rock students to speak French with that accent.

Miss Emily Penton was one of the best teachers I ever had, including Yale College and Divinity School and the University of St. Andrews. I had her for American history in the 12th grade. We had reading assignments, but she also lectured in such a fascinating style that I hung on her every word. She went to Little Rock Senior High, graduated from Hendrix College in history and English, and earned her master's degree from the University of Chicago. When we came to the Civil War, I remember being jolted by her critical presentation of the role of the planters and slave owners in getting into that war, and dragging with them many small time farmers who had nothing to gain and a great deal to lose in that conflict. I had had good history teachers in elementary and junior high school, and a fine world history teacher in the 10th grade, but Miss Penton was the standard against which I measured my history professors from then on. When Governor Faubus closed the Little Rock high schools in 1958-59 over integration, one of the local TV stations provided free time for Miss Penton to teach history to students who were trying in various ways to make up for that lost year. She developed quite a group of fans, including a lot of adults. She would go on the air at 7:30 a.m. and finish in time to return to the shuttered Central High, where she had nothing to do, but had to be present to collect her salary.

All of the other teachers I've mentioned were tried and tested members of the faculty. Elsewhere I have mentioned one new and young one — Kay Mitchell. She came from Marfa, Texas, where her father had a ranch that was measured in sections rather than acres. She grew up on horses and learned to drive a car when she was something like nine. They obviously had a lot of money. She was a riding instructor at the summer camp my sister and others attended for several years. One of those was Lucinda Blakely whose father was on the Little Rock School Board. When Kay graduated in physical education from Baylor University, she was looking for a job, and Little Rock needed a female phys ed teacher. Dr. Blakely made the connection. She came when I was in the 10th grade and Ann was a senior. Ann invited Kay to come to Scott, and Daddy was delighted to have someone ride our horses, so I got to know her in that context. Kay was made sponsor of cheerleading. It was partly because I knew and liked her that I thought of running for cheerleader. She really put us through our paces in training us. I remember after the first session my legs hurt so I could not step from the street level to the curb without leaning to one side. I had a great relationship with Kay through two years of cheerleading. I think our whole team liked her, but I had the special friendship outside that structure. She is the only physical education teacher with whom I've ever had a positive relationship.

I headed this section "Faculty and Staff" mostly because the registrar was the one individual who did the most to hold the school together, even more than the principal. Her name was Miss Ernestine Opie, but she was known to generations of students as "Opie." Before computers were invented, Opie had one in her brain. She apparently never forgot anything or anybody. She knew everyone who had gone through that school for years. It was she who decided which "track" a person was going to be put on— college prep, or secretarial/business, or home economics/manual training. Once a student was assigned to such a type of education, it took an act of Congress to get him or her moved. And even in the college prep group, she categorized people into levels. If she decided you had the potential, you got put in the classes of the best teachers, so it was almost like a small private school inside a large public one. It paid to stay on the good side of Opie!

Not only did she assign pupils to classes, but she also knew somehow at what hour each student was supposed to be in what room, so that people trying to skip class would be nailed to the wall the moment Opie saw them. She was not mean about it. But she ran a tight ship and did not intend to let things get out of hand. Bettye Jane Erwin Daugherty told me recently something I had not known before. Anyone who came to school and wanted to go home because of illness had first to go to the school nurse, and then get a slip signed by Opie. Opie could see through phony excuses like x-ray can see through flesh. Bettye Jane said when girls were having menstrual cramps, they would visit the nurse, then Opie, so they could go home. Opie would say, "I don't think you really need to go. Here is something that will help"—and would pull out from her desk drawer a bottle of whiskey and give them a swig, then send them back to class.

Opie was an awesome presence through the administrations of at least three principals and was much of what made LRHS a first-rate school.

Study in High School

When Art, Ann, and I were growing up, we were never given "chores" to do around the house on a regular basis. If a special need arose and we could help, we were expected to rise to the occasion. If we did something extra, we were never paid for it. It was a part of our obligation as members of the family. Mother was very outspoken that our normal contribution to the family was to be good students. That was our "job." Art and Ann took that somewhat seriously. Art did not have to study hard and made a combination of A's and B's. Ann studied much harder than Art, and made A's and B's. I studied harder than either of them and made mostly A's, with a few B's in the 10th grade.

I can't recall ever going home from school without textbooks and notebooks to use that night, except at the end of a semester. In high school, I would be kidded about the large number of books I'd carry under my arm and rest on my hipbone. Because we lived in the country, once I got home there was nothing to tempt me to go astray. My friends in town might meet at the drug store, or wander over to visit with each other. The nearest person for me to hang out with was five miles away. Even before gas rationing, our family did not drive for frivolous reasons. We did enough driving for necessities. And once gas rationing set in in the middle of my 10th grade year, there was no fuel for running around. There was no TV in those days. We did have radios, but did not keep them on while studying. The one deviation from studying until bedtime was Monday nights when the Lux Radio Theater was on. Normally we had to go to bed at 8:00 p.m., but on Monday nights if we had taken our baths, brushed our teeth, and were tucked in bed by 8:00, we were allowed to listen to those excellent radio plays that ran until 9:00 p.m.! I think after Art and Ann went off to college, that may have eased up a bit and I would study regularly until 9:00. We had to get up at 6:00 a.m. to drive to town each day to deposit our riders and be at High School early enough to do some visiting with friends, for that was the chief socializing time for me.

So, as soon as I drove home from school, arriving about 4:30 or 5:00, I was working on my lessons except for the dinner hour. I was on my own in all subjects except Latin. Because Mother had majored in this language at college, and because I had a poor teacher when I started Latin in junior high, she began to help me at night. Even after I got better teachers, we continued this collaboration. I suppose she got some pleasure from it, too. On the weekends, I had to do my homework on Friday night, during the day on Saturday, or Saturday night. Mother laid down the law that we did not study on Sunday, even if we were having a test on Monday morning. That was hard, and I often wished the Sunday night rule were not there. On the other hand, because I could not study, Sunday nights were free. Often Mother and Daddy would have company for dinner that night. The cook was off, and Mother would take over. When the company left, she would wash the dishes. We used to offer to help. Usually she declined, but occasionally she would let me dry dishes as a "treat." It was good visiting time, and I was free since I could not study.

One of the great benefits from my rather rigorous study schedule was that when I got to Yale as a freshman, I found I had to study no harder than I had in high school. This is not to say I found it easy in college, but it came as no surprise to me as it did to others who had rather breezed through high school.

I think we had one study hall period each day, except for those few people who took five subjects instead of the normal four. There was also a library, and with permission a student could go there instead of study hall. I went there especially when I was working on my debate and had to do research. The library was directly beneath the band room where they would practice, and the noise of the music was quite distracting. In the 10th grade, even more in the 11th, I would also spend some study-hall time working on student council business. In the 12th especially, when I was president of the student body and student council, I would often spend the study-hall period with Miss Edna Middlebooks, working on student council business. Since I grew to dislike her, I did not enjoy those times at all.

When I was in actual study hall, I found it difficult to concentrate. There would be whispering. I also remember in the winter I would freeze to death, for there were usually some boys wearing heavy athletic jackets who would raise the windows. To them, it was for fresh air, but for me it was an arctic blast. Looking back on it, I wonder how much of my distraction in study hall was due to attention deficit disorder (ADD). I certainly did study better at home where I had privacy.

In high school, we had to write papers in English classes. And I studied hard from the textbooks. But I guess the only real research I had to do was for my debate in the first half of my senior year. In preparation for this, I went to both the school library and the public library. This research opened up a whole new world for me. In browsing through the magazines, I remember coming across articles on other subjects that were also eye-openers. One I especially recall was on "Black Jews." It told about the Jewish community in Ethiopia that dated back to the time of King Solomon. I had never heard of it. Little did I imagine this required segment of 12th grade English would be my first taste in scholarship, in research, and in taking a look at alternatives to military force as the way to deal with international issues. And what a blessing it was when I got to Yale and had to do research papers, especially my senior essay.

One other class I enjoyed, and worked moderately hard in, was French. I took two years of that. I knew practically everyone in that class, and I liked Miss Mary Murphy the teacher — in spite of the accent she taught us.

The weakest link in my academic preparation for college was the literature half of English. It seemed to me we were given some of the dullest writings in the world to study. In 10th grade, I remember unhappily *Silas Marner* by George Eliot. I have never since been able to make myself go back to re-read it to see if there was some merit in it. That year, we also read my first Shakespeare play, *As You Like It*, which did not turn me on. We had to memorize the seven stages of man, and the only thing that stimulated our class was the "muling and puking" because that seemed slightly naughty. We also got excited when we checked the date of the marriage of Shakespeare's parents with his birth date and decided the pregnancy was a bit short. I think we also had Coleridge's "Ancient Mariner," from which we changed "Water, water everywhere and not a drop to drink" to "Water, water everywhere, my God how this does stink." In the 11th grade, the dullest thing I remember having to read was Burke's "Speech on Conciliation with America." Surely there must be some better substitute for that. We also read some of Milton's shorter poems — "L'Allegro" and "Il Peneroso" and "Comus." At least we didn't have to tackle "Paradise Lost." Sometime that year, we studied "Macbeth" — perhaps that was with Miss Leidy, whom I did like. I found that play interesting, although the memorization killed it.

In the spring of my senior year, Miss Celia Murphy took us through some of the English and American poets. I remember reading Poe's "The Raven" and Wordsworth's "I Wandered Lonely As A Cloud" and Shakespeare's "Hamlet." Then there was some terrible prose from Emerson. There were also American Victorian poets who don't seem to have made it into *Bartlett's Quotations* — giving some idea of their importance to the world.

I continue to have some resentment about the quality of teaching in literature. I was so turned off that I did not like freshman English at Yale and was completely unprepared for it. In my sophomore year, I skipped the "real" course, which dealt with Chaucer and major writers, and instead took what was known as "Engineer's English" that covered such things as Byron's "Don Juan" and Shaw's plays. After passing that, I dropped English and did not discover my love for literature until later in life.

I took as little math and science as I could and still be admitted to college. I took second year algebra in the 10th grade. I never understood it, but would memorize what we had been taught, and I would make an A on the exam. The day after the exam, I would forget all I knew and would have to memorize it again for the final. In the 11th, I took plane geometry. That made a little more sense to me and I got A's, but had no interest in going to solid geometry or calculus, though they were offered.

A photo of me in 1944.

My exposure to science was even more limited. In the 10th grade, I took biology. We were required to have one "laboratory" science in order to graduate. I feared this was going to mean I would have to cut up a crawfish or a frog. I could have put that fear behind me. I had biology from Mr. S. E. Tanner. I have learned recently that he had been teaching biology at Little Rock High since 1915. We thought he was ancient, but he was probably 50 to 55 years old. He had white hair and was absent-minded and somewhat vague. He was kindly and not demanding. The amount of "lab work" we were required to do was minimal, and I never had to cut up anything. The only thing I can remember was from the botany part of biology. It was in the second semester when leaves were coming out. We had to collect leaves, press them, and then enter them into a notebook. I remember working on that and turning in mine. That may have been a course in which I made a "B." I know I was not excited about the subject matter, and Mr. Tanner was not an inspiring teacher.

In 12th grade, I did think perhaps I should have another science, so I signed up for chemistry taught by a man Art still says was one of the best teachers he ever had. However, on the first day of class he told us to memorize the atomic chart (he said there were 92 elements and would never be any more) by the next morning. At that point I decided I needed Public Speaking more than I did chemistry, and changed. I am amazed my parents let me get by with that, although the public speaking course was helpful during my year as president of the student body.

Discipline at High School

The principal at LRHS, John Larsen, had been in administration since 1911! He was somewhat aloof and could be very stern, although my contacts with him through student council were always pleasant. When someone was "sent to the office," it meant sitting on the bench outside his office. Those who came out indicated it was not a pleasant experience. I do not know if he ever used a paddle or belt—I think not, but I'm not sure. When Mr. Larsen was away, people were sent to Opie, the registrar, and that was deemed worse.

The normal way of punishment was to receive so many days in "detention hall," which meant coming an hour early or staying an hour late. Truman King was always getting punished for smoking or slipping over to the drug store or skipping class. But since she lived in the country and the whole car could not be made to come early or stay late, Mrs. B. Cotton Thomas, the dean for women, would assign her so many lines of poetry to memorize and write in Mrs. Thomas's presence. The problem was Truman was so smart she could memorize that overnight and be out from under any burden.

It went without saying that the response to any female teacher was "ma'am" and to male teachers "sir." Failure to use those terms would have been considered not only impolite, but a direct challenge to authority. I never heard of anyone flatly refusing to do so, but I would not have been surprised if the penalty was not suspension or even expulsion.

Teachers did not administer discipline. That was to be done through the central office or through one of the deans. I do not remember who the dean of men was, for I never was sent there. The teachers did play a significant role, however, in discipline of the school. Attendance was taken for each class period, and the list of absentees sent to Opie. She would compare them against the list of absences reported from homeroom. Those homes she would call immediately, speaking to a parent. If that student had been left home alone, the student had to bring a note from a parent upon returning to school—and Opie knew all the signatures and could spot a counterfeit a yard away. Also, when we went to the auditorium for some kind of program, we had to sit by homerooms, and attendance was taken, with absentees reported. Tardiness at homeroom, or for individual classes, was reported to Opie. I know in junior high, and I think in senior high as well, each report card had a place for citizenship as well as one for academic performance each six weeks.

There was always the potential for rowdiness in the halls between classes, with 3,000 students trying to get from one room to the next in a five-minute period—and sometimes one had to go from one end of the school to the next, two blocks, and up or down as many as two or three floors. Anyone who ran or made too much noise, or got in a fight, could be stopped by any teacher and sent to the office.

The boys' gym, I felt, was another world. The gym teachers were primarily coaches who seemed to tolerate physical education as a necessary evil. It was a rough world, with shouting and cursing and bullying.

At the football and basketball games, there could be rowdiness occasionally, but there were enough teachers in attendance that we knew authority was present. If there was much roughhousing, it would be after the game was over, or before, and off the school grounds. There was a lot of school rivalry, especially with Pine Bluff and North Little Rock, so sometimes things did get a bit out of hand.

I never once felt afraid during my high school years. I was intimidated by the size of the school when I first started. But the sense of having my life or limb endangered never entered my mind. Stealing was something else. Every student was assigned a locker out in the halls, and each of us had a lock. Also, in gym you had a lock to put on the basket that held your clothes while in a sport or in the shower. I think there was some stealing that went on, but I never lost anything. Also, there certainly was cheating that took place in the classrooms — such as writing answers on one's hand, or slipping notes back and forth, or when we graded each other's tests as often happened, giving a friend a favorable "break." I never saw a teacher lose control of a classroom. On the rare occasions when a student was sent from class to the office, I never saw him/her protest or refuse to go. There was no doubt that the faculty and staff were in complete control. They were tested professionals.

I was so fearful of getting a whipping in grade school and junior high, and so desiring of approval, and so fearful of the repercussions at home if I got a bad report from school, that I was completely cowed. I imagine others, if they thought about it at all, considered me a "goody-goody," and I probably was. But I also had high standards drilled into me at home, and it was not hard for me to live by the rules.

Academics in High School

Although there were social, family, and religious developments during my high school years, the dominant factor of my life was school, the academic side of it.

While gas rationing did not start until a few months after I entered the 10th grade, we all became very conscious of limiting our driving because of a shortage of tires. Once I got back home from school in the afternoon, I stayed there. Perhaps I would have anyway. There was no way I could meet friends at Smith's Drug Store, as many of my PIE friends did. And I did not go to parties of the old Scott crowd. On weekends I might go to a dance or party on either Friday or Saturday (and I certainly did not do that every weekend), but the other weekend night I had to study, since Sunday was out. Truman was beginning to rebel and her grades started slipping, but I was very conscious of wanting to go to an Ivy League college and knew I would have to win a scholarship. Therefore it was important for me to keep my grades high. My first year, as I remember, I made a mixture of A's and B's. I'm pretty sure I made A's in algebra, world history, biology, and Latin the first semester. I probably made a B in English, for I hated my teacher.

In the 11th grade, I think I moved into all A's or A-'s, and continued on that way through the 12th. It is really remarkable that I apparently was able to live in both worlds — to take my studies very seriously, yet still be popular. Part of that was because I lived at Scott so nobody expected me to do things at night. I had taken third-year Latin during the summer, once it was clear I wanted to go to an Ivy League college and they all required three years in one language. So in the fall of the 11th grade, I took Latin, English, geometry, and French. I can't remember what took the place of Latin in the spring. I took it as a matter of course that I would be elected to the National Honor Society, and I was. By the 12th grade, we somehow became aware of our academic ranking in the class. I am sure the school did not publicize this, so students who did volunteer work in the school office must have leaked it. (Truman had done that at East Side, and told us our IQ scores.) In the 12th grade, I had French, English, Public Speaking (instead of chemistry), and American history. The top students were Marshall Trieber, Dorothy Hammett, Virginia Dilworth, Margaret Stitt, and then I came—fifth in the class. As always, I was not the most brilliant, nor the most diligent—but came in the next ranking group. As I look back on it, I am surprised I did that well, for I was so involved in being president of the study body, a cheerleader, and secretary of PIE I was not focused on just the academics. Part of my skill was in avoiding courses in which I knew I would be weak. I dropped chemistry after one day, never even looked at physics, and did not take solid geometry or calculus. By senior year, I was very much concerned about how my grades would look on a college application. I was not so motivated by a love for learning as for getting into a good college.

History was the subject that really turned me on intellectually. I had liked world history in the 10th grade, and absolutely loved American history in the 12th.

I was not a rapid reader, nor was I speedy in any subject. I regarded myself not as brilliant, but as good academically and a plugger. (I guess that is still my self-image.) So I usually had to take four textbooks, plus a notebook, home with me every night. This would have presented a real problem had I been within walking distance of LRHS, or ridden the streetcar, as many people did. But since we came in a car, I could pile my stack in.

As soon as I got home from school, I would usually have a snack then would settle down to do as much homework as possible before dinner. The minute dinner was over, it was back to the books. I guess I would usually spend two to three hours a night on homework.

On the weekends I would study on either Friday or Saturday night about the same amount of time. I guess there were times when I would study during the day on Saturday, but I do not think that was the pattern. I remember I got in the habit in my later high school years of going back to bed after breakfast on Saturdays to read *Time* magazine from cover to cover—and discovering, to my pleasant surprise, there was a section on "Religion." Ann would often have guests for the weekend, and I would get involved with them. Saturday was also the one day when I had time to read novels and other things just for the fun of it. At that time I was a member of the Book-of-the-Month club and would get new volumes to read.

Looking back on it, I am sure one cause of my long hours of study (other than being compulsive and wanting to "get it right") was my ADD. That would explain why I was so easily distracted in study hall. I wonder if ADD sets in at puberty for some people.

As I remember, I did all my homework in pencil. I am sure that was true of math, for I would have to erase mistakes and go back over it. I think on occasion I would use a pen. That was before ballpoint pens, so we would have to fill them up from an ink bottle, and from time to time the "bladder" of the pen would empty itself and get over clothes and books.

I had a hard time with memory work and with spelling new vocabulary. That called for my going over it time and time again. I guess I did ask Mother to help me on that. In math, I had no "feel" for algebra—sheer memorization. Geometry made a little more sense to me, but it was still not "my thing." I did much better in the languages, in grammar and writing, in history, even in biology.

While I did well in school, I always looked forward to the vacations—two days for Teachers' Meeting, two for Thanksgiving, two weeks for Christmas—then it was a long haul until summer. School usually ended about mid-to-late May and started up the week after Labor Day. We were not given any kind of reading list during the summers. The only summer that I used for academic purposes was 1943 when I did the first half of third-year Latin.

When I was in high school College Board examinations were not required for admission to most schools in the South, and certainly not to any public colleges. Only those wanting to go to top schools in the East took them. Since I had applied for Yale, they were necessary for me. I don't recall any "cram" course or any other preparation given by Little Rock High for those of us who were going to sit for these exams.

The exam was given on a school day, as I remember. As I left the house that morning to drive the car to town, I felt scared and weepy. I had no idea what I was getting into, but I did not feel prepared. My whole future hung in the balance — although part of me was hoping I would not get in Yale, for I really wanted to go to Washington and Lee (many family connections there) or to the University of Arkansas at Fayetteville, for that was the "in" place to go and was reputed to be a great party place.

As I remember, Donna Davis took the exam that day. I think I drove her to wherever the test was given. It felt like "playing hooky," not being in class, although of course the school knew where we were and encouraged us to go. There was a lunch break in the exams. I remember Donna and I splurged, treating ourselves to lunch at Ole King Cole restaurant at Fifth and Broadway.

I felt I did pretty well on much of the test, but I remember being completely thrown by one section in social sciences in which we were given a mythological country, with a description of its natural resources, and we were supposed to hypothesize its economic and political life. I had never been presented with a challenge like that. Our tests had always been to reproduce information we had read or heard in a lecture. This required creative thinking. I felt I really "blew" it and left suspecting that my prospects at Yale were over.

Cheerleading

I was motivated to run for cheerleader for three reasons. First, it was a way out of taking gym. Second, at that time it was considered a great honor to be one. Third, in the fraternity/sorority world in which I lived, it was important to PIE to have members in this visible spot.

The first year, the hold-overs were Davies Campbell (no kin), Ged Canby, and Marian Tipton. Kitty Rose Wills and Patty Carson were elected for the women. Mickey McSwain, Edward LeClair, and I were the men. The second year, Jim Johnson filled the male vacancy while Marian Davis and either Jeanne or Deanne Mosley filled the female slots. (I could never tell the twins apart. The other

Little Rock High School cheerleaders for 1944-45. I am in the upper right.

one was the substitute, and I always wondered if they did not switch around.)

The cheerleading team spent a lot of time together, for Kay Mitchell made us practice for hours. Then we were together every Friday night in the fall when there was a home football game, and some of the team would go to basketball games—though they were much less important in those days. World War II was on, curtailing travel, so I think we did not go to most of the out-of-town games. At least I do not remember many.

I do recall taking my car to Hot Springs once in senior year, filled with other cheerleaders. I guess I had saved up enough extra gas coupons to allow me to drive the 60 miles there and back. I especially remember Patty Carson was a passenger. We told stories and laughed all the way over and back. On that trip, we went up the observation tower on the mountain overlooking Hot Springs.

When the door of the elevator opened onto the observation deck, I suddenly found myself on my hands and knees in my white cheerleading suit. It was the first time I ever realized I had acrophobia.

Another out-of-town trip was to Pine Bluff. It was the only time I remember being on a train until the night I left for college. There was a special train for the ball game, for playing Pine Bluff was the "big" event of the football season—even more so than playing North Little Rock on Thanksgiving Day. We went down and came back the same day in a coach.

There was a pep rally in the auditorium every Friday before the games. We cheerleaders would line up on the stage and lead the yells, the captain calling them. I think Davies was captain my first year, and Mickey the second. That was a lot of fun. It was exhilarating to be up in front of 3,000 screaming kids. We had white flannel uniforms, provided by the school. We didn't wear them to school during the day for that would have dirtied them, so we had to change just before the pep rally in the afternoon. Occasionally, I would eat dinner at the home of Aunt Alice and Uncle Gordon Campbell, but generally I would keep on my uniform after the pep rally and go downtown for supper before the game. My favorite spot was Franke's Cafeteria on Capitol Avenue where I would often get fish, since we rarely ate it at home. Then I would go out to the stadium, and after the game I would often go to a dance, still in my uniform. We were provided a sweater for the first year, with no marker on the sleeve. At the end of the first year, we were given a new sweater with one black band on the arm, at the end of the second, a sweater with two black bands. Many athletes wore their sweaters to class and other places. I don't think any of the cheerleaders ever did. When our class had its 50th reunion, I found I still had my sweater—and with a little stretching was able to get in it when those of us who survived led a cheer.

Never being athletic, I understood the football game so little I was often not sure of what was going on out on the field, and therefore didn't realize what kind of cheer we should be leading. So I followed the lead of the others.

In those days, cheerleaders did not do acrobatic stunts, performing and entertaining, as was the vogue later. We were there just to stimulate the crowd into supporting the team. We had a limited repertory of yells. This being the big athletic event in the city, the stands were usually filled with students and adults, too.

As I think back on my high school career, cheerleading was one of the highlights. Daddy, who had been a football player, was clearly embarrassed that I was a cheerleader and not out on the field. I was conscious that never once did he and Mother come to see me as a cheerleader — but then they never came to see me preside as president of the student body. It may have been because of the gas shortage, but they did come to town. It may have been because of Mother's obvious decision to stay uninvolved when we went to Little Rock schools, in contrast to her role at Scott. But I think it was due to Daddy's sense that it was "sissy" to be a cheerleader.

A photo of me in my cheerleading outfit.

High School Politics

I guess I have been a political animal from early on. Perhaps I inherited it from my father, who loved to be engaged in Republican politics — although in Arkansas at that period this was purely an "amateur sport." My taste was whetted at East Side Junior High when I was elected vice-president of the student body, then was defeated in my run to be president my last semester.

During my first two years on the student council, I was faithful in attendance and carried out my assignments on committees or in other jobs. It was not a heavy burden. With our principal, John Larsen, as council sponsor, things moved along smoothly as they had for many years. Each spring, the student council nominated officers for the student council/student body for the following year. Each nominee would make a speech from the main stage in the large auditorium announcing his/her platform for the year. Then there would be an election through the homerooms. A majority of the students did not bother to vote, for they were not in close touch with our work, other than seeing the president preside at all student body assemblies. However, for the fraternity/sorority crowd, this was very important, for it was a way to "gain points" over their rivals if one of their number was elected. I think people were also elected as vice-president and secretary, but I'm no longer sure. The student council nominated Tom Johnson, a Delta Sigma, and me, a PIE, to run for the office. I liked Tom, and we had worked together in the council, but I did want to win and worked hard on my speech given to the whole student body. I have no idea what I advocated, but that mattered little, for elections were based on personality and name recognition. I had an advantage in having been a cheerleader for a year, and therefore was often on the stage at pep rallies. I cannot remember the exact count, but I think I won by a vote of something like 384 over Tom's 365. I am convinced the victory came through name recognition (for in a student body of some 3,000, I did not know the vast number of my schoolmates). And it all came about by accident.

I need to give a little background.

When I was growing up, the rate of syphilis infection on the plantation was very high—at least Mother and Daddy thought it was about 100%. All through my childhood, I was told never to eat or drink after a "nigra," as we politely termed the blacks, nor were we ever to share a toilet with them. Of course this was ridiculous, for they milked our cows, cooked, and served our food. But that was Mother's idea of preventive medicine. I let that spill over, or at least inferred it, to include the poor whites on the plantation and at school.

One summer, probably 1939, Chuck McCain was giving his family so much grief in Chicago that Cousin Charlie and Cousin Frances asked if he could come spend the summer with us at Scott. That is another subject, for he livened things considerably. But when he learned that our cook had syphilis, he went "ape." He insisted that we all needed to take Wassermann tests (the test for syphilis), so we all paraded in to Trinity Hospital and had our blood drawn. I don't remember saying it, but Mother claimed I announced that if I had syphilis then I would never get married. All this for background.

During World War II, Camp Robinson was filled with soldiers, and the venereal disease (VD) rate skyrocketed in Little Rock. It became a major public health concern. So the Public Health Service

Tiger Staff Photo

This group is the constitution committee of the student council which has been in charge of drawing up the new student body organization constitution that is now up for adoption. They are, left to right: Tom Johnson, chairman, Jimmie Johnson, Joanne Mayne and Carolyn Scruggs.

A student council committee I appointed. On the left is Tom Johnson, whom I defeated in the election for president of the student body. In the center is Jim Johnson, who was vice-president of PIE.

and Principal John Larsen decided an ounce of prevention was better than a pound of cure. They scheduled two educational programs on the subject—one for the boys and one for the girls. The boys came first. There were about 3,000 students at Little Rock Senior High at that point. All boys were dismissed from their classes and told to assemble in the auditorium—about 1,500. The girls stayed in their classes, wondering exactly what was going on. A doctor from the Army talked about venereal diseases, what they were, and how they were transmitted. He showed a film, then Mr. Larsen stood up and asked, "Are there any questions?" There was complete silence—1,500 silences. Mr. Larsen stood there, expectantly.

At this time I had been active in the Student Council for two years and had been a cheerleader for one. I was moved to try to break the ice, so I stood up. With Chuck McCain's concerns in mind, I asked, "Pardon me, sir, but can you get it from your cook?"

There was another *profound* silence—for about 15 seconds. Then there was an explosion of laughter from 1,500 boys and the entire male faculty, who were about falling out of their chairs. Mr. Larsen, always serious and dignified, also broke up laughing. I never got an answer to my question! And that ended the educational program as 1,500 boys poured out into the halls.

When 1,500 girls heard this roar of laughter coming from the auditorium, their curiosity knew no bounds. And as soon as a girl met a boy she knew, she found out the cause.

I became known in school as "Cookie Campbell." When I would have boys come down to spend the weekend, every time Hattie (our cook) would come into the dining room with food, they would begin to smirk and giggle. I never told Mother and Daddy about this little episode, but they noticed the change in my friends' behavior. Years later, Mother told me Daddy got her aside and said, "Margaret, I don't know what is going on between Donald and Hattie, but I don't like it."

An unintended consequence of my question was its impact on my run for the presidency of the student body, which came not too long afterward. I think there is no doubt that it was "name recognition" that put me over. Everybody in Little Rock High knew me as the one who had asked the "cook question."

And I am pretty sure my being president of the student body was a major factor in my being accepted at Yale College. "For the lack (or presence) of a nail an empire was lost (or won)..."

As I have indicated elsewhere, the summer before my term as president of the student body began, John Larsen retired. I guess the new principal, T. Q. Srygley, came determined to change things. One goal was to break up the "old boy" way of electing officers for the student body. He wanted also to make it more open and democratic, although to me he was just ramming through ideas he was importing from Port Arthur, Texas. Probably a hidden agenda was also to break the hold of the fraternities and sororities on leadership in the school.

There had been Republican and Democratic conventions in 1944, and then the general election in which F. D. Roosevelt won a fourth term. So Srygley decided, working through Edna Middlebrooks, that we students should have similar conventions, to teach people the political process and to get them interested in who the candidates were. One "party" was to be named "Black" and the other "Old Gold," the two school colors. (It certainly had nothing to do with the rights of black people, as there was none enrolled.) There were to be posters and rallies and delegates. Half the student body (I don't remember how they were divided) was to meet one day for the "Old Gold" convention and name a candidate; the next day the "Blacks" were to do the same.

I was named the chairman for one of the conventions (I don't remember which) and Tom Johnson, whom I had defeated for president, was to chair the other. I remember thinking this was a lot of hoopla about nothing, but did my job. I don't recall which convention named whom, but the person elected president was Jack Guenther whom I did not know very well, but liked. He was not a member of a fraternity.

It was interesting that when he graduated, Jack came to Yale College, and the man I followed as president, Ted Lamb, had gone to Yale ahead of me.

Social Life at LRHS

I am somewhat vague about my social life in the 10th grade. I became 15 in October, but still had only a restricted driver's license. That meant I was quite dependent on Ann for transportation. For the first part of the year, gas rationing had not started, but we were conscious that we needed to look after the school car, for we would not have a chance of getting another one until the war was over. Nor would we be able to buy new tires. When gas rationing began, we conserved our coupons. We were able to get a "C" card because five of us were driving in to school. That covered our weekday needs during the school year, but allowed us only a little extra to use on weekends and during the summers. Ann was the "driver" of the car during my 10th grade year. I do not believe we went to Friday night football or basketball games that year. Ann was not interested, and we had to get our other passengers home or make arrangements for them if for some reason we did not return on schedule.

My social life, all three years, centered around the PIE fraternity. I went to the Sunday afternoon meetings each week while Ann went to her DBS meeting. From time to time there would be a PIE party on Friday night, and I would be expected to go. I had several dates with Mary Kay Claxton, who was in DBS sorority. I remember early in the fall of 1942 we had a hayride and I took her. I was shocked at the kissing and necking that took place in the hay. I had been brainwashed by Mother's Puritan stance on how boys should treat girls. I hardly touched Mary Kay that night. But we had a lot of fun looking and being scandalized. Mary Kay was always fun on a date. We were together several times during that year. I also had some dates with Margaret Stitt, who was a member of the other sorority, DAD. Sometimes I would spend the night, after our date, at her house, for her brother, Edwin, was in some ways my sponsor in PIE. He also had a few dates with my sister, Ann. He tells me several times I invited him to ride home with me to Scott to spend the night or weekend in order to keep me awake when I was driving. Perhaps since he was 16 I could drive with my restricted license if he was in the car with me.

PIE always had a big formal dinner dance on Christmas Eve, and I always took a date to that. These were held at the Lafayette, Marion, and Albert Pike Hotels with table cloths, cloth napkins, and waiters or waitresses. At these dinner dances, the dress was formal, the girls wearing long dresses and the boys tuxedos, although both were hard to buy in the stores because of the war. Boys were expected to send, or take, their dates a corsage. The normal one was made of carnations. I'm vague about the price, but I think they cost 75 cents or a dollar. If one really liked a girl, the flowers might be roses or a gardenia. They probably cost a dollar and a half or even two dollars. That, on top of the ticket for the dance and dinner for two, would eat up my allowance for two or three weeks. I am not sure what my allowance was at the time, but I think it was something like five dollars or less, and that included buying lunches at school. As a result, I quit eating lunch altogether until my senior year when the sponsor to the Student Council told me my breath was bad. Then I started bringing an apple from home and eating it at noon.

I can't remember who were my dates for these dinner dances, or again for the spring swimming party, held early each May. That first year it might have been Mary Kay. I am sure in my senior year I took Maisie Lackey, whom I dated several times that year. Her brother had been a friend of mine in PIE. I was "sponsor" from PIE to DBS, so since Maisie was the most sought-after potential pledge, I was assigned to win her over, and did. I would from time to time take Truman King to dinner dances if she did not have another date. And I dated a variety of other girls during those three years, but none of them seriously. I guess Maisie was the closest person whom I would have called "my girl," but she would not have known that. She was very popular, and I did not date often and was very inhibited about showing any affection. The only time I kissed a girl in high school was after the Christmas Eve dinner dance in my senior year. And then I was very awkward about doing it.

My social life picked up a little when I reached the 11th grade. I was in charge of driving the school car, although I did not turn 16 until the middle of October. So I had control of when it went home. Also, by then I had been elected a cheerleader. That meant I had to attend every in-town football game. We did not lead the cheers for all basketball games, but I remember going to one or two. After the football games there was usually an informal dance given on a rotating basis by one of the high school sororities or fraternities. These, by the way, were always chaperoned by parents from the group putting them on. For most informal dances, I would wear the same clothes I had worn at school that day—long pants of corduroy or wool and a long-sleeve sport shirt, with a short jacket in cold weather. For dances after football games, we cheerleaders, both boys and girls, wore our white wool uniforms with great pride. I don't remember owning an overcoat or a hat until I went to college, although I was very fond of wearing a scarf, usually a white rayon (there was no silk during the war) monogrammed one. The fad of saddle shoes with signatures on the white leather part held through all of my high school days. Girls usually wore skirts and blouses, or sweaters in the winter. Slacks for girls at school or dances were unheard of.

During that junior year, I had three friends I want to mention. One was my old friend from Scott, Buddy Craig. He had spent his junior year at a military academy, but had talked his parents into letting him come back for his senior year. He was dating Bettye Jane Erwin that year, and that drew us closer together. Buddy also rode to school in my car. One of his closest friends, but also a good friend of mine, was Buddy Lackey, the son of the colonel who was head of the state military. A third friend I grew close to was Dan Phillips. He was Jewish. PIE took in Jews, and at that point the other fraternity did not, so we got some fine members. Some years later I had a role in persuading his parents to send him to Yale to college.

I shall write later about a deliberate choice I made in the spring of my 11th grade year to throw myself into more contact with people. As a result of that decision, though, I began to date more the last few weeks of my junior year, and also to seek out boys in PIE. That is the time when I ran for and won as president of the student body, was elected by DBS sorority to be their PIE sponsor, and was nominated for the presidency of PIE. I lost the PIE election to my friend Johnny Washburn, but was elected secretary.

By the start of my senior year, I was very much in the thick of social life in the fraternity-sorority circles at high school. I had a lot of friends in the other big sorority, DAD, and was invited to some of their parties, and to dances given by another social group called La Jeunese that included the most popular girls from both of the sororities and some girls who had chosen not to join a sorority. After the dance, we would often go to a drive-in restaurant called "The Purple Cow." The typical treat for the evening was a Coke or Grapette (a drink invented and manufactured in Arkansas) and a bag of Fritos. They had just come on the market. The cost for each was five cents. A girl who ordered anything more expensive was considered a "gold digger." In earlier years when I was staying in Little Rock after a party too late to drive home, I would occasionally spend the night with one of my PIE friends. But in the 12th grade I did that much more frequently, usually staying with Johnny Washburn. His father, a doctor, was in military service and away from home. His only sister was grown and out on her own. His mother was very hospitable and let me know I was welcome there any time. As a result I had Johnny spend some nights with me at Scott, and also some others but I can't remember who. Because we were cheerleaders together, and because he was vice-president of PIE, I got to know Jim Johnson much better and remember spending one night at his house. It was at a party I had on our place for the PIE officers that Mother mentioned the hardship she experienced in the country with only an "A" gas-rationing card. Jim's father happened to be head of the rationing board as part of his contribution to the war effort. Within a matter of a couple of weeks, Mother received a "B" card in the mail! She always had a warm place in her heart for Jim.

I have mentioned elsewhere that in the fall of my senior year I was asked to "rush" Maisey Lackey for DBS. I was glad to accept the assignment, for she was cute and popular, and I began to ask her for dates, although she was just in the 10th grade. That year Truman King was also often spending the night at Bettye Jane Erwin's house, and I would often be over there. I never dated Bettye Jane until the night of our high school graduation. That year also I dated a girl named Anne Bush who had moved up from Mississippi. Because she was not heavily endowed with breasts, boys would often call her "Flat Bush." She lived in Cammack Village, an appendage to Little Rock on its northwest corner. It was the most distant part of the city. With gas rationing, a boy thought twice about asking a girl from Cammack for a date. Also, the houses in Cammack were small, built during the war, and were almost identical. It was hard to tell them apart. When boys, including me, were going to pick up Anne, they would ride down the street, start honking, and yell out "Flat Bush" in the hope she would turn on the porch light to make sure we would go to the right bungalow. Although I did not date a large number of girls, I had many friends in both sororities, especially DBS. It was quite acceptable to go to a party as a "stag," or dateless, for this enabled a lot of circulation for the girls. It was expected that boys could "tag" a girl in the middle of a dance, which meant tapping her partner on the shoulder indicating one wanted to dance with her. The really popular girls would get tagged two or three times in one dance. If you got stuck with a girl whom no one tagged, you would begin to look to other boys to help you out. If that did not work, you would suggest that the two of you sit out a dance or two, and then she would make an excuse to go to the ladies' room and disappear.

I have mentioned dances, but said little about dancing. We had all been to some dancing school, so knew how to do the waltz (very seldom), the foxtrot, and the two-step. But when I was in high school, jitterbugging came in. These were very fast dances in which the partners did not put arms around each other, but would sometime dance apart, sometime barely holding on to each other. If a couple were doing this exceptionally well, others would stop their own dancing and gather in a circle around the performers and clap. I never did learn how to jitterbug. If a fast piece of music came on, I would suggest to my partner that we sit it out. But then if a slow piece of music started, I would take her out on the floor. One fall Friday night, after I had gone to school all day, led cheers at the pep rally in the auditorium, then led cheers at the football game, and wound up at the dance, I was tired. I was dancing slowly with Babe Hodges (whom I came to know in high school but we had been born at the same time at St. Vincent Infirmary). The next thing I knew, Babe had her arms around me and was holding me up. She said, with indignation, "Don, wake up!" I had literally fallen asleep in her arms. She caught me before I collapsed on the floor. She has never let me forget that, and I sure did get a lot of kidding at the time. Looking back, I realize my narcolepsy was at work, but I did not get diagnosed for several decades.

Most of the informal dances were held at the Women's City Club at Fourth and Scott Streets (now owned and restored by the Junior League) in the second floor ballroom. There were always adult chaperones at those dances, though they were not intrusive. There was no drinking allowed (perhaps a few boys would go outside for a beer, but I never actually saw it) and no smoking in the dancing room. One of the favorite activities for many of the boys was to go up to the third floor, where the men's rest room was located, to shoot craps. I never did shoot craps because I was too stingy to risk losing money, as well as I disapproved of gambling (Mother's morality). My friend John Washburn was a good crap-shooter and got all his spending money that way.

I was very happy in my social life during high school, especially in my senior year. I did not have any girl with whom I was in love. I did not have someone with whom I was "going steady" for I liked to play the field. And I certainly did not want to get "pinned" to someone. This meant a boy gave a girl his fraternity pin that she would wear (away from school since fraternities and sororities were frowned on by the school authorities), and they were considered an item. But I had a lot of female friends, as well as male, and there were always girls whom I could ask as a date. For me it was more being part of a social group, an experience I'd never had at Scott since our dancing school group broke up.

A symbol of being part of the "in" gang was the use of my car after school. It was a 1940 green two-door Ford. Of course in those days, all cars were stick-shift, and the front seat ran all the way from door to door, so three people could sit on it. In our commute between Scott and Little Rock, there would be five of us, unless Mother rode in to do shopping or for some noonday social engagement. During the war, not many students had cars, so the small parking lot at Central High was not crowded. Once school was over for the afternoon, a lot of people wanted rides to downtown for shopping, doctor appointments, or trips to the library. People would ask me if I would take them down. I was a pretty easy sell, so would agree. It was not at all unusual for us to have eight people in the car. Once I remember we squeezed 12 people in that little car. Why the tires did not blow out, or the shock absorbers go out, I do not know. I could carry that heavy a load from high school to downtown only because the land was level between those two points. I would never have been able to make it in the west part of the city where there were hills. Cantrell Road was a particular challenge for the car. Even with only two or three in the car, I would have to shift from high to medium to low gear at the top of the hill, and then there would be a "ping" in the motor. Because of the war, the octane level in even premium gas was very low.

That car had a personality of its own. We named her "Bessie." When Art was driving the car, he had picked up an ancient car horn. I think it must have been made for a Model-T, or maybe a Model-A, Ford. Instead of making a "beep" or "honk" sound, it went "ah-oog-ah." I never heard another one like it in the city, so when I honked, everyone knew exactly who was coming. Not part of the car itself, but going along with it were two identifications I picked up that senior year. One was an old felt man's hat that I would put on my head and pull down until the crown reached my ears. Somehow I felt that was distinctive. When I went away to college I gave it, and the horn, to Dan Phillips. My other "symbol" that year was a smoking pipe that I would stick out of the side of my mouth. It never had any tobacco in it. I did not smoke and could not stand the smell of it, although Truman would smoke in the back seat and fill the air with fumes. Even so, I thought it made me look very mature to have that pipe. So car, horn, hat, and pipe were part of my *persona* that year.

There is a sub-section of my social life I want to share. It was probably not until after the first of the year in 1945 that it began, but could have started in the fall. Carolyn Alexander and Truman King were both members of DBS, and I was a member of PIE. Truman and Carolyn and I had grown up together at Scott, being part of the same social group since we took dancing at Miss Dorothy Donelson's every other Friday night when I was in the fourth grade.

By personality, those two were not really congenial. Furthermore, Carolyn's grandmother, Mrs. Moore, who was very rich, helped the Kings financially, and I am sure had told them she would make it possible for Truman to go to college. There may have been some resentment on the part of both girls as a result.

Since the war was on, we had to pool our gas to be able to get to the Sunday afternoon DBS and PIE meetings. I guess I usually took the car, since I had a "C" gas-rationing card. After church, did we go to someone's house for lunch, or did we eat in town? I can't remember. But after the meetings were over, we would usually go to one of our three homes for supper. The bonds among the three of us grew stronger. Carolyn was a year behind Truman and me, for she had lost a year of school due to a childhood kidney illness that almost killed her. Truman and I were facing the prospect of going away to college. We three talked a great deal about what the future held. I remember nothing about the content of what we discussed—just that it felt good. World War II was going on, though V-E Day came before the school year was over. But it was assumed war in the Pacific would continue for a long while. I had applied for Yale, but did not get an acceptance until up in the spring—probably April. Truman was planning to go to Texas State College for Women.

I remember when just Truman and I were in the car, she would often comment that she thought the only two happily married couples in our social circle at Scott were her parents and mine. She felt both of them were still in love with each other. Then she would name off the rest—where there was indifference or fighting or running around. I had not speculated on that (I have never been much given to such speculation), but when she said it, it rang true.

I have one special memory of such a Sunday night drive late in the spring, for the air was warm and the car windows open. I had the sense that a very happy period of my life was about over, and the future uncertain.

Some Special High School Friends

I had a lot of friends in high school, both boys and girls. On the other hand, I never had a "best friend" such as Truman and Bettye Jane Erwin were, or Clyde Gray and Walker Barksdale, or as Ann and Carolyn Alexander were, and Art and Breck Campbell. I guess I was not made that way, for I never have needed (or wanted?) that much intimacy, and I did not want the exclusive aspect of such a relationship.

Truman King was a special kind of friendship, and to a lesser degree Carolyn Alexander. They were really more like family than friends, for our roots went back so far and the various strands of friendship were so intertwined that they could not be described by one simple phrase. Truman was Mother's godchild, though that meant very little to Mother, not having been reared in the Episcopal Church. But we were thrown together from infancy. From fourth grade on, we were in the same grade so had some rivalry between us as well as friendship. Carolyn entered the picture when Miss May Keyes married Mr. Charles Alexander. I'm not sure of that year, but it was before we entered fourth grade and started going to dancing school. When I was little, I used to say Carolyn was my "girl." By the time of high school, I never had a date with her. It would have seemed incestuous. She never asked me to fill in as her date for a DBS dinner dance as Truman did. But she was in and out of our house frequently, because she and Ann became best friends long before I entered high school. I continued to see Truman and Carolyn through high school years.

One of my very good female friends was Bettye Jane Erwin. I'm sure I knew her ahead of time, but it was after Bettye Jane and Buddy Craig began to date that BJ and Truman became such good friends. BJ and Truman would spend the night at each other's home not only on weekends but also during the week from time to time. That meant BJ would ride in our car going to and from school. Bettye Jane was very vivacious and was always entertaining in a crowd and was quite popular. One of the ways boys would show they liked a girl (not necessarily wanting to date her) was to steal a red coaloil lantern that had been placed around a construction site as a warning signal, and hang it on her front porch. Her mother would be dismayed, and her father would remove it the next morning. Bettye Jane's father did not try to return them to their original location, but simply lined them up on a shelf in the car garage. Bettye Jane had the largest collection of red lights of any girl in my acquaintance.

Another good DBS friend was Anne Bush. I dated her some, but we remained good friends afterward. She and Bettye Jane ran in the same crowd, but Anne was much quieter than Bettye Jane. Still another girl in that crowd was Patty Sue Thomas, nicknamed "Runt" because she was only about five feet one inch tall. She, too, was a lot of fun to have around, but I never dated her. Still another DBS girl whom I got to know through cheerleading was Marian Davis who moved over from Hot Springs. And in my senior year I dated Maisie Lackey, who had moved down from Mountain Home.

I also had friends in DAD. Margaret Stitt was someone I dated from time to time. (Neither of us knew at the time we were distant cousins through the Williamson line.) Through her I got to know a number of other girls in that sorority (as well as through being in class with them), such as Jane Cockrill, Mimi Coates, and Elizabeth Ginnochio. Another girl in that group was Donna Davis. She lived in an apartment just south of 14th Street, down which I drove each day to reach Little Rock High. She would stand on the corner waiting to catch the bus. By that point in our daily journey, I would have dropped one or more passengers at East Side Junior High, so I would have room for her. I also got to know well some of the DAD girls who were cheerleaders with me—Ged Canby, Marian Tipton, Patty Carson, and Kitty Rose Wills.

There were many other girls in "our circle" whom I knew and liked, and at dances I would "tag" them at least once during the evening.

But I also had a lot of male friends, more than I ever had had before due to the scarcity of boys my age at Scott. The chief and most important one in high school was Buddy Craig, with whom I had run around at Scott. He was one year ahead of me in school. He was in PIE and I am sure was one of the main reasons I received a bid to that fraternity. During my 10th grade year, he was away at military school, but he came back for his senior year. He rode back and forth to school in my car. We were together at PIE and at All Souls Church, and we double dated some. We also continued playing golf and tennis during the summers. Another person who

My friend Buddy Craig, who served as vice-president of PIE when he was a senior and I was a junior.

guided me into PIE was Edwin Stitt, the brother of Margaret Stitt with whom I had some dates. Edwin was also one of the few people who asked my sister, Ann, for dates. Sometime I would invite Edwin to ride with me to Scott (to keep me awake), and he would spend the weekend with us. He seemed to enjoy being in the country and riding horses. The fraternity system limited my circle of close friends to PIE, but I did get to know fairly well some boys in Delta Sigma fraternity, and some who were good students and not in any fraternity. One of those was Louis Brunck, and in my senior year, Thurman Penn. We became quite close, and I invited him down to spend the night a couple of times.

There are three boys I got to know through PIE about whom I want to write more extensively. One of those is Dan Phillips, whose mother owned M. M. Cohn Company, the most expensive department store in Little Rock, and his father was the president. I did not know Dan when his name was brought up for a bid to join PIE, but he had a reputation as being pretty wild and a very fast driver. I had reservations about him on that score. He told me years later he did not receive a bid until two weeks after his classmates did because he was a Jew. Then Harry Crow and Clyde Gray went to bat for him and got him in. I did not know about anti-Semitism because my Aunt May Campbell was Jewish, and she was very much a part of the family. Dan told me years later that he experienced a lot of prejudice. Most of his friends belonged to the Little Rock Country Club, but he was not allowed to swim with them there, and when there was snow he could not ski on the golf course as they did. In Boy Scouts, he was turned down for Golden Arrow because he was a Jew until, again, Harry Crow went to bat for him. I got to know Dan quite well and spent several nights at his house. By the way, Dan was not called by his name but as "Tubby" because he was overweight. I don't think I ever referred to him as Dan the whole time we were in high school, and it has been hard for me to break the habit in adulthood.

The second male friend I want to write about is Jim Johnson. I first met Jim when PIE was "rushing" him. He and Vernon Markham were very close friends. Getting the two of them to pledge was a great plum that year. He was always friendly, good looking, popular, and universally admired. At the end of my 11th grade, and my first year as a cheerleader, he ran for and was elected a cheerleader, too, so that threw us together. Then at the end of that same year when I was elected secretary of PIE, he was chosen as vice-president. That led to more associations. He was in Student Council when I was president, and I named him to the committee responsible for writing a new constitution for LRSH. So in various ways we were more than casual friends. Once he invited me to spend the night at their house on Crestwood, after some kind of party. I remember how luxurious it was. I also discovered that his mother was a McCoy from Monticello and had known Mother when Mrs. Johnson was a girl.

The third good friend in high school, especially in my senior year, was John Washburn. As I've mentioned, John beat me in the election for president of PIE, but I was quite satisfied, for I had just been elected president of the student body at high school, and I felt that was enough recognition. At the same meeting where John was elected, I was elected secretary, the vice-president was Jim Johnson, and the treasurer was Bill Rule.

Johnny was very much "in and of" the inner circle of PIE. He lived in the upper Heights area, where a large proportion of the fraternity lived. I don't believe his family belonged to the Little Rock Country Club, however. John's father, an M.D. specializing in public health, was away in military service. I believe he was a colonel, but I am not sure. I never met him during the years John and I ran around together. Mrs. Washburn stayed home and ran the house and reared John. Since John and Mrs. Washburn were the only ones in the house and had plenty of room, they let me know I was welcome to spend the night with them when I needed to stay in town — and I took up that invitation on many occasions. Johnny was not one of the leading students in high school, nor was he involved in Student Council activities. I think his major investment was in PIE, and in shooting craps. He was rather short in stature, even shorter than I as I recall. He dated a lot, especially girls who were not tall. He did not have a car of his own, but I gather his mother let him use the family car pretty much whenever he wanted it, so far as gas rationing would permit. I do not know if he used his gambling money to buy gas coupons on the black market, as many people did. I never knew of his doing so. But he was mobile. He had a good sense of humor and was a lot of fun to be around.

Later in life when I moved back to Little Rock in 1961. I looked him up. My wife, Ann, and his wife, Carolyn, were not drawn to each other, so we did not see them socially. But in 1965, after Ann had been in Menninger's and the children went to Knoxville (where Donald was put back in first grade), I brought the children back home. Donald was assigned to the second grade at Brady Elementary at the start of the second semester. He was hopelessly behind, for he had been repeating first grade work. We tried to get him put back in first grade (he had been too immature to benefit really from first grade), but the teacher refused. She said she would get one of the brightest children in class to help Donald. He would come home and talk about how Johnny had helped him. One day I asked, "Does Johnny have a last name?" He said, "Washburn." The two boys became good friends until the Washburns moved to another part of the city. I found it ironical that whereas John was not a good student and I was, John's son helped out my son a generation later.

As I reflect on high school, I have a warm glow emotionally as I recall those years, 1942-45, in terms of relationships with peers. I have the impression of being surrounded by a great many friends, but not even John Washburn was a "best friend" in the sense of being inseparable.

I am sorry to say I "dropped" some people who had been friends at earlier periods of my life. This was true of most of those with whom I had been friendly at East Side Junior High. The east end of town by then was lower middle class, except for a few people who still lived in the large homes that had once been the "gold coast" of the city. So most people from that school were not in the fraternity/sorority circle.

Gordon Campbells

The Gordon Campbells must have moved from Gaines Street out to Edgehill about the end of 1942. It seems to me I remember going from the barber shop at 23rd and Arch, where the PIE hogs got our hair cut, to the Campbell house at 23rd and Gaines. I believe it was in 1942 that Sue had to be evacuated from Alaska after the bombing of Pearl Harbor because of fear of a Japanese invasion, and they were in the Gaines Street house when she came back.

But most of my high school memories of them I associate with their first house on Edgehill, the one that had already been built when they bought it. I remember I used to go by their house to change clothes when I'd been in school all day and was getting ready to go on a date, or to change into my cheerleading uniform if I'd not worn it at an assembly meeting that afternoon. I don't think I had meals at their house, nor do I remember spending any nights with them on Edgehill, but I do remember feeling warmly welcomed by them whenever I needed a place to go.

Gordon Campbell, my Uncle Gordon who gave me golf and tennis lessons at Little Rock Country Club.

I am vague as to when Uncle Gordon paid for me to get lessons in both tennis and golf at the Little Rock Country Club. It may have been in junior high days, for I was not that free during daylight hours once I got into high school. But I do remember playing golf on the Rob-Bell golf course and during the summer would often play with Uncle Gordon. I did not feel close to him in those days, but was very grateful to him. I guess I was somewhat in awe of him.

On the other hand, he could not have been more understanding and welcoming than he and Aunt Alice were during those high school summer nights when I was learning how to play bridge. Sometimes, I would go to the clubhouse and play bridge with them. It seems to me Pud Steele would come down, and we would make a foursome. Or Sue Horner may have been there to make the fourth. Aunt Alice and Uncle Gordon were both expert bridge players, but they were very accepting of my first efforts. It is strange, but I did not play bridge with my parents nearly as much as I did with the Gordon Campbells.

We continued going to the Gordon Campbells for Christmas dinner during those high school years. We did not stop doing that until 1948 when Ann and Hoyt got married.

Aunt Alice continued to be my idea of what a "lady" was like.

The Browning Murder

In October 1943, the radio and newspapers shocked the Little Rock community with the news that Mrs. Browning, a wealthy and socially prominent widow living at 5101 Edgewood, had been found dead on the floor of the sunroom of her house. The sunroom is on the front of the house with a number of windows facing the street. The body was discovered by one of her sons, Bill Browning, who had ridden home from school at Catholic High (then at Roosevelt and State Street) on the back of a motor scooter driven by Jerry Brizzolara who lived across the street from the Brownings.

This murder dominated the front page for days as the police looked for a suspect. There were several strange aspects of the case. No murder instrument could be found. There was no evidence of forced entry. A model ship belonging to Bill Browning was found on the floor, broken. Some days later the keys to Mrs. Browning's car were found on the floor of the attic. Then the headlines announced that the police had arrested Bill Browning, and he was accused of murdering his mother.

There was a highly publicized trial. I can remember being at family and other social events when this was the topic of conversation. People, and families, were divided in their belief as to whether Bill was or was not guilty. Many Protestants felt the Catholic community rallied solidly behind Bill. He had an uncle who was a priest and who was his confessor, thus being shielded from questioning. In the end, Bill Browning was acquitted. That did not stop the talk, or the disagreements as to whether he was guilty. Bill had at least two other brothers, and all of them moved out of town, and the house was sold to the Walton Litz family. (I remember going to a meeting there in the late 40s. It was held in the sunroom, and I recall having trouble keeping from looking around to see where the blood stains must have been.) Once Bill was acquitted, the legal community made no effort to find another suspect because they were so convinced he had done it. The Browning family never pushed for more investigation, nor did they offer any reward for evidence leading to the arrest or conviction of the murderer. One neighbor, who lived directly across the street from the Brownings, said his family was convinced Bill had done it when the family failed to push for further investigation. Jerry Brizzolara has steadfastly maintained Bill's innocence, saying Bill was with him at the time the pathologists said Mrs. Browning died. I never knew Bill Browning myself, although I knew many of his friends. Both the neighbors to whom I referred were in my high school fraternity, and Jerry was later my dentist.

At a dinner party on December 4, 1999, at the home of some friends who now own the house where the Browning murder took place, another guest sat on my right. Somehow we got to talking about this being the "Browning house." After we left the table, we got into conversation with the hostess. They, of course, knew about the murder when they bought the house. One day she and her husband were getting ready to leave for Europe, and she had some workmen in the house. The doorbell rang, and two young men were at the door. One of them said that they were in college with Bill Browning's son, and he had asked these two, since they were going to be in Little Rock, to go by the house. Bill Browning, who had moved to the Texas panhandle, had one son and two daughters. The visitor reported that Bill had never told any of his children about the fact he had been charged with and acquitted of killing his mother, but when his son got ready to go to college, he decided it would be wise to tell him in case he ran into people from Little Rock who might ask questions. The lady of the house invited them in, since there was someone in the house. She said one of the young men asked all the questions and did the talking. The other never said a word. She gave them the names of several people who had lived in the neighborhood and who might be of help to them. (None of the others ever heard from the two young men.) Then she left for the airport. While in flight she told her husband about this visit. He immediately said, "The one who did not talk was Bill Browning's son!"

The owner of the house said a black man who had done some stone work for them before had returned for another job after a few years. He had done the work in his work clothes, but when he came to get paid, he was all dressed up in a suit and tie. As they talked while she paid him, he said, "You know you have a ghost here. She digs out in the yard. But don't be afraid. She is a kind ghost. However, you will never be able to get anything to grow in two spots out there in the yard." The owner said they had planted various kinds of plants, and indeed none of them has survived in either of those spots.

Then the lady of the house said a few years later a couple was spending the night with them. The two men were out late doing something, and so the two women went to bed. My friend said she *never* sleeps on her husband's side of the bed, but for some reason that night she did. She said all at once she sat up in bed and *knew* she was going to hear a scream. Almost immediately there was a scream from the guest room. The visiting lady came dashing in and got into bed with the hostess. She reported that she had seen the form of a woman in the guest room.

Class Structure in High School

We used to say how wonderful it was to have only one high school for the whole city of Little Rock, for while there were economic/social differences among East Side, West Side, and Pulaski Heights junior highs, and even more among the various elementary schools, in LRHS people from all levels got to know one another.

Of course this ignored completely the fact there was another public high school—Dunbar High for black students. That was so far off the radar screen that we white people did not think about that. In addition, there was a small Catholic boys school and a small Catholic school for girls, but even faithful Catholics usually went to LRHS—people like Fred Balch and Elizabeth Ginnochio. Some, such as Harry Hastings and Jerry Brizzolara, did go to Catholic High, but the bulk of white students from all over the city did come together on one campus, and we celebrated that fact.

Looking back on it after my class's 58th reunion with all the names printed out, however, I saw that there were "strata" within LRHS. There was one route for those going into manual training or sales work—boys in the former and girls in the latter. Then there was the route of secretarial and accounting. They took basic English and less demanding courses, with no foreign languages. I guess students or parents or school counselors made that decision. Then there was the college prep route. And within that group, there were those Opie, the registrar, thought had intellectual potential or had social or financial backgrounds, and she would route us to the best teachers in each of the departments, while other college preps who she thought were going to college simply because it was the right thing to do would get the "second runs" of the teachers.

As a result, those of us whom Opie put in the top echelon would wind up together in class after class. I came to know a lot of these people—but practically none in the manual or secretarial routes.

Within the first and second rungs of the college prep, there was also the fraternity or sorority distinction. And within that, there were the "big four" and the lesser groups whom we hardly knew. While I had a speaking acquaintance, and some classroom friends, among the Delta Sigs, none was a really close friend. The PIE "sister" sorority was DAD, but most of the people from Scott were DBSs, and I wound up being the PIE sponsor for DBS. I went to parties with DADs, but most of my dating was with DBS girls. The circle got smaller and smaller.

For some reason there was a "mystique" about people from Scott—at least children of planters. It extended to Peggy McNeill, even though her family had collapsed because of alcoholism, and she had to work as a maid on Edgehill. It did not extend to Imogene Henry or Emelou Helton, however.

Some people would break down these distinctions. One was Gege Dickinson, who was in La Jeunese, but not in a sorority. I don't know why. I remember David Davies's best friend was not a member of any fraternity, and that seemed strange. From the 10th grade on, I was in homeroom with Louis Brunck and liked him a lot. But I think he was not in any fraternity (unless maybe Tri-S), so we did not mix socially outside school. In the 12th grade I became good friends with Thurman Penn, whom I had come to know in Student Council. But I think he was the one exception.

There were people with real intellectual ability who were excluded because of their appearance or "odd behavior." One was Lawrence Witherspoon, whom I did not get to know really until Grace Church was founded. I remember his name was brought up more than once for a bid to PIE, but he was voted down because he was "odd." (And he was, but maybe as a result of exclusion, rather than that being a cause.) Another person was Thomas Spurling. Miss Celia Murphy pushed him because she saw poetic qualities in him that the rest of us missed, or if we saw them, did not value. I think he did continue to write poetry as an adult before dying early. Were we really missing a genius?

Looking back on my years at LRHS, I now realize there was just as much stratification there as at Yale. I was not aware of it because I was in the top level—until I got to Yale and realized I was on the bottom rung there. What a great learning. People not only did not know about PIE and Scott, they didn't even know where Arkansas was!

How Boys Dressed in High School

I really am quite vague about how I dressed during those years, or how other boys did. I know we all wore long pants. Knickers were definitely outgrown during, if not before, junior high. And short pants, even in the hottest weather, would have brought on all kinds of kidding. (That is true during the school year. In the summer it was considered all right to wear tennis shorts or even a bathing suit when playing tennis or golf.) In the summer I wore long white duck pants when I was going to a party.

At school I think we wore corduroy pants a good bit of the time, or in the winter some kind of wool pants. I know we did not wear blue jeans, unless we were going on a hayride. And we did not wear khaki pants. We probably wore some kind of synthetic material, for this was during World War II and one pretty much wore what could be found at the store.

I know we wore long-sleeve sport shirts to school. It seems to me I had about three of them. I would wear each one two days, and that would get me through the five days of school. Alfred Bracy always wore a white dress shirt, with the collar unbuttoned and no tie. He was unusual in that way. It seems to me during my senior year I had to keep a white dress shirt and tie in my locker in case an assembly was called and I would preside at it. I wore a dress shirt and tie but do not believe I wore a jacket on such occasions. As a matter of fact, I don't think I owned a sport jacket.

On Sunday I would wear a suit (wool in the winter, Palm Beach in the spring), with a collared white shirt and tie to church. Usually I did not go home between church and PIE meeting, so I would wear a suit to that meeting. I think most of the boys did. I believe my high school suits were mostly double-breasted ones that I would keep buttoned.

At the end of my senior year, as I was getting clothes to take to Yale, I remember buying a light blue wool suit that must have been single breasted, for I also bought a lavender vest to go with it. I thought I was really dressed for the big leagues. When I got to Yale I found I stuck out like a sore thumb, for at Yale people wore gray flannel suits and conservative ties.

It was necessary for me to have a tuxedo during my high school years, for there were formal dances given by PIE and by the sororities. I remember mine was a double-breasted one. I think I wore it right through college, for I did not grow much after high school.

I remember wearing saddle shoes most of the time, and mine had the names of people written on the white parts of the shoes. For Sunday I would have had a pair of black leather shoes that also doubled for use with a tuxedo. I know we did not wear tennis shoes to school, nor would any boy have thought of wearing sandals.

I did not own an overcoat in high school, but had wool jackets in really cold weather, and sweaters in the fall and early spring. I did not need a real coat for I was rarely outside since I drove to school, and there was no place to walk to in the country. I did not own a raincoat for the same reason, or a hat or an umbrella. These were all equipment I had to acquire when I got to Yale and was without a car.

I believe when I wore my cheerleading uniform I would wear a white shirt under it, but not a dress shirt that buttoned at the neck. It would be a white sport shirt.

If there was a "dress code" for boys at high school, I must have fit in it, for I do not remember feeling "out of step," nor did I feel I was a "trend setter," except with that suit I bought for Yale. But then I have never paid much attention to clothes — either those I am wearing or those worn by others. That was also true in high school.

Part of my "clothes" in high school was a pair of glasses. The "in" kind were clear/ivory plastic rims. I was supposed to wear them just for reading, but I found it so hard to keep up with my glasses that I soon started wearing them all the time.

How Girls Dressed During High School

I am not a good observer of clothes, as I mentioned above. I often am not aware of what I am wearing until I look in a mirror. But my memory is that in school there was almost a "uniform" for girls in high school — skirt and sweater in the winter (sometimes a blouse under the sweater or a "false collar"), and in warmer weather, a skirt and blouse. Skirts at this time went slightly below the knee. Girls never wore hats during the week. They wore white "bobby socks" and usually loafers or saddle shoes. In winter they would wear a wool coat over that, and in fall and spring, an over-sweater. In cold weather they often wore gloves.

I don't think I ever saw a girl in school wear slacks — unless it was for a play or some special event, or during a snowstorm. I imagine she would have been sent home had she tried. They did have something called "culottes" that were slacks cut so they looked like a skirt. That would probably have been permissible.

In the summer girls wore shorts a great deal, or dresses. My sister, Ann, almost never wore shorts because she thought she was too fat—and was at that stage in her life. She did wear "jodhpurs," or pants, when she rode horseback.

For church or semi-formal events, girls might wear a dress, or it could be a skirt and a very nice sweater or blouse. There was often a strand of imitation pearl beads. But I think most girls in those years would have some kind of velveteen dress. If they had several then one of them would be black. In grade school and through junior high, they usually had flat-heel, black patent leather shoes with white socks. By the time they got to high school they would be wearing shoes with heels and "silk" stockings for more formal events. Since this was during World War II, silk was almost impossible to obtain, and nylon was just making its appearance. So the stockings were rayon—which was not as sheer, and which tended to "sag" as the day wore on.

For formal dances the girls would wear long dresses—usually of some pastel color. There were a few very sophisticated girls who would wear a black dress, and some of them wore white. I am not sure of the materials. Some of them were "net" over a silk-like undergarment; some of them were just silk-like, but again, during the war, materials were hard to come by. Most of the dresses had short sleeves and were modest—partly because many of the girls did not have large breasts. A few, who were richly endowed, would wear dresses that were cut pretty low. I think when they wore long dresses, they wore flat shoes so they would be more comfortable dancing. The boy was supposed to send (or take) his date a corsage, and he was wise to find out ahead of time what color would go best with the dress. The corsages were often carnations or daisies. More serious ones could be roses or gardenias. To go all out, there was an orchid. I don't think I ever sent one of those. The corsage was usually pinned to the girl's dress at the shoulder. It could go on at the waist, and if she preferred not to distract from her dress, there were corsages made to wear at her wrist.

For a formal date, if it was cold, the girl would wear a regular wool coat—unless she had a fur coat. This meant almost invariably a mink-dyed muskrat short coat.

Home Situation in High School

I have written a great deal about what happened away from home during my high school years, and that is appropriate, for this is when a young person begins pulling away from family in preparation for becoming an independent adult. I never went through the somewhat violent adolescent rebellion I observed in some of my friends. I'm not sure why. Had my parents so brainwashed me on their values and outlook on life that I was cowed into submission? I never felt that way, but I suppose someone whose spirit was broken would not be aware of it. Or, did my parents lay on me so few restrictions, and give me so much freedom, that I did not have to rebel to get free from them? I do not remember any form of discipline they exercised during those three years. I was never "grounded" or had my allowance cut off. Daddy said I could have use of the car if I did not exceed the 35 mph wartime speed limit. Mother had drilled in me inhibitions about keeping my hands off girls. I guess in that area I was cowed, for I did date a fair amount and I certainly had a strong sex drive. But this was never talked about at home. Mother got in her licks when I was much younger. I think maybe I never went through adolescent rebellion until after my divorce and I moved over to Atlanta where I had a good measure of anonymity.

During my first year in high school, my sister Ann was living at home, a senior in high school. We had always been very close when I was growing up, but that year there were some tensions between us. I confess that I teased her a lot, and she would let me get under her skin. We still had some good times together, and certainly never fought verbally or physically, but we had grown apart—although she really supported me in trying out to be a cheerleader. She rejoiced when I was elected to that, and also when I became a PIE. She dated very little and never seemed to be jealous when I went to dances. She had a lot of girlfriends and would invite them to come down to spend the night or the weekend. She was generous in letting me associate with those friends, who became my friends, too. Ann was the driver of the school car the year I was in the 10th grade. I recall some of my teasing had to do with how she drove. When she left for the University of Tennessee the next fall, I kissed her goodbye, and it shocked both her and me.

From that moment on, our old closeness was restored. During my junior and senior years when she was home on vacations and during the summer, we had a great time doing things together.

I think it was in the winter of 1942-43 that Grandmother Campbell came down from Bloomington, Illinois, to "visit" for the remainder of the winter in Arkansas, living with us most of the time but occasionally going to the Gordon Campbells' home in Little Rock for a short time. Grandfather Campbell died in 1942. Every year Mother and Grandmother would go through a ritual. In the early fall Mother would write, inviting her to come down to "visit." No one ever said "live." Grandmother would take a few weeks to think it over, and then would decide she would like to come. When she arrived, Mother's friends, and Aunt Alice's friends in Little Rock, would all have parties welcoming her back to Arkansas. Then when spring arrived Grandmother would begin to talk about going home. At this point Mother's friends, and Aunt Alice's, would have "going away" parties for her. She would return to Bloomington until the next fall when the ritual would start all over again. She did this for at least 10 years. Mother was so grateful for the way Daddy had welcomed her mother, Main, into the home that she was determined to be just as gracious to his stepmother (whom he regarded as his mother). She had her room in the Guest Room, so when Ann came home from college her own room was waiting for her. I never picked up any friction between Grandmother and any of the family. I did not see a great deal of her, for I was dashing in and out, and was studying at night. But she was a pleasant presence to have around and added depth to the conversation, for she was a learned woman who read a great deal. Whereas we'd had Neoma Lyon living with us when I was in the eighth grade, and Alice Coles when I was in the ninth, from the 10th through the 12th it was Grandmother. Having someone living in was part of the lifestyle of our home.

Mother was the dominant force in the house during those years, as she had been in the previous ones. When Grandmother was visiting, she tried to find some time each day to do something with Grandmother, other than take her to parties and have folks in for meals. One activity Grandmother loved was hooking rugs together. Grandmother, whose eyesight was not what it had once been, would do the background and Mother would do the flowers.

Mother kept up her bridge club, birthday club, and couples' dinner-bridge club round of activities. She also was teaching Sunday School to junior high girls (until she was 50, when she moved to adults). She was on and off the Board of All Souls Church, and at one point chairperson of that group. As soon as we left Scott School, she dropped out of PTA and had nothing to do with it when I was at East Side or Little Rock High. She became very active in a women's study group called Edelweiss Club, for which she had to write and give a research paper each year. She would spend hours studying for that and then writing the paper. She also spent some time in the first half of my 10th grade, then the following summer, and the first half of 11th grade helping me with my Latin. I think she got some pleasure in reviving her skill in it. However, I am sure there were times when this was a real drag on her. It did give us some time alone that we would not have had otherwise.

Mother often said her calling in life was to be a mother and a hostess. She worked hard at both. She wrote Art, and then Ann, a letter each Sunday night, just as she did me once I left for college. There was always room for a guest at our dinner table. I did not invite a lot of people down to spend the weekend, as Art and Ann had done, though I did some—and felt free to do so if I wanted to. Because of transportation limitations during the war, if I had someone for Friday night, he would have to stay over until Sunday, and I didn't want to entertain anyone that long. Also, on one of those two nights I needed to study. Mother's ban on studying on Sunday was firm. But Buddy Craig could drive over for the day, or for one night, and he came often in my junior year after returning from military school.

Daddy was always in the background, solid and helpful. The only person who did not know Mother was the head of the family was Mother. But she always put Daddy in the position of leadership, even if she had pushed him into doing what she wanted him to do. Knowing that whatever she suggested he would object to, she "played" him the way a violinist does his instrument. If she had in mind a major project, she would start out opposing it. Daddy would take the bait and start pushing in its favor, and soon would have the idea that it originated with him. Mother would then praise him for being so foresighted! It worked like a charm. Mother was a nominal Democrat, although I think she often voted Republican as Daddy did.

By the time I was in high school, the war had brought the economy out of the Depression. The prices of cotton and beef went up. The Winooski Savings Bank, for which Daddy had worked from 1927 on, had gone bankrupt in the late 1930s. Daddy was then hired by the Federal Deposit Insurance Corporation to sell off their Arkansas land holdings. I am not sure when he disposed of the last of these, but in doing so he was able to make some fast friends in East Arkansas. Once the price of cotton and rice went up, he was able to help these farmers who had rented during the Depression buy the land they had farmed. Some of them became very wealthy. Daddy was very successful, I gather, in this. But as that workload dwindled, he began spending more time on the plantation, where the recovering economy was making it profitable. By this time he was about as involved with cattle as with cotton, and he enjoyed the cattle end much more. He quit wearing three-piece suits everyday to work, as he had done with the Bank and FDIC, and began wearing khaki pants and shirts. This sometimes embarrassed me, for the fathers of most of my friends in Little Rock were businessmen and wore suits and ties. But when he would invite these friends to ride horses and herd cattle, they thought he was something special.

Daddy was always a man of few words. He was very conservative (in every way except farming, where he was very progressive) and would shake the newspaper and raise his voice in protest over something the New Deal did. He was one of the few Republicans in Scott. In fact, the Republican Party was so weak in Arkansas in the early 40s that it consisted to a good extent of some of those who had come down from Illinois and their friends.

During my high school years, I was not close to Daddy. He was supportive of most of the things I did, except cheerleading. He never protested it, but he and Mother never came to see me lead the yells. I don't remember having any angry clashes with him or rebelling against him. I just kept my distance. Due to a speech impediment in his childhood, he "barked" out his words. This had frightened me as a child, and I still had the same reaction when I was in high school. I did not learn until years later about the speech impediment. I wish I had known about it then, for I think our rapprochement could have taken place during my adolescence instead of after I got out of college. Daddy provided a comfortable living and never raised a question about financing my college education even though I was applying for a much more expensive school than Art or Ann had gone to.

Another part of our household was Hattie Walker, the cook. I think Hattie must have come to us in about 1941, after Neoma Lyon left, so I would have been in the ninth grade. Her father was Lewis Crittenden, a black renter who was a notch up in the black social scale from a sharecropper or day laborer. I don't know how much education Hattie had, but she was intelligent, nice looking, and always neatly dressed. I don't know how old she was. My guess is she was in her late 20s or early 30s. She was a very good cook and seemed more businesslike in the kitchen than my friend Marie had been. And there was no comparison between Hattie and Bea, the incompetent cook who lasted about a year. Soon after Hattie came, I somehow got in the habit of kidding her by calling her "Old Woman," and she in turn called me "Old Man." It was always a pleasant relationship, from my point of view, but I never felt as emotionally close to her as I had to Marie.

Hattie Walker, our cook at Scott in the 1940s.

Tom Cat (Fred) Nowden was also a part of the household until he left for California to get a wartime job. He was followed by Freed Pearson. Freed and Hattie had some kind of relationship going, when she was not having an affair with Deshay Robinson, a married black landowner near the Pemberton plantation. I guess Hattie had refused to come to work for us unless there was better housing than Dr. Robinson's old office had been for Marie (and I guess for Bea). Daddy built a one-room house, with a screened-in porch, and a bathroom with a flush commode for Hattie! (It has been moved to the Scott

Plantation Settlement, although it has at this writing not yet been restored.) The chief thing of note is the flush commode. So far as I know, that was the first time such a convenience was provided for any black person on the plantation, or any neighboring one. There was no bathtub in the house, however. Since her house was some distance from ours, she had more privacy. Often Deshay Robinson's car would be there late at night. After my famous "Can you get it from your cook?" question, Hattie was of great interest to the boys who would come down for a meal or to spend the night.

Bob Hunt, the hostler, continued to be part of the "household" in that he came to

Freed Pearson, our yard man at Scott in the 1940s.

the kitchen every morning for his coffee, delivered the paper, and saddled riding horses when we wanted to use them. In 1942, there were still a good many mules for him to feed and equip. By 1945, they were diminishing in number, although the difficulty in getting tractors because of the war delayed the dramatic transition that took place in the postwar years. Because I would be off to school most mornings before Bob came in, I did not see him much except when I rode horses. Because of some frightening experiences I had early in life with runaway horses, I never enjoyed riding as Ann and Alice, and Daddy, did. But for a couple of years in high school I had a pony named Tony that I did like and rode with some pleasure. Daddy was big into raising cattle at this time, and I would help in herding them.

My memory of home life during my high school days is pleasant. I was away from home enough, due to school and social life, that I did not feel hemmed in. But I was there enough to feel deeply rooted. I had no desire to rebel and break away. I had no serious arguments with Mother or Daddy. I liked having a grandmother around again. Main had died in 1938, and I missed her. Grandmother Campbell did not force herself on me, but was there if I wanted to talk. I guess one of the reasons I suffered so from homesickness once I got to Yale was because I had been so happy at home.

Being an Only Child

By the time I entered high school in the fall of 1942, Art was away at Texas A&M, and then in the Army. This meant I had the upstairs of the house to myself, except when the whole family slept on the sleeping porch.

Starting in the 11th grade, Ann was away at the University of Tennessee, and I had my first experience of being the only child. I loved it! Ann and I had bickered during her senior year in high school (mostly because I picked at her). Our deep friendship did not begin until she went away to college. So there was some relief that first year of not having to "share" with anyone. I also had control of the school car those last two years in high school.

I studied hard during all three years in high school. It never dawned on me that loneliness was a possibility. I was busy during the week with homework, and also on Friday or Saturday night. Sometime I would have a boy come down to spend the night or the weekend, but usually I was by myself. I can remember being alone in the house on Saturday nights when Mother and Daddy would go out to play bridge. I would often listen to the Grand Old Opry. And on Saturday afternoons I would often listen to the Metropolitan Opera. My love of reading, which had flourished so in late elementary school and into junior high, pretty much faded out, not because I did not like to read but because my studies took most of my time.

I don't remember ever, during those two years of being the only child, of yearning to have someone my own age to share the house with me. It was a new, and pleasant, experience so far as I was concerned.

Summers of '43-'45

In the summer of 1943, before the 11th grade, the shortage of labor on the plantation was getting serious. They really needed me. I started the summer again driving the truck for oat harvest and into hay baling. The oats triggered a violent allergic reaction. I don't know how long I kept doing that, but I think I did not last to the end. I did, however, work with the hay that second summer. I don't know if I started taking allergy shots that summer, or the next. But Mother would boil the needle and give me the shots (she had some nursing training during World War I). One summer, and it was probably this one, I helped a bit as a tenant house was being built back near the Perry Field. And I think I did some work with the cattle. However, that was the summer I took the first half of Third Year Latin at home, with Mother as the teacher. During the 10th grade, after I completed Second Year Latin, we realized I had to have three years of one foreign language to get in an Ivy League college. I had started French too late to go that route. Mother had majored in Latin in college, and had helped me along for two years. Gas was rationed, so I could not drive into Little Rock every day for summer school. So they let us work out a deal for Mother to teach me, and I would take the school exam. If I passed it, then I would get credit and be able to go into the second half of Third Year Latin in the fall. I learned more Latin that summer than I had ever known before! Mother really made me get down to it. So much of that summer was spent on Latin.

I also had some pleasant activities. Buddy Craig came back from military school, and he and I got together often for golf, tennis, and swimming. I was in PIE as a member, and there were some social events during the summer, then rush parties toward the end. I recall it as being a good summer. Art was in the Army, but not yet overseas, so not in danger. Ann was getting ready to go away to the University of Tennessee as a freshman. Through the USO (United Services Organization) and chaplain's office at Camp Robinson, a number of soldiers would come down to Scott for weekends. We got to know some of them pretty well. They were invited to picnics, swimming parties, and dances if we had any. They were all two to three years older than I. Since all eligible men over 18 from Scott and Little Rock were in the military, the college girls really liked having the soldiers down.

In the summer of 1944, between 11th and 12th grades, with the war on, Mr. Davis, the postmaster, had lost his assistant to the draft and was needing help. He invited me to be the acting assistant postmaster! Here I was, just 16 years old, and in a position that had always been held by an adult. (I've written about Mr. Davis — "Day" — in my first volume. He was a regular part of our household when I was younger.) Of course I felt comfortable with Day because I had grown up with him in and out of our house, and even after he and Dex married we saw a lot of them. I was able to ride to and from work with him. It was not a demanding job, though enough to keep me busy. There

C. M. "Day" Davis, postmaster at Scott, summer 1944.

were two rural mail carriers: Mr. Dickey was a white man with the longer route, and a black man (whom I called by his first name), had the shorter. Looking back on it, I am surprised a black man could get that job, for it was considered a desirable one. I liked him. He was competent and "kept to his place" — not obsequious, but not pushy. At this time I was a racist, though I did not realize I was. I remember some black newspapers from Detroit would come through the mail, going to black subscribers. I would read them from time to time and was shocked by their presentation of life, which differed so from what I had been taught. They even supported labor unions! I also remember when a post card came to Buddy Craig once, I read it and called to tell him what it said before he received it. That, of course, should have caused me to be fired if it had ever been discovered.

While most people got their mail at home from the carrier, there were a few people who lived near Scott and had mailboxes. They would come in and visit. I remember Mr. George Alexander would come, get his mail out of the box, and throw one envelop after another into the wastebasket without even opening them. I was amazed. I had received so little mail in my life that I opened every one that came. I now understand. I heard a lot of man-talk in the post office, not as openly coarse as what I heard on the plantation because women also came and went, but it was not the polished style I was accustomed to at home.

I remember D-Day vividly — June 6, 1944. There was a radio in the post office, and we kept it on all day, getting reports from the Normandy beach and from headquarters in England. Art was not over there, but was in training to go. There were many people from Scott who were there. It was a tense and emotional day — and continued so for some weeks. The night of D-Day a special prayer service was held at All Souls Church. My family never went to evening services, but we did that night. I remember especially Miss Mildred Pemberton praying for the safety of those involved. (On the Allied side. It would have been regarded as treason to pray for the Nazi people in peril.) This was very moving, for her only son had, a few months before, been shot down and killed over Yugoslavia. For weeks there was doubt whether the Allied invasion would be a success.

By this time, the labor shortage was so acute that Daddy was hiring German prisoners of war to help on the farm. There was supposed to be no fraternization, and they were to work only in the fields, but we had no yardman at this point. Daddy would use them to cut the grass, and Mother would feed them. Mother and Daddy got to be friends with a couple of them, and when the war was over would send them CARE packages.

This was the summer when I had just been elected secretary of PIE, was the newly elected president of the student body, and was going to be a cheerleader for the second year. I was in my prime socially. While gas restrictions were severe, I did some dating in town, and we had a good bit of social activity at Scott. I also, in my off time, engaged in the sports I liked. It was a very happy summer for me, while it was living hell in both Europe and the Pacific.

During school term, my only "sport" was cheerleading. We did have to practice a good bit, and I entered into that fully and enjoyed it — probably more for the social aspect than the athletic. By being a cheerleader, I avoided those games and sporting activities I had disliked before when I had to take gym. Areas that were completely "out" for me were football, basketball, and baseball. At home at Scott, I had no interest in fishing or hunting, and had to avoid diving because I would get ear infections. Things I did like to do, but participated in on a limited basis were ping-pong, badminton, croquet, dancing, and horse riding. Things that I really enjoyed were tennis (my favorite sport), swimming, sunbathing (I spent hours doing this), and golf (mostly because Buddy Craig liked to play—but I enjoyed it mildly.)

Uncle Gordon paid for me to take some tennis and golf lessons at the Little Rock Country Club. The tennis pro one summer taught me to serve in a most unusual way—to turn my back to the net, then spin my body around as I hit to give the ball more speed and less bounce. When it went in, it was very effective—but because I could not count on throwing the ball up the same way every time, it was erratic. I got a lot of kidding about that serve. One of its values, though, was that it would confuse my opponent.

I also took golf lessons, thanks to Uncle Gordon. The golf pro said I had excellent form, but I was never able to "click" on it—partly because I was not physically strong. I suspect it was also the way he kept students coming back, by saying "You have a beautiful swing. Just a little more, and you'll really hit them." It never did work out.

In swimming, I was adequate and competent enough so I always felt safe, but never outstanding. I was never confident enough to swim across Old River. And the fact I could not dive or get my head under water kept me from having any "style." What I really loved, and spent hours doing, was sunbathing, trying to get the deepest tan I could. We never heard in those days that exposure to sun rays could lead to cancer.

The "post-high school" summer of 1945 was only one month long, for I left at the end of June for Yale. However, the month between graduation from high school and my departure was one long idyllic party. There were a number of invitations to homes as farewells, some parties given at Scott, and dates and visits in Little Rock. Cousin Catherine and Ann Williamson had a "cousin house party" in Monticello for my sister Ann and me, Scott Hamilton and Ethel Smart, cousins on the maternal side. I had never met Ethel before, but liked her immediately. Scott was "weird" in high school and stayed that way that weekend. Because of gas rationing, we could not drive to Monticello, but came and went by bus. And while we were in Monticello, there was a bus strike, so we stayed an extra day. All the Williamson friends had parties for us. There were some naval trainees from the Delta part of Mississippi at A&M College whom they invited out for parties. The two Anns, Ethel, and I played bridge—and Scott wandered off to case the town. We laughed, much of it at him, the whole time we were there. It was a wonderful house party. Then we returned to more preparations for my departure.

I remember once during the early 1940s our cousins Adrian and Lamar Williamson came up from Monticello to Scott for some kind of dance at Scott. I think it was a Christmas dance Carolyn Alexander had at her house. Ann came up once, too. I don't know if all three came at the same time. Probably. I remember Adrian and Lamar slept in Art's and my room, and I stayed on the sleeping porch. I was amazed that they played football. Being from a small school, I guess everyone could be on the team. In Little Rock, only the "big boys" did that. I wondered at the time what it would be like to go to a small school. This must have been pretty early in the 1940s, for the Adrian Williamsons moved to Washington when Adrian, Sr., was stationed there, Ann going to the Cathedral School, and Adrian, Jr., graduating from St. Albans.

Transportation to and from LRHS

There were really several ways white people came from all over Little Rock, Park Hill, and Pulaski County to attend LRHS during World War II. There were some who, living in that part of the city, were able to walk, but they were few in number. Benjy Lincoln tells me when the weather was good he and friends around 20th and Gaines/Broadway would walk to and from school — passing Dunbar High and never having any problems there.

The great bulk of people came by streetcar and/or bus, from all over the city. Those who lacked the money could get free tokens. Others bought tokens in quantity, and this let them ride at a lower cost than individual payments. The one that most of my "Heights" friends rode was the "Number 8." They took it to Third and Victory, then walked to Eighth Street where they caught another streetcar that took them to 12th and Park, then they walked two more blocks. I never rode on it, but this is the one that carried most of the fraternity and sorority boys and girls, and I would hear stories of all that happened there. Because there were so many of them, I think they found it to be fun. There certainly was no quiet time on it during which they could study. I am sure there were other buses and streetcars that went in other directions to the four corners of town. (The city had started replacing streetcars with buses just as the war was breaking out.) While there was a lot of noise and horsing around, I don't think I ever heard of any serious troubles or fights, although there was probably a lot of teenage cruelty toward those who did not "fit the mold."

I am sure there must have been black students and adults riding those streetcars and buses. They would have had to sit in the back, and probably had to stand since the whites would have claim to as many seats as they needed. Whether the black and white schools started at different hours so there would not be large numbers of students from the two races on the same buses at the same time, I do not know. It was typical of that segregated world that the question would never have been raised, but some accommodation would have been worked out—doubtless to the advantage of the whites. The housing pattern in Little Rock in the 1940s was probably less segregated than it is in the early 21st century, so there would have been both black and white students from all areas going to school on the same days.

There were those who drove cars—again, not many. With gas rationing, few had enough gas to spend it driving to school five days a week. Lawson Delony tells me five of them would carpool to school—each family driving one day. Usually one parent would have a "B" card because of the nature of his work (Lawson's father, an architect, was building Prisoner of War camps) or because of disabilities (Cal Ledbetter's mother was bedridden). Those of us who came from out in the county could get a "C" card if there were five people in the car each day. We Campbells had the 1940 Ford that Daddy had bought for Art. Art drove it two years, Mrs. Crutchfield drove it one, Ann drove it one, and I drove it two. I have written elsewhere that the one condition Daddy placed on me when he turned over the car to me was that I would never exceed the 35-mph speed limit (which I did only once). As a result it took about 60 minutes from our house to LRHS, with stopping to pick up people and deposit them at their various schools.

Some people came in from Scott with Dr. Richardson, a dentist who lived at Scott, so he was able to get gas. (He was the only person on the road who drove more slowly than I, and I could pass him.) The Dortch clan rode in a station wagon driven by Miss Catherine (who would close one eye to pray with and keep one open to drive with). Carolyn Alexander Thaxton tells me she caught the Trailways bus coming from Memphis each morning, and another to get home. I guess she took the bus or streetcar once she reached Little Rock.

1944 Flood

There had been a disastrous Arkansas River flood in 1927 — one that devastated the whole lower Mississippi River basin. During the Depression, one of the New Deal efforts to provide work for the unemployed, as well as to protect against future floods, was the building of a much larger network of levees along the rivers. I think the one in the Scott area was completed in about 1937.

After that, because there was no system of dams, there were almost annual rises in the Arkansas River that would flood the low land on the river side of the levee. Daddy kept cattle on some of that unprotected land we called "the island." When word came that the river was rising, there would be a push to get the cattle off "the island" and up on the levee to graze on the grass there (Daddy had some kind of lease for grazing rights) or brought over to the main plantation.

I can't remember any of these floods being a serious threat until the spring of 1944. The river got so high that, looking out the west windows of our sleeping porch, I could see water coming right up to the top of the levee — about a mile and a half away.

While water was not coming over the top of the levee, it was undermining it — coming up in "bubbles." This was during World War II, and troops were brought up from Fort Polk in Louisiana and stationed all along the levee — for two reasons. They were there as guards, because in flood season there was always a temptation for people on one side of the river to cross over and dynamite the levee on the other to relieve the pressure on the levee protecting them. The second reason was to build up, with sandbags, a circular tower higher than the top of the levee. Water would seep under the levee, but once it reached the height of the water on the river side, it would match the pressure and stop the undermining. If my memory serves me correctly, I think they stayed for about 10 days or two weeks.

That year I was driving our Ford to school each day with four passengers. The road was clear as far as Baucum, but at that point the highway went on the river side of the levee. Right at Baucum the land elevation is high, and the levee quite low. But farther west, on the way to Rose City, the elevation drops, and the levee becomes quite tall. I knew, from previous days, that the flood waters were over the road in that stretch. I could have gone north to Highway 70, but that was longer and in gas rationing days one took the shortest possible route. Also, since I drove at 35 miles per hour, going up to Highway 70 would have taken longer. So I decided to forge ahead.

We were going through water that came almost up to the bottom of the doors, but having no problem — until suddenly I began smelling gas fumes. I asked my passengers, and they all agreed that was the smell. The farther we went, the stronger the smell got. There was no way to turn around, so we were all sitting on the edge of our seats, wondering if we would make it before exploding.

When we finally reached the junction of highways 30 and 70 at Rose City where Warden's Service Station was located (the one all the Scott people used), I pulled in, threw open my door, and told the other four to run. I shouted, "We're about to blow up!" We and all of the service attendants ran behind the building, waiting for the explosion. Nothing happened. Gradually they came out from hiding, and even more gradually, we did. They looked under the hood of the car and could not find any leak. With reservations, we climbed back in the car and went on to school.

That afternoon on our way home when we reached the flooded part of the highway, the water was coated with a thick layer of black. During the war, in order to get oil and gas from the Texas oil fields to the northeast, two major pipelines had been hurriedly built — the Big Inch and the Little Inch lines. The Little Inch crossed under the Arkansas River downstream from Little Rock. It had sprung a major leak that morning just before we headed into town, and the first flood of petroleum was coming down and spreading over the inundated areas. It was not yet visible and had not been reported, but we were getting the fumes. By that afternoon, though, the gooey mess was evident, and it was on the news that night. In the following weeks when the water receded, the oil coated the trees, grass, and ground. I think it took years for the fertility of that land to recover.

Selection of a College

I am appalled when I realize how little I knew about colleges when I began thinking about where I wanted to attend.

When I was a child, I had been through Conway on our way to and from Petit Jean Mountain and had seen Hendrix College from the road. I liked the idea of a small college near home, and there was something appealing about it, although the only person I had known who attended there was our All Souls pastor, Mr. Hedges, and he was not well educated.

I knew a lot about Randolph Macon College for Women, Mother's alma mater, but of course that was out. In 1937 and perhaps again in 1941, we had stopped at Washington and Lee. We visited Cousins Eleanor and Edgar Shannon (where he was head of the English Department), and I had heard about how happy Uncles Arthur and Howard McCain were there. I found it very appealing. And some people of my generation from Little Rock went there, so it would not be unknown territory.

When we were in Williamsburg we had gone through William and Mary College. I had been intrigued by the architecture and the history of the place, and had some passing interest, wondering what it would be like to live there. But I never knew anyone who went and knew very little about the college.

In 1941 when we were in Washington, we passed Georgetown University, and Mother commented that was where diplomats were educated. So I had that in mind, though I knew nothing about the university.

Daddy had gone to Lake Forest College, but he had never pushed it.

In 1933 when we went to the Chicago World's Fair, we visited Northwestern University where Walter Dill Scott (Grandmother's brother) was president. We had lunch, and I believe we swam in the pool. But it never seemed much of an option, for Walter Dill had retired or died by the time I was considering college.

We had visited the University of Tennessee in 1941. In my junior year, Ann enrolled there, largely because Miss Jessie Harris, a family friend, was dean of the Home Economics College where she would major. But I was not excited about that university, even after Ann enrolled.

Art was enrolled at Texas A&M, but that was a military school, and I was certain from the beginning that I did not want to be a part of that—and also engineering was clearly not my cup of tea.

The Murphy sisters used to talk a great deal about Columbia University, and usually got a scholarship each year for someone from Little Rock.

There was Junior College in Little Rock, which Neoma Lyon had attended. But that was a very second-rate school, and furthermore, I thought I wanted to get away from home. (I changed my mind later!)

The school about which I had heard the most was the University of Arkansas. Swarms of people from Little Rock attended there. Chi Omega and Pi Beta Phi were the equivalent of DBS and DAD, and Sigma Chi and SAE were like PIE and Delta Sigma in LRHS. There was an open channel from one to the other. Pud Steele was up there, after escaping from Sullins College, and would bring back all kinds of reports. But all I heard from her, and from other friends going there, had to do with fraternities and sororities and parties and drinking. I was sure if I went there, I would know lots of people, would have introductions, and would have a lot of fun. I had an idea that no one studied there. (I later found this was not true, but I did not know that when I was in high school.)

All my observations were colored by the fact that all the years I was in high school World War II was being waged. Boys might get in one term, or two at the most, before they got drafted or enlisted. Many went into the military straight from high school if they were already 18. That meant most of the reports on the University of Arkansas came from girls.

There was also the report Mrs. Ross Anderson gave to Mother, of her conversation in the club car of a train with a diplomat who said anyone wanting to go into diplomacy really needed to attend Yale, Harvard, or Princeton because those were the only American universities people abroad had ever heard of. When Aunt Marion heard that, she said, "Oh, don't go to Harvard. They are such snobs." I ruled it out instantly.

I wrote to Princeton, but learned that it did not give scholarships in freshmen year. Once a sophomore, a student could apply for a scholarship. But I could not afford one year without help.

So I applied to Yale University, Hartford, Connecticut. I had never visited there nor known anyone who attended. My lack of knowledge about Yale is indicated by the fact it is located in New Haven, not Hartford. Some kind person in the post office took pity on me and forwarded my inquiry to New Haven!

Looking back on it, I am shocked that my parents let me apply for only one college — and Yale at that. When I got to New Haven, I found that most people had applied to several of the Ivy League colleges. Some got in several and had to choose. My roommate, Dan Howard, really wanted to go to Dartmouth (because he had grown up in New Haven), but did not get in.

Down in my heart, I was half-hoping Yale would turn me down. I really wanted to go to Washington and Lee, where both of Mother's brothers had gone, or to the University of Arkansas in Fayetteville, where most of my PIE brothers were going until they got drafted. Yet there was also a nagging feeling that I ought to go to Yale, if I could get in, for I wanted to be a diplomat.

Looking back on it, admission to Yale in 1945 was pretty casual from the University's point of view as well as mine. During the War, male enrollment was so low that a men's college was probably eager to take any boy who was too young to be drafted. I received a phone call that someone was to interview me. His last name was Tracy, and I remember he said his father was a professor of math at Yale. He was tall and thin, and not very attractive in looks or personality. We met at a coffee shop on Third Street, across from the Rector Building where Mr. Tracy worked. I think I was a bit nervous and anxious. I have no idea what we talked about. I did not feel I had made any special impression on him — nor he on me. I never saw the man again. Since I avoided math at college, I never had his father for class, nor even heard of him — for I stayed as far as I could from the math department.

I got no written report on the interview. I wonder what he wrote about me. I think such interviews were an important part of the admissions formula. How different my life would have been had he written such a negative report that I was turned down.

The time of the year arrived—it must have been April—when colleges were sending out rejections and acceptances. I had been watching the mail carefully every day. It was a Saturday morning. I walked down to the mailbox on the highway—and there was a letter from Yale University! I was terribly excited—would it be "yes" or "no"? I tore open the envelop, and there it said I had been accepted—and given a $294-a-term scholarship!

I remember running all the way back up to the house, shouting as I went. I could hardly believe it. Mother and Daddy shared my excitement and joy. I do not remember getting on the phone, but I am sure I called around spreading my good news.

What a difference the message in that envelop made in my life!

$294 does not sound like much money, but the equivalent in 2008 dollars is $3,516, or $7,032 for a year. I do not have figures on the total cost when I was a freshman, but I remember in 1948 when I applied for scholarship help, the total cost for a year was $1,250, which in 2008 dollars is $10,763. Higher education at a top university was a real bargain in the 1940s.

High School Religious Life

Daily prayer had dropped out of my life in middle childhood, as soon as Mother stopped having me "say my prayers" to her. So had Bible reading at home on a daily basis. It was not that I rebelled against either; they just slipped out of my daily routine. And there were very few places in our house where one could count on, or have, privacy. When I was nine years old, I pushed to "join the church" because I wanted to be able to take communion. Mother tried to hold me back, but I insisted. Uncle Mac MacKrell was pastor at the time. He gave us no instruction and announced he had asked us no questions because he knew we would give only rote answers. It meant very little to me, except Main did give me a Bible for the occasion.

I did, however, continue to go to Sunday School and church—not reluctantly, but as a matter of course, and really with anticipation, for I would see friends there. In church there was no inspiration from the sermons. By that time Wesley Pruden was the pastor, and I had little use for him. I had rebelled against sitting with my parents up front and would sit on the back row with my friends. I was in charge of ushering (how I got that job I do not know) and was responsible for finding some boy my age to help me. When I could get Buddy Craig to come, he was my choice; otherwise, Wayne Douglas. As soon as we took up the offering, we would go up to the balcony or sit in the women's Bible class, and he would tell me dirty jokes. I also liked the architecture of All Souls, especially the Good Shepherd stained glass window. The choir was plus and minus. We would make fun of one soprano who squeaked and an alto who sounded like an out-of-tune piano, but on the whole I liked the music—especially when Bill Fletcher would sing a solo, "Going Home."

I never missed Sunday services unless I was sick or out of town. I was probably regarded as the keystone of our class. I guess when I spent the night in town it was usually on Friday, for I don't remember going to church with any of my friends in town, except once when I stayed with Fred Balch and went with him to the St. Andrews Catholic Cathedral. (This was the only time I went to a Catholic service until once in college with Dagoberto Weisbach and once when Elizabeth Ginnochio came for a football weekend and I went to mass with her.) I would take them with me if they spent Saturday night with me.

Sunday School meant much more to me than church. All Souls had no youth group, but we would do things together, especially in the summer. I don't know who tried to teach our class, but we didn't like whoever it was and made life so unpleasant she quit. I don't know what we did. I don't think we were rowdy or noisy. I think we must have shown our boredom. I know I never studied the lesson in advance, and I doubt anyone else did. Mr. Pruden, the pastor, said he would take over—and meant to straighten us out. We so disliked him that within a few weeks he threw up his hands and quit. But during his brief interval, he taught us what I later learned is the "British Israelite" theory—that the 10 lost tribes of Israel were not lost, but came to the British Isles, and therefore the English-speaking world has a special place in history and in God's sight. This fits in with the racist approach to life. I had little background to evaluate and repudiate this, but I knew it was a bunch of hooey.

In desperation the Sunday School superintendent, since no one else would take us on, turned to Virginia Alexander Brown, who had just returned from Canada where she had separated from her husband. In those days, a separated woman was looked on askance. She was relatively young, vivacious, and a lot of fun. We took her to her immediately. She taught the Sunday School material about two weeks and decided it was dull, so she proposed that we just study the Bible itself. We began with Matthew. She would read all the commentaries and helps she could find, and was obviously working hard at it and was enjoying it. One Sunday she came in and exclaimed, "Kids, I learned something last night. You won't believe it, but it must be true because it is printed here in this book. There are four books in the Bible that are just alike, and they are called the Gospels!" I almost died laughing (quietly) because of course I had known that most of my life. When I went home after church and told the family, I thought Grandmother would flip at the idea of someone knowing so little teaching high school students. But Miss Virginia was EXCITED! And she continued to be excited about what she found in the gospels—and she got us, or at least me and I think most of the rest, excited. She was the best Sunday School teacher I ever had—purely and simply because of her excitement over what she was learning and teaching. That was probably the beginning of my reawakened interest in my faith. I did not want to miss a Sunday morning after she came on board. And she stayed through the end of my high school career, teaching and then having parties for us.

In high school in those days, there was daily Bible reading and prayer in each homeroom. David Davies was always chaplain for our homeroom, so that was his job. I did not object, but it did not mean much to me.

In my last months in high school, knowing that I was going to be leaving home, I realized I did not have the inner resources to survive when I was on my own. In desperation I began to read the Bible on my own—starting with Mark. The call of the first four disciples, the call to lay down one's life, the call to forsake all for Jesus—these words that I had read and heard all my life suddenly came alive and hit me between my eyes. And I began to pray seriously, for the first time. I suppose those nights (by then we had given up the sleeping porch in the winter and I was sleeping in my room) were my real "conversion," for I came to know Jesus Christ in a personal way that I'd never experienced before. If it had not been for this, I don't know if I would have survived that first year at Yale.

Race Relations in High School

Race was a half-conscious factor in my life, and in the lives of most of the white students I ran around with. Segregation was taken for granted. Looking back, I am sure it was both a burning and a simmering issue for black students. We knew there was a Dunbar High School for blacks, designed somewhat like LRHS, but smaller. But we never went there, nor did they ever come to us. Teams played in different leagues. We had black janitors and people who served in the cafeteria. Most of my friends had a black cook, but there was a caste chasm between "us" and "them."

While my racism was "genteel" — never using the word "nigger" but rather "colored person" or "nigra" — some of my friends did say "nigger." I always cringed when I heard it. I remember Bobbie Bird talked about riding down West Ninth Street (the black downtown) and going "coon conking" — hitting people on the sidewalks with things from an open window in a car. I recall being horrified by this.

But I do not remember ever hearing in any class, in Sunday School or public school, a discussion of the pros and cons of segregation. In Miss Penton's American history course, we studied slavery and the Civil War and Reconstruction. She pointed out that a small percentage of people in the South had been slaveholders, but that they had the political power to push for secession. Many of those who fought and died for the Confederacy were from small farms or the hill country where there were no slaves. She was certainly a Southerner, but evidently a critical one. Judging by her actions in 1958-59 when Governor Faubus closed the schools (she taught history on TV for the benefit of students who could find no school to attend), I suspect she had some real problems with segregation but she never expressed them in class — nor did any other teacher. I suppose she would have been fired if she had. It was simply a "non issue" so far as my high school was concerned, 1942-45. No one ever dreamed that this same school would become the focal point of desegregation some 12 years later.

Black Baptizings

Representative of the failure to apply Christian teachings to race relations, and the assumption that black and white churches functioned in two completely separate worlds, was our treatment of baptizings.

Almost all the black churches in Scott were Baptist. And in order to be a Baptist, one must be immersed. The city Baptist churches might have had indoor baptisteries, but out in the country this had to be done in a creek, river, or lake. Since there were no creeks at Scott, and the bayous were full of snakes, baptizings took place in the nearest lake. The church would ask the landowner for permission to have a baptizing on a given day. I never heard of that permission being denied — although I'm sure I would not have heard had that taken place.

It was a familiar scene in the summer, especially after crops were "laid by" in August and revivals were being held, to see a group of black people gathered at the bank of a lake. The preacher and those who were to be baptized were always dressed in white — as were many of those on the banks. There would be a cappella singing, and some shouting, and then the preacher would put them under one by one — followed by more singing and shouting.

I have to confess that when I was a teenager and we heard a baptizing was to take place, we would drive over just to watch from a distance — and to make quiet fun of what was going on. I especially remember doing that over in Steele Bend on the Craig plantation, which was the inside of the Old River loop. Looking back on that, I am sure there must have been great resentment of us. But we were totally unaware of the anger.

Sex Life in High School

I have written elsewhere that masturbation was a part of my life from the summer before I entered seventh grade. I did not know the term testosterone, but mine was developing and constantly in battle with the inhibitions Mother had laid on me indirectly. I don't recall her ever saying, directly to me, "don't" about any expression of sex. She didn't have to. By silence, and by what she said to Art, I got the message.

As Puritanical as Mother was, she was remarkably tolerant in other ways. When Art took his trip to Denver with the Pembertons, he brought back a present for Mother — a cigarette lighter of a nude woman standing up, and the lighter caught fire when her genitals were touched. Mother kept that in the living room for years. Also, there were two crystal compotes she put on the dining table for nuts and candies, and the supporting column of each was a nude woman. Then Art pinned to the ceiling over his bed in our room a picture of some scantily clad movie star. And Mother never had it taken down. I have always wondered about her mixed messages.

I used to have a hard time not falling asleep when I would drive home at night after a dance or some other activity. I used to engage in sexual fantasies to stay awake. In my senior year I had a sexual encounter with another boy. I find it hard to say homosexual, but that is what it was, for we mutually masturbated.

I carried a sense of guilt about all this, while enjoying it. I also knew it was immature and that I would have to cut out all this when I went to college, both because of lack of privacy and because it did not seem appropriate for a college man. And I did.

Death of Franklin Delano Roosevelt

School was out for the day on April 12, 1945, but I was still in Little Rock because Truman King was practicing for a program at high school. I was downtown and happened to pass the door to the Telephone Company. People were standing outside it and said word had just come that President Roosevelt had died. It was a total shock. We had all known throughout his presidency that he was a victim of polio, but the photographs did not show him in a wheelchair. Apparently he had been in declining health for months — probably all during his fourth presidential campaign, but the public was kept in the dark. The coverage on radio and in the printed media was extensive, but the press was far less invasive in those days.

I dashed out to high school to pass on the word. The teacher in charge at first was not sure to believe me. Once the news soaked in, practice broke up, and that program was never put on.

The country went into deep mourning — although some Republicans, such as my father, thought his death was a good thing. The antagonism toward FDR was as intense as was the admiration for him. At least Daddy did not say, "Thank goodness" as some of the people on Wall Street were reported to have said in the elevator. I felt shock, and sadness, and something of being adrift. After all, even though we were Republicans, he had been the only President I had ever known. It is hard, since we have had a succession of Presidents come and go, to grasp the shock at the death of the man who had led the country through the Depression, into World War II, and to what everyone felt would be before long the victory over Hitler in Europe.

For the next few days, all the music on the radio was classical. That was when Samuel Barber's "Adagio for Strings" became so famous, for it was the piece played more often than any other. I remember loving the music on the air, despite the cause. I guess I was more into classical music at that stage than I had realized. I do not believe school let out for the funeral. This was before TV, so the only reports were on radio. I cannot remember if we had radios at school to hear the funeral service, but I do not think so.

One of the nearly universal responses was, "Harry Truman as President!?" He was almost an unknown except as a Senator from Missouri who had led an investigating committee that had done a good job of turning up corruption. But it was assumed a long and very costly war still must be fought in the Pacific, and people had a hard time imagining Harry Truman as being able to conduct that. No one had a clue about the existence of an atomic bomb.

Little was known about his family, for as Vice-President he had received scant attention. Shortly after this, my sister, Ann, heard from one of her high school friends that Margaret Truman was a member of Pi Beta Phi Sorority at one of the universities in Washington, D.C., (or was it St. Louis?) and that she was a lovely person.

Only a few days after President Roosevelt's death, Nazi Germany surrendered, and the war in Europe ended. It was called V-E Day. But I have no memory of that. The country was so focused on the continuing war in the Pacific, and the anticipation of how costly that would be, that victory in Europe made little impression on a teenage boy facing the draft.

Graduation from High School

Prior to graduation, there were a series of preliminary events. The school had a "class day" at what is now War Memorial Park. The PIEs had had the annual swim party, and perhaps a dinner dance, and DBS had had a dinner dance. In those days invitations to graduation were sent out to relatives and family friends, and I received a lot of gifts and was kept busy writing thank-you notes. I think I got more than usual because I had won the Yale scholarship and had really been a leader both academically and in school activities.

Graduation from LRHS took place in the football stadium. In the past, girls had worn long white dresses, and boys wore dark suits and ties. But our year, I think for the first time with the advent of the new principal, we wore academic robes. There were about 500 of us (all white, of course) out on the field, with family and friends up in the stands. Miss Winnie Bess Rawlins, an old family friend, was president of the School Board and signed our diplomas. She had been president for years.

Graduation was a great experience. I felt I'd had three wonderful years. I was not the valedictorian or salutatorian, but I think ranked fifth in the class. I don't remember receiving any kind of award. Perhaps my scholarship to Yale was announced. The one bitter part was I had to receive my diploma from the principal, T. Q. Srygly, with whom I had fought all year.

The normal thing was to go out to "party" afterward, then one of the theaters put on a free movie. I wanted to celebrate with some good friends. I did not have anyone I was dating regularly at the time, and I wanted to make sure Truman King was included. So I proposed to Benjy Lincoln and Thurman Penn that we get dates and go out to Hilltop, a "night club" just south of town where "the big boys" went. I had dated Anne Bush, but I guess we weren't dating at that time. Perhaps Benjy was already dating her. Anyway, he asked Anne Bush as his date; I invited Bettye Jane Erwin, who was a dear friend but I'd never dated her before; and I talked Thurman into inviting Truman. Benjy's cousin, Rose Pickens, and her family gave us a bottle of champagne to take to Hilltop, for in those days it was illegal to buy alcohol and drink it at the same place, so people "brown bagged" it. I was driving my car, for the

Officers

President	John Washburn
Vice-President	Jimmy Johnson
Treasurer	Bill Rule
Secretary	Don Campbell
Historian	Addison Harris
Sergeant-at-Arms	Alfred Bracy
Chaplain	David Davies
Pledge Masters	{ Cal Ledbetter { Buddy Coleman

Officers–Elect

President	Jimmy Johnson
Vice-President	Lawson Delaney
Treasurer	Purcell Smith
Secretary	Charlie Hill
Historian	Ed Smith
Sergeant-at-Arms	Bucky Carson
Chaplain	Owen Lyons
Pledge Masters	

PIE officers listed in the program for the PIE annual inaugural dinner dance in June 1945.

war was still on and gas was rationed. We six crowded into a cubicle. It was my first time to go to Hilltop. Looking back on it, the place was a firetrap. It was made of wood, with wire fencing to keep people from slipping in without paying (but it would also have trapped people from escaping had a fire started). I can't remember if there was a live band or recorded music, but we danced. Then we broke out the one bottle of champagne—for the six of us. And we all got tipsy on that one bottle! I guess it was my first taste of alcohol. I remember in our "drunkenness" we made up a song that ran something like:

> We'll always remember this night
> When we ... all got tight.
> And told T. Q. Srygly
> To go ... back to Texas.

We thought we were very clever.

The free movie started at midnight, and we arrived at the last minute, making a lot of noise and singing our song.

When the movie was over, we delivered the girls (they may have all stayed at the Erwin house, but I'm not sure), then both Benjy and Thurman came down to Scott with me. As I remember, all three of us slept in the big bed in the guest room. Mother and Daddy did not ask me to check in with them.

The next morning we drove back to LRHS where we got our final report cards—and received a lot of kidding about our being drunk the night before.

Self-Analysis in High School

Later in life, I worked with a psychiatrist who used the Transactional Analysis approach. One of its theories is that we have an internal "script" about who we are and what we should do. I have reflected on what "life script" was operative in my psyche during my high school days. Probably it was this:

1. Life is stable and supportive at home—from Daddy, financial comfort (adequate but not unlimited) and physical safety; from Mother, intellectual, emotional, and social security. I know I am privileged.
2. My parents trust me.
3. I am intelligent, not brilliant (as Truman is), and in need of and capable of disciplined study.
4. I am "on my own" in Little Rock in a way I never was at Scott.

5. My assigned slot in life is as a "runner up": Art is better looking, stronger, more popular than I and I will never catch up; financially we are comfortable but not equal to Uncle Gordon or Uncle Arthur or Uncle Howard; I am smart, but not brilliant as Truman is; socially I am "in but not of" the PIE world.
6. Despite that, I am expected to shoot for the top — so I ran for office at East Side, LRHS, and PIE, applied to the very best of colleges — and always made it, to my surprise.
7. Sex, though never talked about, is considered "dirty" before marriage, and I am inhibited about open expressions, but secretly fascinated.
8. Church life and my Christian faith are fairly important, but mostly "second hand" until my senior year in high school when in desperation about leaving home I turn to God and find God waiting.

With this "life script," how did that play out in my life during those years?

On the plantation, I regarded myself as the planter's son, with a distinct pecking order in that society. I "dipped my toe" in manual labor for one and a half summers, but was not comfortable in that role. I was much more at ease reading, studying Latin, eating in the dining room, and playing golf or tennis than I was taking orders from Togo and hearing the rough language of the workmen. Later I found a phrase that, I think, described my self-image during those years (and later) — that Mother had reared me to be "a gentleman, not a man."

In the family I saw myself as the youngest, pushing to find my place in the sun. I was definitely Mother's favorite. I was still afraid of Daddy's bark and kept my distance from him. With the various people who lived with us — Neoma, Alice Coles, Grandmother — I felt very comfortable, and liked them probably more than Ann or Art did. My relationship with Ann was pretty stormy until she went off to college — then we became close. Art was just a distant figure whom I rarely saw, and I did not regard myself measuring up to him, although academically I exceeded. I saw myself as "good" in my outward behavior, inhibited by Mother's expectations, but with a vivid fantasy sex-life. I knew, for sure, that I was not as "good" as others saw me, but I did nothing to abuse their misconception.

In the social life at Scott, I regarded myself as "belonging" in the inner circle, liked and trusted by the parents, respected and liked by my peers — although they would get irritated by my always coloring "inside the lines." But I was completely comfortable in that environment and enjoyed it.

When I went to high school, I felt intimidated and like an outsider who had been "let in" — but was not a part of the inner circle because once I left school I was gone until the next morning. I had no place where I would spend the night during the week — partly because I felt obligated to study,

A photo of me in 1945.

and partly because I had to provide transportation to our carload of others. Especially in my senior year, I got so I spent the night more often in town on either Friday or Saturday night, and felt the Washburn home was open to me. I saw myself as having as many friends who were girls as those who were boys. I tended to shy away from the rougher and cruder conversations and jokes, though I got in on them some. I saw myself as a serious student, not brilliant but smart, and disciplined — the tortoise, not the hare. I saw myself as having leadership skills. I saw myself as being liked, but not intimate with anyone, and respected when not liked. I saw myself as destined to get educated for some serious life work — at that time, thinking it was to be a diplomat. I had enough self-confidence to apply for Yale, doubted I would get in, and secretly hoped I wouldn't so I could go to Washington and Lee or University of Arkansas where I would be "safe."

I regarded myself as a Christian and regular in church life — but this was not a vital part of my life. Virginia Brown had stirred up some interest in the Bible, but it was not until graduation from high school approached that I for the first time seriously began to read the

Bible and pray. As I've mentioned before, I may have looked secure on the outside, but on the inside, I knew I was scared to death and felt inadequate for going out into the unknown world of Yale.

How I Think Other People Saw Me

From 1942 on, my relationship to Scott, with the exception of the summer of 1944 when I worked at the post office, was threefold — on the plantation itself, at All Souls Church, and with "our circle" of planters and their families.

The black and white people out in the fields probably saw me as a smaller, and much weaker, replica of Art — who had thrived on that work. I managed one summer, and then my allergies got so bad the next summer I quit. To the people who worked around the house, I was the "baby of the family," under the shadow of Art (who was older, stronger, more of an outdoors person, and far more daring and rebellious) and Ann (who was a lot of fun, very popular with her friends, had a lot of them spend the night, loved to ride horses). I imagine I was seen as the one who read all the time, who much preferred being in the house rather than going out on the place. I had a pleasant, but distant, relationship with Bob Hunt, Tom Cat Nowden, and Bob Heron. Bob Heron was also the only one who, when I was a child, had said, "You sure is going to make a preacher boy," and I had protested, "Oh, Bob, I am not!" My relationship with Hattie was much friendlier because I saw her much more. We kidded each other.

At All Souls, I was probably seen as a faithful church member, a leader of the young people, quiet, polite, well dressed, somewhat reserved, and "good," and they probably thought I was far more religious than I actually was. I think I had the respect of the adults and my peers, and had little contact with those younger than I.

Among "our group" at Scott, the adults probably saw me as the quietest of the three Campbell children, polite, dependable, smart, someone they could count on, an integral part of the young people of Scott, always included when it was appropriate for a boy of my age to go to something — and sometimes I was included when many boys would not have been since so many of my friends at Scott were girls. I think they felt I would be a restraining influence in any group activity. Among the adults, there were some I felt very close to—Virginia Alexander Brown; Miss Pearl (and somewhat Mr. Tommy) Steele, who helped teach me to play bridge; Mr. Truman and Miss Fannie King, who were almost semi-parents; Miss Margaret Gaston; Miss May Alexander; Mrs. Moore; and in the summer, Aunt Alice and Uncle Gordon.

In my peer group at Scott, I was regarded as being in the inner circle—in Art's shadow, and not as much fun as Ann, but certainly there, and as I grew older more of a leader since the others had gone away to college and then the war. I was probably regarded as somewhat "stuffy" and pious and inhibited, but also reliable and also fun and one of the "leaders of the pack"—especially as I began getting more recognition in Little Rock. I was looked on as smart, because my grades were so good—but Truman knew she was brighter than I, and Peggy McNeill felt she was, too. I think Carolyn and Truman both regarded me almost as a brother; Buddy Craig probably as a younger brother or protégé, but also a buddy.

In Little Rock once I pledged PIE, I was in the "upper level" of high school society. I don't think I realized then that all of us from Scott were considered somewhat special—like a plantation aristocracy. The fact I had a car also gave me some status. My academic achievement gave me some standing among LRHS students who were studious, although I was never the "class genius," for I was too well rounded for that. After I was elected a cheerleader, then president of the student body, I certainly had special status at school, and even in fraternity circles because each fraternity liked to have some "leaders" to boast about. I am sure I was regarded as "good" or even "goody-goody" because I did not shoot craps, smoke, skip school, or get seriously involved with specific girls— although I dated around. I was probably "respected" and "admired" more than I was "liked"—and was seen as a loner, partly because of being isolated at Scott. In my last year, after taking a series of psychological tests (see below) and deciding to try being with people more, I did become much more social and probably better liked. And an invitation to spend the weekend at Scott was, apparently, coveted. I think I was "in, but not of" the inner social circle in Little Rock.

Psychological Testing

In the spring of 1944 when I was in the 11th grade, the Junior League brought to Little Rock a psychological testing group called Human Engineering Laboratory from Boston. I believe the tests were held in Trapnall Hall, which was then the Junior League headquarters. Mother had long since dropped out of Junior League, so I don't know how she heard about it, nor how she and Daddy decided it was worth the investment, for money was still scarce. I don't know how much it cost, but it changed my life.

I spent two days taking all kinds of psychological tests. Then Mother and Daddy and I met with the counselor for his interpretation of them. There were several insights that had a great impact on my life.

First of all, on a scale of objective/subjective (extrovert/introvert), he showed I knocked the end off the objective range. I remember he suggested one of the vocational options for me would be to become a streetcar conductor! He said that should I go into law, I ought to be a trial lawyer and not something like a patent lawyer. I had all my life been a loner, partly because I lived in the country and had no boy contemporaries. None of the three of us could believe that the test was accurate. But I decided that just in case he was right, I would throw myself with people as I had never done before. This was just before the time I was elected president of the student body and an officer in PIE. Whereas before I would go home for the weekend without attending parties on Friday night, I pushed myself to go, to be with people, to work harder at making friends. I found that the psychologist was right, for I blossomed like a rose. It was the first time I discovered how important people and friends are. I don't think I would have probed in this direction without that test.

The second big revelation was my creativity and my ability to write. I remember one of the assignments was to imagine I had boots that would let me take strides of something like one hundred, or one thousand, miles at a step. What would I do? He said most people freeze in the face of such a challenge. He noted I started writing immediately and had fascinating trips to places like Australia. He claimed my imagination was outstanding and my ability to write about it also. I did not put this into effect as immediately as I did the extrovert insight. (During college I never took a creative writing course because I was turned off to the English department by having had poor teachers in high school.) But it did give me some self-confidence in my writing skills. And later in life, I followed up on creativity—not so much in writing as in group thinking. I have learned that I am most creative when I think aloud as part of a group, rather than going off to myself. And I have found that often I can think into the future and see possibilities while others are more tied to the practicalities of the present.

I still have the results of those tests and have seen how he marked certain areas: "extremely high" in creative imagination and analytical reasoning; "extremely objective personality." On the next level, as "High" he had inductive reasoning, large English vocabulary, observation, number memory. He said I was "above average" on accounting aptitude, "slightly above average" on pitch discrimination, "slightly below average" on tweezer dexterity, "low" on tonal memory, and on "Limited Structural Visualization" he simply underlined that several times, which I assume meant I had zilch in this area. I still have the records showing a more detailed breakdown.

On the front cover, in my writing, I see listed as vocational areas:
General law
Diplomacy
Journalism
Teaching
Selling

I went to Yale to go into diplomacy. Once I dropped out of that, I did consider law, journalism, teaching, and selling (both insurance and banking) among others, such as politics.

From this point in my life, I would say the tests were on target. Ministry was not on my horizon at that point. He strongly urged that I should take writing courses, which I did not. Would that I had done that, but I think I have learned through years of writing sermons.

My Predicted Grade Level at Yale

Just days before I was to leave for Yale my cousin Donald Coles and his bride, Polly, came to visit. When Polly learned I was going to Yale, she told me one of her cousins, Ned Noyes, was chair of the Admissions Committee at Yale and must have acted on my application. She said she would write him and ask him to look me up. Then when I went to the first session of my English class, I found out Mr. Noyes was the professor. When I identified myself to him, he said they wanted me to come out for dinner some night. It was several weeks before the invitation came. When I arrived, I found two or three other students had also been invited. I remember one of them was the son of John Hersey, the playwright, who had a show being shown on Broadway. They all talked on a level of sophistication beyond me.

That night, I am sure in violation of confidentiality rules, Mr. Noyes told me my predicted grade average on the basis of my College Boards and school records was 79—which was a "high C." That meant that I was at the bottom edge of those who were admitted, unless they were "legacies." This was a shock to one who had normally made an "A" with a rare few "B's." I determined that night I was going to exceed this level. Of our "crowd" in Berkeley (my "dormitory" at Yale), I think I probably had the lowest predicted average—and was the only one who graduated with high orations and was elected to Phi Beta Kappa. Mr. Noyes did me a great service.

When the night came for me to leave home for Yale, there was quite a delegation of PIEs, family, and girls I had known to wave me off. I was the first one of our crowd to leave for college, because Yale was on a wartime year-round schedule, three semesters a year, and therefore was starting the end of June. Little did I know, as I left, what a jolt lay in store for me in New Haven.

Yale College Years

My First Trip to Yale

My trip to Yale marked a watershed in my life. The month of June had been one of celebration, partying, excitement, and fear. It seemed exciting that I had been accepted by one of the most prestigious universities in the world, and given a scholarship to boot. I knew I was scared to death, and felt inadequate, but I doubt anyone else realized that.

On the night of departure from Union Station, Little Rock, we took the Missouri Pacific to St. Louis. I write "we" because I was to be the chaperone for Alice Vineyard, my first cousin-once-removed, who was probably 10 years old, and who was going to New Haven also to visit her aunt and uncle, Sue and Tap Hornor. The Army had stationed Tap in New Haven at the time.

There was quite a send-off gathering at the station—family, friends from Scott and from PIE/DBS, and Alice's family. World War II was on, so getting a train reservation had not been easy. We went by Pullman, an upper and a lower berth. I had been on a train when I was two years old, but had no memories. The only other time I'd ridden a train was to Pine Bluff and back for a football game. I had been told what to do on a Pullman, but was an utter novice. Alice hadn't been on one, either. There was a lot of waving and well wishing as the train pulled out. I didn't actually cry, but I sure wanted to.

When we were preparing for bed, I put Alice in the upper berth for safety sake. Dressing in a lower berth without bumping my head on the one above me took some maneuvering for a novice. I had been warned to put my wallet in a sock under my pillow. I slept pretty well, although I was already experiencing homesickness. The train arrived in St. Louis on schedule the next morning, so we had a reasonable amount of time before our connection to New York. There was a restaurant in Union Station, and we decided to have breakfast there. I put down my suitcases out in the station and started in. Alice said she thought she'd take hers with her. When we finished eating, I walked over to pick up my bags. A man was standing by them, and he asked, "Are these yours?" I said, "Yes, sir." He replied, "Fellow, I don't know where you're from, but in St. Louis you don't leave your suitcases unattended in Union Station!" Jolt Number One.

When the New York Central train pulled out from St. Louis, it was quite full, for the war was on and troops were constantly being moved from one place to another by train. Enlisted men rode in coach class but we had reserved seats in a Pullman — two benches facing each other at day and two berths at night. I have no memory of how we passed the time as we crossed Illinois, Indiana, and Ohio. There was air conditioning on this train. During the day I began to have strange feelings in one ear. (I had been doing a lot of swimming at parties before I left home.) We ate our meals in the dining car — a new experience for me. In those days, even during the war, dining car meals were served elegantly, with linen cloths and napkins and finger bowls. I can't remember the cost. By

Panoramic view of Yale University campus with downtown New Haven in the background.

today's standards they were ridiculously low, but I remember thinking I was running through money mighty fast. Our berths were made up for the night. By then my ear was really hurting.

We arrived in New York in the morning. Remembering my warning in St. Louis, I carried my suitcases everywhere I went. I had two new ones (they were hard to get during the war), and they were heavy. There were no wheels on suitcases in those days, nor the little carts people use now. I didn't know what a Red Cap was, so didn't use one. It was a long walk from our Pullman to the lobby in Grand Central. Then we had to find Alice's train to New Haven, for I was going out to Scarsdale to visit the Arthur McCains. I guess we did locate it, and I put her on it alone. Then, somehow, I found the one to Scarsdale, jumping up at the announcement of each station, hoping I would not go past Scarsdale. What a relief it was to see Aunt Marion, Mary Wrenetta, Frances, and Arthur! But by then I had a full blown earache and asked if I could see a doctor. They took me to their family doctor who said I had a bad fungus infection in the ear. I was to put some drops in it two or three times a day. He warned it would hurt—and it did. It was like having a red-hot poker inserted. But my ear did begin to heal.

Other than the ear, I had a wonderful time at 75 Morris Lane, the new home they had bought on leaving 17 Rectory Lane where we had visited them in 1941. We played tennis and went to Manursing Beach Club (I think, although surely I did not swim). And one night they had tickets for Mary Wrenetta and me to go into New York to see the popular musical "Carousel," the new

Frances McCain, Aunt Marion McCain, Arthur McCain, Jr., and me at Manursing Beach in Scarsdale, New York, on Memorial Day in 1946.

Rogers and Hammerstein play. It was the first musical I ever saw, and I was enchanted, especially by the song "You'll Never Walk Alone." I felt it spoke to me that night, and I kept humming it all through the coming year. (Mary Wrenetta has absolutely no memory of that play, for the following Christmas she had a severe nervous breakdown followed by two years of hospitalization—and I suppose she was beginning to come apart even that summer.)

After two or three days, the McCains put me on the train back to New York where I caught one to New Haven. That train was not air-conditioned, and it was hot! People kept the windows open. Thinking that I was going North, I was wearing my light blue wool suit, white shirt, and tie. As much as I like hot weather, I was used to wearing cotton shorts and short-sleeved shirts. This was something new.

When I arrived in New Haven, Dan Howard, my assigned roommate, met me. We had corresponded after we were told our assignments. Dan was a New Haven resident and had come in his mother's car so he could take my heavy suitcases and me to Berkeley College where we were to live. Dan was a good looking, dark-haired young man, taller than I, with a clipped accent and a "cool," not "warm" personality. But he was pleasant and helpful.

First, we had to register. Ellie Hutchins, the college secretary and later my boss, told me she'll never forget that registration day. Sweat dropped off people as they signed in—smearing the ink on the pages. It was 95 degrees and 100 per cent humidity—one of the most sweltering days she could ever remember in New Haven. And there I was, a Southerner come prepared for the North, in my heavy wool suit!

Yale had written ahead of time that we would be in room 599—so I assumed the dormitory would have at least five floors, with 100 rooms on each, and I hoped maybe we would have a corner room. Never having seen Yale, I did not realize most of it was Gothic Collegiate architecture and that each residential college was a small community within the larger university. I found Berkeley College was a stone building, divided into South and North Courts, with "cross campus" between them. We were in South Berkeley on the third floor of a four-story building. We did not have "a room" but a suite—a sizeable living room with a fireplace and paneled wall. A hall led back to two bedrooms, each holding a bed, chair, dresser, and mirror. The living room contained two wooden chairs. We were expected to furnish it according to our tastes and finances. We were on the inside of the building, so we looked out on the courtyard through windows with leaded glass. There was another wing, similar to ours, on the other side of the courtyard. A one-story building containing the common room and dining room linked the two. On the first floor of our half was the college library, and the first of four "fellows' apartments" at the north end of our building, looking out over cross campus.

As much as I was in shock, I was amazed at the beauty of the buildings, the spacious arrangement of the suite, and the fact that I would have a private bedroom. This was more than I had dared hope for.

I had arrived at last.

First Sunday in New Haven

The next morning was Sunday. I had always gone to church on Sundays. The day before, I did not get my bearings about the location of Berkeley College in relation to the rest of the university or the town. Coming out of the dormitory, I went through the gate into Cross Campus, and there to my left I saw a beautiful Gothic building with huge wooden doors. I assumed this must be a church, so I tried to get in. The doors were locked. I thought, "I have, indeed, come to the pagan North."

Determined to go to church, I kept wandering. New Haven is full of churches, but I took the one route that led away from them. Finally I saw up ahead another building that looked like a church, and there were lots of people going up its steps. I thought "At last" and headed in that direction. About that time, I saw two or three nuns in their habits ascending the stairs. Realizing this was a Catholic Church (it was St. Mary's), I turned away from that.

I missed the street that would have passed First Methodist and Battell Chapel, but found one that led to a large open space. At last, I saw three churches! When I approached the first one, it said "North Church, Congregational." I had never heard of a Congregational Church so backed away. The next one was Center Congregational, and again I avoided the unknown.

The third church on the Green was Trinity Episcopal Church. While I had never been to an Episcopal service, I had at least heard of this denomination, so I went in. I was pretty much lost in the service and was surprised to see some of the people (but not all) kneeling for prayers. This was new for me. If I am not mistaken, the service that day was the Litany. In 1945, most Episcopal Churches had Morning Prayer as the standard Sunday morning service, with Communion the first Sunday. Often on the third Sunday, they would have the Litany. I was miserably homesick during that service, but at least I was in a church, and that brought some comfort.

Second Sunday in New Haven

On my second Sunday at Yale I attended First Methodist Church, located one block from Berkeley College. All my life I had gone to Sunday School, so I showed up at the appointed hour. There was only one class for adults, and none for students. The "program" that morning was a woman telling her story. She was Caucasian, but she was married to a Nisei (person of Japanese ancestry born in this country). She said shortly after Pearl Harbor, there was a knock on their door, and her husband was led away to go to an internment camp. She described her shock, fear, and the problems she had, plus the conditions under which he had been living for almost four years. This was in July 1945, and the war was still raging. I was dumbfounded. I did not know our country had done that to American citizens. I later learned there were two Japanese internment camps in Arkansas, but I had never heard of them. I was conscious of the German Prisoners of War at Camp Robinson, because Daddy would hire them to come down to work on the plantation.

At this point, I was not a gung-ho patriot eager to go to war. I had very little social conscience. But I do remember being shocked by this woman's story.

I never went back to First Methodist Church, for I got started at Battell, the university chapel.

First Days at Yale

Berkeley College had been closed for at least a couple of years because enrollment dropped so during the war. (Let me explain here that "college" is used in two ways at Yale. The liberal arts part of the university is Yale College, an academic unit. But students enrolled there, and in the School of Engineering, were housed in facilities that other institutions would call dormitories. Yale, patterned after Cambridge and Oxford, had 10 of them called "colleges." The one to which I was assigned was Berkeley.) ASTP (Army) students were housed in Old Campus, the place where freshmen normally lived before moving into one of the colleges. The navy V-12 was occupying Branford and Saybrook Colleges. I guess Jonathan Edwards and Calhoun had stayed open throughout the war, and possibly Timothy Dwight. But after V-E Day, some servicemen were beginning to return. They, plus our class, enabled Yale to re-open Berkeley and Silliman Colleges. A few freshmen went into JE and Calhoun, but the bulk of us were in the two re-opened ones. I believe I remember there were 155 in Berkeley that summer, all but 15 freshmen. The others were veterans who were "senior advisors" or "counselors" or some such title.

Dan Howard, having met me at the train station, helped me lug my two suitcases and a footlocker trunk up two flights of stairs. After unpacking, I went next door to meet our neighbors. I shall never forget walking into their living room, which had only one wooden arm chair as furniture, and seeing a rather chubby man/boy standing on the chair, waving his arms and reciting one of Shakespeare's plays. It blew my mind, for that was not what boys in my circle in Little Rock did. I found out his name was George Kearns, from Bridgeport. Then I soon met his roommate, Dagoberto Sarmiento, a handsome man with a heavy Spanish accent who came from Bogotá, Colombia. I hardly knew where Colombia was. They were uncertain where Arkansas was.

There was a third suite on our floor, of the same size, except their living room (as did the Kearns/Sarmiento one) looked out on High Street, with Trumbull College (also closed) across the street. There I met Peter Crosby, from Binghamton, NY, and Danny Jacobsen from New York City, I think. Danny never was a part of "our group," but the other five of us stuck together and became good friends — although I never really got close to Peter. They all commented on my accent, never dreaming they also had accents — and never did, in four years, admit it.

There was a communal restroom — with two shower stalls with metal swinging doors, two commodes, and three lavatories.

The first floor in our "entry" was empty because the space was taken for the college library and a Fellow apartment. The third floor had the same floor plan as ours. So there were 12 of us in that entry.

All meals were served in the beautiful college dining room. Before the war, they had china plates, silver utensils, menus, and waiters or waitresses who would come to each table to take orders. But those had been packed away during the war, so we ate on army-style metal trays with stainless steel knives and forks, and went through a serving line in the kitchen. They served soup, one meat, potatoes and one other vegetable, bread (often what we called "light bread" in the South), dessert, and a drink. This was in the summer in the midst of a heat wave. Coming from the South, where we had light food and lots of ice, I could not get over the fact we had hot soup every day at lunch, and "iced tea" was regular tea in a glass with one lump of ice floating forlornly.

I was impressed by the ornate dining room — and common room, through which we entered. There was a lot of intricately carved oak all over both rooms, and some very large portraits on the walls — one of President Seymour (the first Master of Berkeley) and one at the end of the room of Bishop Berkeley and his family. The tables were heavy oak ones, some for four people, some for six to eight.

Yale was built for the academic year. There was no air conditioning, no fans, no cross ventilation. That summer, especially those first days, was humid, with the temperature in the upper 90s. Even I was hot.

We also learned that we had to wear coats and ties for every meal, including breakfast. Without them, we would not be served. In Arkansas, only "old men" wore seersucker suits. Seercord was unknown. The only suits I had were wool, for the winter. So I sweltered. I think we also had to wear coats and ties to class — at least, I did.

The whole registration process — taking tests, meeting with an advisor, and getting assigned to class — was a blur that I can hardly remember. That first semester I took French, English, human zoology (we were suppose to take a lab science but I found out this fulfilled the requirement), classical civilization, and American history. My preparation was good in French reading and writing (not speaking), excellent in American history (after Emily Penton), and the only science I had ever taken was biology, so I had some preparation for that. I knew how to write, but I was utterly lost in literature, and I had no background for classical civilization.

The testing revealed I was in the lowest quarter of the class in speed of reading and the highest quarter on comprehension. So they put me in a course for speed-reading. The only problem was I could not "speed read" French, T. S. Eliot in English, zoology, or classical civilization (the professor wanted us to memorize dates and names). So the speed-reading did me no good.

A photo of me in 1945 or 1946.

But the BIG memory of those first days at Yale was homesickness. I had heard about it before, but having spent only one week away from family (Boy Scout camp—which I hated), I was not prepared for what it was like. My body was in New Haven, but I "lived" back in Arkansas. I wrote home every day and wrote to every family member and friend I could think of. They were kind and would respond. I would often get 10 to 12 letters a day, and respond to each of them. How I ever passed my courses, I do not know.

On top of that, the carillon in Harkness Tower each day at noon played from the New World Symphony the section which Bill Fletcher used to sing as a solo at All Souls Church, using the words "Going Home." Every time I heard it, the wound of homesickness was opened up afresh. I don't think I ever cried, literally, but I cried constantly on the inside.

On one of those first days (probably that Sunday), the Master of Berkeley College and his wife had a tea for students. His name was Sam Hemingway. I later learned he was a professor of English, with a specialty in Shakespeare, especially *Henry IV, Part II*. The tea was the most elaborate one I'd ever seen, with maids (white) bringing food out. We were served "iced tea" that was tepid, with one cube of ice. When I introduced myself to Mr. Hemingway, he said, "I saw you are related to Charles McCain. We were in college together. I asked especially to have you in Berkeley College." Even though I barely knew Cousin Charlie, that did make me feel better. This tea was out in their beautiful garden, which was part of the Master's House.

Introduction to Dwight Chapel

At the beginning of the term, I came in from class one day and found on my dresser a notice about noonday chapel services in Dwight Chapel. The speaker the next day was President Charles Seymour. I was not sure where Dwight Chapel was located, but I was curious to see what the president of the university looked like.

I asked Dan Howard, my roommate, if he had put the notice there. He said he had not. I asked him if he had left the door unlocked while we were away. He said he had not. I could not imagine how that notice arrived on my desk. There was not one on his. To this day I still don't know who put it there. (The Jesuit Gerard Hughes has written that for a person who is *in Christo* "nothing happens by chance." I have come to believe that.)

The next day, since I did not have a 12:00 noon class, I went to the service at 12:10. I walked into this Gothic style chapel, quite narrow but long, with a very high ceiling—and up front the most beautiful stained glass window, predominantly deep blue, but with various figures in primary colors. When I arrived, the organ was playing. I sat toward the back of the first half. There were not more than 12 people present. We sang a couple of hymns, there were some read prayers (which were strange to me), and President Seymour spoke briefly.

I have no idea what he said. I was not particularly moved by his remarks. What I did find in those quiet moments was the presence of the Lord, whom I had come to know in my desperation as I read the Bible and prayed back in my room at Scott. I had some peace, some consolation in my homesickness, some strength to go on.

As I left, I knew that I would be returning to this chapel and this service.

Noondays at Dwight Chapel

That semester I had a class at noon on Tuesdays and Thursdays, so I was able to go to the noonday service at Dwight Chapel only three days a week. But whenever possible, I would arrive a couple of minutes early. I kept this up throughout my undergraduate career. Some semesters I could make it all five days, some only two.

I would come in, listen to the organ music, and pray—in desperation. There were never many present—a couple of professors maybe, and five to 10 students. Luther Tucker was the associate chaplain in charge of these services. Buckner Coe, a Yale divinity student, was an assistant at Battell Chapel and often led the Dwight services. I am sure I met them that first semester and through the years, but I never became a friend of theirs, nor did I get involved in the other Dwight Chapel programs. One year Ned Sherrill was on the staff, and I remember he did join me for lunch one day at Berkeley—and shocked me by saying that the Church is older than the New Testament. I thought this was heresy and protested. Of course, later I found out he was correct.

During those years I came to have deep appreciation for many things. The architecture made a lasting impression. I had always thought All Souls was a lovely church, but this was far more beautiful, yet rather simple. That blue window was imprinted on my soul. In a later remodeling, it was almost covered up with organ pipes. But I can still see it in my mind's eye.

I had grown up with extempore prayers and at first was shocked to hear "read" prayers. But through the years, I came to appreciate them, their beauty, and their range.

I also came to know, and finally to love, hymns that were not part of the repertory at All Souls. One with special meaning, as I was struggling about my life work, was "Spirit of God, Descend Upon My Heart," especially the second stanza: "I ask no dream, no prophet ecstasies, No sudden rending of the veil of clay, No angel visitant, no opening skies, But take the dimness of my soul away." I did come to have a sense of the presence of God, but I was groping in the dark as I searched for how I should spend my life after I realized I was not cut out for the diplomatic service.

It was toward the end of my college career before I began to kneel in prayer. At first this seemed "popish," but it came to have deep meaning for me, and at Yale Divinity School I continued even though most people there did not.

As my spiritual life began to come more alive, I had no privacy in my room for Bible reading and prayer. Dan Howard, reared as a Catholic, was rebelling and was very scornful of my religious life. If he had caught me reading the Bible or praying, he would have made a mockery of it. The one place I could pray without embarrassment was in Dwight Chapel. Even there, when I would turn off the walkway in Old Campus to go up the steps to the chapel, I would hope no one would see me.

Walking to Dwight at noon meant I would, on the way, be hearing the carillon in Harkness Tower playing "Going Home," and I would pray for healing from homesickness. The carillon played various pieces of music (even "Boola, boola" on football weekends) on that powerful range of bells, but "Going Home" was always included at noon. I gather it was Mrs. Harkness's favorite.

Throughout my four years as an undergraduate, those noon-day services were a sustaining source of nourishment.

Although these did not take place at noon, Berkeley College had a service in Dwight Chapel each year on All Saints Day, remembering fellows and members of the college who had died. I had never heard of All Saints Day. It was an Episcopal service, since the Hemingways were Episcopalians, and Bishop Berkeley, for whom the college was named, was an Anglican divine. I am not sure I went the first year, but after I became a Master's Aide, I felt obligated. I think that was the first time I received communion with wine. I was shocked at first. I never got really comfortable with that service during my four years as an undergraduate. But it was an introduction.

Battell Chapel

On some of the weekends during that first summer, I would go out to Hamden to stay with Sue and Tap Hornor. What a blessed relief that was. But they were not going to church in those days, so I didn't either when I was with them. I may have attended one of the Congregational churches on the Green once. Battell, the university chapel, was closed for some or all of the summer. But then the sign outside began announcing who was going to be the preacher the next Sunday. I decided I ought to give it a test.

I have often said Battell is a help to worship because it is so ugly. There is nothing else to do there *but* worship. It was a barn-like "preaching station" kind of structure with "stained glass" windows that were just opaque white—nothing like the window in Dwight. The church was wide, and on the two sides there were slightly raised pews where faculty, some alumni, and their families sat so students could see them. President Seymour's wife was always there; former President Angell and his wife sat there, and after he died, she came alone. Up from there was an eagle lectern on one side and a barrel raised pulpit on the other. In the middle was a five-seat bench on which the president and four deans sat, in academic robes. Behind them a curtain raredos hid the organ, and behind it in a semi-circle sat the robed all-male choir. The choir processed in, followed by the academics and then the chaplains and the guest preacher. All of this was new to me. The organ was magnificent, and so was the choir. I had not seen such hoods and robes before, nor was I used to seeing clergy who were robed. Ours at Scott never had been. There was no air conditioning, nor any fans, in Battell because normally Yale was closed in the summer; and when winter arrived, I discovered the heating system was far from adequate, for my feet would freeze, and often I would wear my overcoat throughout the service.

At first I was put off by what seemed to me a very formal service—the unison prayer of confession, the other prayers, the hymns with which I as not familiar. I left thinking I would have to find some other place for worship.

Maybe it was at this time I found where the Presbyterian Church was located and went there. It was almost empty, seemed dusty and lifeless. The architecture was was worse than Battell. It had the reputation of being the ugliest church structure ever put up. It was some kind of "memorial" church in name. The oral tradition is that it was given by a woman in memory of her husband's first wife!

After that I guess I decided I should try Battell again. Sidney Lovett was the chaplain. He was excellent in leading worship—but was one of the world's poorest preachers. I understood later that he was called as chaplain partly because he was a Skull and Bones man, but also because he was pastor of a Congregational church in Boston at the time of the Socco and Vanzetti trial and had taken a very courageous stand that the university liked. I guess he knew he was not a good preacher, so on most Sundays (except when there was a holiday and there were not going to be many present) he brought in some of the leading theologians and preachers in the country. Some of them seemed to be on the "team," for they would come once every year—Reinhold Niebuhr from Union Seminary, John McKay from Princeton Seminary, Clelland from Duke Divinity, Paul Tillich, Hal Luccock, and Liston Pope from Yale Divinity, Willard Sperry, dean of Harvard Divinity School, etc. Some of them were like Morgan P. Noyes, a Trustee who (even though he produced an excellent book of prayers) was not much as a preacher. However, one of his sermons did "speak" to me vividly when I was wrestling with my vocation—so much that I asked him for a copy. When it came some weeks later, I could not find anything in it that moved me. I guess the Spirit can work through anything.

One Sunday in my first year, I must have arrived late, or it may have been deliberate, so instead of sitting on the main floor where I usually did, I went to the balcony. The preacher (I do not remember who he was—perhaps he was black, perhaps Howard Thurman—I don't know, for that name would not have meant anything to me at the time) gave the South a hard time because of its treatment of blacks. I was INDIGNANT. I was tempted to get up and walk out, but didn't. That afternoon at tea, I told Mrs. Hemingway, who quietly said, "I am certainly glad you didn't."

Gradually I adjusted to the Battell order of worship and came to love it. The organist was a professor at the School of Music. The male choir was magnificent. The words of the anthems were printed in the bulletin, with translation when they were in some other language. The preaching was on a level I had never heard before at Scott—a quality I didn't know was possible. Some were funny, such as Hal Luccock—and when our defenses were down laughing, he would turn on us like a prophet. Some were more profound than I could understand, but I knew I was being exposed to first-class theology. Listening to Reinhold Niebuhr was a draining experience because he was so powerful. I had had the idea that a sermon that was read was not really a sermon. But he read in a way I had never dreamed of. He would hang out of the pulpit with that eagle-like face looking to his left, then swoop down on his way to his right, and in passing read his text and preach it like a prophet.

Going to Battell became a part of my weekly routine. I never did appreciate the architecture, but the music, prayers, and preaching expanded my horizons. Also, we had communion the first Sunday of every month. That was new for me, because we had received it only once a quarter at All Souls.

I am sure there was much about Battell Chapel that was phony. Some of the guest preachers were invited for college political reasons. Many in the choir came because they were paid, and they studied during the rest of the service. There were student deacons who served as ushers and received the offering. I don't know whether being a Battell usher was one way to climb the snob-ladder, or ushers were selected from those who had arrived in the upper reaches of undergraduate life (namely, members of the Senior Societies), but they all wore the "required" gray flannel suits, regimental stripe ties, white shirts, etc. George H. W. Bush, who was a member of my class, was a regular usher. I never met him, but saw him there often.

Despite that phoniness, if it existed, Battell Chapel contributed greatly to my spiritual life, expanding horizons and deepening my understanding of theology and the Bible and worship. I am deeply grateful for it.

First Contact with Latourette

One night in July or August, Peter Crosby, who lived across the hall and who was a slob and a big beer drinker and never went to chapel, came over to tell me that he had just come from a Bible study group with one of the Fellows of the college. He thought I might be interested and suggested that I go with him the following week. I did—and that was the last time Peter ever came to the group. (Again, "nothing happens by chance.")

Kenneth Scott Latourette, a professor of history in Yale College and also the Divinity School, had just been made a Fellow of Berkeley College. To contribute to Berkeley, he offered an informal Bible study group. There must have been about six of us in his office in the south court, on the other side of the court from our room. He suggested we start studying the Letter to the Ephesians. The second verse begins "Grace to you, and peace...." I remember saying, "I have heard of grace all my life. But what in the world does it mean?"

We spent several weeks talking about grace. While Virginia Brown had opened up the Bible for me at All Souls, it was in an enthusiastic but certainly not a scholarly way. This man, who was not only a history professor but also an American (not Southern) Baptist minister, took us deeper into the Bible than I had ever gone before.

In my homesick misery that summer, this one hour a week was like an oasis in the desert. Not only was there learning about the Bible, but here was a man who knew who I was, and who cared about me. I also found some fellowship in this group that was deeper than I was getting on our floor in Entry E. I am not sure how many of these students were there from the very beginning, and how many came in later. But some of those I remember were Bill Andersen, whose father was an Episcopal priest and who was a graduate of Andover, majoring in classics. He became the coxswain on the Yale crew. He was on scholarship and supplemented his income by winning endowed prizes for "the best Latin poem" or "an essay in Greek." So few people were taking those classical languages that no one else could compete, but the endowment kept making money — so Bill always walked off with the prize. He was a real brain.

Another was Steve Chamberlain, who came from New Britain, Connecticut. I think he was a graduate of Putney, a co-ed prep school committed to a simple lifestyle. He was quiet, solid. I never did get really close to him, though we stayed in the group together for several years. When I failed my physical exam and could not go to Yale-in-China, Steve was the one selected to take my place in February 1949. The folks at home had quite a send-off. Then the State Department stopped him in Oshkosh, Wisconsin, because the Communists had taken Changsha, where Yale-in-China was located.

I think George Van Buskirk was in that group. He was drafted into the Army and was sent to Camp Robinson in 1946. If he had just been in Berkeley College, I doubt I would have known he was at Robinson. Anyhow, when I went home the summer of 1946, we started having him out to spend the weekend at Scott. He was there on July 4, 1946, preparing to go to the Scott picnic at the Kings' house, when the phone call came that Art was flying in from Memphis. We piled him in the car with the rest of us, so he was in on the greeting. George was from Pittsburgh. When he came back to Yale after the service, we saw each other, but did not continue as close friends.

Joe Gall must have been in that group for a while, at least. I knew him fairly well, and I don't know how else that would have happened. He was very quiet, very studious. He graduated with "philosophical orations" (summa cum laude), went on to get his Ph.D. in biology, was a professor at Yale, and became very distinguished in his field.

Another was Joe Lieper, although I think he came in later. He was a Presbyterian. His father was involved in the National Council of Churches, or the national YMCA, or some such. Latourette knew his father. Joe thought seriously about going into the ministry, but I think in the end did not.

Frank McClain joined that group, but he was certainly not there that first summer, for he was still in the Army. Frank moved across the hall from us and became one of my very good friends. Frank was a "new Episcopalian" from Water Valley, Mississippi, with an acquired English accent. He was planning to go into the ministry, and did. He visited me at Scott, and we kept in touch until his death.

I am sure there were other people, but at the moment I do not remember them.

One of the things that drew Mr. Latourette to me was the fact that I knew some of the "old" hymns that he had grown up singing. They were the ones we had sung at All Souls. I was the only one in the group who had ever heard most of them.

That group helped hold me together that first summer, through all that painful first year, and beyond.

Bible Study/Cell Group

At the end of June 1946, Mr. Latourette, after the final meeting of the group, asked me to stay behind and inquired if I had ever thought about going into the ministry. I said I had not and dismissed the idea.

When we returned in the fall of 1946, he suggested instead of having a Bible study group that we turn it into a sharing group, or "cell group" as it was then called. We would continue to study the Bible, but we would also share our stories, and our current concerns, and could pray aloud. I was frightened at first. I had not prayed in public since my disastrous experience at All Souls for some kind of Sunday School program when I was a child, and I had dissolved into tears. I can still recall my fear at the first meeting, and especially when it came my turn to pray in the group. But I did manage.

We met once a week during term time, right after dinner in the office assigned to Mr. Latourette in the basement of an entryway in South Court. I guess it was when we changed from Bible study to cell group that Mr. Latourette asked us to call him "Uncle Ken." That was the custom at Yale, when a professor and a student, or a group, were very close. And it certainly did increase the sense of intimacy in the group. Most of the people who had been coming before continued in the cell group. (This was before the McCarthy era of Communist hunting when such a term as "cell" would have been suspect.) Even though I am having trouble remembering the names of all the participants, this was my major support group beyond those friends in my entryway.

Between this group, Dwight Chapel at noon, and Battell Chapel, my spiritual life that had "hatched" in the months leading to my departure from home began to grow. I did learn how to pray aloud. I was introduced to names and books. I began visiting churches during the week when I passed them (in those days they were unlocked) and would pick up booklets on spiritual life. I remember one I cherished was *Prayers, New and Old* printed by the Forward Movement of the Episcopal Church. They had quite a publishing program from which I benefited greatly.

Pattern of My Quiet Time

When I was growing up, once Mother stopped having us "say our prayers" to her, I had no regular "quiet time." As I have written before, toward the end of my senior year in high school I began reading the Bible every night. When I got to college, I did not continue that, but I did go to Dwight Chapel noon services as many days as my class schedule permitted and to Battell Chapel regularly on Sundays. I was in Uncle Ken's cell group where he would talk about his "quiet time," but that was out of the question as long as I was living in 599 Berkeley, especially after there were four of us in the suite, and two of us in a bedroom. After I moved out of 599 at the start of my senior year (over sharing a bath with a black), I was in a single room with one roommate the first semester. Three times a week he had a class right after breakfast and I did not, so there was that time I knew I would be by myself. I began some Bible reading and reading of prayers that I found in various resources. My last semester, I had a room all to myself. There, I began praying at night, before I went to bed, if I did not fall asleep.

Early Catholic Worship

In my home, there was not outright prejudice about religion, but the underlying tone was more sympathetic toward Judaism than toward Catholicism. When Daddy grew up in Pontiac, Illinois, there were three families of boys who played together all the time—the Campbells, with a Presbyterian minister father; the Mallorys, with a Methodist minister/chaplain father; and the Greenbaums, whose father was the banker. Eventually, Uncle Bruce married May Greenbaum. After Uncle Bruce's death, Aunt May would come down to visit and was part of the family.

I never knew my Grandfather McCain. He apparently was a warm, out-going, and loving man—but he had a mental block on Catholics. Why, I never learned. His other scorn was for soda-jerkers at drug stores. Mother used to tell us how when Uncle Howard would get mad at his brother, or one of his half-brothers, he would describe them as a "Catholic soda-jerker." I had heard this told many times.

All Souls Church, where I grew up, was a Protestant interdenominational church, but Mrs. Rebo was a Catholic and she participated.

As I've mentioned elsewhere, when I was in high school, Fred Balch invited me to spend a Saturday night with him. The Balches were devout Catholics, so we knew that would mean going to mass on Sunday morning. We talked about that. I think the Balches offered to take me to some Protestant church, but I didn't know any of them, either, so I went to St. Andrews Cathedral. Of course the service was in Latin. I didn't have a clue as to what was happening. I think I did not kneel when they did because I didn't know how. It was not a "bad" experience, but an alien one. I had no desire to go back.

When I was at Yale College, I invited Elisabeth Ginnochio, a high school friend who was studying at Marymount College outside New York City, to come up for a football weekend. She had to go to mass, and I felt obligated to go with her. We went to St. Mary's, a local parish. (My Catholic friends later said I should have known better—that we should have gone to the Catholic student chapel, St. Thomas More, run by the Jesuits, for the priests at St. Mary's were so dumb they had only three sermons—one against communism, one against Protestantism, and the third against birth control.)

The church was very full that day. This was pre-Vatican II. Everything was in Latin, and the saints and candles were in full display. I felt totally out of place. As the prayers began, everyone knelt—but I was determined I was not going to. So I sat bolt upright. Finally the woman behind me, hindered in her devotions, punched me and said, "Kneel, sir." I turned around and said to her, "I can't," meaning my religion forbade me from such practices. As the service went on, I realized I had not been kind. This was shortly after World War II, and Yale was full of veterans, some of whom had been injured in the war. So when the service was over and we started out, I limped very badly as I passed the woman—and hoped she felt guilty!

Related to this, showing the chasm between Catholicism and Protestantism in the 1940s, Dagoberto Sarmiento was my best friend. He was a devout Catholic. My roommate, Dan Howard, and next-door neighbor, George Kearns, were also Catholics—but not very good ones. But Dagoberto was 100%. One time, he invited me to go to mass at St. Thomas More chapel—I guess partly to get over my experience at St. Mary's. After doing that, I invited him to come with me to Battell Chapel one Sunday. Before he could agree, he had to talk to his priest and get permission! That was granted, but with the instructions that he was only to observe—that he was not to sing any of the hymns, nor was he to stand when the congregation did. I remember seeing Dago sitting there for the whole hour.

What a joy it was for me when, in the summer of 1996, I visited Dago in Basel, Switzerland. I was there on a Sunday morning. He insisted on going with me to the service at the Anglican Church there, and we worshipped together.

Bursary Jobs at Yale College

Everyone at Yale College who got a scholarship also had to have a bursary job—which paid for meals, $144 per semester. To earn this, freshmen had to work 20 hours a week, sophomores 19 hours, juniors 18, and seniors 16. There was a wide range of such jobs. Some were in the refectory, helping serve the meals. They were at the bottom of the pecking order. Some were clerical, and some were in research. My first one was to be a "runner" for the *Yale Daily News*, a publication that during peacetime was run by students, but during the war was taken over by paid adults. I worked for the secretary of this organization, not unpleasant but not someone I enjoyed. There would often be two of us on at the same time. She would have copy that needed to go to some advertiser for approval or some information that needed to be picked up. So we were sent out, by foot, all over downtown New Haven. I came to know it pretty well. And I never walked so much in my life. My feet grew a half size in four months. It did make me get exercise, but I was at the same time taking a required "muscle building" program at the gym and didn't need it.

One of the real prices I paid for being a bursary student was that when there was an announcement of a try-out for cheerleaders, I had to work at the time of the try-outs. Having been a cheerleader for two years in Little Rock, I thought I might be able to do it—although with Yale politics that probably would not have happened. Had I tried out and been chosen, that would have made a major difference in my college experience. I would have traveled to out-of-town games. I would have met a whole circle of people outside Berkeley. I would probably have come to know the circles that went into fraternities and senior societies. When this door was closed, however, I was herded into other directions and developed deeper relationships with my Berkeley circle than would have been possible had I spread out more.

At the end of the first semester, the war was over, and service men were returning to college. I guess the wartime *Yale Daily* closed, and students began to take it over again. At the start of my second semester, I was switched to the office of Yale Service for Returning Service Men, located in Strathcona Hall, the engineering building. It was a madhouse, for applications were flooding in. Most of what I did there was filing papers. I also made the mistake of letting them know I typed, so I did a lot of that. It was more pleasant than having to walk all over town, especially since winter weather was setting in, but it was very impersonal and was just a matter of "putting in the hours." It did give me some good experience in office management and helped me brush up my typing skills.

Toward the end of my second semester, I was told that Mr. Hemingway had asked that I come to work as one of the Master's Aides in Berkeley College. I was surprised, honored, and relieved to be leaving a high-pressure job. Being a Master's Aide was one of the "top" bursary jobs in the college—the highest being "Chief Aide." It opened up a whole new aspect of Yale for me. There was a "personal" touch in that office—partly because of Mr. Hemingway, but mostly because of Eleanor Hutchins, the college secretary, about whom I will write separately. She and I hit it off from the start and remained close friends through college and Divinity School days, and even after that we kept in touch until she died. In many ways she became a "surrogate mother" for me.

The other aides were also interesting, far more so than the people I had worked with in the other two jobs. When we were not actively working we could go to a room a half-story above the main office and study, or have a bull session. At first I spent a lot of time studying. I had decided I would not let Mrs. Hutchins know I could type, for I realized I would get a lot of it assigned to me. Then one day she was in a real bind, and I weakened and told her I could type. From then on, I got less time studying. While bursary work did cut down on one's time, most of the time I was in the Berkeley office was pleasant.

Mrs. Hutchins and Mr. Hemingway both seemed to be interested in my Southern way of life. One spring when the "magnolia trees" were blooming in New Haven, I was talking to her about what we in Arkansas called "magnolias." She had never seen them. So as soon as I returned to Arkansas in June I picked some magnolias and gardenias, boxed them up and sent them special delivery. She sent me a thank you note, but told me the next fall she had been out of town when they arrived, so when she opened the box they were all brown. But we had that kind of personal relationship. She would also talk about her only son, Todd, who was having trouble in school. When he was thinking about colleges, I had him for lunch at Berkeley and let him see the college from the viewpoint of a student. When my parents visited twice, I invited her to have a meal with them.

I'll never forget one spring day in 1948 when Mrs. Hutchins handed me a list of people who had been elected to Phi Beta Kappa, and I was to deliver to each one's room an announcement. As I started on my rounds, I looked at the list and could not believe my name was on it! She had known it, but let me find out for myself.

That change in bursary work began to make life more bearable in the spring of 1946, but I was still homesick through 1946-47. It was not until the fall of 1947 that I really began to enjoy Yale College. And much of that was due to the Master's Aide job.

Hiroshima

World War II was still raging in the Pacific when I entered Yale in 1945. I would not turn 18 until October and would already be in the second half of freshman year. I hoped I would be allowed to finish that before being drafted, but this was not certain. I did not like, at all, the thought of going into the Army. It was not so much the fear of death. I doubted I would ever get that far. I had never heard of conscientious objectors until I did research for my high school debate. That was not an option I considered. But I felt I would not survive the lack of privacy, the rough and tough world of being with people of all types, the physical brutality of basic training, and then the thought of being trained to shoot guns and to kill people. The whole thing was something I dreaded and tended to pull a Scarlet O'Hara—"I'll think about that tomorrow."

Because of the war, we started classes in July. I had an afternoon class—I think it was French. I went into the hot classroom in Harkness Hall on August 6, and as people gathered for class, someone had in his hands one of the New York tabloids. Printed all across the page, taking up the whole front, were the words "Atomic Bomb." I don't think there was even a picture of a mushroom cloud, for pictures could not be transmitted instantly as they are today.

We were all in shock. "What is an atomic bomb?" we asked. There had been no prior talk of this. We knew about mass bombings, and the V-1s and V-2s the Germans had sent against London. The atomic bomb project had been kept so secret that even the people in Las Alamos and Oak Ridge, we later learned, did not know what they were working on.

That afternoon we had no idea how many people had been killed or injured, or the extent of damage. I, at least, had no idea where in Japan Hiroshima was located. We all knew that after V-E Day troops and war equipment were being shipped as rapidly as possible from Europe to the Pacific. As various islands were captured, we assumed that an assault on Japan lay ahead, and everyone knew that the casualties on both sides would be enormous. But the end of the war, while beginning to seem inevitable, we all assumed could be a long time off, and at great cost.

Then all at once, this "atomic bomb" thing. What was it? What would be the outcome? President Truman in announcing the bomb called on Japan to surrender.

No wonder I do not remember what class was being held that afternoon. I am sure the professor accomplished little of his lesson plan for the day. Nothing else was talked about in our suite and at meals.

In a few days there was an announcement that a second atomic bomb had been dropped on Nagasaki. Rumors began to fly about a possible Japanese surrender.

As I recall, practically every sermon preached at Battell Chapel that year touched on the implications of the atomic bomb. In that afternoon class on August 6, 1945, I learned of one of the turning points in the history of the human race.

V-J Day

Following Hiroshima and Nagasaki, rumors were rife that Japan was about to surrender. It was hard to concentrate on study, though I think classes were held. We would hear the surrender had taken place, then that it had not. Finally in the evening of August 15, the official word came that Japan had surrendered! Even though the official surrender did not take place until September 2, the war was over! Yale, like most of the rest of the country, went wild. Students took to the streets.

I remember going down to the New Haven Green, probably with some of the people on our floor in our entryway, for they were the only people I knew. As I wandered the Green, I saw that the doors of Trinity Episcopal Church were open. This is where I had worshipped my first Sunday in New Haven, so it was not totally unknown. I had a strong desire to go into a church, and to pray, and to give thanks. As I recall, it was not a structured service, but a time when people could come and go for prayer. None of my friends went with me. I think they kidded me about wanting to go.

I was thankful that the war was over, thankful that Art would not have to go from Europe to the Pacific, thankful that I would not have to go to war. The draft was still on, and I assumed I would be called up, but at least I would not have to go to war. I was deeply grateful.

There were many stories in the following days about what people did on V-J night. Four people in a first floor room in Silliman College were playing bridge. One, who was dummy, said, "I just saw something fall past our window." All four got up to look out the window. There was a "dry moat" around Silliman with plants growing in the soft dirt at the bottom. There they saw a student. He lived in one of the upper floors. He was so drunk that he had fallen out of the window of his room — and was so relaxed that he was not hurt when he hit the soft dirt. There were many ways of celebrating.

My Finances—Yale College

During my four years at Yale College, I felt financially "restricted" for the first time — not poor, but definitely living within a tight budget. I knew Daddy had strained to the limit to be able to send me to Yale. It was far more expensive than the University of Tennessee where Ann was going, simultaneously. And Texas A&M had cost them almost nothing for Art. I was at Yale on a scholarship — something no one in our family had ever done before. I always feared that for me to show any excessive expenditures would threaten my chance of keeping the scholarship.

I don't know that I put it all together at the time, but I was assigned a room with another scholarship student, and one of the men next door was on scholarship. I think the boys across the hall were not on scholarship. But none of the really wealthy students in Berkeley were my neighbors.

I remember one afternoon soon after that July semester started my roommate suggested we go down to the drug store to get some refreshments. Having grown up in the country, the idea of being able to walk to such a place was new. The idea of having to pay for refreshments was also new. (They had always been free, and available, at home, and I was homesick and wanted some "comfort food.") I remember getting a caramel sundae, enjoying it tremendously, and feeling very grown up to be able to do such a thing

Mary Wrenetta McCain, Francies McCain, Mimi Bradford, and me in Scarsdale, New York, in 1947.

without checking with parents or anyone—and then, when I paid the tab—something like 35 cents—realizing I could not make this a pattern on my budget.

I did not have a real "budget," but every Sunday night when Mother wrote her weekly letter (more frequently I think that first term, because I wrote home every day!), she would include in the letter a $10 bill (the 2008 equivalent of $120). That was to be my living expenses for the week. Out of that I was to pay for laundry, haircuts, church donation, soap, movies, etc.—and save up enough to let me pay the train fare to go down to Scarsdale, which I did over Labor Day, I believe. I guess that was when I tried hitchhiking. I knew this was the way Art came and went from Texas A&M and assumed that it was what all college students did. I did manage to get a ride to Scarsdale, even right to the McCains' door. But they somehow let me know that in the northeast that was not the proper thing to do—and I never did it again!

Whereas in Little Rock High School I had been surrounded by people who were at the top of the financial pile in Little Rock, I was still surrounded by the "Scott mystique." At Yale, I was surrounded by the elite from all over the nation—not only intellectually, but also financially. People did not talk about their parents' finances, but it was pretty easy to pick up. And far from there being a "Scott mystique," people at Yale did not know who the Campbells were, nor that Scott existed, and many of them had only a vague idea of where Arkansas was, though they had a faint memory of having heard of it. I was really "nobody from nowhere," and that did not feel good. I don't think I have ever put this together before, but the misery I called "homesickness" was probably partly a sense of loss of status.

There was a fraternity rush (although fraternities did not play a big role at Yale), but they were not the fraternities I knew of in Arkansas—SAE and Sigma Chi and Kappa Sig. I did go to a party or two, but had had no letters of introduction and got nowhere and knew it instantly. I comforted myself by saying that it would not be appropriate for a scholarship student to spend money on something as unnecessary as that.

That first year at Yale was a struggle—actually, the first two years. It was not until the fall of 1947, halfway through my junior year, that I felt comfortable being at Yale and began to enjoy it. Even after that, I kept a pretty close eye on my expenses, although I did have girls over for football weekends and a couple of times took excursions to other places. I remember going to Princeton one year for the Yale-Princeton game.

My salvation was the McCains who welcomed me to their Scarsdale home and gave me "free" vacations; and toward the end, the Charles McCains welcomed me to Ten Gracie Square and showed me a side of New York I would never have been able to afford. The latter also set me free from my desire to make money. I was going through a struggle on what I was going to do with my life, and one of the temptations was to make a lot of money. I saw at Gracie Square that money could not deliver on happiness.

I guess I felt "almost poor" most of my time at Yale—until about the last year. (Not as poor as roommate Earl Schultz who did his own laundry and could not go home on vacations.) Once I decided that money was not that important to me, the sense of being strapped financially was lifted from me. It was part of my Christian growth.

Traveling to and from Yale

One way in which I tried to economize was the means by which I traveled back and forth to New Haven. As I mentioned earlier, I first went there in a Pullman. I wound up traveling in coach, but I never did descend to going by bus!

One great exception to frugality was in October 1945. I was so miserably homesick, my parents offered/gave in to having me come home. The time between terms was so short that the only way I could get there and back was by flying — the only time I did that in my years at Yale. The war was just over, and seats on a plane were almost impossible to reserve. Uncle Arthur McCain said he would see what his secretary could do. The next day she told him she had a seat going and returning. I was impressed. So was he — until he realized the name of the vice-chairman of the Board of Chase Bank was also Donald Campbell, and the airlines thought they were giving a seat to an important financier. That flight was on a DC-3, propeller (of course). It was a "local" that, as I recall, put down at Washington, D.C.; Roanoke, Virginia; Bristol, Knoxville, Jackson, and Memphis, Tennessee, and Little Rock. I think it took all day. The same was true going back. But that trip was a lifesaver for me. It did not cure my homesickness, but it enabled me to go on.

By Christmas, I felt so guilty about the cost of travel that I began traveling on coach. I'd catch a train from New Haven. Because the best connections were through Pennsylvania Railroad, I'd try to catch one from New Haven that went to Penn Station, but there were not many of them. If I went to Grand Central, I would have to catch the shuttle subway, lugging my heavy suitcase. (I never have to this day learned how to pack light. And my suitcases were heavy even when empty.) In those days there were a few non-smoking cars, but on most of them people could — and did — smoke cigarettes, pipes, and cigars. The air would be so filled with smoke that it would descend almost to the floor. When I could find a seat only in a smoker, I would begin to get a headache and stop up before the train pulled out of the station. In 1945 and 1946, the

Our dining table at Scott set for Christmas dinner in 1948.

trains were filled with troops, so every car was full to capacity. There was not enough room in the luggage racks for all the suitcases, so often we would have to put them on the platform between cars. The dining cars were always full, so one would have to wait in line to get in, and the quality of food and service began to decline. Sometimes, I would travel with one of the Little Rock men studying at Yale, but usually I was alone and did not enjoy talking to my seatmate. There was an exception one Christmas—when Uncle Ken was traveling with me but staying in a Pullman—when the person seated next to me was a student from Harvard. We had a lot in common and I enjoyed him greatly.

The only other time I took a Pullman was at Christmas 1947. Dan Phillips was at Yale by then, and I think Lee Hall was coming home. Dan organized an evening in New York where we all met under the Clock at the Biltmore (agreed upon meeting place for all the Ivy league men and women) with some women they knew from various colleges. I remember feeling so "old," for I was about to start my junior year and the rest were all freshmen. We did go by Pullman that trip—either everyone having a roomette or two sharing a bedroom. I guess we came back the same way, though not all at the same time. I think I arrived in St. Louis on the return trip by myself, except for Mantz Sussky who had come up by coach. I felt guilty about such luxury and never tried it again.

At that point in history, the railroads were trying to get out of the passenger business, for their money came from freight. At best, they did not encourage their staff to be pleasant; we all suspected they were instructed to be as rude and uncaring as possible. If so, they succeeded admirably! The Pennsylvania was the worst of all. The Missouri Pacific between Little Rock and St. Louis was OK, but not good. I found that if I went through Washington instead of through St. Louis, the Southern Railroad to Memphis was cleaner, the scenery better, and the staff much, much more polite, and the ambiance was "Southern," not "Northern." I was especially drawn to this route because Ann was in school in Knoxville, which was on the way. A couple of times, I stopped there to visit her before going on. In Memphis, I could catch either the Missouri Pacific or the Rock Island, usually the latter.

But on the whole, I developed a strong dislike of rail travel, from which I have not recovered. In later years when I got on the train in Little Rock, I would take a benedryl pill, wake up in St. Louis, take another one as we started for New York, and wake up when I arrived. That is exaggerating a bit, for I often had to study. But those trips were something to be endured.

I never had a car at Yale, as undergraduate or at Yale Divinity School (YDS). During and right after the war, they were not available. Even when they did begin to come on the market, they were expensive, and most students in Yale College did not have them. Some did at YDS, because it was necessary for their fieldwork. But since mine was being secretary for Uncle Ken, I did not have to have one. Daddy was more than generous in supporting me through college and divinity school, but that generosity did not extend to providing a car!

Architecture of Yale College

It was impossible for me to live for four years surrounded by the Yale College buildings without their having an influence on me. Having never seen the campus prior to enrolling there, I had no idea what to expect.

The buildings are quite a hodge-podge of styles. The oldest structure on campus, Connecticut Hall, sitting in the middle of Freshman Campus, is a rather modest three-story redbrick rectangle of simple colonial design. It was a dormitory at the time of the American Revolutionary War. Nathan Hale lived there. He was the young martyr who said, "I regret that I have but one life to give for my country."

Connecticut Hall is surrounded on all sides by the Freshman, or Old, Campus made up of Nineteenth Century redbrick collegiate Gothic dormitories and class buildings—rather ugly. Normally all freshmen are housed here before going into the residential colleges at the start of sophomore year. However, the Army ASTP program was still using those buildings when I entered in June 1945, before the war ended, so we and a handful of early returning veterans went right into the colleges.

In the late 1920s and early 1930s Yale set out on a program of breaking up the undergraduate student body into smaller residential colleges. They did this with a fortune left by a Mr. Sterling who had made his money in Standard Oil. The stock was sold just before the 1929 stock market crash, so Yale got top dollar value. Then when the Depression came, it was able to build with the low wages and cost of material of that era. As a result the new colleges were beautifully constructed. They were in a variety of styles. Calhoun, Berkeley, and Trumbull were collegiate Gothic, as were Saybrook, Branford, and Jonathan Edwards, although the latter three I think were built with Harkness money, rather than Sterling funds. Pierson and Davenport were redbrick New England Colonial. Silliman had an early 20th century front and redbrick inside. Timothy Dwight was Colonial brick, but with some white columns. The Sterling library, the major classroom building, and the Payne Whitney gymnasium were all Gothic. Yale even had a Gothic smokestack!

Unfortunately, Yale was built in downtown New Haven, a city not noted for its beauty. To compensate for this, each college was built around a courtyard that was beautifully landscaped, so students did not get the feeling of living in a metropolitan setting.

Breaking the undergraduate student body into residential colleges was very successful, for it gave me the feeling of living in a small college. In our classes we were thrown with people from all

Entrance to Berkeley College at Yale.

the colleges, but all my real friendships were formed with Berkeley students. The few married students who lived off campus were assigned to a residential college. In that way I got to know Bard Smith. Those who became involved in extracurricular activities, such as fraternities or the Whiffenpoofs, would not have been as insulated as I. Berkeley had both liberal arts and engineering students, so there was cross-fertilization of ideas.

Since I was so centered on Berkeley College, its architecture had a real impact on me. It was divided into two sections by "cross campus," an open space leading up to the Sterling Library. The two parts were connected by an underground tunnel, as well as by large gates opening out onto cross campus. While Gothic on the outside, I suppose the interior would have been more Tudor. The Common Room and Dining Hall had a great deal of intricate woodcarving, and the walls were lined with paintings. Attached to the North Court were the Master's House and garden, and office. These were beautifully appointed on the interior. Sam and Mary Hemingway were often described as "the last of the Edwardians," They served tea each afternoon, and had an "open" tea for all students and fellows on Sunday afternoons. It was a genteel way of life that took the edge off the sometimes-crude aspects of undergraduate life and behavior.

For the first three years, I lived in a suite that had been designed for two people, but due to the overcrowding after World War II, we wound up with four of us in it. It had a living room with a fireplace, and a hallway leading to two bedrooms. There were also single rooms. In the first half of my senior year, I lived in one of those, in North Court, with a roommate. In my last semester, I had a single room to myself in North Court.

The "symbol" for Yale University is the Gothic Harkness Tower that looms over Branford and Saybrook Colleges. It must be eight or 10 stories tall. In it is a large carillon that tolled the hours, but had such a range of bells that it played all kinds of music at specified times.

I have often said that if the Yale buildings had been located on the Princeton campus, it would have been the ideal university setting. The Princeton buildings are not nearly as substantially built as Yale's.

Gym at Yale

I hated gym from my first exposure to it at East Side Junior High, and again at LRHS, and worked hard to avoid it. When I arrived at Yale, I found that freshmen had to take one year of physical education and go through a "muscle building" course established by the Navy V-12 program. If I had known this in advance, I might have been tempted to turn down Yale. I don't guess so, but it was not appealing.

The Payne Whitney Gymnasium at Yale is the only Gothic gym I have ever seen. It was large, expensively built, beautifully equipped. I guess there were 40 to 50 of us freshmen who were herded into one of the rooms and told we were to be checked out on a number of events. The only one that did not frighten me was swimming, for I knew I could pass it since I'd been swimming all my life, and had done a lot of it just before leaving Arkansas. But I was taken back when I found that we had to swim in the nude. I did pass the swimming test, but I vowed I'd never go back there again.

I can't remember all the tests we had to take—push ups, sit ups, long jumps, high jumps, running, weight lifting—but worst of all, we had to climb a heavy rope hanging about 20 feet from the ceiling (and looked like 100). I remember on the push ups I was teamed with someone named Burnside from South Carolina. He was as unenthusiastic as I. We decided the South should unite. One of us was to count while the other did push ups. I think we counted "by two's," so managed to declare the other had met the requirements. I did not do so well on the other tests, so had to continue returning to the "muscle building" class all that summer and most of the fall. I gradually passed one test after the other. The last hurdle was climbing that damn rope. I have always hated heights, and the thought of being up that high (if I ever got there) and having to come back down scared me to death. But at long last, about two-thirds of the way through the second semester, I somehow managed to get up, not freeze, and come back down without breaking my neck. I was one happy person!

After that we were allowed to do some things we liked. Tennis and golf were not among the options, but volleyball was, and I rather enjoyed that.

When I cleaned out my locker at the end of the second semester, I vowed I would never come back in that gym again! And I didn't except a couple of times when I was taking people on a tour of Yale and they wanted to see the place.

Physical Activities at Yale

Even though I shook the dust of the gym off my feet, I did not lead a completely sedentary life as an undergraduate.

The biggest physical activity I had at Yale College was walking. I had not realized until I got there that, living in the country, I rarely walked anywhere, for we had to drive. Even after I changed to a different bursary job, students still had to do a lot of walking around campus.

I could not play tennis or golf—partly because I did not have time, and partly because they were far from the main campus, and

I would have had to take the streetcar to get there since I did not have a car. Berkeley College did have some squash courts in the basement. I had never heard of that sport, but Dagoberto Sarmiento had played it in Colombia and said he would teach me. It was enough like tennis so I was interested. It is played with a racket that has a smaller head than a tennis racket, but is stringed. The ball is small and solid rubber. The ball is bounced off all four walls of the cube, and can also hit the ceiling. I was never really good at it, but I did enjoy it and from time to time would play.

Some people would go to Payne Whitney "for fun." That was not on my agenda!

When I would go to Scarsdale, we would play tennis. I was never in the league with the McCains, but they graciously played with me. And in the summers I would swim and play tennis and golf.

Me playing tennis in Scarsdale, New York, in 1945.

How Men Dressed

When I arrived at Yale, I found the style of clothes was radically different from what I had known at Scott and Little Rock. I was used to wearing long-sleeved sport shirts. White dress shirts were very hard to come by during World War II. I did have a few, but it was a shock to discover I had to wear shirt/tie/coat for every meal, including breakfast. I had never seen a button-down dress shirt, but I soon discovered that was the proper dress. Nor had I ever seen a blue dress shirt, other than ones farmers would sometimes wear with suspenders. Thinking I was going North, I had wool clothes. In Arkansas in the summer, I had worn white duck pants and white short-sleeved sports shirts. I don't think I had a summer suit. At Yale, I found people wore seercord coats and usually gray flannel pants, even in the summer. In the South, middle aged and older men wore seersucker suits, but that was different from seercord. I am not sure how I dressed for class that first summer. I know I did not wear a coat to class, and probably not a white shirt and tie. I think we could wear sport shirts to class. The requirement for coat and tie at meals was so absolute, though, that a few extra ties were kept in the coat closet so if someone arrived and had forgotten the tie, he could borrow one rather than having to go back to his room.

Yale was certainly not air conditioned, and since other than in wartime it was open only for the academic year, those Gothic buildings did not have cross ventilation. I suffered more from the heat during the summer of 1945 than I ever had in Arkansas.

But once we got into the fall, my Arkansas clothes were definitely "out of step" with the Yale dress code. There was nothing I could do about clothes that first year, for I was stuck with what I had. I did rather quickly get into wearing gray flannel slacks. The darker they were, the more stylish—Oxford gray was darker, Cambridge gray lighter. I think for the fall of 1947 I bought a gray flannel suit in Little Rock—but it was Cambridge gray. I began to replace plain white dress shirts for button down ones—though they were still hard to acquire, for clothes were short even after the war. I also scuttled the garish ties I had bought before going to Yale and started wearing regimental stripes. The other "in" tie was a narrow black knit tie. I resisted paying the prices at J. Press and the Yale Coop, and would shop elsewhere. As a result, my clothes were not "quite right," but close. I also finally started buying seercord suits. They are the coolest clothes for summer I have ever found, and I have been "hooked" on them ever since. One of the status symbols at Yale was white buck shoes. (Snobs were called "the white shoe boys.") But they were expensive and I never bought any.

Many of the veterans returning had been officers and wore "pinks," which were tan slacks with a slight pinkish tint. That was all they had, so they wore them, and they did it in such numbers it became "in." Also, many who had not been officers were mustered out with cotton khaki pants. They caught on, and people began to wear them—with a sport coat, preferably tweed, over them.

Black shoes were looked down on. Brown ones were much more in vogue, especially the reddish brown called Cordovan (made out of horse, rather than cow, leather—and it lasted much longer.) I finally got some of those. I also found that the proper kind of tie at Yale was a regimental stripe, or a "college" tie, for each college had a crest, and the Yale Co-op had a supply for each college. The "in" socks were Argyles—wool knits with various colors in a particular design.

The "uniform" for church, a Master's tea, or a date would be Oxford gray flannel suit, or gray slacks with a blue blazer with brass buttons (and many people would have a college emblem on the suit pocket, but I never did), or a tweed sport coat; white buttoned down oxford cloth white shirt; regimental striped tie; Cordovan shoes for a blazer or sport coat; for a gray flannel suit, either Cordovan or black shoes. White buck shoes were also very popular.

We all owned raincoats, for we walked everywhere, and many also had umbrellas. I had never owned either, for living at Scott we drove everywhere and did not need that kind of rain protection. I also eventually got a rain hat, which most people owned.

Toward the last of my undergraduate days, people began wearing blue jeans to class, and would even wear them to meals—with a sport coat and tie on top of them. Until then, I had never seen denim except in overalls and in blue jeans that cowboys wore. I remember, toward my later years, noticing how many jeans were being worn and thinking that if I had any money to invest, I would sure put it in whoever manufactured denim. (And I would have made a fortune—and it was Cone in Greensboro, NC, where denim was developed.)

No students at Yale wore caps or hats, other than rain hats.

We all had overcoats for the winter. We knew nothing in Little Rock would be sufficient for a New Haven winter, so I bought nothing until I got there. I got Tap Hornor to go down shopping with me. I kept saying I wanted the heaviest thing they had in the store, for I have always been cold-natured. I got one that was so heavy I was almost stooped when I wore it. And it lasted into the 1980s when I would go north on my seminary trips.

Wool scarves were used a great deal. In Arkansas I had always had white silk scarves, but they were for dress and not warmth. I never saw a white silk one in New Haven. I also began to wear leather gloves in the winter.

I wore pajamas, as did most of our freshman class. The veterans were used to sleeping in their under shorts, and this became fairly common—a mixture. I never did get into that pattern. Some of the veterans had boxer shorts left from the military, but the rest of us wore briefs, and undershirts that had the straps over the shoulders, not T-shirts. They began to come in with the veterans, too.

While many did not wear coat and tie to class, I always did — gray slacks, white shirt, tie (I had to use up old ones), and a sport coat.

When I arrived, I think our hair was not cut too short. But veterans had been used to burr haircuts in the military, and many continued with them. So the longer I was there, the shorter I had my hair cut. I would go to the barber and say "I want it just long enough to be able to part, but no longer." Many of the students at Yale did not shave daily. Most of us freshmen did not really need to, but I was unusual in shaving daily whether I had to or not. I think that paid off for me in being asked to be a Master's Aide, for they knew I would always be presentable.

I got so addicted to this Yale uniform that I would wear my gray flannel suit to church at All Souls in the summer — without air conditioning — and would stick to the varnish on the pews. People would try to talk me into getting out of it, but I would not.

My style of dress to this day is still pretty much that of Yale College in the late 1940s.

How Women Dressed

I do not know how girls in the Seven Sisters Colleges (the female equivalent of the Ivy League), dressed during the week. At that time, all the prestigious northeastern colleges were single sex, either men or women, except right after the war when veterans were having trouble getting a space at a college, and Vassar took in a few men, and Miss Finch's Finishing School took a few — including Bobby Hardy from Little Rock. I heard that women liked having no men around during the week because they felt free to dress sloppily and not to bother about hair and make-up.

When they came to Yale for a weekend, it was a different story! They were dressed "to the nines" (whatever that meant). Even for a football game when they were going to be riding the streetcar out to the Bowl, they would be wearing hose and high heels. They might wear a skirt and sweater if they were staying where they could change before the post-game parties. Otherwise, they would wear what was appropriate for a cocktail party, then dinner. In

1945, because of wartime regulations, skirts were short and rather skimpy to cut down on the amount of material used. I guess it was in 1946, when the restrictions were removed, that "the new look" came in — with skirts much lower, at least to the middle-calf range, or lower. Since girls were fitted out to go to college, almost a trousseau, many were stuck with a wartime wardrobe. There were creative ways of lowering the hem line, such as putting a matching band at the bottom of the skirt, or even ruffles at the bottom.

Girls coming for the weekend would always bring a hat. They probably wore one while traveling on the train to New Haven (most came that way), and certainly would have one if they were going to church. My dates always did, at Battell Chapel if they were Protestants, or in the case of Elizabeth Ginnochio, to mass — for hats were required for the latter, and were expected in the former. When the weather was cold, many of the girls would wear a short fur coat, usually mink-dyed muskrat. If there was a formal dance, they would wear a floor-length dress. One of the nice things about Yale was a tradition that corsages were never sent! Bringing a date in was expensive — and that was one item that could be eliminated.

When I would go to Scarsdale for vacations, Frances and family friends would wear skirts and sweaters, with loafers or saddle oxfords and white socks, when we were visiting around the house, or if we went out for a movie. She may have worn slacks when I was the only one around. If we went in to New York for a play, Frances would wear a dress, heels, and hose, but I think not a hat.

When I was at Scott during the winter, I think girls wore skirts and sweaters, with low heels — although for parties and church, it was good skirt/sweater or dress with heels and hose. I don't believe college-aged girls wore hats to All Souls, although they probably did to the big churches in town. Catholic and Episcopal churches required hats on all women.

In the summer at Scott most girls wore shorts, but my sister never did except when playing tennis, because she felt she was fat and wanted to cover her body as much as possible. I don't think she even wore slacks except when she was horseback riding.

One thing I never saw with girls who came to Yale, but I am sure went on wherever they were spending the night because I saw it at Scott when girls spent the night with Ann, was the ritual of rolling up their hair (except the few who were blessed with naturally curly hair.) Because they wanted a curl in their hair, but scorned permanents that their mothers employed, each night they would roll up their hair around small empty frozen juice cans (or they could buy rollers), or tie up their hair with a number of socks that would dangle down, so they looked like Medusa.

Lipstick was worn by girls, but I don't remember at that stage any were using powder or rouge or eye treatments (though they may have done it subtly enough so I was not aware of such efforts.) At that stage NO ONE who was "nice" had pierced ears. I guess most, but not all, wore earrings, but they were clip-ons. Jewelry would have been kept simple, perhaps a necklace or locket around the neck, and maybe one bracelet, and no rings unless it was a college class ring.

The "grown" women I saw around Yale tended to dress much more simply than those in Arkansas. They often wore "tweedy" suits or dresses, even to church. They all wore hats to church, but I do not remember seeing earrings or jewelry (other than engagement rings) among the University women. They would wear hose and heels, but the heels were low, for many of them did a good bit of walking. Some would wear fur coats, but most wore cloth ones, with perhaps a bit of fur on them. I never was present when they went to "adult" parties at country clubs, so they may have been more dressy then, but I doubt it.

Laundry and Cleaning

When I went to college, we could have our laundry picked up outside our room by one of the student-run enterprises. I thought this was too expensive, so I would take mine down to a laundry on the street behind Trumbull College, next to the barbershop. Everything in it would be ironed, just as it had been in Little Rock when we took things to the laundry. I remember I would have my shirts done with "heavy starch." If the collar was frayed, it would cut into my neck like a saw. I don't think I ever had a shirt other than white ones. One of my roommates, Earl Shultz, was on a very tight budget. He used to do his laundry in the bathroom, and hang it out to dry on clothesline in his bedroom. I think the only laundry I did was perhaps my wool socks, which I would then dry on the radiator.

One other "housekeeping" item that might be of interest to later generations that I'll insert here because I don't know where else to put it: Before World War II, there was maid service in all the college rooms. When we arrived in 1945, this was re-instituted. The women who did it did such a poor job that we used to complain they tracked more dirt in than they took out. This service was dropped during my undergraduate days, and we were responsible for cleaning our own rooms. As a result, many of them were never cleaned.

Yale Football Games

The weekly football games during the fall had a place in Yale life that games in other fields did not approach—except for a race in the spring called Derby Day between Yale and some of the Ivy League crews. I never went to the latter. Every undergraduate was given a season ticket to the football games, so even those of us on limited budgets could go. Also, all the hierarchy of the University, with wives, would turn out for the games, sitting together on the 50-yard line.

At that time, Yale College had Saturday morning classes. We were allowed one or two absences a semester in each course. Dates usually arrived Saturday morning. One hoped their train got in after class; hence many people wanted their Tues/Thur/Saturday classes to be at 8:00. For out-of-town games (I went to very few), we would leave on Friday, skip all the Saturday classes, and then come home on Sunday afternoon. Dates who came to New Haven would spend Saturday night, go to lunch or a party, and then leave on the Sunday afternoon train so they could get back to their colleges. This meant most dating was with people in New England or New York colleges. Vassar was about the limit one could go. Smith and Mount Holyoke were easier to reach, plus Connecticut College for Women.

The local games were played at the Yale Bowl, once the site of major football battles. Compared to stadia in the Midwest and South, it was rather small, a complete circle, half of it set down below ground level.

The Bowl was out on the edge of town. Only a few people owned cars, and they were used only on weekends because there was no place near the university for parking. Those who lived near New Haven might get a car for the game, but most undergraduates went to the Bowl on the streetcar. These were "open" ones, with wooden seats facing the front, each one running from one side to the other. There was a roof over each car, but there were no side walls. Also, there were "running boards," two levels, on the outside of each car, so people who could not find a seat would stand and hang on for dear life. All along the way, little boys from New Haven would line the street containing the streetcar rails, yelling "Throw me a penny, Mister." Before leaving for the game, we would get a lot of pennies and when throwing them to the boys would yell "Scramble." (At that time I had never been to Mardi Gras in New Orleans, but it was very similar, only pennies were thrown, not trinkets.)

The weather varied greatly during the fall. In September, it could be quite warm, so we would take off our tweed jackets. (People normally dressed well for the games.) By the end of the season, it could be freezing cold. Some people, whose father or grandfather had come to Yale, would wear the old raccoon coats from the 1920s. There were other times when it would be raining. Old flannel or khaki pants would be worn (there were no blue jeans until about my last year in college), with every kind of rain gear that could be rounded up. I remember once when the edge of a hurricane was passing New Haven rain fell in sheets. It was very hard for the players to hang on to the ball, so there was a lot of punting. When a ball would be kicked, if it headed into the wind it would go up and forward until the wind caught it, then return by about the same angle, so that it would gain about five yards. On the other hand, the team that had the wind at its back would kick and the ball would go up into the stands at the end. I remember after that game we went home drenched and had to change clothes.

There were no football scholarships to Yale. In fact, people who ate the hearty meals at the Training Table, had to pay extra for their food. This was true of the other Ivy League colleges, too, and as a result it was truly "amateur football." Many of the players were serious scholars. Walker Barksdale, who had been president of PIE in Little Rock, was a star player and an excellent student. Although I did not get to know him until YDS, Bob Raines, who was one of the stars, was an honor graduate at Yale College and YDS and won a Fulbright Scholarship. Also, the "yells" led by the cheerleaders were very sedate, such a "Go, Go" and the singing of "Boola,

Boola" or the Yale song (the name of which I cannot remember) which ended "for God, for country and for Yale." During the singing of the Yale song, all Yale men would pull out a white linen handkerchief and wave it back and forth. The cheerleaders were dressed in gray flannel slacks and blue blazers. I guess it was the fall of 1947 when Daddy took me to the first Arkansas Razorback game of the season before I left Little Rock. When I saw the way football was played in the Southwest Conference (where amateur had very little meaning—full scholarship with probably some money slipped in on the side), I realized football there and in the Ivy League were two different sports. Also, cheerleading, with fancy uniforms and all the acrobatics, was in another league.

Having a date to go to a Yale football weekend was desirable for many girls in the nearby colleges—and sometimes, from far away. I remember once a group came up from Randolph-Macon in Lynchburg, Virginia. (They were curiosities, for they were on the honor code, and were not allowed to drink.) Men with plenty of money would have a date for almost every home game. My budget did not allow that. I usually tried to have a date for one of them a fall. That was a major expense. First, one had to find a place for her to stay. The big downtown hotel was the Taft. It would get booked for football weekends weeks, if not months, ahead. If a residential college was having a "weekend," sometimes some dorm rooms were emptied, and girls could stay in those. The best option was to take up the Hemingways' offer to let girls stay in the guest suite or in their home. When that happened, it entailed sending flowers to the Hemingways, usually large mums. Then there was the expense of feeding the date. Some of that could take place in the refectory, but it was not "in" to have all meals there. Those who belonged to Mory's could eat there. I did not belong. I also had no car, so I was not free to drive out to some of the restaurants along the Long Island Sound. There were a couple of nice restaurants in downtown New Haven.

Then there was the matter of entertainment after the games. (All games were played in the afternoon, for the Yale Bowl had no night lighting.) About once a year, Berkeley would have a dance, held in the refectory. I think once I remember going to a dance over in Paine Whitney Gym. Perhaps that was "junior prom." Generally, people in an entryway would go together to have a drinking party in one of the rooms. That would go on for hours, but I think we had to eat somewhere afterwards. We would all put in money ahead of time for the beer and liquor and mixers and snacks. At that time I was a tee-totaller, so I put in money but did not get the benefits. I remember once, in 1947 I guess, the rest of our "crowd" decided since I would be the only one remaining sober, I should tend the bar. Just before the party started, I explained that I had no idea what drink went with which mixer — and they panicked when I suggested mixing sherry with orange juice. They gave me quick instructions.

As the drinking went on, there would be a lot of singing, getting more bawdy as the night progressed. One of the favorite songs at the parties was "Roll me over in the clover, roll me over, lay me down and do it again."

I can't remember how many times I had dates come up. I think once Dago invited Frances McCain, and I had someone else — perhaps Elizabeth Ginnochio. I remember visiting Ethel Smart at her very strict prep school in Boston, and Pog Gay from Boston — but I don't think I ever had them down.

Then on Sunday morning the thing to do, except for those who were hung-over from drinking, was to take your date to church. Many would go to Battell Chapel, but they had to sit in the balcony or on the side, for the main body of pews was reserved for undergraduates (which meant men). I've written elsewhere about taking Liz Ginnochio, an ardent Catholic, to mass at St. Mary's, a big parish church near the campus, run by the Dominicans. My Jesuit-trained friends all looked down on those priests as being uneducated — saying they had only three sermons, one against communism, one against Protestants, and one against birth control. Well, the Sunday Liz and I went was the "anti-birth control Sunday." Right in the middle of the sermon, a woman got up and walked out with six children following her!

As I think back on those fall football games, even though I never appreciated or understood the sport, they were fun times, whether it was just our crowd being stags, or having a date.

Once I went to Yale Divinity School, I attended only one Yale sporting event.

Berkeley Players

Berkeley College was opened, I think, about 1935. Between then and the exodus of male students in World War II, certain traditions were established, then abandoned during the war years when it was closed. One of those discontinued traditions was the Berkeley Players, a college dramatic presentation. I guess they were not able to get it together by the spring of 1946, but by 1947 Mr. Hemingway and Tom Mendenhall resurrected it. Because Mr. Hemingway was a Shakespeare scholar, Berkeley always put on an Elizabethan play.

For the play, a platform was built in the Berkeley dining hall, right in front of the portrait of the Bishop Berkeley and his family. Curtains around it made the background and the front curtain. Erecting it was a major production, put up a week or so before the play, and taken down shortly afterward, for the space was needed for tables. I do not know if Berkeley had a store

The Berkeley College Players putting on Shakespeare's Taming of the Shrew *in 1947. I am on the far right playing the part of Bianca.*

of costumes or if they were borrowed from the Drama School, but there seemed to be a bountiful supply of Elizabethan clothes and accouterments. Tickets were required for admission (I think we ran two nights), but they were free to the Berkeley students and others in the university. It was always full.

Since Yale College was all male, the plays were put on in the Shakespearean manner, i.e., men playing the female roles. In 1948, I had some minor and innocuous male role in *Much Ado About Nothing*. But in 1947, I was "the beauteous Bianca" in *Taming of the Shrew*. They kept taking away my lines in order to shorten the play, so the plot was well advanced when I finally had a speaking part. All the other actors were from New England or the West Coast with their "Yankee" accents. When I opened my mouth for the first time, out of it came, with full Arkansas accent, "If Ah'm yo' burd, Ah mean to shif ma boosh." At every performance, the house roared with laughter. I had a hard time seeing why it was so funny!

The play was one of the few events in the year for the whole college, except I think we always had one formal dance. But the important thing for me was that this was the first thing I got involved in at Yale other than study, bursary job, Uncle Ken's Bible study, and the chapel services. I don't know if it was George Kearns or Frank McClain, but someone on our floor talked many of us into going out for the plays. It was the first time I had any serious contact with many from Berkeley who did not live in our entryway. And it was the first time I got out of my "shell" enough to feel a part of Yale. This play in the spring of 1947 (at the start of my junior year) was the real turning point, for the next fall I looked forward to returning to New Haven.

Political Ethos at Yale College

When I started Yale in June 1945, the war in Europe had ended, but the one in the Pacific was still raging. President Harry Truman was still pretty much an unknown figure. There was talk of one million casualties if the Allies had to invade the Japanese mainland. The university was still in a wartime frame of mind. Then came the atomic bombs and the Japanese surrender.

There was at first an assumption that things would loosen up immediately, but severe shortages existed in various areas, so rationing continued for a while. The war clouds were gone, and there was relief and thanksgiving. But it seemed to me every sermon at Battell Chapel dealt with the moral issue of the atomic bombs. I did not really understand what the issues were. I don't recall a lot of discussion of the bomb in the bull sessions in our room. We were all "fodder" for the draft and were so relieved we probably did not consider the long-term consequences of the atomic age.

Returning service men flooded back into the colleges, including Yale. The suite Dan Howard and I occupied had three, then four of us living there. The age level and sophistication of the student body shot up. But the draft continued, for those who had been in service wanted out, and there was need for warm bodies to fill their places. A good many of my classmates were drafted as they reached 18. Shortly after my 18th birthday, I was called up for my physical. Because of a letter written by the allergist who had been treating me since I arrived at Yale, I was given a 4-F status and was free of the draft. I cannot say I was disappointed! What a relief. I could assume I would continue on with my academic career.

I do not remember a lot of discussion with other students about national politics. I remember one student on the floor below us was Ed Rockefeller, but he was not part of the moneyed side of that family. He was very liberal and was a great advocate of unions.

In the fall of 1948, I was opposed to Harry Truman because I thought the Democrats had been in power too long. I was not enthusiastic about Thomas Dewey. I must confess that I toyed with voting for the States Rights Party, with Strom Thurmond as the candidate because I was a segregationist and Southerner and conservative! But I finally cast my first vote (I had just turned 21) for Dewey. I do not know how my closest Berkeley College friends voted. By then I was living in a single room in North Court. Had I still been in Room 599, perhaps I would have been more aware of the political climate.

Intellectual Expansion

I suppose anyone who takes college seriously goes through many intellectual and emotional revolutions. I certainly did. I did not have to study any harder at Yale than I had at Little Rock High, but with the same amount of work I did not achieve my previous high level as far as grades were concerned. The difference was that in high school, there were people who were sharper and better students than I, but they were few in number. At Yale, most of the people I knew had as good, if not better, academic backgrounds. In freshman year, I guess my English course was the biggest jolt. I had not a clue as to how to read, and understand, poetry, especially modern poetry. I think I took Economics 101 that year, and recall how shocked I was to learn prices were not set by cost of production plus a fair return, but rather by supply and demand. I was stretched in my faith by participating in weekly and some mid-week chapel services, but I never took a religion course. I had so little theology, I was not really upset by evolution or how the Bible came to be, or by the repercussions of the atomic bomb.

I found American history fascinating, and it was taught in more detail than in high school, but I had been so well prepared in this field, there were no shocks. I had no background at all in other aspects of history — diplomatic, economic, world. I found political science fascinating, but soon it seemed a bit empty so I switched to history. Writing the senior essay was not only a lot of work, done under time pressure, but it opened up an aspect of teaching history that I did not like, i.e., research. I could do it (and still can), but I found it tedious and decided I did not want to spend the rest of my life doing that.

A photo of me in 1948.

One of the most stimulating courses, with lifelong repercussions, was Epistemology by Brand Blanshard — reflections on how we know what we know. This atheist deepened my faith immeasurably, and probably prepared me for seminary and later theologizing by helping me realize we do not "know" anything, but live by faith. Even science is based on the faith that what our senses tell us is real.

As I progressed in French, especially that first semester, I realized I was out of my league since most of the other students had grown up with French governesses.

I took one course on the History of Art. This taught me a lot, but most of my growth in the arts came from my circle of friends. I went to a Shakespeare play my first year — I think it was *Othello*. I grew to love the pipe organ, mostly from the playing at Battell Chapel, but also Dwight Chapel. Even though my knowledge was limited, from conversations in the room and at the Hemingways' teas, I became conversant with some of the figures in literature through the centuries.

While in college, I became aware of the larger world. Before, I had been interested in Republican politics, and listened to the news regularly, and read *Time* magazine faithfully every week. But to have people like The Provost, from Kings College, Cambridge, visit at Berkeley and to get to know him; to have Dago from Colombia as my closest friend; to get to know Jim Boyes so well my senior year—all this was mind-expanding. Also, to have my Southern customs and prejudices challenged was painful, and I fought a rear-guard defense, but I was having doubts from intellectual and spiritual encounters.

My frequent visits in Scarsdale with the Arthur McCains was an education. They were so basic and down to earth, but they lived in a rarefied atmosphere—especially after Uncle Arthur was elected President of Chase Bank. I got a glimpse of the inner circle of the financial world in New York. I learned to be comfortable in the New York-New England world, outside academic circles. Somewhere along the way, I learned how to make conversation in almost every level of society.

The amazing thing is that with all the expansion and revolution of my intellectual world, and in many ways my social world, I never really rebelled against my background, as many people did, nor did I lose my basic values. I attribute much of this to my parents who had firm convictions but did not force them on me.

Myself as the Last Speaker

In the first half of my senior year, the spring of 1948, I took a political science course in which we were assigned a book, *A Modern Symposium* by G. Lowes Dickinson, which hypothesized a series of speakers at a conference, each one representing a particular worldview. The assignment for the term paper was to write "Myself as the last speaker," giving my philosophy of life. I am including excerpts from this paper to show the philosophy of life I held at that stage of my development.

> I am rather reluctant even to try explaining my philosophy of life to you, for since it is based on the belief that the only ultimate values are those of the spirit, a communion with God, some of you will from the first

dismiss my beliefs as mere "superstition" or "wishful thinking." Others will have a comprehension of them so much more profound than I do at the present time that my talk will seem like that of a child.... My first point is that most of the values in this life are not the materialistic ones that are subject to the scrutiny and investigation of the scientific method....

While the mysterious system we observe in the universe hints that there must be a plan, and the occasional saintly acts we hear of indicate that deeds can be done that are above the imagination of those who feel capable of directing the affairs of the world, I think that the only way even to begin to comprehend the magnitude and indescribable kindness of the Christian God is to know Him. After once having realized this new aspect of life, there is no more doubt as to His existence than there would be about the reality of a friend after having met him. I also think that the interpretation of this divine being which we get from the teachings of Jesus Christ through the Bible is the correct one....

One problem that always must be confronted by a person holding God to be both good and omnipotent is the presence of evil, for it cannot be denied.... Men are not merely automatons controlled by their environment, but do have some degree of free will....

But first I might begin by giving just a brief idea of those values that I would hold dear if this new influence had never come into my life—those that I did live by and those from which I must start building with supernatural help. I think that my ideal was a life of ease and beauty. Not one of laziness, but a world in which all of the people with whom I would come in contact would be cultured and would have the will and capacity for social responsibility.... I would have called for an aristocracy of talent and graciousness.... There was one great exception to this rule of the value of talent combined with culture, and that was the Negro. I was reared in the South, and while I was glad to give a colored person equal economic and political opportunities, I could not admit him to social equality at any level.... Here I would like to explain my conservative approach to this, and other, matters by saying that it is one of my most profound beliefs that no part of human personality should be destroyed before something has previously been supplied to take its place. In fact, the old element should be forced aside only by pressure from the new, or something will rush in to fill the vacuum. No one can tell what this new filler will be....

Take the problem of property and the distribution of income. Now for me, this is not an ultimate question, for I can see no way in which a comfortable living *per se* can have intrinsic value if value is defined as a relationship between man and God. But I do think that these things can be of extreme importance as a means, for the presence or absence of dire need can to a large extent determine the extent to which a man is able to grow and develop spiritually. I think the ideal environment for such a growth would be Christian communism or anarchy, for they would be about the same.... But unfortunately men are not prepared now for a society where such unselfishness would be demanded. I would say that it is better to keep the bulk of our present property system, mitigating the worst evils, than to rush into something new—or what is more likely to be the case, to rush out of something old without knowing what the new "filler of the vacuum" will be....

Another realm of life where my Christians ideals and my natural desires are widely divergent is the race problem that I, coming from the South, have to deal with so often. There is no doubt in my mind that this spiritual power and reality that I am so certain exists is open to all men regardless of their color. If this is so, and it is what makes life valuable, it would seem that the only just way in which all men could be treated is on the basis of complete equality—at least opportunity. But I cannot do that, though I feel it to be theoretically true...

As a final illustration of the limitless ramifications of this premise on which I base my reasoning in regard to the problems of life, I would like to mention the problem of war and pacifism.... My first reaction would be that there can be no justification for killing a man in war since that destroys a bit of the eternal. But on the other, I do believe that only by the freedom of thought and religion can man even try to accomplish his mission on earth.... I doubt if I could force myself to kill another man in battle, but on the other hand I realize that it is only because of the willingness on the part of others to do this in the last war that I am free to express such beliefs. The answer is not clear, but I think this may indicate to you some of the tremendous implications that follow from an application of such an ideal as mine to actual life....

All the social wrongs demand correction, but they assume only the role of means. They are necessary, but there is something much greater beyond them. This final goal is sad in its great happiness, for it is perfect and impossible of achievement here. There is constantly present the humbling realization that one falls short, but all of those richest meanings of life come in the striving for it.

T. S. Eliot

I had never heard of T. S. Eliot when I went to Yale as a freshman. The only poetry we had studied at LRSH was Victorian English and some American. I knew nothing about modern poetry — that did not rhyme! In my English class we were assigned to read "The Love Song of J. Alfred Prufrock." I was at a total loss. I not only did not understand, but did not like it — to put it mildly.

A year or two later, Eliot came to Yale to read some of his poetry. I remember he spoke in the auditorium at the School of Music. This must have been in sophomore or junior year, for I was "sophisticated" enough to know he was important, and this was probably the only time I would ever see/hear him in person. It did come alive a bit more, but I was really lost during much of it.

The first time Eliot really came alive for me was one weekend I was invited to New York by the Charles McCains and Chuck was there. They had purchased tickets for us to see *Cocktail Party*. I had never heard of the play. This was the original cast with Alec Guiness in it. Our tickets were on the very front row. As they spoke (it seemed like "raced through") their lines, I could tell what they were saying was profound — deeper than I could comprehend instantly. I kept wanting to say, "Go back and repeat that again." I was really "turned on" by the play. The theme of giving up one's life in service resonated with me, for I was wrestling with the idea of ministry.

In my first year at YDS, the students put on *Murder in the Cathedral*, which I had never read. Bill May played Thomas á

Becket—and did a magnificent job. The other roles were also well played. It, too, "turned me on."

After that, I bought a copy of the complete (then) works of Eliot and have gone back many times to read, especially, the three works listed above. I have especially quoted from Prufrock in sermons.

Unfortunately, that was one of the books destroyed in my 1998 fire, but I replaced it, and re-read it in 2008. The older I get, the more poetry speaks to me.

Charles Fielding Affair

The first time I became aware that I was racially prejudiced was in the summer of 1945, my first semester at Yale. I was sitting in a window seat on a streetcar, with the window open. The seat next to me was vacant. A black person got on and sat down next to me. I was "polite" enough not to say anything, or to get up and move. But I still remember the deep "gut" feeling that rose up from somewhere within me. I almost went out the window. I was completely caught off guard and surprised by my reaction. It was not that I had not many times sat next to black people—but never as an "equal."

I was so homesick at Yale for two years that the longer I stayed there, the more "unreconstructed" a Southerner I became. I had a Confederate flag that I insisted on putting up over the fireplace in our room in Berkeley. One morning it was missing. I found it stuffed in one of the toilets in the rest room. I was furious. No one admitted being the culprit, but it could have been any one of a number. Dan Howard, George Kearns, Pete Crosby, and others from the north had no sympathy with my position—although I doubt any of them had ever had extensive contacts with blacks. But in "theory" they were opposed to segregation. I got to know Walter Lowrey and Frank McClain who were from Mississippi, and they were fellow conservatives, especially Walter. But he was also prejudiced against Jews and everyone else who was not a white from the Delta.

There were black people in the student body, and a few in Berkeley College, but I never met or spoke to any of them. In the fall of 1947, Charles Fielding from Hot Springs, Arkansas, returned from military service and was assigned a room in our entry way, on the third floor (I lived on the second). We never spoke—but then, social status at Yale was measured by the number of people you did *not* know, so it was not unusual to bump into people all the time but never speak to them. Then at the end of my junior year (which would have been in January), there was a vacancy in the suite across the hall from our room, and I heard that Charles and some of his friends (white) were going to move down to our floor. That meant sharing the bathroom. At this point my "gut" again reacted violently. I was *not* going to share a bath with a black person, even if he was a Yale student. I announced to my roommates—Dan Howard (with whom I had lived for three years), Earl Schultz (two years), and John Hewson—that I was moving out and invited them to come with me. They all said "Goodbye."

At that time, I was a Master's Aide and worked closely with the Master of Berkeley College, Mr. Sam Hemingway. I went in to tell him of my problem. He was wonderfully wise. He said, "Don, I completely disagree with your attitude on race, and I could force you to stay in that room, for you have signed a contract. But I'll do everything I can to find you another space." His confrontation, plus his compassion, touched something deep inside me. He did find me a room on the third floor of the North Court with a sophomore whose name I no longer remember. He had gone to Groton prep school, was going to med school, but was majoring in philosophy. He probably had thought he was getting a single (for it was just a single room instead of part of a suite) but he suddenly found me as a roommate. He and I were never close, but we did get along all right.

I was very active in Uncle Ken's cell group at this point. I talked with him about this. He, too, let me know where he stood, but also allowed me leeway. At this point, I was thinking about going into the ministry. I remember saying to him that I did not see how I could go into the ministry feeling as I did about race, but I could not change. He said, "Don't let that stand in your way. God can work wonders in your life."

I wrote home about this. The Arthur McCains happened to be visiting at Scott when my letter came, and the Graham Halls were down to see them. Apparently there was a general discussion about my position. All of them thought I was wrong—except Daddy, the one of the group who had come from the north. But my decision became widely known and much discussed. I graduated from Yale in January 1949 — still a segregationist, but with a guilty conscience about it.

My Senior Essay

In order to graduate with honors (actually, high orations or *magna cum laude*, for Yale did not give a simple honors or *cum laude* degree), it was necessary to have a certain grade average, to get honors on one's comprehensive examination, and to get honors on a senior essay. (We did call it an essay, for the word "thesis" was reserved for the Master's or Ph.D. degree). I had to make a decision of whether or not I was going to shoot for this before my senior year began, for it would take the place of one course. At this point, I had not been elected to Phi Beta Kappa. I am surprised I thought I had a chance of graduating with honors. I made that decision during the fall of 1947. I was still struggling with the issue of my life work, but I had a strong sense of wanting to return to Arkansas to do whatever I was going to do. Since I was majoring in American history, I decided I would like to write on "Changing life on a cotton plantation" or "southern plantation," since that was what I knew most about.

I have forgotten the minimum length, but we were told it could not be longer than one hundred pages. I thought "Never fear about that!" I went to the library and discovered to my dismay that a Donald Alexander from Pine Bluff, Arkansas, had written a senior essay on "Changing life on the cotton plantation" just before World War II, and therefore this topic was ruled out.

When I returned to Little Rock that Christmas, I got an appointment with Mr. Ned Heiskell, publisher of the *Arkansas Gazette*, to see if he had ideas about Arkansas topics for such a study. He told me the Missouri and North Arkansas Railroad had filed a petition for bankruptcy in 1946, and suggested a study of the factors leading to that action would be a good topic. I don't believe he offered any other ideas. That seemed to me to be a good one. So when the essay seminar started, I was ready with my subject. The instructor agreed it would require research and was worthy of tackling.

During the spring of 1948, I went to the seminars and did research in the Sterling library at Yale, but found very little information. It seemed I was going to have to do a lot of my research in Arkansas, but that I might find some of the necessary documents in the Library of Congress in Washington. My sister Ann was living in Washington that spring. Instead of going to Scarsdale for my spring break, as had been my custom in previous years, I decided to go to Washington to do my research. Unfortunately, before I got to the library, I went to Capitol Hill where important hearings were being held before some Senate committees. I attended those and was so enthralled that I kept going back to them, then to see the full Senate in session, and briefly to the House of Representatives. I never even put my foot in the Library of Congress. Then Ann had a few days free from her teaching nursery school at the National Child Research Institute. We decided to take a trip into Virginia by bus. We went to Williamsburg, Lynchburg, and Lexington and had a wonderful time together. By the time we returned to Washington, I had to return to Yale.

Since I had accomplished so little research in the spring, I felt I really needed to work on my senior essay during the summer. However, I had four impacted wisdom teeth the dentist said had to come out. He was not an oral surgeon (I don't know if there were any at that time). He took out those on one side. I had a lot of difficulty afterward and was laid up for three weeks. Then he did the other side, and again, it took me three weeks to recover. By this time, the

Me at Bearskin Lake at Scott in 1948.

summer was wearing on. I managed to get up to Fayetteville by bus and did a little research in their library. Then I took a bus to Harrison where the headquarters of the M&NA had been located. I found very little information there. I had hoped to get permission to get a handcar, or motorized one, and ride down the rails of the M&NA so I would have a feel for the terrain through which it passed. However permission was denied for safety reasons. I remember the only bus from Harrison to Little Rock was not due for several hours, so I decided to hitchhike. This was my second attempt at that. A man in a pickup truck stopped and wanted to know what I was doing with the Yale sticker on my suitcase. He never did believe that was where I was in school.

By this time, Ann and Hoyt's wedding on September 3 was getting close. Our household was focused on that. Ann and Mother were up to their ears in preparations, parties, dresses, etc. I found they were disorganized in their activities. I had not realized before my organizational skills, but they let me fill the vacuum, and I did a lot in terms of preparing guest lists, getting the church redecorated, cataloging gifts, working out the details of the wedding. The senior essay was forgotten until the wedding was over.

When I returned to Yale for the fall of 1948, I had a room to myself. I really did settle down to doing research and gathering data on such things as miles of line built, tonnage of various kinds of materials hauled, miles of paved roads in the counties crossed, population, income figures, etc. This was the same period of time when I was struggling with my vocational decision. I found the research and writing so unpleasant that I decided a career of teaching and writing was not for me, so being a historian was dropped from my list of options. I was distracted when I accepted the idea of going to Yale-in-China, and then was turned down for that. I did not get started on the actual writing until almost Thanksgiving. As I recall, I went to Scarsdale for Wednesday night and Thanksgiving Day, but came right back to college to write. That was the Christmas when I invited Dagoberto Weisbach and Jim Boyes to spend Christmas with us at Scott, so I was busy then. When I returned after Christmas, I was still working on my first draft of the essay. By then, I had more than enough material and was beginning to realize I was going to have a problem with the maximum length. And even though I could type, my typing was not good enough to meet the required quality, so I had to pay a professional. She charged by the page, but she normally used wide margins to make the document look better. I had to pay her extra to use narrow margins so I could get as much material on a page as possible. I also had her put the footnotes at the end of the paper instead of at the bottom of each page, and we did not number the footnote pages. I wound up with a 99-page paper! I did not have it ready by the deadline and had to get an extension. It was still at the typist's when that second deadline came, so I had to get a final extension. I turned it in one hour before the absolute deadline. I'd never turned a paper in late before in my whole career. And I've never turned one in early since!

I was delighted, and amazed, that I got an "honors" on the paper. This paved the way for my graduating with "high orations," depending on the outcome of my eight-hour comprehensive examinations. And there is a story about that, too. One of the questions, for which we were allowed two hours to answer, was "Take any invention you choose and trace its effect on American history." I immediately picked the cotton gin. However, half an hour into writing about it I realized I could not remember just when the cotton gin was invented. Was it in the 1790s or the 1830s? I knew Eli Whitney, a Yale graduate, invented it in South Carolina. It was this invention that gave slavery, which had been dying out, a new lease on life. Somehow I managed to write in such general terms that I never had to commit myself as to the exact date of its invention. And I got honors on my comprehensives! You can be sure I looked up the date as soon as I got out of the exam. If you are interested, it was in the 1790s!

Spring in North Court

Even though I had moved out to North Court (and it turned out Charles Fielding, the black man, did not move down to our floor), the people on my old floor were still my best friends. In the past we would often wait and go down together to meals. Now I would go on my own, therefore often sitting alone or joining someone not in "the gang," but if they were eating, I felt perfectly free in sitting with them. And I would visit in their rooms.

With two people in a single room, I did a lot of my study at night in the Berkeley Library — where Dan Howard was the chief librarian, or I would go to Sterling Library, which was just across the street.

By this time, I was very serious about my faith and was really struggling with the possibility of going into the ministry — and fighting it every inch of the way. One of the high points of that spring was having some privacy when my roommate was in class.

He had an eight o'clock class Monday, Wednesday, and Friday. That meant I could be certain I would not be interrupted, so I was able to read the Bible. I had discovered some books of prayers that "primed the pump" in my own prayers. I had begun to like to kneel when I prayed. I could do all these things three mornings a week, and I cherished that time. In addition, I was in Uncle Ken's cell group and was going to Dwight Chapel almost every day and to Battell on Sundays. I think I may have started going to the pre-ministerial group, also, although I might have started that only in the fall.

It was good for me to get out of the rut of living in the same place, with the same people, since freshman year. I was also comfortable in my job in the Master's Office. That was the term when I started working on my senior essay. We had weekly meetings with our advisor about how to do research, the requirements of an essay, etc. They were pretty boring.

It was this spring that I learned I had been elected to Phi Beta Kappa — something I had not really thought about, for I didn't believe my grades were that good. It was a real boost to my morale. That is the first and only long distance call I made from college to my parents! By this time, I was very much at home at Yale and was enjoying it. I had learned that I was going to get a private room on the same floor where I had spent the spring, and was eager to return in the fall.

My Last Semester

My last semester at Yale College was tumultuous, critical, and very happy.

When I returned in September, I could hardly wait to get back. Yale had become "home." What a far cry from my trip up there in June 1945, and even September 1946. But at last I had made the adjustment, and my self-definition was that of a Yale man.

I was moving into a single room. It was the first time since freshman year that I had had a bedroom to myself, and even then I shared a living room with Dan. Now I was all on my own and could do what I wanted to when I wanted to. So I began decorating the room. I had brought some things up from Arkansas. Then I bought a used rocking chair at Goodwill, or some such place, and some material and decided I would recover it. I remember I bought some gold upholstery material and some brass upholstery nails. I had never done anything like that before in my life, and I spent an inordinate amount of time on the project. But I did finish it. At the time, I did not know I would be staying in New Haven, but when I went to YDS, I took that chair with me and used it for three years.

I was facing many major hurdles. I had accomplished very little on my senior essay during the summer. I had done some research, but not all I needed. I had not even started to write it, and during the fall I kept putting it off, claiming I had more pressing matters before me. I also had my comprehensive exams coming up in January — eight hours of written exams on various aspects of American history.

I was also dealing with the fact that within four and a half months I would be graduating from college, and I did not know what I was going to do. I had narrowed my vocational choices down to studying law, teaching history, or going to divinity school. If I went the last of these routes, I would go to Union Seminary in Richmond, Princeton, or Yale. On my visit to Richmond the previous spring, I liked friends who were students there, but I was so turned off by the architecture, I did not think I could stand three years in those ugly buildings. That was the "in" place if I was going to be a Southern Presbyterian. But the big emphasis there was on preaching, and that did not appeal to me. I had met a number of Princeton students the previous year at a one-day conference set up by the national office of the Presbyterian Church, USA (Northern), and I thought they were arrogant and stuck-up, and I did not respond well to them, nor think I wanted to be part of that mix.

Soon after I returned to New Haven, Uncle Ken had me for dinner one night at the Graduate Club. I was telling him about my confusion. He said, "You seem to be having such a hard time making up your mind. Have you ever thought of going to China? Yale-in-China each year sends two 'Yali bachelors' to the Yali Middle School in Changsha, to teach English. That would give you a couple of years to think about this decision. I think we could get you an appointment. I am chairman of the Board." This was a bolt out of the blue. I told him I had never given any thought to going to China. I had always been fascinated by India and wanted to go there, but China was not on my horizon. But I would think and pray about it. By this time, I should have known better than to pray about one of Uncle Ken's suggestions.

I went home that night and prayed about it. For two or three weeks, I wrestled with the Lord about this. Because I had a room to myself I was able to read and pray with complete freedom. So I prayed at Dwight Chapel at noonday services, at Battell Chapel on Sundays, in the cell group—and back in my room. I guess I wrote home and told my parents about this possibility. Uncle Ken had said the Communists would be taking Changsha in the not-too-distant future, and Yale-in-China knew that once they captured the city, no more American staff could come in. But they thought if they could get two more in at the last minute, the Communists would let them stay. Since I was graduating in January, this would be perfect timing.

One night, the moon was bright. I was kneeling by my bed. Harkness Tower loomed ahead. I could see down in the courtyard of North Court. As I prayed, there was a sensation of light—no voice, no figure, just very bright light. I got up off my knees and knew that I was to go to China. Then I went to bed and fell asleep. The next morning, I made my second long distance call to Arkansas, to tell Mother and Daddy, then I called Uncle Ken to say I would go. I shared the decision with my friends.

My Yankee friends kidded me a lot about the poor Chinese who would learn English with an Arkansas accent. They would roar with laughter at the thought of someone traveling in the western part of China who would meet an English-speaking person who would say, "Ah just caint doo th-at." My "Christian" friends were excited and supportive.

The wheels began to turn so I would be ready to go right after graduation, due to the Communist take-over. I had to fill out all the paperwork, and that went smoothly. Then I had to take a physical exam. I had never before, nor have I since, had high blood pressure. But that day it was high. Also, in reading my chart, the doctor saw that I had allergies and was taking shots.

A couple of days later, there was a knock on my door. It was Uncle Ken. He came in and said he had never hated so much telling someone bad news, but I had flunked my physical and I could not go to China. He said the doctor told the Board under normal circumstances he would not rule me out because of allergies, but with the Communists coming they had no idea what kind of medical facilities would be available or if the shots would be possible, and he would not approve of my going. I felt so bad for Uncle Ken that at the moment I was not aware of my own pain. He said that if as a result of this I decided to go to seminary, and if I chose Yale Divinity, he would like for me to be his student secretary — a pattern he had developed the last few years.

Once he was gone, however, I felt crushed. It was the most unselfish decision I had ever made. I was so certain that I was responding to God's call. The whole world seemed to fall down around me. I was pretty much in shock for two or three weeks. When the dust finally began to settle, I realized in the process of deciding to go to China I had also decided I would go to seminary — for one year, on a trial basis. And Uncle Ken's offer of being his secretary tipped the scales, so it was easy to decide I would go to YDS. But I did not want to start in the middle of the year. I wanted to enter in September with the class. So then I had to do the necessary paperwork to apply to YDS. With my academic record, and recommendations from Uncle Ken and Mr. Hemingway, there was no question I would get in.

At the first meeting of the Pre-Ministerial Group in the chaplain's office (I guess this was the first time I went, for up to then I was trying to hide my consideration of going into the ministry), there was a suggestion that we form some small prayer groups. I volunteered to form one, since I had a single room, but warned that I was not sure I was going into the ministry. They said if I had decided to go to China, that was enough. So Bard Smith, Rudy Everest, and I formed a group. It was at the second meeting, probably in October, that Bard urged us to come to the next Pre-Ministry Group meeting, for his mother was going to tell about her conversion. I thought to myself, "The last thing I want to do is hear about your mother or my mother or anybody's mother talk about her conversion!" I was repelled by the idea, but because of my friendship with Bard I went. There I heard Gert Behanna (for about the second time in her life) tell in a powerful way how she, a wealthy alcoholic, had hit bottom and had been saved by God from self-destruction. I was spellbound, and I was shaken to my foundations. Hers was one of the most compelling accounts of what it means to follow Jesus Christ that I had ever heard. (More about her elsewhere.)

The man who lived across the hall from me was Bill Conway, one of the stars on the Yale football team. I had known him only casually until I moved into that room, but we had become friendly, although he was around very little. One day, on a weekend, I heard a sustained knocking on his door. I went into the hall, and a man told me Bill had told him to come by, for he was going to lend him some money—perhaps it was $10 (a fair amount in those days). I told him Bill was gone for the weekend. He said his need was desperate and asked if I could give him the money until Bill got back. I agreed. When Bill returned, he knew nothing about this man. I had been conned! I reported it to the campus police. When the officer was writing it up, he said, "Where do you live on Old Campus (where freshmen lived)?" I said I was in Berkeley. He asked what class. When I said I was a senior, his response was "I can't believe it. How naive can you be?" Eventually the man was arrested and taken to court, and I had to go identify him. I did learn one more lesson my last semester.

By this point we were into November. Because of my distraction, I still had done very little work on my senior essay. But election night 1948, I forgot about academic obligations. I invited Jim Boyes, an exchange student from Clare College, Cambridge, to listen with me on my radio as the results came in. I was for Dewey, and he was for Truman.

The senior essay was becoming a serious issue. I came back from Scarsdale on Thanksgiving night so I could work over the weekend, and I really plugged away at it until Christmas. I should have worked on it during that break, but I asked my parents if I could invite Jim Boyes and Dagoberto Weisbach to spend Christmas with us at Scott, and they agreed. Looking back on it, I was asking a great deal. Ann and Hoyt had married in September and would be there. Art was coming home. (I think he had graduated from Texas A&M and was working in Clarksville, Tennessee). Grandmother Campbell was spending the winter with us. That would be nine people sleeping, plus all the guests who would come for various parties. But they said, "Of course."

Dagoberto was taking the train. Jim Boyes was strapped for funds, and I was trying to economize. Ted Lamb and his sidekick from Little Rock said they had learned used cars brought a much higher price in Arkansas than on the East Coast, so they were going to buy two cars in New Haven and drive them to Little Rock and sell them. They invited Jim and me to ride with them and share expenses. Ted had been my predecessor as president of the Little Rock student body, but I did not know him well, and barely knew his friend. When we got in the cars, the heater in one of them did not work. The other one ran smoothly until we got to 30 mph, then made an awful noise—until it got to 60 mph when it became smooth again. So across the country we went, day and night, taking turns driving. It was pretty miserable. On the second night, we were in the boot heel of Missouri. I was in the second car. Suddenly our car died, and the lights went out. So did the horn. We could see the other car pulling ahead, but could not honk or attract their attention. So there we sat in the middle of a farm. We hoped eventually they would look in the mirror and realize we were not following. About an hour later, back they came. It was about 4:00 a.m., and the next town was several miles away. Clearly we could not push the dead car that far—and if we did, it had no headlights. The only hope was to pull it. But we had no chain or rope to tie them together. Having grown up on a farm, I knew what a disastrous thing it was to take down a fence around a pasture. But there was a three-strand barbed wire fence. I decided the bottom two ought to hold the cattle, so we managed to cut the top strand and wired the two cars together with barbed wire. We drove slowly and finally reached a filling station where we were able to get a new battery, or get whatever was wrong fixed. And so we made it to Rose City where someone in my family drove up to get us.

That Christmas of 1948 was memorable, and much fun. Dago had visited before, so people knew him and liked him. Jim was charming and quickly won folks over. There were dinners and parties at Scott and in Little Rock. I guess we must have had the Kings down for Christmas Eve dinner. Dago said he had to go to mass. Jim wanted to go to a Christmas Eve service—something I had never attended. Truman said she'd go to St. Andrews Cathedral with Dago, and Jim and I went to Trinity Episcopal Cathedral. I was still struggling with what I was going to do with my life. I had had enough of doing historical research on my essay to know that I did not want to go on for a Ph.D. in history. I was down to law or ministry. The quietness of that communion service was very precious to me, for there was little solitude in the home at Scott that year.

Dago and Jim left on the train before I did, so I had a few days alone. The unfinished essay was hanging over my head. I think I did a little work, but very little. I left a New Year's Eve dance at the Women's City Club to go to Union Station to catch the train to New Haven. I still had not decided if I was going to law school or divinity school. If I was going to divinity school, I did not want to enter at mid-term, having been a mid-term student all through Yale College. If I was going back to Yale for divinity, then I wanted to come back to the University of Arkansas for the spring, mostly to get reacquainted with Arkansas people and to take some courses I'd never had time for at Yale. The night I was leaving, Carolyn Alexander and Marvin Thaxton called to say that if I was coming to Fayetteville, they would try to find me a place to stay and would meet me at the train. I was still undecided — but while they were on the phone, I said, "Yes, I will come to Fayetteville. Thank you." So the decision was made to return in the fall to YDS.

When I got back to New Haven, I told Uncle Ken and asked if the offer of the job was still good. He said it was. Then I settled in, working very hard on the essay.

The comprehensive exams loomed ahead, also. My handwriting had never been good, and the longer I was in college the worse it got, for I took extensive notes and had to write very fast. I had begun getting points taken off my grades because my exams were so hard to read. So I asked for permission to take my exams on a typewriter — in a room with a proctor. This had never been done before, but permission was granted! There were four or five others who also got permission.

Once the essay was turned in and the exams over, we were moving into graduation, right at the end of January. Mother and Daddy came up for it. The Hemingways invited them to stay in the guest suite, a gracious thing for them to do. They were making a trip of it, going to New York first, then up to Hartford to see the Ross McCains who were having some kind of family gathering. I took my parents up to Yale Divinity campus. A new snow had just fallen. It was beautiful indeed. The Divinity School quadrangle is patterned after Thomas Jefferson's University of Virginia. Mother was waxing eloquently about what a quiet, beautiful environment this was going to be when out of Taylor House burst a bunch of students engaged in a snowball fight. So much for the quietness.

Uncle Ken had my parents up for lunch. They also met the Hemingways and Ellie Hutchins, and perhaps the Beazleys, as well as my circle of close friends. It was a wonderful few days. They had been there only once before, in the spring of 1947 when I was in *Taming of the Shrew*.

I went to graduation and was sitting toward the front, for I was one of the few who went forward to get diplomas for the Berkeley contingent, to be handed out individually by Sam Hemingway back at Berkeley. We were given a program. I looked down and to my utter amazement saw that I was graduating with "high orations." I knew I had received an A- on my essay. After my fiasco on my comprehensives, it had never entered my mind I would get honors. Needless to say, my parents were thrilled.

Immediately after graduation, I caught the train to New York, then to St. Louis, then to Fayetteville, where Carolyn and Marvin met me. They had found me a room in the half-basement of the McKinney house, and I enrolled at the University of Arkansas.

Mother and Daddy went up to Hartford. They told me Cousin Ross announced to the family gathering that I was the brightest star in this generation of the family. (He had met me only once.)

What a last semester that turned out to be—so far from the miseries of the freshman year.

Pilgrimage on Vocation

I have included bits of this story in other places, but because it is so central to my life, I think it is good to have it all linked into one account.

The reason I went to Yale was because I wanted to be a diplomat and I had heard the only American universities people abroad had heard of were Yale, Harvard, and Princeton. I had decided in ninth-grade civics class that I wanted to be in the Foreign Service and never wavered from that all through high school, so when I enrolled at Yale, I signed up for a major in international relations.

When I landed at Yale, I was miserably homesick and stayed that way for almost two years. When suffering from that complaint, it was very clear to me I did not want to spend the rest of my life far away from home. I prayed a great deal about this matter of vocation and talked about it in Uncle Ken Latourette's Bible study group. At the end of my first calendar year at Yale, he asked me if I had ever thought of going into the ministry. I said I had not. When we parted for the summer, I thought no more about the ministry.

But I was wrestling frequently with what I was going to do since diplomacy was no longer an option. I realized that diplomats only carried out instructions from the State Department anyway, so I thought about planning for that. Then I decided that the State Department carried out instructions of the politicians. By this point, I had given up my junior high dream of being President, but I did think about running for public office, as a Representative or Senator. However, at that point I was a Republican, and they were only a shadow party in Arkansas. That was not a realistic goal. Then I concluded I needed to get involved in shaping the political thinking of the state (for I was determined to get back to Arkansas) so the Republican Party would have a chance. I asked myself what kind of profession would give me that leverage. Three came to my mind — being a lawyer, editing a newspaper, or teaching on the college level. About this time, I decided to switch majors from international relations to American history. I was able to do that without losing a single credit or having to take any extra courses. So the thought of teaching history on the college level looked attractive.

A photo of me at Yale.

About this time, Uncle Arthur McCain was elected president of Chase National Bank in New York, and Cousin Charles McCain was president of Dillon Reed, a major investment-banking firm in New York. I wondered if banking might be a place for me. Along the way, I also thought of insurance, for Uncle Gordon had done very well in that field, and Cousin Ross McCain was president of Aetna Fire and Casualty.

At the end of my second calendar year, about the same time I decided to switch majors, Uncle Ken again asked me if I had thought any more about going into the ministry. I said, "No, sir, not since you raised the question last year." And I left for the summer in Arkansas. But I thought, "He's a nice old man, and he has been very kind to me. The least I can do is give it some consideration." I told my parents he had raised this issue. My father was dismayed. I am not sure whether he thought the ministry would be bad for me (his father had been a Presbyterian minister, so he was aware of some of the pitfalls) or I would be bad for the ministry. Mother did not express any negative feeling, but did not push it, either.

That second summer (it was 1947), I found I could not shake loose of Uncle Ken's question about the ministry. I was repelled by the idea, for until I met Uncle Ken, I had never known a minister I really respected. (Grandfather Campbell had been a minister, but I didn't think of him as one for he had been retired for many years when I came along.) Even though I was repelled by the idea of ministry, I was also fascinated.

As I returned to Yale in the fall of 1947 for the last half of my junior year and the first of my senior, I had pretty well reduced the possibilities to history, law, or ministry. The matter of my life work was very much on my mind. I had no private prayer life at the time, but when I prayed in chapel or the cell group, that was the subject of my supplications. At the start of my senior year, in February, I began work on my senior essay, and found it very tedious to look up and pull together the detailed kind of information required. I did a good job, and got honors on the paper, but it convinced me I did not want to spend my life doing that kind of research and writing. So my choices had pretty well narrowed down to law or ministry, law school or divinity school.

After much prayer and sweating, and cringing at the idea, I decided at Christmastime 1948 that I would return to Yale Divinity School in the fall for a one-year trial, with the option of switching to law school if that did not feel "right." When I graduated from Yale College in January 1949, I knew that I was coming back to New Haven the next fall. For how long was uncertain, but at least I'd try it for one year.

Adults Who Influenced Me at Yale

Sue and Tap Hornor

Sue Campbell, my favorite first cousin, was married to Tap Hornor, Jr., of Helena in a large, socially prominent wedding in about 1939. Tap had graduated from Law School. I don't know if he ever practiced, for he was in a National Guard unit that got called into service in 1940. They were sent to Alaska. Then all women were sent back to the lower 48 after Pearl Harbor.

Later, Tap, who was in the Quartermaster Corps, was brought back to the lower 48. When I decided to go to Yale, I had no idea they were living in New Haven. Perhaps they were transferred there after I made that decision. Anyway, when I arrived in June 1945, they were there. When I arrived, and was so homesick, I

A Campbell family gathering in our living room at Scott in 1945. Front row: Laura Campbell Nichols, Sue Campbell Hornor, Louise Scott Campbell (Grandmother), Alice Robinson Campbell (Aunt Alice). Second row: Margaret Campbell (Mother), Shuford Nichols, Margaret Campbell Vineyard, Arthur Campbell (Daddy), Tap Hornor, and Gordon Campbell (Uncle Gordon).

doubt I would have survived if the Hornors had not been there. They lived in Hamden, a suburb. I would take the bus out and often spend Saturday night. Mary Sue was about two or three, and Laura was a baby, in diapers. I remember once when I was there, Laura needed to be changed, and I did not know how to change a diaper. Mary Sue had to tell me. Another time, when Alice was still there, I tried to fry chicken for us. I knew Mother said Hattie used flour and a beaten egg, but I never learned how the two functioned. Instead of dipping the chicken in egg, then rolling it in flour as I later learned to do, I mixed the egg and flour so it came out dough, and tried to stick that on the chicken—but it would not stay. Our chicken was not a great success.

I remember Sue and Tap used to drink Southern Comfort. Having grown up in a dry household, I knew nothing about such things. Tap would make breakfast on Sunday mornings, and I remember he would cut up fresh mint in his scrambled eggs, and they were delicious. Tap's immediate superior was a major, Bill Beasley, whose wife was called Tootsie. How Bill got a New Haven assignment I do not know, for he was a native of there and had been in real estate before (and went back into it after the war and was very successful). The Beasleys and Hornors were great friends and took us out to the Long Island beach once to look for clams at the home of some friends, the Halls, who owned one of the large dairies in town.

Once the war was over, Tap got an early discharge, leaving in the fall, but he stayed long enough to help me buy a winter coat. I got one so heavy that it made my shoulders slump when I wore it.

Kenneth Scott Latourette

I have referred several other places to Mr. Latourette or Uncle Ken, but because he played such an important role in my undergraduate days, I want to let you know who he was.

He was born in 1884 (two years after Daddy's birth) in Oregon City, Oregon. The Latourettes came to America in the late 1600s as Huguenot refugees. They, and other ancestors, migrated west in stages as far as Kentucky and Indiana until in the 1840s they took the Oregon Trail to the west coast where they were among the early settlers. His father was a lawyer and banker. Ken Latourette attended a small Baptist college, McMinnville, in Oregon, graduating when he was 20. He then went to Yale College to take another senior year, which he completed so successfully he was elected to Phi Beta Kappa. He stayed on in the university and earned his Ph.D. in history, writing his thesis on the first ties between the United States and China. While at Yale, he volunteered to be a missionary to China through the newly formed Yale-in-China at Changsha in Hunan province. He contracted amoebic dysentery and had to return to Oregon where it was assumed he would be an invalid for life. After a couple of years, he was able to start teaching part time at Reed College in Portland, Oregon. From there, he went to Dennison University in Ohio to teach history, and he inserted a course on China. He also became chaplain to students. This required that he be ordained as a Baptist minister, although he had never been to seminary.

In 1921, he accepted a call to Yale Divinity School as a full professor in missions and oriental history. He had already published books, but his publications grew in number, and with them his reputation as a scholar. Between 1937 and 1945, he published the seven-volume *History of the Expansion of Christianity*, the first time church history had been presented from an ecumenical and worldwide perspective. In recognition of this achievement, honorary degrees were awarded by many universities, he was made a Sterling Professor (the most prestigious rank at Yale), and he was invited to become a Fellow of Berkeley College.

From his undergraduate days he worked with small groups of students. That is how I got to know him, as a member of a Bible study group he formed in the summer of 1945, just after he had been made a Fellow of Berkeley. At that stage, I called him Mr. Latourette. Yale professors in the sciences are addressed as "Doctor," but those in the rest of the university (all of whom have doctorates) are called "Mister." As I have mentioned elsewhere, when there is a close bond between students and a professor, he often invites them to call him "Uncle," hence the term Uncle Ken.

Of all the faculty during my undergraduate, and later my divinity school years, he had the greatest influence on me. He reached out to me in my freshman and sophomore years when I was so homesick. He was the one who suggested I consider the ministry. He proposed that I go to China, and when that did not work out offered me a job as his secretary if I decided to go to Yale Divinity School. He became a friend of my family, visiting my parents twice at Scott, and later came to both Crossett and Grace Church in Little Rock as a speaker. I did not know the term at the time, but he was my "spiritual director" for years and helped form my prayer and devotional life. He had planned to preach the sermon at my ordination to the ministry, but had to cancel due to surgery.

After his retirement, he lived on at Yale Divinity School. On Christmas night in 1968 while walking to the mailbox to post his Christmas thank-you notes, he was hit by a car and killed instantly.

Ellie Hutchins

Next to Uncle Ken Latourette, Ellie Hutchins, the Berkeley College secretary, was probably the most influential adult in my undergraduate days, followed by the Hemingways.

Ellie's ancestors came to New Haven in 1630, whereas Mr. Hemingway's did not come until 1640. She would call him a parvenu. But some of Ellie's forebears had been "merchants," and in New Haven society that meant she was not acceptable on the highest levels. I gather her parents did not have a lot of money, but she went to a prep school and evidently was "reared right" by her mother. She did not go to college, but at an early age married Bill Hutchins, brother of Bob Hutchins who had been the child-dean of the Yale Law School, and then the innovative President of the University of Chicago. I am not sure what Bill did, but I assume he was a teacher at some private school, for that is what he did later.

They had one son, Todd, who was probably six or seven years younger than I. He was good-looking and very attractive, but had real problems in school. Ellie finally had to send him to a very small (about five to 10 students), expensive, private school out in the Rockies where they did a lot of horses and outdoor things. Evidently, he learned in that context, for he did get in Yale and graduated.

I do not know when Ellie was divorced, but Bill fell in love with someone else. After that, she lived a frugal life. The Hemingways knew her, and he hired her as the secretary. I don't know when, but she had been there a while when I arrived in 1945. I am sure I met her in those first days, but I really don't remember her before I went to work in the Master's Office in the spring of 1946. She was much lower key than the two women I had worked for in previous bursary jobs. She was a "lady." While she had never been to college, she was one of the most educated people I'd met. She read widely and well. She had all the sophistication anyone could ask for. She gave us work to do, but when work was slack (as it often was), she would visit with us aides down in her office, or let us study upstairs.

I'm sure she picked up on how homesick I was, and probably reached out to me more than to some others. She was intrigued by my Arkansas accent, and when she learned I came from a plantation, she wanted to know about our culture. She shared a lot about her life as a single mother, and talked about Todd and his problems. She would also share some of her own experiences. She told me that after her divorce she decided she would never have a drink by herself. If she wanted a drink at night, she would invite a cousin or neighbor to come in to have it with her. I don't know if her ex-husband had a drinking problem, but she was scared of it.

She also told me once when her cousin and her cousin's daughter were visiting, she was talking about some dress she was thinking about buying. The daughter said, "Ellie, I don't know why you bother. Once you're past 40, all you can hope to do is be neat and clean." Ellie said she could hardly wait for the girl to turn 40! She had a great sense of humor.

At one point she was invited to come out to Alma College in Michigan to see about being a housemother, or a dean of women. She took the train out, and I was scared she would go. But she came back saying that was not the environment for her.

Theodore Greene, a professor of philosophy, was also Master of Silliman College. His wife died. He had to have someone as hostess on weekends when students would be putting up their dates in the Master's House, and also expecting teas and other kinds of entertainment. He asked Ellie to fill that role, and she did while also being at Berkeley. She needed the extra income.

When my parents came to visit twice, I made sure we took Ellie out for dinner. They liked her very much.

When I started at Yale Divinity School, I was to be Uncle Ken's secretary. I was supposed to learn shorthand during the summer, but I was so busy working at Second Presbyterian Church, I postponed it until the two weeks before I left. I studied hard, but I was totally unfit to take dictation. As soon as I got in town, I looked up Ellie, because I wanted to see her, and also to ask her if she could help me on my shorthand. So I would go down, and she would dictate to me, to help me build up my speed.

While I was at YDS, I kept up with her fairly often and invited her up to the campus for a meal. I guess it was while I was at the University of Arkansas in the spring of 1949, the wife of the Dean of the School of Engineering—an expert on mushrooms—served some one night for dinner. Her husband said he did not like the looks of them. She insisted they were good, ate them, and soon was sick from mushroom poisoning. They rushed her to the Yale Hospital, but there was nothing they could do to save her. After some decent period of time, Walter Wohlenberg, the Dean, began to take Ellie out, and soon they got married. So, suddenly, she had gone from being the secretary in a college to being the wife of the Dean, and therefore moved in all the higher circles in the University. She resigned her job, and I gather served well in her new role—to the delight of the Hemingways.

Dean Wohlenberg put all his savings in annuities. Then, after I graduated from YDS, he got sick. Ellie knew it was terminal. They could have changed the annuities into other investments, but she did not want him to think he was dying. So on his death, she had almost nothing from his estate—and she was back into frugality.

In the meantime, Todd was married and had children, but he was having mental and physical problems, and finally divorced his wife. Ellie was supportive of her and their children. His problems had to do with small strokes in the brain, I think—an inherited trait.

The Assistant Dean of Engineering, Grant Robley, was very solicitous about her after Wohlenberg's death, and before long she wrote that she and he were getting married. So she again had an income, not as large as before, and status in the university, though not as high as before. When I would visit New Haven in the 1970s, I several times went out to see them. He was gracious to me. Then Ellie began to have the kind of strokes that had killed Todd. The last time I went out, she was in a hospital bed and barely knew me. After her death, I tried a few years to keep in touch with Grant, but got no response so gave up.

Hers was a hard life, but she sailed through it with style. I learned a great deal from her about the good side of New England life. And I learned that while it may take longer to become friends in New England than it does in the South, once a New Englander becomes a friend, he/she is a friend for life.

The Hemingways

In the first days at Berkeley College, the Master and his wife, Professor Sam and Mary Hemingway, had a "tea" in their garden. Most of the college went to that. What we did not know was that the Hemingways had a formal tea every Sunday afternoon during term time, and had "informal" tea every afternoon. The Sunday teas where open to all in the college. A good number would come—mostly the same people. The "elite" of the college, such as the Gimbel twins (their family owned the second largest department store in New York, next to Macy's), and later Chuck McCain, would be off to parties in New York or Boston or Greenwich for the weekend. But those teas were a very civilizing experience for me. They were more formal than the life I had known—but they were the closest I found to the kind of social life at Scott. I got to know better some of the other Berkeley people, and also met some of the Fellows of the college, and visitors from time to time. I came to feel close to the Hemingways that first year. I would see them at Battell Chapel, and they were like substitute parents—which is what a college master was meant to be.

Even though we were aware that any student could on any day drop by the Master's House where there would be tea served from a silver tea service and some "goodies" to eat, I did that only two or three times. But it meant a lot to know that was available.

I suppose it was from my contacts with Mr. Hemingway that he got to know me—and had sized me up enough to select me at the start of my third semester to be a Master's Aide. That was an honor, and it certainly was more pleasant than the work I had been doing. And it let me get to know Ellie Hutchins, the college secretary.

The Hemingways had no children. Later I found they were drawing from their investments to maintain the kind of life they lived, and the hospitality they offered the students. We used to laugh and describe them as "the last of the Edwardians," for with their maids and fancy foods they really did live something like pre-World War I. What a privilege it was to sample that, for I had never been exposed to it before. It was a crucial part of my "education." I learned how to balance a teacup on my knee and how to make small talk with people I had never met before. I was introduced to something about art and music and literature. There were always candles burning in their drawing room. Even during the week, there would be candles—they bought remnants from a candle factory on Cape Cod where they had a summer home at Chatham.

After I became a Master's Aide, I saw a lot more of Mr. Hemingway. He taught only one course a semester, on Shakespeare. It was for English majors, so I never thought of signing up for it. He seemed to have time on his hands, and often sat out in the secretary's office and would visit with us.

At Yale, when people got very close to a professor, they would often call him "Uncle," as I did "Uncle Ken." Mr. Hemingway was a member of one of the lesser "senior societies"—I forget which—and those students who belonged to that would refer to him as Uncle Sam. I never did. But after I went to Divinity School, and he retired from Berkeley, I would go see them on Lincoln Street. Mrs. Hemingway when talking to me about him would say "your Uncle Sam" as though she thought I was in the inner circle.

One of the greatest things Mr. Hemingway did for me was handling my crisis when I learned Charles Fielding, the black man from Hot Springs, might be moving to our floor. I went to Mr. Hemingway and told him I could not handle that. I shall never forget his conversation with me. What a wise man he was to confront me, show me the power in his hand, then allow me room to move and find a face-saving way to do it. I think that was key to my later conversion on race. And I told him so later.

The Hemingways had extra bedrooms in their house, and also a guest suite. They would take in out-of-town dates, and I used them several times. Dagoberto taught me the proper way to respond—in this case, with flowers.

Mrs. Hemingway, while less prominent, was a quiet presence in my life—partly in her gracious ways at the teas, her interest in me and my life. When I was an aide, I remember once she wanted to send some clothes to someone she knew in England, but they had to be "used" clothes. (This was after the war, but things were still desperately short in Britain.) She thought I could wear the shirts for this person, and she asked me if I would wear each one for one day so she could wash them and send them, honestly, as used. Another time when she had fallen, or was sick, and not able to walk their Dachshund, she asked me if I would walk him for her. By the end of the four years, I was sure I was not just another student, but a friend. And in YDS days, that proved to be true.

I found the Yale concept of residential colleges, each with a master and some fellows, a wonderful way to make life in a large university more manageable. We had classes with people from all over Yale College, but practically all my significant friendships were with people in Berkeley College.

Some Yale College Professors

I have little or no memory of the majority of the men (and they were all men) I studied under at Yale College. But a few stand out — because they were very good, or very bad.

David Potter taught American history. I already loved that subject, but he was an excellent lecturer — though not one bit better than Miss Emily Penton at LRHS. I never did get to know him as a person. But his lectures were interesting and informative. He was a Southerner, which helped at that stage in my life. He gave a series of hilarious lectures on the various Union generals who tried to capture Richmond, and failed. He opened areas for me that were new. It was through him that I read *John Brown's Body Lies A-moldering In The Grave*. Even though I was "un-Reconstructed," it did make me look at things differently. I think my Christmas gift to Daddy that year was a copy — which he did not appreciate!

The first semester of my human zoology course was taught by Dr. Baitsell, the head of the department. This was the course that those of us who could not pass a lab science course sought out, and he knew why we were there. He began his first lecture saying, "This is the 30th time I have taught this course," dusted off his notes, and began to read them wearily.

A younger man, Dr. Boell, who was very good and who made it come alive, taught the second semester — but not alive enough to move me to take another science course.

My Classical Civilization course was taught by the head of the department, Mr. Bellinger. We had full professors as freshmen because most of the younger faculty were away in the military service. He was not exciting, and wanted us to memorize the minutiae of dates and names, and killed any interest I had in pursuing that aspect of history.

Mr. Noyes, Polly Coles' cousin, taught my first semester of English — maybe my second, also. He took us into an analysis of literature, especially modern poets like T. S. Eliot, far beyond my comprehension. I was more poorly prepared in this area than any other. At the end of the second semester of English, we were required to take a second whole year of English. My friends were excited about Beowulf and Chaucer, which were required for going on further in that field. I wanted to get out of English as quickly and easily as I could, so I took "Engineers' English." I don't remember the professor, but that was the first time I ever really enjoyed an English class. I remember we read several of George Bernard Shaw's plays and Byron's "Don Juan," and I liked both.

S. R. Driver was a popular political science professor. He was English and a brilliant lecturer. I think about four times in my undergraduate career a class would break into applause at the end of a lecture — and three of them were for Driver (the other was for Ralph Gabriel). Attendance was so large he had to lecture in the Law School auditorium. There was no contact with him as a person. In this, we studied the forms of government not only in the United States, but other countries as well — and this was brand new for me. Graduate students would lead the small group sections — and during exams, would proctor them dangling their Phi Beta Kappa keys as we were struggling with our blue books.

Samuel Flagg Bemis, professor of diplomatic history, was probably the most pompous professor I ever had. He had written the textbook. If anyone asked a question, he would say, "I explained that in my book," and that was the end of conversation. If a student was one minute late to class, he was not allowed in the room. If a paper was one minute late, he refused to accept it. Probably this was the course that helped me decide I was not going to major in international relations (in the Political Science Department) as I had come to Yale to do, but to go into American history. If Bemis was part of the diplomatic world, I wanted nothing to do with it — having already decided, because of homesickness, that I was not going to be an overseas diplomat. But I had thought about working in the State Department — until Bemis.

I do not recall the name of the instructor in my fourth semester of French, but I remember him. When I came to Yale, I made a 92 in French, because I did know how to read and write it. As we moved on and conversation became more important, I began to slip—to a 90, then to an 85. My last semester of a required foreign language was "Conversation and Composition" that was supposed to prepare one for the diplomatic service. I had come to the point of being able to "think in French," but speaking it was something else. At the end of that semester, in which I got an 80, the instructor said, "Messieur Campbell, I did not know one could speak French with a Southern accent, but you do. You do not sound like anyone anywhere in France unless it is Languedoc, and that is the worst French spoken. I suggest you drop French." And I did.

Ralph Gabriel, professor of intellectual history, was almost as good as David Potter. His course was "The Cultural History of the United States." He, too, had written the textbook, but it was interesting, and I found the subject matter fascinating, for Miss Penton had not covered this aspect of history. I kept his books until my 1998 fire. He opened up aspects of our national life for me. He was the other professor who got a round of applause at the end of one lecture.

A. Whitney Griswold taught a course called, I think, "The Constitutional History of the United States." I thought this would be very exciting, for constitutional law interested me. But he was so self-important, and so interested in impressing the "white shoe boys" and those in Senior Societies, that he could have cared less about the rest of us. He was also narrow-minded. I would now probably agree with some of his prejudices, but at that time I was at the other end of the political spectrum. But I am still incensed by the way he treated John Quincy Adams. We had spent a long time on Jefferson, Madison, and Monroe. Then he said, "And there was John Quincy Adams—ha, ha, ha." And that was the end of the subject. We moved on to Jackson. Certainly the second Adams was not a great president—but he is worth more than a laugh. For instance, there we were in New Haven where the slave ship *Amistad* found harbor, the slaves were arrested, and where John Quincy Adams took their case to the Supreme Court and won their freedom. And Griswold did not even mention it. Later he "ran" to be elected President of the university and won—and I think was a disaster as President. I did not like Bemis, but I had no respect for Griswold.

At one point, in my wanderings after deciding not to be a diplomat, and after Uncle Arthur was elected president of Chase Bank, I thought about going into banking. I saw there was a course on banking taught by Mr. Westerfield—one semester on commercial and one on investment. He, too, had written the textbook. He was a dull lecturer. Halfway through the investment course, I found that if one read an outside book, and reported on it to Westerfield, he would give extra credit—one or two percentage points over exam grades. I did not discover this until toward the end, but having caught on began to read as fast as I could. I think I got my grade up to about 96—very high for a liberal arts class. At the start of the second semester, I vowed to make 100, if he would do so. I read like crazy. I think I had enough points to reach about 104, for safety sake, but he could give me only 100. I think that was what made the difference in my graduating *magna cum laude*. It was poor pedagogy on his part, and I'm not particularly proud of doing it.

We were required to take two semesters of a "laboratory science" (I have already described how I got out of that) and two semesters of "systematic thinking" (they had in mind mathmatics). I found that this could be met by taking philosophy. People who went this route were meant to take a course in Logic, I think, but I found that I could meet the requirement by taking a course in Ethics. Brand Blanshard was the professor—probably head of the department. He was an agnostic, if not an atheist. The class was relatively small, maybe 30, so there was some chance to have discussion, and also I wrote a term paper "Reason, the Servant of Mysticism"—on which he gave me an "A", so he knew of my Christian stance. I am not basically a philosophical thinker, but I did like his course. And I had to take one more semester. Since I liked Blanshard, I looked to see what else he offered and found that his course on "Epistemology" would satisfy my requirement. I didn't know what epistemology was, but I signed up. (Epistemology is the study of how we know whatever we know.) I'll never forget the first day of class. He said, "I would like for someone to tell me something which he absolutely knows is true." There was no response. He looked around, evidently not knowing most of the class, but he spotted me in the front row and said, "Mr. Campbell, what do you know, absolutely, about which there can be no question?" Knowing his skepticism, and deciding to stir up the snakes, I replied, "Well, I know there is a God." His mouth fell open, and in shock he whispered, "*Really*, Mr. Campbell," and we were off to the races. It proved to be a wonderful course, and has had a lot to do with my theology ever since.

The Sociology Department at Yale had a reputation of being very liberal, and I was very conservative. I held off, but finally decided I should take at least one course. The professor, I think his name was Turner, taught the introductory course. Intellectually, I "fought" with him on much of what he said. But that was the year the Masters and Johnson study on "Male Sexuality in America" came out, so I was able to read it "for credit." It was an eye-opener for me — to learn about the frequency of premarital sex, homosexuality, masturbation, frequency of sex in marriage, etc.

I don't remember the name of the professor, but I took two semesters of the history of art. It was an expanding experience. It made me appreciate painting, sculpture, and archaeology.

I do not remember the name of the junior faculty member who worked with a group of about five or six of us who were going to write senior essays in history. This was not required for graduation, but was if one wanted to get honors. He met with us once a week or so for the spring semester (the first half of my senior year) while we learned some of the skills of research, how to write an academic paper, etc., and began to narrow down on a subject. The advisor worked with me through the fall of 1948, my last semester in Yale College. He was not exciting, but he stuck with me and was a help.

Uncle Arthur McCain

Arthur McCain was my mother's older brother. They lived in Scarsdale, a suburb of New York, where he was a vice-president of Chase National Bank. My contact with Uncle Arthur increased tremendously from 1945 on. I visited them in June 1945 on my way to Yale, and then spent all my short vacations and breaks from Yale with them, so that they became my second home. I was there during the tragic years of Mary Wrenetta's mental breakdown and as they recovered from their house fire at Christmastime 1945. I was there when he was elected President of Chase Bank, and from a distance witnessed the excitement of being on the top of the financial world. He did not change, except he began bringing home work each night—something he had never done before. But he would play tennis (although I was not in their league), bridge, or anything else going on. He and I would have heated political and economic debates, to Aunt Marion's distress. We liked and respected each other. He was pleased I was at Yale and doing well. They came up to Yale several times.

I had gone to Yale to be a diplomat, but gave that up and ran through a series of possible job routes. After he was elected President of Chase, I thought about banking. When I began talking of the ministry, he was not happy with this. They went to church regularly, but he was not a deeply committed churchman. Because I had almost gone to China with Yale-in-China, he got National City Bank to offer me a job in their overseas department, and was disappointed when I turned it down to go to seminary. It was the only non-church job I was ever offered. It was fun being so near that level of society. They would talk about going to formal dinners in New York. He belonged to the Knickerbocker Club on Fifth Avenue and would take us for dinner there. He had the Chase limousine pick us up. He had us for dinner in the President's Dining room at Chase once. He would talk about how the Seraphic Secretaries, secretaries of the top financial people in New York, would work with each other—one borrowing another's boss's plane or some other perk for her boss. He would talk about meeting people from Saudi Arabia, for Chase was financing their oil expansion. What a rare treat it was for a country boy to get that insight—and never with any condescension on Uncle Arthur's part.

Several times when I visited in Scarsdale, I had a cold. I learned from Aunt Marion that it made Uncle Arthur angry when anyone was sick, but he never expressed that directly to me.

Aunt Marion McCain

Aunt Marion was an extrovert, very energetic, lots of fun—and determined to keep family ties strong. Even as a child, I knew she was a "force to be reckoned with."

For Labor Day 1945, I came down to Scarsdale—the first of many, many short holidays I spent with the McCains. Aunt Marion was always welcoming and always did things to make the stay fun.

On my way back to Yale at the end of the Christmas break, I called the McCains from Grand Central and went out. But when they took me from the Scarsdale station, it was not to Morris Lane but to a rented house, because their house had been set on fire. They had not told us in Arkansas, nor had they told us Mary Wrenetta (a student at Vassar) had had a nervous breakdown and was in the hospital. They had not wanted to spoil our Christmas, so it was my task to pass this on to my family. I visited them in the rented house, then went back to Morris Lane when it was beautifully restored. That was a very dark time for them. Not only had the house burned (and Arthur was responsible for the electrical fixture that started it), but Mary Wrenetta had had a serious schizophrenic break. Frances had had to sit with her as she was coming un-glued while the parents went to get her in the White Plains unit of New York Hospital—a very good, and very expensive, psychiatric facility.

I went back there at breaks in the winter and spring of 1945, and was very much a part of the family during those trying days. And Aunt Marion was the one who always welcomed me. This continued throughout my college days and into Divinity School. When Uncle Arthur was elected president, Aunt Marion loved it—but refused to get her feet off the ground. By this time instead of having two Irish maids, they had one black maid—Ethel. When Aunt Grace Walker told her she should have a second maid, Aunt Marion refused.

When Uncle Arthur and I would get into a heated discussion, she would try to change the subject, but never stopped us. All through this time, both Aunt Marion and Uncle Arthur would go to White Plains to see Mary Wrenetta and would come back so discouraged, for she would make some progress, then regress.

The McCains came to Yale for an occasional football game, and when Arthur started to Choate, they would stop on their way, and once took me up there with them.

I would never have survived those first two years at Yale without the Arthur McCains and their haven in Scarsdale. They were my family-away-from-home. I grew very close to Frances. Arthur was pretty much a pill at that stage. Mary Wrenetta was in the hospital for about two-and-a-half years, I think—finally recovering when they gave her a combination of insulin and electric shock treatments.

When Mary Wrenetta was released from the hospital, they asked if she could spend the summer with us at Scott, for one of her problems was jealousy of Frances. The relationship between the two families was that close—that either one felt free to ask the other for help when help was needed. I felt that if Mother and Daddy were killed, it would be the Arthur McCains, rather than the Gordon Campbells, who would step into the parent role. Some of that was because of Uncle Arthur, but more due to Aunt Marion. When Mary Wrenetta went to Hood College and had no one to invite down for a weekend, I went down to Frederick, Maryland. I was filling in the role of a brother, for Arthur was too young.

The McCains listened to me through the years as I floundered over my vocational future. They were distressed when they heard I was thinking about the ministry—and Aunt Marion resented the influence Uncle Ken had over me. I did finally get them to meet each other once in New York City.

When I returned to Yale Divinity School, the relationship with the McCains continued. I would go down there for all the short vacations and holidays. I found myself becoming uncomfortable with the very "posh" atmosphere of Scarsdale by then, but the McCain warmth drew me back.

During my Clinical Pastoral Education (CPE) year, while I was at Bellevue Hospital, I would run out to Scarsdale on weekends. Ann Williamson, then at Union Seminary, also was out there, for as a relative she had the welcome mat out too. It was during that year she and Frances became good friends. I guess it was during my last year at YDS that Uncle Arthur (having been demoted at Chase because he did not agree with Winthrop Aldrich) was made president of Union Planters Bank in Memphis and moved down. That was a major change for me, but by that time I had established a relationship with the Charles McCains in New York, and they filled the gap—but never emotionally.

Some Undergraduates Who Influenced Me

Fellowship in Berkeley

Because of the circumstances in which I grew up (in the country and only one other boy of my age in our circle), I had always acted, and saw myself, as a "loner"—in, but not of, a group.

When I went to Yale in June 1945 and started living with a roommate and in a dormitory, this was the first time in my life I had been thrown into intimate contact, over an extended period, with people outside my family. There were times I felt a bit claustrophobic, and for the first couple of years, I was hurting so badly from homesickness I held back part of "me," but still I developed closer friendships than I had ever known before. Dago Sarmiento soon became my best friend, but I also felt very close to George Kearns and Dan Howard—less so to Peter Crosby because while he was always there, he was such a slob and boor. Later, Frank McClain and Walter Lowrey became very close friends. This was the group with whom I would often go to meals. If I came late, I never hesitated to sit with them, for I knew I was welcomed. They were all bright—most of them far more intelligent and sophisticated than I. They could be terribly funny. Of the five I have mentioned, two remained good friends until their deaths, and three are still close—Dago, George, and Walter.

This group taught me most of what I know about literature, art, and music. Dago taught me much about "formal manners" to which I had not been exposed in Arkansas. Subtly, they taught me how to dress in an Ivy League way. Although they made great fun of my Arkansas accent, they never made me want to lose it, nor did I cease to identify myself as an Arkansan.

When I write about the closeness of our friendships, I need to put a qualifier on that. We talked, and argued, about politics, the ecclesiastical side of religion, the social mores of the nation and world, art and literature, philosophy, regional differences, types of entertainment, a very little bit about sports—really only football in our group, the post-war future, jobs, university rules and requirements, what courses to take, sex in a generic sense and in jokes and apocryphal stories, etc. Looking back on our bull sessions, we did not discuss the inner aspect of our faiths (spirituality, although I didn't know that term at the time). I did this far more in Uncle Ken's cell group and would not have dared expose this private side of my life to the ridicule I would have received from the guys on the floor, with the exception of Dagoberto. They did know of my participation in chapel and the cell group, and I got some kidding on that, especially from Dan Howard. But they never got a glimpse of what those activities meant to me. Also, in regard to sex, we never shared with each other our fears or hungers or lack of knowledge. In many ways, I put my own sex life "on hold" for those four years. The lack of privacy and fear of ridicule shut me down.

I do not know who assigned people to rooms in Berkeley, but I am grateful that our constellation was placed where we were. I wonder if we would have sought out each other if there had not been that propinquity.

As I look back on my years at Yale College, I think I benefited as much from my friends, in the way of education, as I did from my professors. What makes an institution like Yale special is the makeup of the student body. There are more books in the library of even a community college than anyone is going to have time to read. And in almost any college there will be one or two professors who can "turn on" a student willing to learn. But what one does not find in other places is a constellation of students who are very bright, who bring with them rich backgrounds, and who create an environment in which ideas are debated, challenged, and encouraged.

In addition to this close group, I also made friends with the people in Uncle Ken's cell group—not as close as those in our entryway, but close. Of those, Bard Smith has been the one lasting friendship.

When I moved out of 599 at the beginning of my senior year, there was a major shift in my friendships. I still was very friendly with my old floor-mates, but did not see as much of them as before. By then I knew enough other people in Berkeley to join at meals. That spring I participated again in the Berkeley Players and that took a lot of time, and so did beginning on my senior essay, and I was reading like crazy in my Banking course to move up my grade. I never felt lonely during senior year. I had long-since learned to live alone. My last semester, when I had a room to myself, was great. I began entertaining, against college rules, with teas in the afternoon. I was absorbed in what my future would be, and I was pushing hard to complete my senior essay. My need for friendship was partially met by Ellie Hutchins down in the Master's Office.

As I've mentioned earlier, the college plan was a great way to break up a large university into manageable bits in which people could find their place. The negative was that I never made any real friends in the other colleges. I knew some of them through classes, or at Dwight Hall, but real friendships were within the walls of Berkeley.

Dan Howard

Dan Howard and I were assigned to be roommates before we ever arrived at Yale. I don't know who made the match. He was kind to meet me at the train station the first day, and his family invited me to go to Hartford for Thanksgiving that first year when we were on a wartime schedule still and did not have Thanksgiving off. His uncle once invited me to have lunch with him and Dan at the Union League Club, one of the "in" places in New Haven. When my parents came on their first visit, and perhaps the second, we took Mrs. Howard out for dinner.

Dan's father died when he was relatively young, but I don't know how early. He was reared by his mother as a single parent. She had some kind of job that was not a big one. I was never invited to their home. She had a car. Dan had gone to the public schools in New Haven, not Catholic ones. But they were practicing Catholics until Dan came to college. After that his attendance was sporadic.

Dan and I were congenial, but never were really close in the sense of confiding in each other. I never was as close to him as I was to Dagoberto. I now wonder how he put up with me, especially that first year when I was so homesick and psychologically unable to put down roots at Yale. He rebelled against his Catholic background and was sarcastic about my increasing interest in my faith, especially my ties to Mr. Latourette. I remember once when those of us in Uncle Ken's cell group were following him after dinner to his office, Dan called across the courtyard, "There go the Christers." I cringed. But he was a vital part of "the group" of those of us who lived on the third floor of that entry. He loved to tease me about being from the South—my accent (he declared he did not have one). Phrases like "I'm waiting on you" would elicit an "ouch." I am sure I was a trial for him, especially when I put a Confederate flag up over our mantle. I think it was after John Hewson moved in. Later when I found it stuffed in one of the commodes in the restroom, I put it back up! Dan was very bright, but did not study hard or in a disciplined way. His drinking did not get out of hand, but he did often go out for a beer at night and could get a little under the weather on a football weekend. I am not sure when he began to date George Kearns' sister, Maureen. I don't remember their dating during our college days. Maybe it was in graduate school. But they did eventually marry and had one daughter, Loretta.

After our first year, Dan got a bursary job of being one of the librarians in the Berkeley College library — where there were a few books, but it was mostly a quiet study room to which few people went. When I would go there to read, I would often (not knowing about ADD then) fall asleep. One of Dan's favorite tricks, when he caught me sleeping, was to turn the pages of my book back about 30 pages, then make a noise that would wake me up. I'd begin reading hard — and he would die laughing, knowing that I was re-reading it all. That may have been when I started marking books, so I'd know where I had been.

Dan started out in economics, I think. After graduation he went out to Indiana to work for one of the railroads. I don't know if he switched to an English major or if he had just taken enough courses to be able to get in Yale Graduate School in English, but he got his Ph.D. in that and then taught at Rutgers where he eventually became chair of the department. I visited him and Maureen once. It must have been in 1971. I had been to the Amish country and bought an Amish bonnet. I showed it to Maureen who grabbed it and said she was going to wear it to the next cocktail party in New York. She was a blithe spirit, began writing novels, and has become a major figure in New York literary circles. Eventually Dan and Maureen divorced — but Dan and George remained the closest of friends.

When I was working in Atlanta and traveling to the seminaries, on my visits to Princeton I would often see Dan and/or George. Dan had by then married Barbara, from England. On one visit I was to have dinner with Dan and Barbara, and George was to pick me up from the bus. When I got off, George told me Dan had suffered a stroke that day, was in the hospital, and they did not know if he would live. He did make it, but was impaired, and the impairment grew more serious. Toward the end, George was having to co-teach with him, to carry his courses. Finally, he was forced to retire.

The last time I visited him, he was very limited physically, in speech, and in his mental capacity. After his death, I kept up with Barbara. She says I am one of the few of his friends who has done that—other than George. When I stayed with George in 2002, they invited Barbara over for dinner. She and Dan had two sons, Peter and Matthew, who graduated from college and seem to be doing well.

George Kearns

George Kearns lived next door to me. He was the one who, on the first day I was at Yale, was standing on a wooden armchair in the middle of their living room waving his arm and reciting one of Shakespeare's plays. That was an appropriate introduction to

George Kearns and me at Yale in 1947 with the Harkness classroom building in the background.

George. He was a blithe spirit. I liked him and felt closer to him than to Dan, but never as close as I did to Dagoberto, his roommate.

George came from Bridgeport and had gone to Fairfield Prep, a local Catholic school that apparently was very good. His father was a detective in the Bridgeport Police Department, but I gather his mother had inherited some money, for they lived on a level I don't think a detective's salary would allow. As I mentioned earlier, his younger sister, Maureen, eventually married Dan Howard. She was too young to come to parties in our first year but was invited by senior year.

I met George's parents many times, but never got to know them well. I was never invited to their home in Bridgeport, although that became Dago's "second home," and I think Frank McClain visited there. Nor did I ever invite George to come to Scott. But through my four years as an undergraduate, we were part of the same "crowd." He was much more given to partying, kept his room like a pig-pen so the maid eventually refused to go in there, and was totally undisciplined in his study habits. He was an English major, but also was excellent in Spanish, and having Dago as a roommate helped that. I don't think I remember George having dates very often. He could do the most absurd things. He was a lot of fun. His bursary job was working on a research project concerning James Boswell papers and later in the Rare Book Room of the library.

When we graduated from college, George had no idea what he was going to do. He eventually got a job with Coca-Cola, or Pepsi-Cola, as their representative in the Caribbean and would go from island to island. He was good at it because he was so fluent in Spanish. I remember his writing once that he came into some town and every hotel was full—except the local brothel, so he stayed there. He was never explicit about how the night went. He was "loose" enough to decide since he was there he might as well try out all the "facilities." On the other hand, he could have decided to entertain the "ladies" by a reading of Shakespeare. But he would have enjoyed the night, whichever way it went.

George was a Catholic—not as serious about it as Dagoberto, but not as lax as Dan. I think he would go to mass occasionally at Yale, but I am sure always did in Bridgeport. He said his family were "lace curtain Irish" (as distinct from "shanty Irish"). However, when he eventually married, it was important that his wife convert to Catholicism even though she had been teaching at Princeton Theological Seminary.

After his Caribbean episode, I think George started graduate school—and took forever to write his dissertation on Ezra Pound and get his Ph.D. from Boston University. Then Dan found him a job at Rutgers where he started teaching the very basics to freshmen, but finally became a full professor and upheld Dan after his stroke.

When I took my children on the trip up the East Coast in 1973, I checked the AAA book and found a hotel right on Times Square because I thought it would be good for them to see the theater district. Then I contacted George. He wrote, "Donald, I know you have become liberal, but I really don't think you want to put up your children in the Dixie Hotel. It is where all the pimps and whores in New York hang out." So he told us about another hotel near Washington Square where we stayed.

Once when I was in New York, I spent the night with George in an apartment he owned in lower Manhattan. I am not sure exactly where it was, but I think near Soho. It was a walk-up, about the fourth floor. It was the first time I had ever stayed where there were not only three locks on the door, but also a metal rod that fit in a socket on the floor and leaned against the door so if anyone tried to push the door in, there would be metal backing for it. George owned this, but rarely used it—yet did not rent it out or sell it, with New York real estate being very expensive. I never did understand why he had it and why it sat empty.

Perhaps it was on that same visit that Dan and Barbara came into New York and had dinner with us. George excused himself because he had to make a phone call to Maureen, his sister and Dan's ex-wife. He came back saying, "She is the most difficult woman to work with." Dan, in his typical cryptic style, replied, "Tell me about it."

It may have been on that same trip that we were driving around lower Manhattan when we passed a bar. George asked if I had ever been to a gay bar. I had not. He said he needed to broaden my education, so we went in to have a beer. It was an eye-opening experience for me to see men dancing together, kissing openly, flirting, and moving toward heading off for the evening for some "fun."

Quite late in life George married Cleo, who had her doctorate in English but could not teach at Rutgers because George was on the faculty. She had a hard time finding a position, and I think never did get a satisfactory full-time one until George retired and she was eligible for a post at Rutgers. I guess they could not have children, so they adopted a boy, Chris, from Latin America. I stayed with them the fall of 2002 in Princeton. George has also had a stroke. His mind is still good, but his speech is impaired. He speaks slowly and not distinctly. After I left, Cleo told me he had talked more during my visit than he had in months, and that after I was gone he seemed improved. George and Dago and Cousin Walter are the only three of our "crowd" still living. I feel close to him.

Dagoberto Sarmiento Weisbach

I met Dagoberto the first day I arrived at Yale. He and George Kearns lived next door to Dan Howard and me. First I had met George Kearns, the blithe spirit standing on a chair waving his arms and reciting Shakespeare. Before long, this good-looking Latin American came back to the room. He had been in New Haven for a little while, having come up from Bogotá, Colombia. He was as different from George as any two people could be, except they were both Catholics — but totally different in their observance of that.

Dago spoke English fluently, but with an accent. I was to learn that the accent came from both Spanish and German, for he had attended a German-speaking school in Bogotá. His training and world-view were "old European." It was clear that his family was affluent, and he had been trained in all the social skills. His clothes seemed a bit strange. They were beautiful, but formal, and had a "cut" that was different from the American style. He had built into him a very rigid structure about what should be done, said, and how one should act. He thought that until a certain hour a man dressed in one way; after that hour he dressed differently. On some occasions one took a hostess candy; on others one sent flowers, etc. He came from a world totally different from my Scott world, but we hit it off almost immediately.

Along with his courtly manner, he could also be very arrogant. When I finally started to replace my Arkansas clothes with ones that fit in better with the Yale styles, I would take him with me to the clothing stores. I shall never forget the first trip. We walked into the store—probably J. Press, one of the very good ones near campus. When we entered, Dago said to the salesman, "My good man, bring us some suits!" I cringed. I would never have addressed anyone, especially an older man, with that haughty a voice. When he brought out some suits, Dago would turn them inside out, tug on the seams to see if they were well stitched, and if they did not meet his requirements, he would throw the suit to the floor and say, "Simply not! Bring us some more." By this time, I was ready to crawl behind the nearest suit rack. Finally, we found one that I liked and, more important, met his requirements, and purchased it.

With the passing of months, and semesters, he was the person on the floor to whom I felt closest. I talked about him so much to the McCains that they told me to bring him down for a visit in Scarsdale. They found him charming. He invited Frances up for some football weekend, or perhaps even a formal dance. She was terrified when some Spanish music was played and he swooped her across the floor in a samba or tango or some such dance. Then I invited him to visit me at Scott. He made quite a hit with people there, for he was good looking and he was charming.

This was prior to Vatican II, and Roman Catholicism was rigid. Dago was convinced that non-Catholics were going to hell. But he seemed to be impressed by my quality of life and my piety. He told me one day he was convinced I was a "secret Catholic," and he prayed for my eventual conversion. He urged me to go to St. Thomas More chapel with him, and I did. Then I invited him to visit Battell Chapel with me. He had to talk to his priest ahead of time and get permission. I was impressed that when I visited Dago in Basel, Switzerland, in 1996 and was there on a Sunday, he insisted that we go together to the Anglican church for worship. He had loosened up a great deal, as had the Catholic Church.

Dago talked about having a half-sister who lived in this country, and he talked often about his father in Bogotá. Then one day he came to me and said he had something to tell me. He said his name was not Dagoberto Sarmiento but Dagoberto Weisbach. His father had been head of I. G. Farben, the German dye manufacturer, in Colombia. As World War II was approaching, he decided to apply for Colombia citizenship, instead of German, but Pearl Harbor came before that was finished. His business was confiscated, but he was far along enough so he was not interned nor were his finances

Dagoberto Weisbach Sarmiento, Frances McCain, Elizabeth Ginnochio, and me in the Berkeley College courtyard after the Yale-Brown football game in 1946.

seized. But when Dago, in 1944-45, decided he wanted to come to the USA, there was no way a person with the name of Weisbach, whose father had worked for I. G. Farben, was going to be let into this country. So he took his mother's maiden name of Sarmiento. I learned many years later that his mother and father were never married. In Colombia at the time, the only legal marriages had to be performed in the Catholic Church. His father was a Protestant and would not convert. So his mother and father simply lived together.

The reason this had to come out now (it must have been in 1947) was that his father was coming to this country for medical treatment and would visit him at Yale, and we would all meet him. So we had to be told. Needless to say, this was quite a surprise. It did not seem to make any difference to anyone but to Aunt Marion McCain, who never invited him back. Her maiden name was Vinsonhaler. During World War I, there was such strong anti-German feeling that they felt pressure because of their name; then her father was in the American forces going to France in 1917. She still had a strong anti-German feeling.

When World War II was over, there was desperate hunger in Europe and many of us were sending CARE packages. Dago came to me one day saying he had noticed I was sending those packages. Would I consider sending one to his father's brother, who had been conductor of a symphony orchestra in Germany? Because he had played before Nazis, he could not work anymore and was in desperate condition. I did send such a package. Some time later, I received a thank you letter, in German. He said he did not know who I was, or why I had sent it, but he wanted me to know what a help it was.

Dago did come down to Scott once in the summer, I think — and Frank McClain and Walter Lowrey came over from Mississippi. Then at Christmas 1948, I invited Dago and Jim Boyes to spend Christmas with me.

Dago had dropped out of Yale for a year earlier ("to rest") so did not graduate until the spring of 1950, I think. He may have taken another year of "rest," and then went to the University of North Carolina in Chapel Hill to get his Masters. He had started out in chemical engineering, but switched to chemistry. We corresponded through the years. After graduating from UNC, he went to Germany to get his Ph.D. At his leisurely pace, that took years. While he was there, George Kearns was stationed there in the Army awhile, I think. And Walter Lowrey got a Fulbright Scholarship to Rome, then a civilian job with the Army in Germany, and married Kjerstin. They visited back and forth a lot and became very close friends.

I have kept up with Dago through the years by occasional letters and phone calls. In 1969, when I went to Brazil and found I would be returning through Bogotá, I left the group and stayed behind in Bogotá for five days and visited with Dago and Charlotte and Pancho in their home that was secured against robbers in a way I could not imagine. As indicated earlier, I visited him and Charlotte again in Basel in 1996 on my way to Scotland, and then they visited me in Perth that fall. Dago now has early Alzheimer's and is beginning to get vague. Charlotte has died, and he has moved to an apartment near his son, Pancho, who owns a home in Basel. Dago has become a Swiss citizen.

Walter Lowrey

I am not sure at what point in my Yale career Walter appeared. I think it must have been the fall of 1946, as I began my fourth semester there. He had been released from the Army and was coming on the GI Bill. He had not studied at Yale during the war, as Frank McClain did, but was encouraged to come by a Yale graduate, Lomax, who lived in, or came from, Marks, Mississippi, Walter's hometown.

Walter was, and still is, small in size and trim, and has looked middle aged since I first met him. He has adopted a "role" to play—that of an aristocratic Southerner, sophisticated, condescending to those he considers boors, deferential to people in positions of power (although condescending if he considers them also boors), skeptical, irreverent, droll, well read, humorous, quiet, slow-speaking, steadfast in his friendships.

I think he and Frank McClain must have arrived about the same time. As I remember, they both roomed across the hall from us, and very soon became good friends. They had not known each other in Mississippi, but they had so many mutual acquaintances that they began to call each other "Cousin Frank" and "Cousin Walter"—and that spread through the floor so all of us in the "inner circle" began, and we still do, to refer to each other from time to time in that way.

Marks is a small town (a county seat, I think) in the Mississippi Delta. His father died when he was young—I'm not sure how young. I don't know if his father was a merchant, lawyer, or planter, but he evidently left enough of an estate so they lived comfortably, although they were not rich. He had a younger brother, Mark, whom I did not meet until 1969, who graduated from Tulane and was an architect. Walter's mother, later in life, moved to New Orleans where she died in the 1990s. I think I met her only once. If the Lowreys did not have a lot of money, they had "connections" with the wealthy in the Delta—which is a sub-society of its own.

Walter, at Yale, was both rejecting that Southern culture while at the same time relishing it—the "mystique" it has in the North, the arrogance, the bigotry, the pseudo-sophistication. This combination made him entertaining company, with his droll sense of humor, his undergraduate skepticism, his obvious intelligence, and his skill in both conversation and writing. He majored in English and only tolerated engineers. I never was in a class with him, so do not know how he functioned scholastically. He was well liked in our circle and was at the core of it. He also enjoyed going to the Hemingway teas, and the Hemingways liked him. I do not remember his ever bringing a date to Yale, although there were some girls who came up from Randolph-Macon for a football weekend, and he may have invited one of them.

I think Walter graduated a year before I did. Perhaps he got a scholarship, or had saved up enough, to go to Paris where he met a young Swedish student, Kjerstin, whose father had been the chief veterinarian in Sweden, and whose sister married a count. Kjerstin was only about 17 or 18. They got married. He did not want to move back to this country, so got a job as a civilian employee of the Army in Germany writing news releases, I think, and translating the writings of generals into literate English. Along the way, he won a Fulbright scholarship and spent a year in Rome. When they came back to the U.S., they went to Mexico for a year or so, and Walter wanted to write a travel book on Mexico. I don't think it ever got published. However, he did publish a novel, *Night Watch* that was somewhat autobiographical. It was quite good. They were traveling in a trailer and came by Crossett, visiting Ann and me. That was the first time I'd ever met Kjerstin. Then after my divorce, they came to visit me in Little Rock—the same time the Weisbachs were there.

I got to know the Lowreys even better when I moved to South Louisiana. They were living in the French Quarter of New Orleans, and I would drop by to see them from time to time.

Frank McClain

Frank McClain came to Berkeley College in 1946, I think. He had been in the Army Specialized Training Program (ASTP) during the war, so had a right to return.

Frank's mother lived and worked in Memphis, Tennessee, but he had grown up in Walter Valley, Mississippi, where I think his grandparents lived. I never knew anything about Frank's father. I assumed his parents were divorced. His mother was with Southern Airways, but in what capacity I do not know. I never met her. But in Frank's mind, he was from the Delta society of Mississippi.

Frank had grown up a Methodist, I think, but he had "moved up" to the Episcopal Church, with a vengeance. He was a member of St. John's Episcopal Church in Memphis where Mag Loring-Clark Jones' father was rector. By the time he came to Yale, he knew he was going into the ministry. For a while, he was in Uncle Ken's Bible study group, but I don't believe he stayed until his graduation.

Frank was a strong personality, always reaching out to meet new and interesting people, always proposing activities or projects. He came to know a Mrs. Yeats, who sat at the exit to Sterling Library checking people's books to make sure they were not stealing any. It turned out she was the widow of a Rhodes Scholar who married her in England. He came back to Yale as a chemistry instructor, but was killed in a laboratory experiment. She was left without children, and without means, but knew a lot of the faculty. She became a friend to all of us.

Frank affected an English accent, although he had never been there. He became more and more high church, liturgically. He had a wonderful sense of humor and could be a lot of fun — sometimes on the bawdy side. He used to go into a mock orgasm whenever he heard Wagner's "Triston und Isolde" prelude. He also had a lot of naughty limericks, such as this one:

> From a crypt in the Church of St. Giles
> Came a scream that sounded for miles.
> Said a monk, "O, good gracious,
> Poor Brother Ignatius
> Must have forgotten that Father has piles."

He was far from a prude. I liked Frank a lot, but never felt "close" to him as I did to Dago and George and Walter, and even Dan. But he contributed a lot to my education — about the Episcopal Church, music, art, sophisticated manners. The Hemingways were very impressed by him because when he was there in ASTP, the Archbishop of York came for a visit. Frank, on his own but acting on behalf of all the students, bought some suitable book as a present and addressed him as "Your Grace." Where in the world he learned that etiquette I do not know. But he is the kind who would do the necessary research.

One of his greatest contributions to my education was to talk several of us into participating in the Berkeley Players. The play in the spring of 1947 was *Taming of the Shrew*. I hesitated about getting into something that would take so much time, but finally was persuaded. We had a professor from the drama school as our director; the producer was Tom Mendenhall, a history professor who was Senior Fellow for Berkeley. As we practiced, I got to know the two professors and the other members of the cast. Looking back on it, I suppose participating in that play was the "turning point" in my Yale life. In the fall of 1947 when I came back to Yale, for the first time I looked forward to returning. I had become a Yali. And much of that was due to Frank.

After Yale, Frank went to General Theological Seminary in New York and was ordained at St. John's in Memphis on "The Feast of the Circumcision of Our Lord." How typical of him to chose that day. Then he went to Nashville where he lived at the home of the bishop. I spent one night there with them. Then Frank went to Oxford and got his doctorate. I think he must have gone to a parish in Virginia where he met Missy and they got married. He was rector for a long time in Winnetka, Illinois. When I took my children to Chicago, we drove out there. I warned them he would speak with a heavy English accent and would be dramatic. When we left, they said I was right.

We exchanged Christmas cards through the years. The next time I saw him was at Caroline Lowrey's wedding in New Orleans, where he officiated. Then once when Marnie and I spent some time in Charleston, after Frank had retired and moved there, we called on him and Missy in their gorgeous tri-plex, looking out over Charleston Harbor. The next day we went to worship at the small, inter-racial church where he was supplying. That was a good visit.

A couple of years ago Frank went in for heart surgery and died on the table. I called Missy a few months later and had a good visit with her.

Fringe People on Our Floor

Peter Crosby was the third person to move in with George Kearns and Dago Sarmiento when Berkeley began to fill up and rooms got crowded. I believe he had lived on the second floor before the consolidation. Peter was from Binghamton, New York. It was obvious he was from a well-to-do family, and the one time his mother came to visit, she seemed like a charming lady. But Peter was "unpolished" to say the least. He was not crude or rude, but always bordered on one or the other in the way he talked. I got used to being with him when I was with other male students, but when we had girls around, I always felt Peter was a misfit. I understand he returned to Binghamton and ran the family business, which I believe was in lumber. I do not know what his major was, but I would imagine economics. My guess is that he was an average student. He was on the "fringe" of the inner core of our third-floor group.

Another of those I call "fringe" was James Bassett from Bristol, Connecticut. His father owned some kind of business there. He went home many weekends. He was very quiet and reserved, and people referred to him as "quiet Jim." He had lived on some other floor, but when we had to have four people in a suite, I think George and Dago took him in. In looking at my 1949 graduation program, I was surprised to see he got a BA with "high orations" (*magna cum laude*). I do not know his major, but my guess is it would have been economics. I guess I never wondered whether he was smart or dumb, he said so little. He did participate in the Berkeley Players, I see from some old snapshots, but I don't remember his being there. I think George Kearns told me he went into his father's business and lived in Bristol.

Earl Schultz was the third person in the suite with Dan and me. He came from McMinnville, Tennessee, where his father was the county agriculture extension agent. Earlier, he had filled the same job in Wynne, Arkansas, where my father knew him. Earl was pleasant, but mostly absent from our fellowship. He was studious, I knew, but I am surprised to see he, too, graduated "with honors" in chemical engineering, from the Engineering School. I know Earl was very strapped for money. He never went home, even at Christmas. He would stay and get work with the Post Office prior to Christmas, and get some other job until school restarted. I don't think he ever had a date. He would do his own laundry in the bathroom and then hang it on cords strung across his bedroom. I exchanged Christmas cards with him for a few years, then that played out. I do not know where he lived.

John Hewson was the fourth person to move into our suite. He was older than we three. He had been in the military, but I don't know if he had been sent to Yale during the war and thus got in, or if he just applied. I know he was an engineering student. He came from the Los Angeles part of California, where his father was inventing some kind of "new" car that I think had only three wheels. He was very seriously in love. I don't know if she came from California or was from Connecticut. I got the impression that they were sleeping together pretty often. He used to kid about sticking his hand in front of a radar machine, for in the service men had accidentally discovered if they got in front of radar, they would be temporarily sterile. Whether that was true or not I do not know. I think he must have married, because his place was taken by Lew Starke.

Lew Starke was a mathematical genius. He was in electrical engineering. He would regularly get 95 to 99 on exams. (In the liberal arts that was almost impossible.) He did not have to study hard. While more than bright in his field, he was totally uneducated in other areas and murdered the King's English. I remember someone once urged him to take an English literature course. He said, "I ain't got no need to take English." Perhaps he moved in after I moved out. I know I never got to know him well. I don't even know where he came from. He must have taken either John Hewson's place or mine. I think he and Earl Schultz shared a bedroom.

Milt Colvin, from New Orleans, and Blake McFeely, from Baltimore, lived across the hall from us. They were both older and out of the military, so really operated in different circles. I rather liked them, especially Blake, but never got to know them well.

In the floor above us, Hal Steinberg and Al Greenway lived, and I think they were joined by Danny Jacobsen. I liked them, especially Hal. Al Greenway was my first encounter with an Orthodox Jew. In the dining hall, he had a hard time following his dietary laws. I especially remember that he would always eat his ice cream first, then vegetables, then meat, on the theory that by then the ice cream would have melted and left his stomach and thus not violate the law against eating a kid at the same time one ate the mother's milk. None of them wore the skullcap, and certainly not the flat brimmed hats. The Jews I had known in Little Rock were all Reformed (although at the time I did not know the distinctions), and I thought mixed comfortably with the Gentile world (although since then I have learned they did not feel that way). I had to tell Mr. and Mrs. Arthur Phillips that I had encountered more anti-Semitism at Yale than I ever had in Little Rock.

In the dining room, we could sit at any table where there was an empty space. But with the passing of time, it became pretty obvious who the various "circles" or "cliques" were. Many of the wealthy rarely ate there, but would go out to restaurants or clubs.

Other Friends in Berkeley

After talking with Walter Lowrey, I am recalling some people in our circle who did not live in our entry.

Arthur Salisbury lived in the North Court and was a friend of Frank McClain and Walter Lowrey. He was sophisticated and pretty cynical. I was not close to him, but enjoyed him. He went into medicine, never married, and lived and died in the Boston area.

Frank Shivers was an English major who belonged to the Elizabethan Club and talked often of going there for tea to visit with various professors. As I remember, he came from Cherry Hill, New Jersey, where his father farmed. He was tall and thin, not good looking, but quite interesting, and trying very hard to be "ivy league." The thing he said that I remember most was after someone had behaved boorishly at a party: "One has some responsibility for the behavior of one's friends, but none for that of one's friend's friends."

Elsewhere, I mention people I got to know in our cell group — Steve Chamberlain, Bard Smith, George Cox, Joe Lieper, and Jim Boyes.

In my last semester in Berkeley, I came to know Jim Boyes, who had graduated from Clare College, Cambridge, and was over for a year on a scholarship. I am not sure how we got acquainted, for he did not live near me. Perhaps Mr. Hemingway asked me to seek him out. However it was, we hit it off. I believe he joined Uncle Ken's cell group, for he had been under the influence of Bishop Steven Neill at Cambridge. I remember I invited Jim to come to my room on the night of the 1948 presidential elections because he did not have a radio and I felt it was part of his learning about America to get in on an election.

I am here going to deviate from my list of friends to comment on the election of 1948. Harry Truman was completing the term he had inherited when F. D. Roosevelt died. My father was a died-in-the-wool Republican, although he had wanted Robert Taft to get the GOP nomination, not Dewey. I did not like Dewey, but I felt strongly the Democrats had been in too long — 16 years — and there needed to be a change of parties. At that point, I was an un-reconstructed Southerner. That was the year Senator Strom Thurmond of South Carolina bolted the Democratic party and formed the "Dixiecrats," mostly on a "states rights" platform, which was a euphemism for racial prejudice. I knew he could not get elected, but I was leaning toward voting for him as a "protest" vote.

I guess I mentioned that to Mr. Hemingway at a Sunday afternoon tea. I remember he urged me never to vote for someone unless I really would like to see him in office. He said once, years before, in a New Haven election he did not like either of the two main candidates, so in protest he voted for the Socialist — knowing that it was a lost vote. But to his dismay the Socialist won! And they had to live with the man he had supported.

I thought about that. I certainly did not want Thurmond as President. So in the end I wound up voting for Thomas Dewey. All the polls predicted that he would win by a wide margin. Jim was very keen for Harry Truman to win. It was a close race. That was when the *Chicago Tribune* came out with the famous headline, "Dewey Wins" only to have to eat crow the next morning. I was disappointed in the outcome, but we remembered that time together.

Also, I found that Jim did not have plans for Christmas. I invited both him and Dagoberto to come to Scott for that Christmas. He was very popular with my family and friends in Scott. When he returned to England, he taught at Rugby, the "public school" he had attended. He married Diana. When Ann and I were in Scotland for Christmas in 1953, they invited us to spend it with them. Later Jim and Diana divorced, and he married April. When Mother and I went to the U.K. in 1975, we had dinner with Jim and April at their flat in London. By then he was headmaster of the City of London School for Boys. Again, in 1996 I stayed with Jim and April in their home in London. Since then, I gather Jim has developed dementia and I have not heard from them in some years.

Bardwell Smith

I first met Bard Smith in Uncle Ken's Berkeley cell group. Perhaps I had eaten at a table with him before, but it was just an acquaintance. Bard was married and living off campus, but sometimes would eat his noon meal in the refectory. But it was in Uncle Ken's group that I really got to know him.

Then as I began to think about going into the ministry, I attended the Pre-Ministerial Group that met in the office of Chaplain Sidney Lovett. One night Bard said he hoped we would all come to the next meeting because his mother was going to tell about her conversion. When I entered the room there was a small middle-aged woman, beautifully dressed, sitting at one end. I sighed and prepared for the worst, but as she began to talk, telling her life story, I was mesmerized. Her name was Gert Behanna. I'll not go into detail about her here, for I'll be writing about her elsewhere. But I learned that Bard was the elder of her two sons, both out of her second marriage—which was to Winthrop Smith, head of Merrill, Lynch, Pierce, Fenner, and Smith. Her father had been very, very rich, so Bard was reared in the lap of luxury. He had gone to private schools, graduating from Andover, and entered Yale in 1943, I think. He had been a playboy. When he left Yale for the military, he was in the bottom one percent of his class. Yale had told him they hoped he did not get killed, but if he didn't, not to come back to Yale. He had then gone into either the Marines or Army, where he was some kind of medical technician in China. Shortly after his return from the war, his mother tried to commit suicide, and he found her and got her to the hospital. Shortly after that, she had her conversion experience. She told Bard about it. He said that made sense, and he quietly turned over his life to God.

Bard talked his way back into Yale, and the first semester he was in the 99th percentile of his class! I did not know all these details about him when our group was meeting in my room that fall, but I could see some of the ways this showed. His wife Nancy's engagement ring was a pearl, not a diamond, and was as big as a small marble. They did not live in a tiny apartment, but had a house. He had a car, but he dressed very simply—always in khaki pants and a blue buttoned-down collar shirt. (I have rarely seen him dressed any other way through all these years.) It was clear he was very bright and a very serious student who had left behind the kind of life in which he had been reared. He was going into the Episcopal ministry. We became very good friends in those few weeks we had before my graduation. I shall write more about him when I cover my Divinity School years.

McCains at Yale College

When I went to Yale in 1945, there were no McCains there. As people got out of military service, three came back.

Mr. Hemingway let me know the reason I got in Berkeley was because he had known Cousin Charlie McCain when they were in college together. (Cousin Charlie could not remember him.) So when I heard Chuck was getting out of the Marines and coming to Yale, I told Mr. Hemingway, and he got him in Berkeley. Chuck lived in a suite directly beneath ours. We spoke in friendly ways, but moved in totally different circles, so I saw him rarely. I do remember going down to his room one night and watching him polish his Marine shoes to a glow such as I never got. He was going to New York the next day for a dance, wearing his Marine dress uniform. Another time I remember going down was when news came that Uncle Arthur has been elected president of Chase Bank. He was very excited about this. His father, Cousin Charlie, had been president of Chase back in the 1930s and had had to resign because in a Senate hearing it turned out he had made some investments contrary to the best interest of the bank. He then went into "exile" in Chicago as head of some large utility company. Then he made a "come back" (my banking professor said it was unique in New York banking history) by becoming head of Dillon Reed, one of the largest investment banks in New York. Chuck was one of the most handsome men I have ever seen — trim, well dressed, always polite — but I never felt I got close to him then. I got to know him better later in life.

Bill McCain, Chuck's older brother, was also at Yale during those years, but he was in the Graduate School, getting his master's in English. I guess I saw him there, but if so only once or twice. I got to know him better in later years

About the same time Ross McCain, Jr. — also a second cousin, but our families had never been as close as my parents were with the Charles McCains — came from West Hartford, Connecticut, where his father was president of the Aetna Fire and Casualty Insurance Company. He lived in Calhoun College, which was next door to Berkeley. I went to see him when I heard he was there, but that was about the end of our contact until out of the blue he invited me to come spend a weekend with them in Hartford. That was the longest visit I ever had with him, or with Cousin Ross and Cousin Dorothy May. I remember Ross told me at that time he was majoring in economics, and especially the economy of transportation. He explained to me how integral that was to the economy. After dinner I remember he took me to an ice hockey game, the first (and one of two) I had ever seen. The next morning we went to the Asylum Hill Congregational Church that was obviously "the" Congregational church in town. Cousin Ross was ushering that morning and wore a cutaway coat and striped pants.

The night of my graduation from Yale College, after I had left for Fayetteville, Mother and Daddy were at the Ross McCains for dinner. Cousin Ross announced that I was the brightest member of this generation of our family. (Having met me once.)

It was pretty clear that these McCains did not consider me part of their world, although they were always polite.

While Chuck and Ross moved in different social circles than mine, Chuck's parents, Cousin Charlie and Cousin Frances, who lived at 10 Gracie Square in New York City "discovered" me. I had been going out to Scarsdale to the Arthur McCains' home for vacations ever since I had come to New Haven. But during the last year or year and a half I was in Yale College, Cousin Frances began to invite me down to escort the daughters of their friends who were in colleges on the East Coast. I guess Chuck and Bill had grown weary of doing this and rebelled. Also, they may have graduated by this time. But I would take the train down to New York and get a cab to Gracie Square where the doorman would let me in. The McCains had a very large apartment on about the third floor, looking right out on the East River. This was one of the most exclusive neighborhoods in Manhattan. My date and I would have dinner at the apartment. The McCains would have tickets to a Broadway play. Cousin Charlie would give me money to take the date out to a nightclub afterward. We'd take a taxi back home that night. The next day, they would drive us out to their country club on Long Island for lunch. Then the date and I would catch our separate trains back to school. I can't remember how many times I did this, but it was several. The girl I liked the most was Thirza Jones from Minneapolis. I still saw her after I went to Divinity School.

Dan Phillips

Of all the people from Little Rock who went to Yale College in my day, the one I had been closest to in high school was Dan Phillips. He was a year behind me in school and had transferred from Little Rock High to Exeter prep school.

On Christmas Day 1945, Mr. and Mrs. Arthur Phillips asked me to come down from the Gordon Campbell house on Edgehill to theirs a couple of blocks away. They wanted to know how much anti-Semitism there was at Yale. I very much wanted Dan to come, but I had to tell them I had encountered more at Yale than I ever had in Little Rock. But Dan came to Yale anyway. When I told Dan about this in 2003, he was not aware that such a conversation had ever taken place. But he said the reason he went to Yale was because they found there was more anti-Semitism at Princeton, the other college he was considering.

Despite our friendship in PIE in high school, during Yale College days I used to see Dan mostly when we traveled up in the fall and at Christmas; then as I took more economical ways, we did not meet, for I guess he flew or took the Pullman. I always felt Dan was much more accepted socially at Yale than I was, but he indicated there were certain areas he had to avoid because of anti-Semitism. After graduation, he returned to Little Rock where he worked at the family store, M. M. Cohn, and eventually became president of it. I had very little contact with him until I came back to Little Rock to start Grace Church. I was invited to his home for a party or two, given by the Phillips and the Frank Gordons. Then when I performed Walter Clancy's wedding, Dan and Barbara gave the rehearsal dinner at one of the clubs downtown.

There was a maxim at Yale College that one's social standing was measured not by the number of people one knew, but by the number one deliberately did not know. I never liked that and was much happier at Yale Divinity School where this was reversed.

My College Summers

I was very lazy and spoiled during the summers of my college years.

In 1946, I did not arrive home until very late in June because Yale was on the wartime three-semester year. George Vanbuskirk from Pittsburgh, who was in Berkeley College with me and in Mr. Latourette's Bible study group, had been drafted and was at Camp Robinson. I invited him to come to Scott for July 4. As we were preparing to go to the Kings' for the neighborhood picnic, Art phoned from Memphis that he was on the way home from the Army. We piled in the car and met him at the airport. He planned to return to Texas A&M in September to get his degree, but was home for the remainder of the summer.

It was the first time since 1940 that the three of us — Art, Ann, and I — were around in a leisurely setting. Art had just returned from battle duty and the occupation in Germany. Ann was getting ready to go into her senior year at the University of Tennessee, and I was back from a homesick year at Yale. So far as I can remember, none of us worked that summer. Ann had some of her college friends come to visit. Art started dating Carolyn Alexander. We played a lot of tennis and golf and swam and ate and dated. I do recall the three of us sitting on the front porch and talking about how difficult it was to remember to "ask" if we could use the cars or go off to play bridge or have some friend in for a meal. We had all three been used to coming and going on our own. We knew our parents would agree to anything we wanted to do, but we realized they would like to be "asked" and not "told." It was good to be able to check this out with the other two.

In 1947, Art graduated from college and went to work. I suppose he was home briefly before he left for work, but I don't think it was for long. Ann had also graduated from UT. That was the summer the Reverend Clifford Barbour, pastor of the church Ann attended and her dear friend and counselor, came over for a visit with his son, Cliff. I remember we invited all our "crowd" to come down to the house to hear him talk and let him answer questions. It was not until later, after he married one of Ann's classmates, that it dawned on me he was interested in Ann as a possible wife until he realized she was falling in love with Hoyt Payne, another of his parishioners. I think some of Ann's college friends came to visit again. I don't think I did anything that summer except "play" (tennis, golf, bridge, swimming).

During college days, the focus of our swimming shifted more and more to Bear Skin Lake, and especially the Kings' place. Bob Bevis, son of the Little Rock gambler and neighbor of the Kings, had lost a foot in World War II, so he could not swim. But he had what was then considered a very powerful speedboat. He seemed to have endless patience in pulling us around the lake on what we called "water skiing," although instead of skis it was a single aquaplane. I was not a natural, but could get up. I found it very frightening, especially when he would swing us around so we almost caught up with the boat. I remember once being very frightened and promising myself if I got back safely I would not ride the aquaplane again. And I didn't. But I would get in the water and sunbathe and was part of the group — and very much part of the picnic that would follow, and the bridge games.

That was the summer after Mr. Latourette raised for the second time the possibility of my considering the ministry. While I had no idea of doing that, I did tell myself I ought to give it some consideration. I also shared with Mother and Daddy this possibility. Daddy was opposed to it, not so much for me as for the sake of the Church! Mother was more open. I remember a scene in which I was helping her make beds on the sleeping porch. I told her one reason I thought this might be a possibility was I was so conservative in every area of life except religion, and there I was quite liberal. This did not seem to make sense to Mother, but it did to me.

That summer, All Souls Church was looking for a new minister. Mother, being a Presbyterian, went to Dr. Adams at First Presbyterian Church, Little Rock, and Dr. Boggs, at Second Church, for ideas. I went with her. In both conferences, she shared with these pastors the fact I was thinking about the ministry. Dr. Adams responded with the corny old story about the boy who saw "P.C." in the clouds and misread it to mean "Preach Christ" whereas it meant "Plow Corn." Dr. Boggs took it very seriously and invited me to come in for lunch with him when we could talk about this more fully.

That summer, before Ann left for her first job, Mother dreamed up the idea of having a "house party" for our old "gang" at Rob-Bell. Aunt Alice said they would all go to town, and we could have the

The club house at Rob-Bell in Scott where house parties were held in the summers of 1947 and 1948.

whole place to ourselves. I can't remember if Art was there, but the rest of our crowd who had been together since dancing school were. Mother and the other mothers provided us with lavish food. We swam and played golf and played bridge and played "the game" (charades) and talked and laughed for two days and two nights. It was one of those experiences none of us has ever forgotten.

In the summer of 1948, I spent the first six weeks suffering from having four impacted teeth pulled. Then I did a little work on my senior essay, though very little. I did have Frank McClain and Eric Sundean come over to visit early on. Perhaps Walter Lowrey came at the same time.

I know Art was working that summer in Tennessee, but he did come home for Ann's wedding. I don't think he was there for the second house party. However, Mother did decide to do a repeat of the house party of 1947, and it was just as much of a success. Peggy and Bob Rochelle, and Hoyt, were all present for that house party. So it must have come fairly early in the summer.

Between the wisdom teeth, the senior essay, and the wedding, I don't think I had a lot of free time. But I know I did not work.

When we were growing up, we were never given "chores" to do around the house because Mother always said our work was being good students. My guess is she (and therefore, Daddy) felt that what I was doing at Yale was demanding and what I needed to do in the summer was relax and recover. I was on scholarship, but there was never any suggestion that I needed to get a job and earn money during the summers.

Ann and Hoyt's Wedding

Hoyt came over to Scott during the summer of 1947, and I think again at Christmas, and visited Ann several times in Washington where she was teaching nursery school at the National Child Research Institute. It was clear things were getting serious, and he proposed during the spring. The wedding was set for September 3, 1948. The wheels were set in motion for a "big" wedding—a socially prominent one.

I got very much involved in preparations for the wedding, doing mostly organization work. I also was instrumental in getting Frank McClain and Eric Sundean, from the Yale Art School, to come over, and Eric made some helpful suggestions about redecorating the interior of All Souls Church. These changes were needed anyway, but with the wedding coming, Mother pushed to get them completed, and they greatly improved the looks of the church. I also helped set up a system for figuring out how many people could be invited to the church (which seated only 120 downstairs and 30 upstairs) by measuring "bottoms" and pews. More people were invited to the reception than to the wedding. Then I also helped set up a system for recording gifts as they came in, and a check list of things to be done, week by week and day by day.

A little before the wedding, we had our second "house party" at the clubhouse. Peggy and Bob Rochelle came, but they could not be part of the wedding, for they were getting married at the same time. That house party was as much fun as the first one—something we all remember with pleasure. I wonder how Mother, Hattie, and Lizzie held together that summer.

There were many parties for Ann that summer, most of them for women only. Some were at night, though, when I would be involved, but with Hoyt in Knoxville, they were few in number. Mother went all out on this wedding, and Daddy backed her—the only wedding they would ever put on. And it was the first "big" wedding at All Souls, except for Lucille Blann's, since Margaret and Lewis Gaston married. Therefore, it set the standard for others to follow — Carolyn's and Mary Carolyn's, etc.

Wedding gifts poured in by the dozens. Every time we would go to town, we would stop at both Stifft's and Cave's, the two big jewelry stores, and bring back a carload. The gifts were displayed on tables made of plywood on sawhorses covered with white tablecloths. I guess Lizzie must have dusted them every day, for without air conditioning the windows had to be open, and in the summer drought, dust was everywhere.

Both Art and I were ushers at the wedding. (No sibling was present at either Art's or my wedding.) To Art's disgust, we wore "summer tuxedos" — regular winter black wool pants and white jackets with black bow ties. I don't know if there were other ushers. Oke O'Callaghan, Hoyt's brother-in-law, was best man. I think Carolyn Alexander was Ann's maid of honor, and other attendants were Laura O'Callaghan, Mary Carolyn Gaston, Pud Steele, and Mary Wrenetta McCain, so there must have been some other ushers. Ann had a formal white gown with the "family" lace from Aunt Alice that had been made in Brussels for her wedding. (When Mother took the lace to the cleaner's to be cleaned, it was in a box with the Gordon Campbell satin gown. When it came back, the dress was missing! That was one of the low moments for Mother when she had to tell Aunt Alice — who was her usual gracious self.)

There was no air conditioning in the church, only fans. People were dressed in formal clothes, and they were packed in like sardines. During the wedding, several of the candles melted. This was an old Southern custom before air conditioning — to speculate before going to a summer wedding about how many candles would melt before the service was over. We had tried everything to prevent this — from putting the candles in the deep freeze until the last minute, to running a metal wire hanger up the center of the candle. We had experimented, and none of them worked.

After the wedding, we drove down to our house for the reception, which was held outside. I guess Daddy had sprayed with DDT, for mosquitoes were not a problem. It was hot, but clear. Tables for the food were set up all over the yard, including the new area to the west. There were a few electric lights in the trees, but most of the light came from candles with hurricane shades. I remember wandering around the yard as the reception was going on. It was so beautiful, as the wedding had been. We were all very happy about this marriage. Ann was the first one of the "crowd" to get married. It was clear that this was the end of an era in our family history, and also of the social life we had grown up with at Scott. I remember thinking "the old life I have known is 'Gone With the Wind.'" It was that, but it was also the beginning of a new and happy chapter for all of us.

The decorations for a couple of the tables were watermelons, split in half, and scooped out, then filled to overflowing with watermelon balls, cantaloupes, honey dew, grapes, strawberries, etc. To give the "overflowing" effect, newspaper had been crammed into the watermelons before the fruit was added. When people began going through the food line, they thought the fruit was part of the meal and began taking it out of the watermelon. When the reception was over Mother, to her dismay, discovered all that was left was soggy newspaper. The other shock to Mother was that they ran out of some of the food. This she considered to be close to, if not indeed, a sin. For the rest of her life when she entertained (which was often), she was so scared of running out that she always had way too much.

Daddy had bought a new car just before the wedding—I think partly to have an extra with all the out-of-town guests. I was a very careful driver, but that night I decided I wanted to follow the getaway car, driven by Oke. I took some people with me—I know Truman was one of them. Instead of heading for the paved road to Little Rock, they went through the back of the plantation. I set out to chase them, and we whirled around corners, stirring up dust in a way I had never done before. They finally escaped us when they went through a gate, and Hoyt had arranged for someone to close and lock it. But in the process I raced that car as fast as it would go. In those days it was necessary to "break in" a car by driving a certain number of miles at a slow speed. I am sure I ruined that car. Daddy sold it shortly afterwards. He never said anything to me, but surely he knew I was the culprit.

When all the guests had left that night and I went to bed, I had a hard time thinking of Ann and Hoyt having intercourse. I was certain Ann was a virgin. I thought Hoyt was, although he had been overseas during the war, for if there ever was a "straight arrow" it was Hoyt. I had never had sex myself, and it made me uncomfortable to think of what was going on between them.

Arkansas Interlude, 1949

New Haven to Fayetteville

The day of my graduation from Yale College, I had already packed to leave, and had also stored some things for my return to New Haven the following fall. Mother and Daddy left immediately after graduation for Hartford for a McCain family gathering. Dagoberto went with me to the train station to say goodbye as I headed for New York, then I caught the Pennsylvania Railroad for St. Louis on an overnight trip, arriving I guess in late afternoon. Then I caught a train to Fayetteville. I don't know what rail line it was, but there were not many cars on it. When I arrived in Fayetteville, Carolyn Alexander and Marvin Thaxton met me at the station and took me to the room they had found for me in the McKinney's basement, next door to Bob McKinney who was in Sigma Chi with Marvin.

One of the first nights I was there, Carolyn and Marvin invited me to see a student production of *The Mikado* by Gilbert and Sullivan. They had listened carefully to the D'Oyly Carte records of all the music and sang it well with clipped British accents. But evidently they did not have a recording of the speaking parts, for they were all in Arkansas Southern drawl. When one of the characters said, passionately, "Nankee Poo Ah Jus Lo-ve You!" I burst out in laughter—but no one else in the theater thought it was funny. It reminded me, in reverse, of the response to my beauteous Bianca line in Berkeley Players. I realized four years in New Haven had made a difference.

Some of my good friends from high school days were in SAE fraternity, but Marvin, Buddy Craig, and Buddy Lackey were in Sigma Chi. The mid-winter fraternity rush was in swing. They invited me to the parties and, I think, could have certainly given me a bid. After not being in a fraternity at Yale, I first thought I would like the experience. But then I began to feel "too old" to go through the hazing and to be associated with 17-year-olds just out of high school. I also realized there was a limit on how many bids they could give. This would mean so much to someone who was going to be there for four years, and I would be leaving at the end of the semester. I decided to ask them to drop me from consideration.

That decision made a profound difference in my experience that spring. Since I would not be eating at the Sigma Chi house, I signed up at a boarding house near the McKinneys' and the people there were definitely not the "fraternity" type, nor the intellectuals. I never did get close to any of them. And while on a few occasions I would go by to see one of the Buddys at the Sigma Chi house, I did not frequent it. In some ways, it was a semi-lonely life.

I had been in Fayetteville only a day or two when, at the Student Union, I ran into Adrian Williamson, Jr. I couldn't believe it. I thought he was at Washington and Lee. He said he had decided to transfer, although I think he had been kicked out for drinking. Anyway, we saw something of each other through the spring, and at least a couple of times he rode down with me to Little Rock where his parents picked him up and took him to Monticello for the weekend, or for spring break. I am not sure how I got down from Fayetteville to Little Rock the first time, but my folks lent me a car after that. I don't know whose it was—maybe Mother or Daddy's old car that they were about to trade in. But having it enabled me to get around Fayetteville and to go down to Scott for weekends. It made a great difference in my life that spring—the first, and only, time I had "wheels" when I was away at school, for I never had a car at Divinity School or in Scotland.

Academics at the University of Arkansas

While I went to Fayetteville mostly to get reacquainted in Arkansas, I also wanted to get a taste of some areas of academics where I felt deficient. I remember signing up for German, historiography, American literature, perhaps a Shakespeare course, and a history course in some area I had not studied. Before long, I dropped German because I was having trouble with the German script, and I knew that with only one semester of the language I would not use it in the future. I found historiography interesting, for I had never taken that before. Out of that, and my acquaintance with the instructor, someone made the suggestion that I submit my senior essay, "A study of some factors contributing to the petition for abandonment by the Missouri and North Arkansas Railroad in September, 1946" to the *Arkansas Historical Society Quarterly*. To my amazement, they said they would like to print it, but I would have to reduce it somewhat in size. Editing that took a good bit of the spring, but in fact it was published!

The American literature course was interesting, for I had read very few of the authors. It seems to me I also took a Shakespeare course, but it must not have made much of an impression since I am not sure. Instead of another history course, I may have taken a psychology one, for I don't think I ever got any of that at Yale College. I did not take any of these courses for credit, although I did the assignments and I think I took the exams. It was a wonderfully free time to explore and learn, without any thought given to grades.

All I had heard about the University of Arkansas was parties, fraternities, sororities, and football games. By not being part of a fraternity, I found there is a circle of people who are serious about their academic life, and some who are very bright indeed. Most of them were not of the Little Rock/social set. Some were from out of state, and some were from small towns around Arkansas. I found myself much more at home with them than I did with my old high school friends. And I came to have much more respect for the University as an academic institution than I had previously.

The library was a disappointment after Sterling Library at Yale. I remember overhearing one of the librarians fuss, "If these students don't quit coming in here checking out books all the time, they are going to wear them out!"

Life in Spring of 1949

My social life in Fayetteville was two-tiered. My old Little Rock friends were all in fraternities and sororities. When I first arrived I, and others, assumed I would fit back in with the old crowd. But when I decided not to be available for a bid to Sigma Chi fraternity, that began to diminish. I would still see them from time to time, but that was no longer my "world." Probably my strongest contact became Adrian Williamson, Jr., who had been a member at Washington and Lee of a fraternity that did not then have a chapter at the UofA, and thus he was "loose."

Maybe I should say my life was three-tiered, for I ate in a boarding house with people at the other end of the social scale—pretty basic, sometimes crude, boys and a waitress who could hold her own with them. I never became really friendly with this group, but they were part of my world.

A third tier consisted of some of the serious graduate/undergraduate students I met in my classes, and even more those I met through Central Presbyterian Church. Dr. and Mrs. Spencer (parents of Margaret Spencer who had been a roommate of Mary Carolyn Gaston and had visited at Scott) really gave me a welcome, and they belonged to Central. When Margaret Spencer and Walls Trimble got married that spring, they included me as a peripheral member of the wedding party, and I enjoyed that. The owners of the home where I rented—Mr. and Mrs. McKinney, and Bob, also belonged to Central. The head of the English Department (whose name I cannot now recall and with whom I was studying Shakespeare) and his wife did, too, and welcomed me into their home.

I was always surprised that I got so involved in the Spencer/Trimble wedding, but it was fun. It took me back to my sister's wedding the summer before. I knew a lot of the people who came. It was also interesting to me that Ed Brubaker, who performed the ceremony, wore not a robe but a tuxedo.

Parking was difficult at the University, so I normally walked to and from classes, and back for lunch and supper. In some ways it was a solitary life. I did not have the camaraderie of Berkeley College. There was a student union where I ran into some people, but I did not spend a lot of hours there. I spent a lot of my time in my room in the semi-basement of the McKinney house, studying, although I did go to the library some. Most nights I was in my room studying, even with my light academic load. I had a radio on which I could, on occasion, get good music—from Tulsa, I guess. One of my distractions was a barking dog (that belonged to the Dean of the Agriculture College) in the yard adjoining the McKinney's back yard.

There were a few good eating places in and around Fayetteville, but since I paid for my meals by the week, and because I was trying to cut costs as much as possible, I did not eat out in restaurants. There was one "steak house" north of town where I could get a steak dinner for something like $2.50 or $3.00, but that seemed high at the time. There was also a good Italian restaurant, Mary Maestri's, where I ate a couple of times.

At the church "college age" activities, I got to know Ed Brubaker, the pastor, and his wife, Doris; a Disciples of Christ woman who was in Fayetteville on a Danforth Fellowship; and a public health RN. I will write later about growth in my religious life that spring, but one event stands out clearly in my memory. The nurse covered the whole of Washington County in her rounds and used to talk about how primitive some parts of it were. There was no electricity in that part of the county, or telephones. The next county east of Washington is Newton Country, the one that in my research for my senior essay I had discovered had not one mile of paved road in 1940. I talked her into taking me on her rounds for a whole day—skipping classes, an unheard of event in my life up to then. It was a beautiful, clear, cool day when the trees were just getting green. We rode to the top of Gaylor Mountain, then went right down the east side. I remember we drove to a point out in the woods where the road stopped. She was to go see a woman with a newborn baby to put drops in its eyes to prevent future blindness. She said I should not go on this trip, but left me in the car with a book. The only way she could get to this house was to walk down the bed of the railroad. The cabin faced the rail bed, but no road led to it.

Later that afternoon we drove past a field in which a man had a mule pulling a single-row plow to open up the soil for planting corn, and behind him came a woman, in a sunbonnet, dropping grains of corn *by hand* into the furrow. This was farming as it had been done in 1900, or probably even 1850 (one century earlier). Not even with sharecroppers in the Delta had I seen such primitive agriculture.

Late in the day, she took me by to meet the Don West family. They lived in a log house without electricity or running water, although the house was kept up and not run down as were many I had seen that afternoon. He was a writer whom the head of the English Department liked, and I had read. My copy burned up in my fire, but I think the title was something like *The Sunny Side of a Horse*. They had children who were attending the basic country elementary school. The wife was also educated. I heard later they divorced, and she began to teach English at the University. I shall never forget the tranquility of that setting, and the stimulating conversation we had in very simple quarters. It was a very different world from what I had known at Yale, yet the ideas we could discuss were just as stimulating. This was a side of Arkansas that was totally new to me, even though I had read about it somewhat in my essay research. I had the feeling that, not more than 25 miles from Fayetteville, I had stepped back in time.

During the spring, I went back to Scott several times on weekends and during spring break. I got to know the highway quite well. It was not an easy trip. From Fayetteville to Alma, over Mount Gaylor, the road was narrow and winding, and when I was behind a truck, there was no way of getting around it. The halfway point of the whole trip was Russellville where we would often stop for a drink, or even a meal. Then from Conway to Little Rock, the highway was a nightmare. It would take about three hours to get from Fayetteville to Conway, then that last 30 miles would often take another hour. It was two lanes, with many curves. It seemed always a pick-up truck would pull out of a side road just before I got there, travel at about 20 mph, then want to make a left-hand turn but would have to wait a long time because of on-coming traffic. I usually had several passengers on these trips, for many people at the UofA did not have their own cars, and all the Little Rock people liked to go home (except during the fall football season, unless the game was in Little Rock). I enjoyed having company.

When I would go home, most of my time was at Scott being with Mother and Daddy, for all my age group were away in college or had jobs elsewhere. A few of them had started farming, but not many, for the servicemen who were older than I were behind in their education. The same was true in Little Rock. I would call on adult friends—such as Cody Moore, the Kings, the Birds, Cousin Lizette.

This was a relaxed spring. I was under less academic pressure than I had been since junior high school, or would be again for another four years. My chief purpose was to get reacquainted with Arkansas, and that I did on several levels. My parents were very generous in financing this semester, letting me have a car, providing spending money. I look back on that spring as a very pleasant interlude.

Religious Life in Fayetteville

When I left Yale for the University of Arkansas in February, I was closing a major chapter in my growth as a Christian. In corporate worship at Dwight Chapel, and Sunday chapel at Battell,

I had solace and strength to survive in the first two years, and then enlargement, challenge, and appreciation for good church music, fine preaching, and the value of corporate prayers. When I arrived, I yearned for All Souls Church. By graduation, I found church life at All Souls quite inadequate for me.

I was also ending four years in a Bible study/cell group that had come to have deep meaning for me. And I was, for a time, leaving Uncle Ken Latourette behind, not realizing he had been my spiritual director (for I had never heard the term) for four years. I was also ending the first term when I had ever had a single room, and was free to read the Bible and devotional material, and to pray when I wanted to.

I had gone through four years of struggling to know what God wanted me to do with my life, had surrendered to what I thought was a call to go to China, had been turned down, and had at the last moment finally decided to go to seminary—and to Yale Divinity School. In my spiritual life, I had moved from "childish" ways to the beginnings of a "manly" level.

When I decided to take a single room in a home instead of becoming part of a fraternity, I continued to have the freedom to spend as much time as I wished in prayer and study.

When I began looking for corporate worship to replace Dwight and Battell, it was another story. Even though I was not a Presbyterian (but inclined in that direction), I expected to find my home there. There were two Presbyterian churches in Fayetteville: First Presbyterian was PCUS (Southern Presbyterian), and Central was Presbyterian, USA (Northern). Since the churches in Little Rock were PCUS (if I knew that at this point), I assumed I would go to First church in Fayetteville. David Davies and Adrian Williamson were attending there. But Dr. Butler was the pastor, and while he was a good man, he was deadly dull as a preacher. So I tried Central Church—which the McKinneys attended. Ed Brubaker was the pastor. He was young, good looking, interesting. I also liked his wife, Doris. The church was more alive and had a larger Westminster fellowship. I soon found myself going there every weekend I was in town. There was also a student group on campus. I am not sure whether it was joint PC US/USA, or just the latter.

Not too many weeks after I arrived, there was a meeting of Westminster groups from universities in Arkansas and Oklahoma—

and perhaps more. When Ed sought people to go from Fayetteville, the only two who were free and willing were the Danforth intern and me. She was a member of the Disciples of Christ, and I was a member of All Souls. We drove out to Stillwater, Oklahoma, and when we arrived, we were told we were supposed to supply one of the worship services. She agreed to do the prayers, but they turned to me to preach the sermon! I had never preached a sermon in my life. I had only that night to prepare for it, and had no resources to use. This was in March 1949, and I preached on "Christianity Must Be Passed On." I am amazed that my handwritten outline (from which I spoke) survived my 1998 fire and is the first one in my notebooks. The notes for what was to be a short sermonette cover three pages, handwritten. It was in outline form, but I think must have been almost the full text. I was scared to death. I had not spoken in public (except for two Berkeley plays) since my senior year in high school. Apparently it communicated, judging by the response I got. At this point I was not certain I was going into the ministry—I had just decided to attend divinity school for one year, on trial basis. But all at once, I was dumped into preaching.

I found the Westminster Group at Central stimulating, and more and more identified myself with it. It was through that group I became aware of the fact that black students in northwest Arkansas who wanted to go to high school had to move to Fort Smith and board, for there was no high school for them in the whole northwest quarter of the state. I had been such a racist at Yale, always defending the South, and had behaved so badly regarding Charles Fielding. But at the University of Arkansas, I no longer had to defend the South. Even I could see this was not "separate but equal." Here was the first crack in my segregationist wall. My horizons began to widen. I had already, at Yale, realized segregation was not Christ's will, but I was not able to turn loose of my bigotry. I had kept telling Uncle Ken I did not see how I could be a minister in light of my feelings. He had said I should not let that stand in my way, for he was confident I would be released of them eventually. Here in Fayetteville, I kept struggling over this issue, but still was not ready to turn loose.

I can't remember if it was just the Westminster group or an ecumenical one that had daily worship services during Holy Week. I had usually been away from Yale during Holy Week, so had never experienced services that followed the progression of Holy Week events. In Fayetteville, I think I had a hand in planning them. They came to have a lot of meaning for me. I guess I left Fayetteville on Wednesday. On Thursday, I missed those services. I don't remember whether we had Maundy Thursday communion at All Souls, but I don't think they were yet observing that.

I do remember calling Cousin Lizette Whipple and asking her to have lunch with me on Friday. She said she would like to, but she wanted to go to the three-hour service at First Presbyterian Church and could we eat early. I had never been to such a service, for they were not held at All Souls, nor at Yale—since we were always on break. We were a little late arriving, but I remember being deeply moved as the various Presbyterian ministers reflected on the Seven Last Words, then there was silence, and music. I was still very much in the mode of seeking to know God's will, and asking not only for guidance, but for strength and courage to carry it out. I remember one of the ministers looking much younger than the others and wondering who he was. It turned out to be John Spragens (who later played a role in my life story), the Synod Director of Christian Education.

I don't remember where we went for Easter, but I assume it was at All Souls. Then I left that afternoon to return to Fayetteville.

At that point, I had no denomination. All Souls was interdenominational, and so was Battell Chapel. Mother and Daddy both came from Presbyterian families, but I did not feel closely tied to that tradition. But I wanted to get a feeling for it, and for the Episcopal Church. On one of my trips back home that spring, I went by to talk with Dr. Marion Boggs, who had expressed a great interest in me after the summer of 1947 when Mother, chair of the search committee for a new pastor at All Souls, had gone to him for suggestions and had spilled the beans that I was thinking about going into the ministry. He had invited me to have lunch with him, and we had a long visit. So in the spring of 1949, I went to see if he could give me any ideas how I might "get my toe in the water" by working in some Presbyterian church. He bowled me over by offering me a half-time job at Second Presbyterian Church, working with college age and young adults, at the grand salary of $75 a month. I'll write about that later, but the end of the spring semester found me lined up with a half-time job in a field I knew nothing about, but with a lot of zeal. It was a glorious end to the spring in Fayetteville.

My First Church Job

I had decided at Christmas I was going to go to seminary for one year on a trial basis. My thought was not to enter the parish ministry, but probably to teach church history. But I thought it would be helpful for me to start Yale Divinity School with a little local church experience. I don't know if I had in mind serving a little church, or what. I probably was so vague I didn't really have any idea. Then Dr. Boggs proposed that I come to Second Church, Little Rock. They had a number of college students, and there were also a lot of young adults just out of college. Many of the men were veterans, some still in school. At that time, the staff of Second Church consisted of a pastor, Dr. Boggs; Director of Christian Education, Ruth Puckett; church secretary, Sara Draper; and janitor, Will Boston. Ruth had come only recently. The church had never employed a DCE until about three years before when Margaret Boozer came. She had not worked out well and resigned. Before Margaret came, Miss Draper and Mrs. Boggs had been in charge of the youth work. That is hard for me to imagine. As I got to know them, I realized Mrs. Boggs was a very prim lady. And Sara was cynical and biting in her tone of voice. (I gather Sara felt Margaret Boozer had taken away her place in the life of the church, and Sara proceeded to make life miserable for Margaret. Then Ruth had been hired. Her chief emphasis was on children and young people. She was aware of the relationship between Sara and Margaret, and worked very hard to keep from irritating Sara.) I doubt Dr. Boggs had talked to the Session about another spot. My guess is he, who was usually so cautious, jumped into the unknown when I came to talk. And I'm sure there was nothing in the budget for my salary. When he offered to pay me $75 a month for half time, I accepted on the spot.

This was an ideal situation for me. Many of the older college students and a good many of the young adults I had known in high school, or through my sister and brother. I suppose the total number of people who could be involved would have amounted to about 40, plus their dates or friends. I don't think Dr. Boggs had any kind of program in mind, and I doubt Ruth did. As a matter of fact, I did not meet Ruth on that initial spring visit. It turned out she was my direct supervisor. She and I hit it off immediately. She was a very wise person, but she did not have the "sparkle" to attract this college and young adult group.

The fact that I was "one of their own" seemed to work. There already was a Sunday School class for this age group. I had nothing to do with that. I have an idea Frank and Marion Lyon taught it. I know they were vitally concerned that this group should flourish. It was my job to start a Sunday night group and to provide mid-week activities.

This was shortly after World War II, and there was an acute shortage of ministers. Many small churches were without pastors. Dr. Boggs suggested that our group might provide worship services for some of them. Instead of putting the whole responsibility on one person, he proposed that we have what we called "deputation groups" to split up the responsibility. I remember we went to Sylvania (the second oldest Presbyterian church in the state), Jacksonville, Cove Chapel, and Woodson, and perhaps some more. We would have someone read the Scripture, someone to provide "special music," someone to pray, someone to preach, and someone to take up the offering. If the church did not have a pianist, we would provide the musician. The group responded enthusiastically to this call for service, individuals taking on jobs they never dreamed of doing. Very seldom did I fill one of the slots. I would go along to coordinate the activities. But prior to our going, I would drive to the location, talk to an elder or other leaders, find out what their order of worship was, and tend to other details. In the process, I found that no two churches had the same order of worship. I began to wonder why they did what they did. I would come back and ask Dr. Boggs why things happened in a certain sequence. He was not always sure, unless they did it the way Second Church did. This was the cause of my first interest in liturgy, although I did not know the word at the time.

We also had Sunday night programs. I would line up speakers from the outside. After the presentation, there would be a chance for discussion, and this group was full of questions on any topic. One day Dr. Boggs showed me a document the General Assembly had approved for study in the churches. It was entitled "States Rights and Human Rights." It was probably the first social action document the PCUS (Southern Presbyterian Church) sent down for study. Dr. Boggs, being a loyal churchman, decided Second Church should look at it, and this group would be the ideal venue. However, he and I knew that it was an explosive topic. I consulted with him and with Ruth Puckett. We got three middle-aged, tested leaders in the community to agree to come one Sunday night to make presentations. I remember one was Mrs. Lillian McDermott, a civic leader and, I think, a School Board member; one was a Mr. McQuistion, head of the State Board of Education. I have forgotten who the third one was. This was considered such a revolutionary topic that we set up as ground rules that no questions would be allowed that first night after the presentations, but would be reserved for one week later, to allow for some cooling-off time. In the meantime, I was to have lined up tours during the intervening week to various parts of the community to let our young adults see if in fact "separate" was "equal." We took them to factories, schools, hospitals, libraries, social agencies, etc. Because Dr. Boggs was such a leading figure in the community, a request from him opened doors that otherwise would have been shut to such an inquiry. I went to all these places in advance to talk to the people in charge. I remember we went to Winburn Tile, as a factory; to the State Hospital, to look at the wards; to Baptist Hospital; to the Salvation Army. In the process of this, I met two individuals who changed my life. One was Lt. Norma Roberts with the Salvation Army. The other was the Reverend Franklin Henderson, pastor of the Allison Presbyterian Church. It was a black congregation in the Presbyterian Church, USA (Northern Church). I, who had grown up on a plantation and thought I knew all about black people, and who had refused even to speak to Charles Fielding at Berkeley College, met two people who were as educated, as cultured, as moral, as clean, as humble, as intelligent as I was. They did not fit any preconceived ideas I had of black people. I was drawn immediately to each of them. My stereotype was shattered. It was the closest thing I've ever had to a Saul of Tarsus conversion. Within one week, I turned 180 degrees! It was so obvious that "separate" was not "equal" as we went to these various institutions. And it was equally obvious that Lt. Roberts and Dr. Henderson were as qualified as anyone in our group.

There had been some rumblings in the congregation about this study on race relations. It had never been talked about openly at

Second Church, or most any other white church in the South at that time. Dr. Boggs said he had to calm down some of the men on his Session, assuring them I had grown up at Scott and knew the situation, and would not do anything revolutionary.

When we met the second Sunday night and had our discussion, it was clear that many of the group were jolted by what they had seen of "separate but equal" and were ready for some changes. It is important to realize this was five years before the *Brown vs. Board of Education* Supreme Court decision. The South as a whole was complacent about its "accommodation," although there was a lot of discontent in the North, and in certain circles in the South. But on the surface things were calm. The questions were open and frank that night. There was dismay that white Presbyterians were hardly aware there was a black Presbyterian Church in town, and they certainly did not have fellowship between the two. In response to my visit with Dr. Henderson, he issued an invitation to our young adults to come to a worship service at their church put on by their young adults. At this time, Allison Church was located on Ninth Street, the heart of the black community. Dr. Boggs, and I guess the Session, approved of this. It was held at night, when our two groups were off from work. There was great concern for the safety of our young adults, especially the women, going "down there." A few of the parents would not allow their daughters to go. But the service went off beautifully. I came out a changed man. Ties between Frank Henderson and me, and between Normal Roberts and me, were established that lasted until he died, and still she and I keep in touch.

The success of that young adult group was phenomenal. Attendance was high and was maintained all summer. There was an excitement and energy that brought some new life to Second Church. It gave me an insight into the workings of a Presbyterian church, and I grew to respect Dr. Boggs and Ruth Puckett. While I had said I would go to seminary on a one-year trial basis but was emphatic that I was not going into parish ministry, I began to waver on that. I loved everything I did that summer. I worked far more than half time and did not begrudge one minute that I gave. I also began to love the Presbyterian Church, for up to then, other than the family connection to the denomination, the only tie I'd had was at the Northern Presbyterian Church in Fayetteville on the weekends I was in town. The summer of 1949 was a turning point in my life.

I returned to New Haven a changed person in regard to race. Having my prejudice challenged in a Southern context, where I was not defensive, enabled me to see the absurdity of the position I had been defending. I knew there would be black people at YDS, and I was ready to accept them. However, I know there were traces of reluctance on my part. I made friends with the few blacks on campus, but I did not seek them out as closest friends. That took a little while longer. But the change Uncle Ken had predicted had begun, and to a large extent had been accomplished. I thank God for the summer of '49.

Life in Summer of 1949

As I said, I was working half time at Second Presbyterian Church—and doing far more than half time. Daddy would from time to time grumble about my being exploited, although he did not really object. He had protested strenuously when I first told them I was considering the ministry. I think he was jealous of Uncle Ken's influence over me, for indeed Uncle Ken was my spiritual father at a level Daddy had never been my emotional father. But Uncle Ken had visited Scott twice and had hosted my parents when they came up for graduation; and Daddy liked Dr. Boggs, so his resistance was melting. I think his opposition came not for fear of what the ministry would do to me, but what I might do to the Church. However, once I decided I was going to seminary, he told me he would finance my education, as far as I wanted it to go. And he certainly did that—without any grumbling or restrictions. I could not have asked for more support than I got from him, and from Mother—but hers had been there almost from the start.

The summer of 1949 was, I think, good for all of us. By this time, Art was working in Louisville, and Ann had married the previous summer. There were just the three of us in the house. My focus was shifting from Scott to Little Rock, although I had come to be friends with Mike Carozza, the pastor of All Souls. And All Souls wanted to give me financial aid for seminary. I protested that I did not need that, but Mike urged me to accept it gracefully, for if I did not, no one else from All Souls would—and Lucy Thibault and Tom Hathcote were both thinking about going into the ministry.

I had time that summer to swim, play tennis and golf and bridge, and date some. However, I realized my interests had changed so, as had those of the girls I had dated in high school, that I found most of them uninteresting. I do remember calling Marguerite "Grite" Rice and asking her for a date. But there were other girls who were friends — Pud Steele and Carolyn Alexander (I guess that was the summer she got married and I was involved in their parties and the wedding festivities). I think Truman had already left for Houston for her first job. And some of my PIE friends were still in college, and thus home for the summer. I also was involved socially with the people I was working with at Second, for many of them were friends from high school or family friends. One way or another, there was no lack of social life. In fact, I had a glorious time.

One thing I remember from that summer was going to a worship service at the newly organized Westover Hills Presbyterian Church where the newly ordained Richard B. Hardie was the pastor. It must have been his ordination service, although I do not recall that ceremony. But I do remember the little church was full of people. Second Presbyterian Church has been the motivating force in organizing this new congregation in the growing western part of Little Rock.

One person not at Second Church was Lamar Williamson, who was summer student at Pulaski Heights Presbyterian Church, under Bill Oglesby. I had always liked Lamar, but had limited contact with him. But while we were both busy, we did have some time together. I especially remember one night we decided we would go "church slumming." We went to a storefront service in North Little Rock put on by the Rescue Mission, then to something else that as going on in the city (I think), then to Immanuel Baptist where they were having a revival. We got there late and sat up in the balcony. I had never been to that church before (the largest Baptist church in the city) nor had I ever been to a Baptist revival. I have no memory of what was said, but it was the first time I ever heard the hymn "Amazing Grace" — which has become one of my favorites.

At the end of the summer just before I left for New Haven, we had a retreat for the Second Church group at Ferncliff. We asked Lamar to be the preacher at our worship service. I remember reflecting on Psalm 121, "I lift up my eyes to the hills…" in that setting. It was a time of real dedication of myself to the adventure of going to seminary, and I suspected, into the ministry.

My fieldwork at Yale Divinity School that fall was to be secretary to Uncle Ken. That had been what settled the issue of where I would go to seminary. This meant that I had to learn shorthand that summer, if I was going to take his dictation. I bought a shorthand book and made a few stabs at it, but procrastinated terribly. There were more interesting things on the agenda. Finally, ten days before I was to leave for New Haven, I settled down and started working on simplified shorthand—way too late. But I did concentrate almost exclusively on that and made some progress.

Art's Impending Marriage

While the summer of 1949 was mostly a joyous time for me, there was one negative aspect to it. Art was working in Louisville and had met Florence Hill and proposed to her. The problem, as far as my parents were concerned, was that she was Roman Catholic. They objected strongly to this. They would have to be married in the Catholic Church and Art would have to promise that their children would be reared as Catholics. This disturbed them greatly, especially Daddy. The problem was aggravated when a priest from Little Rock came down to talk with them and asked them to sign some papers. This was prior to Vatican II, and Roman Catholicism was very strict. They fretted about this all summer. Daddy said that he was not going to attend the wedding. Mother was as opposed as he, but she said she would go to the wedding. They thought they had expressed their opposition to the marriage to Art, but I did not feel they had communicated to him the violent opposition they felt.

Art had asked me to be the best man in his wedding. I, too, was aghast at his having to rear his children as Catholics, but I was not as opposed as our parents, and agreed to be best man. I felt that Art needed to know before the wedding just how strongly Mother and Daddy felt. I also wanted to meet Florence prior to the wedding. So I went through Louisville on my way back to New Haven and told him how violently our parents felt. He was completely surprised. I urged him to drive down to talk to them, which he said he would not do. Then I urged him at least to phone them and talk it out rather than having our parents act it out at the wedding. I am not sure, but I think he did phone, or write, or do something. Aunt Alice Campbell said she was going to the wedding, whether Daddy did or not, to show her support of Mother and of Art. Aunt Marion McCain, from Scarsdale, said she was going to do the same. In the end, Daddy did decide to go. He drove. Mother and the two aunts rode with them. Years later, Ann Payne was looking at some pictures from the wedding, and she asked, "Mother, what dress is that you were wearing?" Mother replied, "My black dress." Ann was shocked. "You mean you wore a black dress as mother of the groom?!" Mother said, "What else would I have worn?" I don't understand all the symbolism of women's dresses, but apparently that told a whole story.

Years later Florence told me her parents were just as opposed to her marrying a Protestant as the Campbells were to this marriage.

Eventually Florence won Mother and Daddy's hearts when they went to Morocco to visit Art and Florence. But she had to work at it. Later, when Florence's mother came to live with them, she and Mother came to be very good friends. Florence remained faithful to her religion. She urged Art to participate in Presbyterian churches when there was one on their construction sites. They had two children. Both were reared as Catholics, and both rejected it. I don't think Bruce had any church life when he was killed in an automobile accident. Bonnie's children were baptized in an Episcopal church because of Steve's membership there. I think they go to the Episcopal Church at Christmas and Easter.

It turned out neither of Art's siblings was present for his wedding. My appendicitis came back with a vengeance, and I had an appendectomy about 10 days before the wedding. I was not able to travel. Ann was pregnant and threatened to have a miscarriage, so she could not drive from Knoxville to Louisville. Hoyt wound up being the best man at the wedding.

Yale Divinity School Years

Returning to New Haven

An outsider looking at the Don Campbell who boarded the Missouri Pacific in September 1949 might not have noticed much difference from the one who left in June 1945, since he still looked so young he was mistaken for a high school student. One difference might have been observed in clothes (for he now had an Ivy League wardrobe), and there would have been no quivering of the chin or tears in the eye. Beneath the surface, though, there was a radically different person. Instead of fear, there was excitement and anticipation; instead of wondering about his ability to cope, there was self-confidence; instead of a flicker of faith growing out of desperation, there was a growing relationship with God and a pretty clear sense of call. I had received great affirmation through my work at Second Presbyterian Church that summer. Between Fayetteville and Little Rock, I had experienced a Saul of Tarsus conversion on race relations. After being elected to Phi Beta Kappa and graduating *magna cum laude*, and with the publication of my senior essay in the works, I knew that although I was not brilliant I certainly had what it takes intellectually, and so I had decided at Yale Divinity School to study to learn and enjoy, and not to worry about grades. Instead of launching forth into the unknown, I was heading back to familiar territory. Even though many of my closest friends had graduated and moved on, I did know people at Berkeley College and some at YDS, and most of all, I had a job as Uncle Ken's secretary and companion. One other change since 1945: I was traveling by coach and not Pullman! I could hardly wait for the day of departure.

The first stop on my trip was in Memphis. Frank McClain and Walter Lowrey were coming up from Mississippi to meet me. We had dinner in the formal dining room at the Peabody and then spent the night there before I took the train to Louisville to talk to Art about our parents' opposition to his upcoming marriage. The dinner was great. The dessert tray was tempting. I had never eaten a French pastry before, so decided to try one. Then in the middle of the night, I woke up violently ill and vomiting. I assumed I had food poisoning. We had eaten the same main meal, and the other two were not sick, but I was the only one who had had the French pastry. In retrospect, I am sure this was my first attack of appendicitis, but that never entered my mind at the time.

When they delivered me to the Louisville train, I was weak, nauseous, and aching all over. It was a miserable trip. I remembered that when children are sick at their stomachs pediatricians give them *warm* carbonated drinks, so all the way up I sipped on warm ginger ale and cokes, and ate nothing.

The Hills had all the family together to meet Art's brother. I had to apologize and pass up most of the food, and was not very good company. When I went to Art's room to spend the night, I told him about the situation at Scott. As sick as I was, I felt I had fulfilled my mission. I knew I would not change his mind, but I felt it was essential he be aware of their reactions.

From Louisville, I headed to New York and on to New Haven. I don't believe I stopped in Scarsdale this time, for I was needing to cram on my shorthand before Uncle Ken got back in town. How excited I was as the train approached New Haven — the familiar tones of the conductor — "Noo Haven, Noo Haven. All going to Hartford exchange trains here." I think someone — perhaps George Kearns or Dan Howard — met me and took my suitcases up to YDS.

When I walked onto the YDS campus, I was elated, excited, and felt a whole new chapter of my life was opening. The only fly in the ointment was my continued nausea and weakness from the spell in Memphis.

First Days at Yale Divinity School

I must have arrived at YDS as soon as the rooms were open, and before most of the students and faculty returned for the fall. I still had a very queasy stomach. It was hot, and I had to walk the two miles down the hill for food, then back up the hill, because the dining hall was not open. I remember thinking New Haven food in hot weather was as inappropriate in 1949 as it had been in 1945 — heavy and hot. I longed for some of the light dishes served in Arkansas in the summer!

I had to get settled in my room in Stuart House. There were eight small "houses" on the Quadrangle (which was patterned after the University of Virginia). Seven of them were rooms or suites for students. In the past, there had not been enough YDS single male students to fill them (especially during World War II), so a lot of students from the School of Forestry, just down the hill, lived there. But most of them were being pushed out this year to make room for our large class. Stuart House was an exception. Most of it was given to offices for the faculty. Uncle Ken had an apartment at the far end of the second floor. I think there were four other rooms on the second floor for students. I had a room of my own, with a shared bath for the whole second floor. I had stored some furniture I'd acquired during Berkeley days, especially my last semester—such as the rocking chair I'd spent too much time re-upholstering. Mother had a green corduroy cover made for my bed, with pillows, so my room could serve not only for sleeping, but also I could have company there.

Once I got fairly well settled, I sought out Ellie Hutchins at Berkeley College, partly because I looked forward to seeing her and considered her one of my best friends in town, but also because I wanted to ask her if I could hire her to improve my far-from-adequate shorthand. I dreaded Uncle Ken's arrival. She agreed to give me dictation, slowly at first, then speeding up. I think she stayed in the office after hours to do this. She also gave me some professional hints. I was lousy! I had really failed to do my homework. Fortunately, Uncle Ken was kind, patient, and accepted dictation that was full of errors. He had had student secretaries before, and I guess counted the companionship important enough to get incompetent dictation.

With a sick stomach and dreading my first dictation, I still was wonderfully happy to be back in New Haven. What a change from 1945!

YDS Orientation

I remember how excited I was—by being at Divinity School; by being an "old boy" because of my undergraduate years at Yale, and therefore able to help people find their way around New Haven; but most of all by the quality of my classmates. I think we were the largest entering class YDS had ever had (this was at the start of the "church boom," which would last through the '50s and '60s), and they said we had the largest number of Phi Beta

Kappas of any class. If I am not mistaken, more than half of the class were Phi Bates.

The people I was meeting were extremely stimulating. Perhaps six to eight of us had gone to Yale College—most of whom I had not known or known only by sight as an undergraduate. I did know Dick Vieth, Chet Miller, and Herb Bainton, but I did not find them terribly stimulating. Rick Mapes and Kelly Clark were much more so. And simply because we had all been at Yale, and because Uncle Ken soon invited them to be in our cell group, I got to know them well.

But the bulk of the class were from other colleges—from all over

Marquand Chapel in the Yale Divinity School quadrangle.

the country, both private and public, large and small. Each had been outstanding in his/her own class. About 10 percent of the class were women. I think they had a "quota." They were even more outstanding on the whole than the men, for the competition for their slots was intense. A fair percentage of the men were married and lived off campus, so I did not get to know them as well. But there were about 90 people for me to meet and relate to. For an extrovert, this was heaven! I'd go into the refectory and sit down at table with strangers, without any apology, and strike up a conversation. At the College, this would have turned off some people. At YDS, it was not only accepted, but expected. Once classes started, we were all under pressure, but in those orientation days we were free. We went to lectures and orientation talks, and had some parties.

I had also, over the summer, decided I wanted to get some exercise. (I did not realize how much walking I was going to have to do, being two miles from the center of the university and downtown.) I had brought my tennis racket and got in some games in those days. I played with John Fesperman, who was a Presbyterian from the South and was the organist at the chapel. He later became the organ expert at the Smithsonian in Washington. There was another guy with whom I played some—but at the moment I cannot dredge up his name. I think he and John were roommates. I had also stored my squash racket from Berkeley days. There was a squash court at YDS, and I inquired about others who might know how to play. I was not an athlete, and was not really good at any sport, but these I could do enough to enjoy them.

I remember meeting Ann Austin in those first days. She was obviously bright, was good looking, and from the start talked about social involvement. I have a dim memory of meeting Marnie Smith, and Bobbie Hall, her roommate, and found both Bobbie and Ann were Presbyterians. I think I met Bob Bailey and Bill Ward in that first week. The individuals have become something of a blur, but the overall impression was that these people were brighter than my class at Yale College had been, were much more open to forming friendships, and shared many of the same values. I don't know if it was during orientation or just in the early weeks of the fall, but Dan Howard and George Kearns came up the hill to see me in this "strange" environment. When they got to my door, they looked frightened, almost harried. They burst in, saying, "Who are these people? Everyone we met on the sidewalk *spoke* to us as though they knew us—and we have not even been introduced." There was a tremendous cultural difference from the College to YDS on friendliness—and from the start, I was more comfortable in the latter.

We had some worship services during that orientation. Marquand Chapel was a lovely New England-type sanctuary. I had become "hooked" on kneeling and from the start would sit over to the side so I could kneel and not be conspicuous. Pretty soon, Kelly Clark was doing the same.

The largest group of our students were Methodists, then Congregationalists, then I think came the Presbyterians. We had a whole mixture — Episcopalians, Baptists, two Greek Orthodox, and a number of people from overseas. From the start, I found this a "heady" mixture. I had a clear sense that I was where I belonged. I still had doubts about being a parish minister, but I was pretty sure I wanted to be ordained. In what denomination was still very much an open question.

Start of School at YDS

I had applied for, and received, a scholarship at YDS. It was not a terribly large one, but did help my parents. Later, after realizing how many students were struggling financially, with my parents' consent, I gave up the scholarship. At YDS, unlike the College where only scholarship students had to have bursary jobs, everybody had some kind of "field work." For the overwhelming majority, this meant working in a local congregation, often being in charge of youth work — and this required them to be there every weekend. Perhaps there was a shortage of churches to employ our large class, but to my surprise I found that my job as Uncle Ken's secretary would qualify as field work — on the grounds that it would expose me to the Ecumenical Movement in a rare, if not unique, way. Since I did not have a car, working in a church would have presented real transportation problems — although others managed it somehow. But it also meant that I was free to continue worshipping at Battell Chapel. The music there was outstanding, it was familiar, and I would continue to get to hear some of the outstanding preachers in the country.

Being a secretary was a challenge, to say the least. I was quite unprepared to take dictation. I did pretty well on typing, if I could read my shorthand. I typed on my portable manual Royal and had to make a carbon of each letter. I shutter when I remember how many mistakes I would make. Uncle Ken would write in corrections. If there were more than five per letter, I would rewrite it, but usually Uncle Ken would say, "Life's too short to waste time doing that," and would send it on out. I wonder what his correspondents thought about the quality of help at YDS. It was indeed a learning experience, for he wrote to everyone who was anyone in the

Ecumenical Movement around the world — most of them on a first-name basis. We'd write to "Pit" (Pitney Van Dusen, president of Union Seminary in New York), John (John Mackay, president of Princeton Seminary), Visser (Visser t' Hooft, president of the World Council of Churches), etc. When these people would come to the YDS campus for a visit, he would often invite me to join them for dinner. He would pay me by the hour. When I felt extremely guilty because I was so slow, I would trim my hours.

What I did not realize when I took the job was how much of it was as "companion." I thought he was an "old" man, though I now realize he was in his 60s! He was a bachelor. The secretary was to live on the same floor in Stuart House. We did not eat all meals together, but usually did have breakfast and often other meals when he was on campus. I did not realize how that would "identify" me on campus, and how it kept me out of much of the dormitory social life which went on in other houses. It also meant that I was responsible for providing him with Sunday night supper. We were not supposed to cook and eat in our rooms, but many people did. I had a hot plate and toaster, and acquired some dishes and eating implements. I had no refrigeration. In the winter, I could put milk out on the window ledge. I don't know what I did in hot weather. Maybe I would put it in the sink and run cold water over it. That is when I discovered Pepperidge Farm bread. I would on Saturday go to a small store on Whitney Avenue at the foot of the hill and buy some bread, margarine, soup (usually tomato), tea bags, milk, and often applesauce. It was simple, but seemed to meet his need for food and fellowship. (The refectory was not open on Sunday since most students were away.)

I found it a bit strange to share the bathroom with Uncle Ken. There were three other people living on the floor — George Lindbeck, Richey Hogg, and a Japanese graduate student. The showers at Berkeley all had doors, but the ones at YDS did not. I felt uncomfortable at first seeing Uncle Ken in the nude, but it did not seem to bother him.

When the second- and third-year and graduate students returned, the regular schedule of classes and chapel began. We had chapel every morning. It was led by a faculty member four days a week and a student on Friday, as I recall. The service lasted 20 minutes — from 10:10 to 10:30, and it was meant to stop promptly at

10:30. When someone, usually a student, ran over 10:30, Roland Bainton, though a Quaker and pacifist, would be very angry. He taught the introduction to church history course right after chapel. He wrote out his lectures in shorthand, then memorized them. They were designed to last 50 minutes, starting at 10:35. If class was late in starting, he did not get to finish his lecture, and the pacifist was angry.

Roland Bainton was a wonderful human being, and a brilliant scholar. His specialty was the Reformation. He had done a lot of work on the Quakers, but he had recently published *Here I Stand*, at the time considered the definitive biography of Martin Luther. He had a reputation of being a magnificent teacher, and his lectures were certainly polished. Most students loved him. I had thought when I came to seminary on a trial basis that I could not ever be a pastor, but that I could stomach being a professor of church history. But Roland Bainton turned me off completely to church history. At the College, history was taught in terms of great sweeping movements, and little attention was given to details. (Witness: I got honors on my senior exams writing for two hours on the cotton gin and did not know when it had been invented.) Bainton saw history in terms of individuals, and he demanded knowledge of dates and names and particulars. This was not history as I had come to love it. I never took another church history course, except in my last year when I took Uncle Ken's "World-wide work of the Church."

My First Semester

I did not come under care of Washburn Presbytery until Christmas 1950. But in the negotiations leading up to that, I had managed to get a waiver from both Greek and Hebrew in that they were not degree requirements at Yale, and in fact the school discouraged people from taking them unless they were going on for graduate work in Bible. This was shocking to Southern Presbyterians. But Dr. Boggs managed to get me the waiver. Then having done that, I decided I did want to take Greek! This was koine, not classical, Greek. We had a young man getting his Ph.D. in Greek, downtown, teach it. He was rather colorless, and I do not remember his name. I am not a linguist. I had to work hard, and was not great at Greek, but I am very glad I took it. Once we began to get the basic grammar and some vocabulary, we started reading the Gospel of John. I remember he said that if people read only John without the Synoptics, they would not like Jesus! And I found that to be true.

The New Testament course was a great disappointment. Paul Schubert came from Germany, many years before, but still had a heavy accent, and he tended to mumble. His lectures were dull, in my opinion — and that of most people. The only parts of his lectures which were interesting were the "asides" he would mumble out of the side of his mouth, and which only those sitting near him could hear. I finally learned this and started sitting up front. And when I later took seminars from him, where he made more such off-the cuff remarks, I found him much more interesting. We plugged through the New Testament, but it was a chore, and I caught little love for it.

The Old Testament course, on the other hand, was one of the most exciting I ever had the privilege of attending. B. Davie Napier had been chaplain at the University of Georgia, and I guess the year before was on sabbatical on the YDS campus. Second- and third-year students had known him as a "senior colleague" and said after dinner he would often go to the Common Room and jazz up gospel hymns to the great delight of the students, and to Uncle Ken's dismay (although he liked everything else about Napier). In comparison with most of the other faculty, he was young — probably in his late 30s. He was enthusiastic about the Old Testament and conveyed his excitement to I think everyone in the class. One of his great skills was reading the Old Testament aloud. He did this in class so we could "see" the characters, and he did it in chapel, along with excellent preaching. He adopted the Class of 1952, and we adopted him — witnessed by the fact he flew from California for the 50th anniversary of that class, although his wife was very ill and he was almost blind. From the first day, this was my favorite class, and remained so the rest of the year. I was about ready to become a Jew because the New Testament failed to excite me as much as the Old.

Davie Napier was not the only new senior faculty member. David MacLennan had been pastor of the largest United Church of Canada congregation in Toronto, the largest city in Canada. There, he was highly regarded for his preaching and was a major "citizen" in the city. When he came to Yale, he found he was one of several hundred full professors at Yale, and at the Divinity School homiletics was regarded by the rest of the faculty, and especially by most students, as the lowest level on the Totem pole, unless it was Christian Education. Mr. MacLennan went into shock. In the first semester, I took his course "The Art of Preaching," which included a study of the history of preaching. I found it very dull, having to read all those old sermons. I did not find him interesting or inspiring. But somehow I got to know him on a personal level. It must have been through Uncle Ken. I think I had a date or two with one of his daughters. I was able to see how he, and his wife, were suffering and had compassion on them as people, and saw how cruel Yale, and YDS, could be.

On the other hand, all year long I took a course called "Platform Personality" taught by William Muehl. Despite the name, it was a course on public speaking. Mr. Muehl had never had one day of theological education. He had graduated from the University of Michigan Law School. I was never sure how he wound up at YDS. He had the reputation of being one of three of the most politically liberal faculty on a liberal campus. At this time, despite my conversion on race, I was still a conservative Republican. I went into his class with a prejudice against him. The first day, he had each of us get up and talk for two minutes about any subject so he could hear us speak. When I sat down, he asked, "Mr. Campbell, where are you from?" When I told him from Arkansas, he asked, "Where did you go to college?" When I told him Yale College, he exclaimed, "You mean you have been gone four years and you still sound like that?"

This was the beginning of what became, and remains, a real friendship. I took every course he had to offer. Of the four professors of preaching, he was by all odds the most helpful one.

So these were my professors my first two semesters. The daily chapel services were also an inspiration for me (most weeks). The faculty would rotate, preaching four of the five days. On Friday, a student could volunteer to preach (the quality ran from excellent to awful), and the all-male choir would sing. The choir was always excellent, as was the organ music. I very rarely missed a chapel service, although many students did skip them. In addition, I would normally go to Battell Chapel downtown on Sunday mornings, and I continued to find the music, the prayers, and most of the sermons uplifting.

The only course change in that first year was in the spring when "Art of Preaching" was replaced by "Church Music," taught by Luther Noss, who was the University organist and director of the Battell Chapel choir, and a professor at the School of Music. I had admired his work at Battell ever since I came. I was not, nor am, a musician. But I found his insights about music exciting. He probably made me more of a "musical snob" than I already was. It was he who said "In The Garden" was the worst hymn ever written. I grew in my appreciation of the role of music in worship, and it has led me ever since to give that great attention in trying to integrate the whole worship service into a whole. I never had any personal contact with Mr. Noss.

As we moved past orientation to real school, I found the other students even more stimulating as I got to know them better. I don't think there was a "dumb" or even "mediocre" student among the 400 student body, including Ph.D. candidates. There were a few who were "dull," but not many of them.

Once Uncle Ken got back on campus he began to invite people to be part of one of the cell groups that he organized and that met in his living room. Being his secretary and having come out of a group in Berkeley College, I was of course invited. He had two groups. With the passing of years, I realized one was more "Ivy League" and the other was more "South and Midwest." (I wonder if he ever realized this stratification.) I was in the former. He usually set a limit of 12, wisely, for past that number there would not be time for all to participate. Rather than go into the dynamics of that group here, I'll write about it separately. But I want to note that Uncle Ken had two weekly groups at YDS and one at Berkeley College, taught a Sunday School class at First Baptist Church, and may have had a group at the Missions House (though I am not sure of that). I never ceased to be amazed how, with his teaching load, his heavy writing schedule, his out-of-town trips to meetings and to give lectures, he was ever able to keep these commitments. But they had top priority for him. Except when he was out of town, I don't remember his ever having missed one.

During that first semester, I continued to play a little tennis and found one or two people who would play squash. But soon my hope of being more athletic faded away.

First Year Cell Group

Although Uncle Ken had in the 1920s made the motion to admit women to YDS, at this time his cell groups were all male. (Later on, I am told, he did have women in them. I think Susan Walker Graybill was the one who blasted her way in.) We met in the living room in Uncle Ken's apartment in Stuart House, just down the hall from my room. I can't remember whether we met for an hour or hour and a half. I think the former. We always began promptly and ended promptly.

In many ways this was similar to the group I'd been in at Berkeley, but I felt closer to the others at YDS because we had such similar commitments, and I was therefore freer to open up some of my inner life. It was a very stimulating group. I can't recall all who were in this, but I do remember Kelly Clark, Rick Mapes (both from Yale College, but not my friends there), Kentaro Buma, Elick Bullington, Dewitt Farrabee, Al Allenby (whose parents and brother had drowned in a sailing accident just before school started), and Frank Geddes. There were surely also some people in second and third year who had been in this group before.

Each year, as a group was formed from old and new members, Uncle Ken would begin by telling his "story" and then would invite us to do the same. Usually two or three people could do that in an evening, with some time for questions and comments.

I remember Frank Geddes telling about his experience with a para-church spiritual group in California and somehow I found it was the same one Bob (Cluck) Martin from Little Rock had been in. Cluck was one of my brother's best friends and had participated in the group I had just led at Second Church, Little Rock.

I remember Kelly Clark telling how he had grown up in an unchurched family in southern California. (I knew from other sources that they were very wealthy, for his grandfather had been a "leather baron" in the late nineteenth century.) His only contact with church had been when, once a year, his "horsy" prep school would have all the students ride their horses down to a nearby Episcopal Church for one worship service. He had come to Yale College and had never been in Battell Chapel or met any of the chaplains. In his senior year (he was in one of the senior societies — but not one of the Big Ones), he had been asked to organize and run the fund-raising dinner for Dwight Hall. In the process, he met the chaplains and was so impressed by them he decided to go to Battell Chapel one Sunday. Then he went a few times to the noonday services at Dwight Chapel. I remember seeing him there, but did not know him. He did not know what he wanted to do on graduation, and the Dwight Hall staff were so impressed by his possibilities that they asked him to be on their staff for 1948-49. During that year, he felt called to the ministry and applied to YDS. He came totally "unscathed" by religious upbringing and was wide-eyed with enthusiasm for what was being unfolded. Once in Old Testament, Davie Napier told everyone to turn to Numbers. Kelly raised his hand and said, "Numbers what?" He did not know there was a book in the Old Testament by that name. Another time I saw him in the library studying. He was racing through page after page. I asked him why the rush. He had started on the story of David and "wanted to see how it came out." (Kelly later got his Ph.D. in Old Testament, taught and was dean in a theological seminary in Singapore and later in the Philippines, then wound up as headmaster of St. Paul's Prep School.)

But the story that made the most impression on me came from Kentaro Buma, a Japanese student. (You need to realize this was just four years after the end of World War II.) He said his father had been pastor to a Japanese congregation in Manila. His father was very much opposed to the increasing militarism in Japan. At the time of Pearl Harbor and the Japanese invasion of the Philippines, he was in a very difficult situation. Because of his age and occupation, he was not drafted into military service. He did everything he could to keep Ken and his young brother, Kyoji, from being forced into the service, but finally he could protect Ken no longer. He was in the Japanese army when the Allies re-took the islands, and he was put in a prisoner-of-war camp until the war ended.

There was a silence at the end of his story. Then Rick Mapes asked, "Which POW camp were you in?" Ken gave the name. Rick asked, "What dates were you there?" Ken told him. Rick quietly said, "I was a guard at that camp at that time." There was electricity in the air. There was bonding. (At the 50th reunion of the class, in 2003, Rick Mapes organized the reunion, and Ken Buma flew back from Japan to receive an award for outstanding service to the worldwide Church.)

This cell group played a major role in my growth at YDS. It sustained and challenged me. Some of the people in it became some of my best friends.

Beauty of the Fall

I had been in New Haven four previous falls and had seen some of the foliage. But I was downtown and rarely got very far from campus. The one exception was one weekend the Arthur McCains came through New Haven on the way to Wallingford to see Arthur, Jr., whom they had sent to Choate Prep School. (He was out of hand in Scarsdale.) Up there, the colors were spectacular, far more so than in New Haven.

But that fall of 1949, I remember the autumn colors as being outstanding. That may have been partly due to my frame of mind. I was glad to be back in New Haven, and I was really happy at YDS. The elms in the Quadrangle were beautifully yellow — almost anything could be in that Quadrangle — and the Virginia creeper on the walls was crimson. Also, I was walking down and back up Prospect Street several times a week — partly to go to church, some to run errands, but also several trips a week to get Ellie Hutchins to help me build up speed on shorthand.

On Prospect Street, there were many trees and also a Yale garden that had some unusual trees in it, and then there was the Grove Street Cemetery with its old trees, and those on the Green. I remember it as a time of golden leaves, blue skies, warm but not hot weather. Is this all a fantasy? Whatever it may be, I recall a happy time in the midst of great beauty.

Appendectomy

One night toward the end of October, Uncle Ken had invited me to go with him to hear the Boston Symphony orchestra. I was very eager to hear and see it in person. But I became violently nauseated and ached all over, so had to cancel on him. The next morning I was still sick. Uncle Ken insisted I go not to the student health center, but to his friend and doctor, Dr. Deaton — the one who had turned me down for Yale-in-China. He checked me out and said it was appendicitis and sent me to the Yale New Haven Hospital for surgery that afternoon by one of the Yale surgeons. The doctor called my parents and told them what was happening, that it was routine, and that he would let them know when it was over. Then he forgot. Mother and Daddy were to go out for dinner with Aunt Marion, but several hours had elapsed, and Mother would not leave until she got a report. Finally, by the hardest, they tracked down the doctor who apologized for forgetting.

This surgery meant that I could not go to Art's wedding. I was ambivalent. I was disappointed because I wanted to support Art, but I was also relieved because I was opposed to the promises Art was having to make to marry Florence in those pre-Vatican II days. I was back in my room on the YDS campus on the wedding day, and I spent the afternoon in prayer for them.

When I could not be best man, Art invited Hoyt, and he accepted, although Hoyt was much more anti-Catholic than I. He and Ann were going to drive up from Knoxville, but at the last minute Ann, who was pregnant, was showing signs of distress in her pregnancy, and the doctor would not allow her to make the drive. So neither Ann nor I got there; Hoyt and Mother and Daddy were there, but very much opposed. Breck Campbell drove up and was one of the ushers. On the way to the reception, he honked the horn of his car and got arrested and taken to jail. Mr. Hill spent most of the time of the reception getting him out.

It was not an auspicious start. Yet it turned out to be a great marriage.

It was the first surgery I'd had since my tonsils as a baby and then having my ears opened. It was the only time I could remember being a patient in a hospital, except right after my high school PIE initiation. I did not feel lonely in the hospital, and certainly was not scared (it happened too fast for that). I was first put in a room with three other men, and it was noisy. I was loaded with homework and had hoped I could at least do a lot of reading while I was missing classes, but that was impossible in that room. I surely did yearn for privacy and quiet until I got a private room. That was much more pleasant—although I still did not get much reading done.

Uncle Ken came to see me almost every day. I remember Sidney Lovett, the university chaplain, came to see me. I was very impressed, for even though I had been going to Battell Chapel for four years, he did not know me. It was probably routine for him to visit all Yale students in the hospital, but I was still grateful.

The person who surprised me most was Dick Stazesky, who came over three or four times. He did not have a car, so that meant he walked four miles each way. I had come to know Dick since arriving the month before, but he was not one whom I was seeing every day. I have felt close to him ever since. And the way he has kept the Class of 52 together shows this was just part of his pastoral touch.

When I returned to YDS, I was severely limited in what I could do. I had my whole belly taped. Rickey Hogg told me that there would be just a small round hole in my stomach, for they did not have to cut people open any more. So I was very curious when they removed the tape—and found Richey had been lying, as he often did. I think for the first couple of days they brought me food from the refectory, for I was not up to going up and down the stairs. But before long, I could walk over there—slowly.

One of the distresses I felt (or was it a subconscious desire to escape?) was that I had to miss Art's wedding to Florence. I knew there would be a lot of tension in Louisville. I don't believe my dislike of conflict could have caused my appendix to act up—or could it?

I had been warned that it would be six months before I would feel really good again. I dismissed that idea. Within a month I was walking at my usual speed, and even began to play squash, I think. I thought I was completely well. Then six months later, all at once I began to feel *really* strong and full of energy. I have had it explained to me since then that anesthesia is a poison that almost kills you, but not quite, and it takes the body six months to get it completely out of one's system.

I guess I was out of school for a week to 10 days. That really threw me behind, for the workload was heavy.

First Year Friends

When I returned to New Haven, most of my closest friends at Yale College had left, though there were a few I knew. Bard Smith was one of them, and Rudy Everest. I continued going to Battell Chapel most Sundays, but I don't think I ate any meals at Berkeley. The downtown people I felt closest to were Ellie Hutchins, and Mr. and Mrs. Hemingway who were still in the

Master's House. I also re-established contact with Bill and Tootsie Beasley, the Hornors' friends whom I had seen off-and-on during undergraduate days. I would also see Mrs. Yates at the Sterling Library check-out desk.

The center of my life definitely shifted up the hill to YDS. Because I lived in Stuart House, I was not in hourly contact with other students the way most were. Uncle Ken had an apartment on second floor. Most of the other rooms were offices for faculty. There were four of us living in rooms on the second floor — Richey Hogg (one of Uncle Ken's first secretaries and soon to be the husband of his niece) who was finishing up his Ph.D. under Uncle Ken; a Japanese scholar working on his Ph.D. on the nature of Christ based on the Psalm "the Lord said to my Lord" — and who never got the Ph.D.; and George Lindbeck who was finishing up work on his Ph.D. in the history of doctrine and who may have been an instructor or reader for Robert Calhoun. Soon after I left, he became a full-time faculty member and has had a very distinguished career in academic theology. He was one of the observers at Vatican II. All three were working very hard on their theses and were not in the market for friendly chit-chat, except Richey was somewhat.

At first I did not feel especially close to Dick Stazesky, but after his several trips to see me in the hospital, I felt much closer. I clicked right away with Bob Bailey, a Methodist from Minnesota, and Bob Ward, a Methodist from Michigan. They were almost inseparable. DeWitt Farabee and Elick Bullington, both from Georgia, became friends. In the fall I got to know George Chauncey, from Southwestern in Memphis, but was not especially close to him until we rode together from Memphis to Rock Island for the Interseminary Conference after Christmas. From then on, we were very close friends. On that same trip I met Mag, Bill Jones's wife, and got to know Bill much better. They were both from Memphis, also.

I got to know Kelly Clark and Rick Mapes much better, especially Kelly. I guess it was in the winter or spring that students put on T. S. Eliot's play *Murder in the Cathedral* with Bill May as Thomas á Becket. He did a magnificent job. I had not known him well, but I learned that he was thinking about transferring from YDS to the English Department downtown. I asked him if he would like an introduction to Sam Hemingway and ended up taking him to a mid-week tea in the Master's House. Bill was nervous as a cat on a hot tin roof. In the middle of tea, he looked down and realized he was wearing socks of very different colors. He tried to hide his feet under the chair and almost fell forward.

Bob Lynn was close to Bill May, and soon gravitated to Bob Batchelder and John Turnbull, George Todd, Betty Carpenter, Ann Austin, and Gregor Thompson as the core of the "social activist" clique, with Professor Ken Underwood as their "den daddy." They put on a weekly radio program called "Religion at the News Desk." I was not part of this group at all, for I was still very conservative. I think we liked each other, but we were operating on different wavelengths. But when I went back for 50th reunion, they were some of the people I most wanted to see.

Will Campbell sat next to me in Bainton's church history class. Bainton had us sit alphabetically to help get names and faces together. At the time I thought Will was the most "country" person in the class, with hayseed almost coming out of his hair, and probably the last person in the class from whom we could expect anything. He has turned out to be probably our most productive and influential member. Through the years, we have become good friends, even up to the present, for we have worked together on race relations through the decades.

I also "clicked" with Frank Geddes and his future wife Ginny, Winthrop Nelson, Jim Borden (who became choir director), John Eigenbrodt (organist after John Fesperman left), Jack Gessell (doing graduate work), and some of the women at 401, the women's dormitory down the street—Marnie Smith, Bobbie Hall, Betty Carpenter, and Ann Austin.

My pattern throughout life has never been to have one "best friend," nor even to be pretty well identified with a small group. I saw that happening on campus. My living in Stuart House would have made that difficult anyway. In many ways my closest associate was Uncle Ken, and I think people identified me with him. That suited me fine, for by not being linked to any one group of students, I felt free to sit and visit with any. This has been a lifelong pattern—not to have any intimate friends, but to have a large collection of friends on the next level of intimacy.

Even in the first year, and more in the second, I found that my room, which was right at the head of the stairs to the second floor, became a waiting room for people who had signed up for appointments with various professors, but especially Albert Outler who did a lot of counseling. And sometimes, when they emerged from those sessions, they would come to my room to "decompress" before facing the world. This is how I first got to know Marnie Smith well.

I found the variety and intelligence and commitment of students that first year exciting and stimulating.

First Year Disillusionment

It is very common for undergraduates, taking their first academic course in the Bible or theology, to find all their beliefs shattered. It is also common for people entering a liberal theological seminary such as Yale Divinity, if they have come from a conservative background, to have a similar experience.

My disillusionment was not like that. I had so little knowledge of the Bible, and no real theology I could articulate, that I never went through the demolition phase of construction. Also, I had the steadying hand of Uncle Ken in our daily contacts and in the cell group.

What I did experience was the disillusionment of finding the Bible not uplifting or challenging, but just plain hard work—mastering the facts, studying the theories, facing up to the inconsistencies. Up to this point, since my re-awakening in the 12th grade, I had had to "hide" my Bible reading; I had gone to chapel, but did not bring it to the attention of others. Now reading the Bible had not the allure of "forbidden fruit" but was just a routine class assignment, and I was usually behind in it.

Also, I was finding that the love I had always had for history was turning into dust under Roland Bainton's presentation of church history. It became clear to me that I did not want to spend my life in this field.

The New Testament course, under Schubert, was plain dull.

I was also going through disillusionment with Uncle Ken. I had always put him on a pedestal, and now, as I lived with him day by day, I found he was a human being who had clay feet.

And some of my stimulating classmates, who seemed so exciting in orientation, disappointed me. There were some who regularly skipped chapel and derided it. There were those who secretly made fun of Uncle Ken, and of his emphasis on prayer. While I don't think anyone was dropped from our class for low grades, some certainly did not seem to work hard. I was pretty sheltered in Stuart House, but it was clear in other houses there was a good bit of drinking and smoking. Cliques began to form — the social activists, the campus ministry group, the missionary group, the small group interested in prayer. The married students tended to live apart from the singles living on campus. And I suppose some thought the "Ivy League" crowd set ourselves apart.

What I was learning was that theological students are human beings, and I guess I expected a gathering of angels. I'm glad I got hit with that early.

Glimpses into Uncle Ken

While I had known Mr. Latourette, then Uncle Ken, for four years at Berkeley College, there was a radical shift in my relationship to him when I became his secretary and companion at YDS. What a rare privilege it was to see this world-renowned scholar "up close" and in intimate ways.

He was a bachelor who lived in an apartment in Stuart House, at the other end of the hall from my room. He had a living room and one bedroom, with no private bath. He kept a "slop jar" in his room for what in China they had called "night soil." Every morning he would bring it down to the rest room, empty it, and wash it out. He showered there and went to the toilet where the other four of us did. He rose so early that usually he was finished before others woke up, but not always.

Once he told me that shortly after World War II, when fuel was still severely rationed in Great Britain, he was giving a series of lectures at a Quaker College. He came down with a cold that went to his chest. The rooms were always chilly. So he decided to draw a hot bath and soak in the tub in the communal bathroom. A student came in as he was soaking. When the student realized who he was, he said, "I didn't know you looked like that" to which Uncle Ken replied, "I usually don't." Most people did not know he had a good sense of humor.

He was very patient and kind — I Corinthians 13 spelled out. When I think of the mess I made of his correspondence, especially in those first months, I am ashamed. My shorthand was terrible, and my typing not much better. I would make up to 10 mistakes in a long letter. Some of them I insisted on re-typing after he had made corrections. But if there were only three or four and I offered to re-type, he would say, "Life's too short for that" and sign them.

He was a "loner," but also at times "lonely." I am sure that is why, as he got older and Mrs. Lincoln retired as his secretary, he began having student secretaries. I think I was about the fourth. I discovered after I got there that part of the job was to fix Sunday night supper, since the refectory was closed. He was always grateful.

Every so often, on no schedule, he would invite me to have dinner with him (usually on Sunday) at the Graduate Club. There was also

Kenneth Scott Latourette.

a Faculty Club, to which he belonged, and we ate there once or twice, but he preferred the Graduate Club, which was "stuffier" and more sedate with no frills, but quite expensive. This is where the senior faculty and wealthy citizens of New Haven went. The waiters all knew him, for he ate there often. That is also where he got his haircuts. There was very little to cut, for he was bald with only a fringe of white hair around the edges. One of his favorite sayings was "Hair won't grow where there is the most activity. That's why there are so many bald-headed men and so few bearded women."

I have never seen anyone else as disciplined as he was. He set himself a quota of writing 5,000 words a week. If he was going to be out of town for a week, he would write 10,000 the week before he left. Other professors kidded that they might produce a baby in nine months, but Uncle Ken produced a book every nine months. His publication list was staggering.

But despite his work ethic, I never knew him to turn down any present or former student who wanted time to talk with him. He carried a little black book with his appointments in it. If someone wanted to see him, he would turn to the book and suggest a time. If people came knocking on his door, he would set aside whatever he was doing and invite them in—for as long as they wanted to stay. He was not a "counselor" in the sense that Albert Outler was. He was a mentor and friend. I came away from my years with him with a sense of inferiority about my self-discipline, but committed to make time for people whenever they came, since, as he used to say, "interruptions are often God's way of telling us to slow down and listen."

I gather when this young bachelor, already a full professor, came back to New Haven, he was involved in the social life of the Yale academic community. He would refer from time to time to dinner parties he attended and the people with whom he associated. He also let me know that at one time he had proposed marriage to someone who turned him down. He never told me who it was.

He did tell me that he dropped out of the social life in New Haven when he decided to write his seven volume *History of the Expansion of Christianity*, the work that made him world famous. The first volume was published in 1937, the last in 1945. He must have started his research about 1934 or 1935. I know that when he was working on his five-volume *History of the Church in the Nineteenth and Twentieth Centuries*, I asked him why "five." He said his mother had made him promise never to do another seven-volume project. And he didn't want to "fudge" on her by doing six large volumes! I guess she saw what the seven-volume project did to his personal life. It was on the completion of the seventh volume that his fame and reputation exploded. It's significance was that it was the first time anyone had written a church history that included the whole world. All other histories had been written for a particular country, or if they claimed to be inclusive, dealt only with Western Europe and North America. Uncle Ken had worldwide concerns, from his involvement in missions. He also read about 10 languages, including such difficult ones as Chinese, Japanese, and Russian.

Visiting professors would ask where his research assistants were, assuming others had done a lot of the digging for this information. There were none! He had done all the research himself, traveling to various parts of the world for the information he could not get in the U.S. He spent a lot of time in Rome at the Vatican Library. He told me he was invited to have a private audience with the Pope. I guess this would have been Pius XI, during the 1930s. He gave the Pope one of his books, bound in white leather. He had to wear white tie and tails at the audience. He said he remembered how foolish he felt as he rode the street car in the middle of the day in such formal dress. Later, when he would go abroad, he would take a clerical collar (although he never wore one in the U.S.) because a clerical satisfied the needs of any occasion that called for formal clothes. Maybe he learned that after the visit with the Pope. But this was one Baptist who did have a clerical collar.

I had no idea at Berkeley that Uncle Ken was anything more than a typical Yale professor. Perhaps it was not until 1945 that his reputation really exploded. That was the year Sam Hemingway asked him to become a fellow of Berkeley. No college had sought him out before. With the completion of *Expansion*, honors began coming from all directions. It was good to see his "feet of clay" in the pride he took in the number of honorary doctorates that were awarded to him. He probably had received some before 1945, but that is when the flood started. I think in 1953 when he retired, he had 14 honorary degrees! The one that pleased him most was from Oxford, given in 1948 when he was in Europe for the founding of the World Council of Churches. That same year he also received one from Glasgow. Those were the two, being in red, which made him stand out in any academic procession. He was also proud of the one from Princeton. And he used to tell about when he was given one by Baylor. The president said, "Sir, Baylor University bestows on you this degree even though you are a damn Yankee and an evil old bachelor." Uncle Ken owned only two suits, I think, but when he was going to be in an academic procession, he would look over the hoods and robes the way a lady might review her hats or dresses before a big occasion.

Uncle Ken always wore a three-piece blue suit with a watch chain and his Phi Beta Kappa key across the vest. During my Yale days, most professors would wear their keys all the time. I never wore mine once, nor do I ever see anyone these days wearing one. I bought Malcolm one, but he has never worn it I am sure. Neither has he worn a three-piece suit! It was a different academic culture.

Uncle Ken was really at the top of the academic ladder at Yale. He had been the Willis James Professor of Missions until the University decided to make him a Sterling Professor, the highest rank at Yale. I think there are about 10 throughout the whole university. There was a little question about the Divinity School getting a Sterling professorship, because Mr. Sterling was anti-religious. But the secretary of the University said Mr. Sterling was very interested in history, so Uncle Ken was Sterling Professor of Church History and Missions. I don't know what the annual salary was for a Sterling, but it was generous. He spent very little and saved a lot. He told me in his will he was leaving his estate, after some family gifts, to the Day Missions Library. I am told toward the end of his life he was so unhappy with the direction the Divinity School was taking that he was about to change his will and give it elsewhere, until Ray Morris, the former YDS librarian, talked him into leaving it to the library. I think it was well over half a million dollars in 1968, when that was a lot of money.

Uncle Ken was chair of the Graduate Studies Committee at the Divinity School. This was the group that accepted or rejected candidates for higher degrees, approved their programs, and made the final decision on whether or not they were granted the degree. And they did turn down a number. The Japanese scholar who lived next door to me never got his, and Harriet Taylor, I am told, never got hers. Just before I graduated, they made a new rule. Up to that point, most of the doctoral candidates who did not get the degree had been ones who had left after their comprehensive exams "with all but the dissertation" and had failed to complete that, or with an acceptable quality. Under Uncle Ken, the rule was changed to say that a dissertation had to be written in the New Haven area so there could be regular and early supervision to prevent these too numerous disasters.

After I left, there was a big fight. The doctoral programs were all shifted to the Graduate School downtown. The faculty were put on two levels. The "real" faculty, of high academic stature, were made faculty in the Department of Religion downtown, but could teach at YDS. The "lesser" ones, and those in "lesser" fields such as Christian Education, preaching, etc., were Divinity School faculty. I gather there were real battles, hurt feelings, and strained relationships as a result. I don't know if this is the direction that made Uncle Ken almost change his will. I do not think he would have approved of having first-class and second-class faculty.

One other comment about the inner workings of Uncle Ken and YDS has to do with women. Back in the 1920s, not too long after Uncle Ken came on the faculty, Dean Brown opened up a discussion on whether or not to admit women. Uncle Ken was, I guess, the only bachelor on the faculty. He told me he asked for the privilege of making the motion to admit women. I was shocked a few years ago when a woman graduate wrote an article about what a male chauvinist Uncle Ken was, opposing the admission of women and downgrading them in his classes. I know those statements to be false.

Generally Uncle Ken was quiet and reserved. I'm sure many regarded him as stern, for he did not smile a great deal. However, knowing him as intimately as I did, I knew there was a lighter side of him. He did enjoy a good story, and he could tell one. He also is the source of the only "clean" limerick I ever heard:

> There once was a woman named Bright
> Whose speed was faster than light.
> She got up one morning
> Took off in the dawning,
> And came back the previous night.

Even though it is out of order chronologically, there is one story I want to tell about Uncle Ken, for it represents how he was identified with Yale, especially Yale Divinity School and Stuart House where he lived from the time the new YDS campus was opened.

Bill Muehl came on the YDS faculty as an instructor in public speaking but wound up a professor of preaching. He, like Uncle Ken, had never had a theological education. He had graduated from the University of Michigan Law School. Politically, he and Uncle Ken were at opposite ends of the spectrum, for he was extremely liberal and Uncle Ken was one of two Republicans on the faculty. Bill was a "this world" political activist, and no one would ever have accused him of being sentimental or into "spiritualism."

On Christmas night 1968, Bill said he had been cooped up at home all day, and the children were driving him crazy. He made an excuse for leaving by saying there was something he needed to check in his office, which at the time was located in Stuart House. In fact, all the rooms in that building were offices except Uncle Ken's suite on the second floor. Bill said he was about ready to go back home to face the ruckus there when he heard the outside door of Stuart House open and close and footsteps come up the first steps, across the hall, up the flight to the second floor, and down the hallway to Uncle Ken's rooms. At that point according to Bill, Uncle Ken had suffered a mild stroke, so he dragged one foot slightly, producing a special sound as he walked—step, drag, step, drag. "It's sad for Ken to be here alone on Christmas night," Bill thought. "I'll go up and wish him a Merry Christmas."

He knocked on Ken's door, but there was no answer. He knocked again, more loudly. He thought, "There's no way he could have gone to bed and fallen asleep this quickly," so he went down to the communal bathroom, but there was no one in it. He thought, "Perhaps some tramp has come in," so he checked the doors of every room in the building and found them all locked. Finally, he shrugged his shoulders in puzzlement and went home.

He said, "You can imagine my amazement the next morning when I read in the New Haven paper that Ken Latourette had been hit by a car and killed instantly on Christmas night in Oregon City, Oregon, his hometown." Typical of Uncle Ken, he had already written all his thank-you notes and decided to walk down on a dizzly night to drop them in the mailbox. He was wearing a black coat and carrying a black umbrella, and a woman driving down the street did not see him and ran over him. Bill went on to say, "I've tried every rational explanation I can think of, but have finally given up."

I asked him, "What time of night did this happen?" He thought for a minute, then replied, "About 8:30." I sat there in silence a minute, then said, "Uncle Ken was hit and killed at 5:30 West Coast time."

First Year Social Life

Looking back on it, I don't recall much about my social life that first year at YDS. Since I was pretty much isolated in Stuart House, most of it took place in the refectory at meals. Sometimes, especially at breakfast, I would eat with Uncle Ken, but not most meals. I felt free to sit with almost anyone there—much freer than I had been at Berkeley College. I rejoiced in the more open, more democratic atmosphere at YDS. I guess there were some to whom I gravitated more—George Chauncey (especially after Christmas), Kelly Clark, Bob Bailey, Elick Bullington, Jack Gessell (graduate student), Harriet Taylor (middle-aged graduate student), Bobbie Hall, Marnie Smith, Ann Austin, Frank Geddes, etc. There was usually a gathering in the Common Room after dinner, often with Kim Underwood playing the piano and some people singing. I did not sing and usually felt pressure to get back to studying, so would pause, then go to my room.

On weekends many of the students who had church assignments would be gone much of Saturday and all day Sunday, so the campus emptied to a large extent. The refectory was closed all day Sunday. I would have breakfast at George and Harry's on my way to church. I can't remember what I did about the noon meal on Sundays. From time to time, Uncle Ken would invite me to the Graduate Club, but that was not a standing invitation. I don't think I ever went back to Berkeley. Then on Sunday nights I would serve Uncle Ken supper when he was in town, which was most of the time.

Sometimes we would go to movies on Friday or Saturday nights, especially to the Lincoln Theater that had foreign and art films. We had to walk everywhere. I never went to any of the football games or concerts downtown.

I did not date any of the women at 301. Some of the students did, and several of them paired off rather quickly. I liked the women there, but I was not drawn to them date-wise. Marnie was the most attractive of the lot to me, but I thought she was too fat.

The Charlie McCains, in New York City, had friends from all over the country whose daughters were at boarding school or college in the area, and Cousin Frances and Cousin Charlie invited me to serve as an escort for them. I don't remember the name of the first such date, although I think she came from Nashville. Nor do I recall the play, but afterward they suggested we go to the Plaza Hotel where Hildegaard was performing at the Persian Room. I had heard her on the radio for years, especially her theme song, "Darling, je vous aime beaucoup, Je ne sais pas what to do." It was a real thrill for me to be there. My date had a drink. I was a teetotaler at the time so had a coke.

Another weekend, with another girl, they suggested that we go to the Blue Angel nightclub after the play. It was "the" in spot, I had read in the *New York Times*. When we got seated, my date went to the ladies' room. A middle-aged man sitting next to me leaned over and said, "Son, do you realize how expensive this place is?" I responded, "Thank you, sir. But I have the money to pay for it."

Of the various girls they paired me with, Thirza Jones from Minneapolis was the one I liked best. Her father owned the major newspaper there, and obviously the family had money coming out of its ears. They were members of Westminster Presbyterian Church, the big fashionable one. That first year I think Thirza was still a student at the Masters' School in Dobbs Ferry.

Ben Marais

Among the many fascinating people on the YDS campus that fall of 1949, Ben Marais stood out. He was pastor of the largest Dutch Reformed Church in Pretoria, South Africa. The prime minister and most of the cabinet belonged to his church. Under that regime, apartheid was growing stronger and stronger, and the Christian community around the world was in protest.

While his church members were the ones pushing apartheid, he was opposed to it. He was in a minority in his own denomination. At table in the refectory at lunch, we would have a chance to talk to him. I was just coming out of my American racial prejudice, but even I could see the evils in South Africa. Ben was very open to discussion and was able to hear the black/white criticism of young American theologians who had all the answers.

He lead worship services some, especially for the Presbyterians. He did it beautifully, and it was wonderful to experience South African liturgy first hand.

He and his wife were returning to South Africa at the end of the term. The women at 401 had a party for them, and I was invited. I remember in a private conversation asking him how he felt about going back to that situation. He said, "I have mixed feelings. Of course I want to return to my family and friends and congregation. I have missed them very much. But I feel as though I am walking into a fiery furnace. I see no way out of this without a blood bath." That was in 1949.

There was much blood shed between then and 1990 when apartheid ended. One of the miracles of the 20th century was the fact that change took place without fighting. On the whole it was peaceful, but there were certainly pockets of resistance. Without Archbishop Desmond Tutu and Nelson Mandela, I do not believe that miracle could have taken place.

In the years since 1949, I have thought often of my last conversation with Ben Marais. I wonder how he spent the rest of his life.

Episcopal Bishop

While I was still interdenominational, my love for liturgy pulled me toward the Episcopal, Lutheran, or Presbyterian Church. My work at Second Presbyterian Church, Little Rock, in the summer of 1949 had certainly pushed me toward that denomination. But I thought it would be good for me to have a similar experience in the Episcopal Church before I made any commitment.

When I came home for Christmas, I made an appointment with Bishop Mitchell. I told him about myself, where I was educationally, and the kind of experience I had had the previous summer at Second Presbyterian, and then asked if there was any way in which I could have a similar experience in one of his congregations.

He said I certainly could not unless I had been confirmed in the Episcopal Church. He also wanted to know where I had been baptized, and by whom, and seemed to have serious doubts about the validity of that. I was furious.

I went directly to Dr. Boggs (whom I had forewarned about my plan) to describe what had happened. He said, "You just come on back here to Second Church next summer, and we'll find a full-time job for you." While I still had some reservations, the tide really turned in his welcome of me.

I guess it was the next summer Mr. Andrew Friberg told me that as a member of the Diocesan Council he always got a copy of the Bishop's calendar/diary showing what he had been doing. He said he noticed one entry that said young Don Campbell had been to see him. He was surprised when I told him what had happened.

Later on, I told Cotesworth Lewis, the dean of the Cathedral, about this. Perhaps he had asked me if I had ever thought of the Episcopal Church. When I told Cotesworth about this run-in with the bishop, he said, "Oh, I wish you had come to my office instead of his. I was looking for someone to help me on my staff that summer. I would certainly have given you the job."

"Nothing happens by chance." How many times a life is maintained, or changed, by some seemingly trivial event or word.

Inter-Seminary Conference

Through my undergraduate years, I had never gone to one of the many conferences held right after Christmas, nor had I given serious thought to getting a summer job, such as tutoring the children of wealthy families spending the summer on Cape Cod—because my yearning to be back in Arkansas as much as possible slammed those doors before they even got open.

But in the fall of 1949, I heard about the Inter-seminary Conference to be held at the Lutheran Seminary at Rock Island, Illinois. This was one agency of the National (or was it still Federal?) Council of Churches. It brought together theological students from a whole range of denominations and schools. I don't know who first told me about it. Maybe it was George Chauncey. But it excited me enough to be willing to leave home the day after Christmas and not return. This was the same Christmas when I had the encounter with the Episcopal bishop.

I am not sure how I got to Memphis, but there I met George Chauncey and Bill Jones (whom I had known) and his wife, Mag—whom I had not met before. Bill and Mag were driving in their car and took us on as passengers. Mag had grown up in Memphis, but as we headed up the west bank of the Mississippi River, this was the first time she had ever been to West Memphis. We could not have left before about noon, if I came from Little Rock. I think we drove that afternoon and all through the night in order to reach Rock Island in time for the start of the conference. I have found the best way to get to know a lot about people is to take a cross-country car trip with them. As the miles pass and there is nothing else to do, people talk, and if they talk enough, they reveal a great deal about themselves. The other three already knew each other from Southwestern, but they too probably disclosed things they had not talked about. Then we drove from Rock Island back to New Haven, day and night, and therefore had more sharing time—including talking about what the conference had meant to us. It was the basis of three of my real friendships.

Attendance was in the hundreds, if not a thousand. But George and I roomed together, and we saw a lot of Mag and Bill, so I did not feel overwhelmed. I do not remember all the speakers, but they were top-flight. I do recall the worship services in which we did a lot of chanting. I especially came to love the "Glory be to God on high." But what I will never forget is the series of sermons given by Bishop Stephen Neil, who was then the assistant to the Archbishop of Canterbury. I had heard Jim Boyes talk about him during his Cambridge days. Neil had been a missionary in India. There was some mystery about his having to leave because he had struck an Indian student, and then was sent off for psychiatric treatment. I think there was also a hint, but only a hint, that his anger might have grown out of a homosexual advance. Whatever his background, he was eloquent—magnificent—in what he said and how he said it. I had gone to YDS expecting it to be a mountaintop experience and had become somewhat disillusioned during the fall. Suddenly the Bible was no longer a source of inspired religious experience, but a textbook that I had to take apart and learn. Especially was this true of the New Testament. But Bishop Neil lit the candle of my faith again and made it glow. I had gone to seminary on a one-year trial. I remember on New Year's Eve spending a long time alone in the chapel in prayer. That may have been the time when I decided it was no longer a trial year, but that I really was called into some form of ministry. I did not know what kind.

I returned to YDS with renewed enthusiasm. That was heightened in the spring when Bishop Neil was invited to be the speaker at a Religious Emphasis Week at Yale, preaching each night at Battell Chapel. It was the first time Yale had had such an event since about 1900 when Billy Sunday came. There was a lot of nervousness on the downtown campus about this, and not a little at YDS where many students looked down on it as a "revival," which lots of them had had too many of in earlier years. But I went, and my cup was filled. I shall never forget at the end of the last sermon he invited each of us to bow in prayer and said, "I invite you to give as much of yourself as you know to as much of God as you know." It could not have been more challenging yet more realistic. It did "revive" me, the way a glass of cool water does a weary traveler on a hot day.

I don't think Yale has had such an event since.

First Year Spiritual Life

There were ups and downs in my spiritual pilgrimage that first year in Divinity School.

I was taking both Old Testament and New Testament Survey. I was learning the history of how each was written, and collected, and how it would contradict itself in places. I was having to read fast in the Old Testament, but was inspired by Davie Napier. In the New Testament, Paul Schubert's lectures were so dull I lost interest. I recently found my grades from the end of the spring in 1950, and the lowest grade I made was B- in New Testament.

Also, before many weeks, the idealized image of YDS students I had projected on others developed cracks as human weaknesses became evident. Some were plain boring. Some were driven by ambition — ecclesiastically, or academically, or socially. It is always hard to discover the feet of clay on those I have put on a pedestal.

I was also finding myself in a small minority as a conservative on campus. I had experienced my "conversion" on race the previous summer, but the "sanctification" process was proceeding slowly. Bill Philpot, a black man, was in our class. I was friendly with him, but did not seek him out as a friend and would have been uncomfortable living on the floor with him. The overwhelming majority of students and faculty were very liberal politically and socially. In my head I suspected they were right, but in my gut I was not ready and often felt defensive or isolated. I would find comfort in Uncle Ken on the political issues, but not on race.

On the other hand, there were some real positives.

I had a room to myself. I had enjoyed having my own room during my last fall at Berkeley College, and again in the spring in Fayetteville. Now I had one I assumed I could hold for three years. There was no reason I could not pray or read the Bible devotionally or read prayers and other inspirational material. Also, Uncle Ken was on the same floor, and I knew he was setting aside what he called his "quiet time." In some ways his example helped. In other ways, it so intimidated me I was tempted to give up. As a result, my private prayer life was sporadic.

A great plus for me was having daily chapel services. There had been terms at Yale College when I could go to Dwight Chapel every day, but usually I had noon classes either three or two days a week.

Also the YDS chapel services were longer. The singing and music were excellent, and most of the sermons were really good. I had missed this terribly in Fayetteville and during the summer. I think it was in my first year that I began to kneel for the prayers—so sat off to one side so I would not be conspicuous.

It was a great privilege to be able to go to Battell Chapel most Sundays. When the guest preacher was someone I knew from previous experience that I did not want to hear, I visited other churches a bit. But Battell remained my "church home."

Being so intimately related to Uncle Ken produced mixed reactions. There were times when I felt "cornered," not free to mix and mingle as classmates did. But on the whole it was very positive. He was my "spiritual father"—had been for some years, but this was much more intimate. We talked about many things, but there was never a discussion of sex or dating. I don't know if he would have been open to that. He was an Edwardian Puritan (if there can be such a mix), and it would have been unthinkable for me to talk about the inhibitions Mother had drilled into me, or wet dreams, or any such.

I was also still very much in the "deciding" phase of my pilgrimage. I had come to YDS on a one-year trial basis, but if I stayed, what would I do? The summer work at Second Pres was deeply satisfying, but I had terrible doubts about the parish ministry. I rationalized, "But graduates from YDS would not be like those other dull pastors." Then on alumni day, I went out into the Quadrangle and saw all these alumni dressed in black suits with copies of their bulletins bulging out of the side pockets of their coats (to share with friends). I went back into my room, crawled into bed, and pulled the covers over my head.

The physical environment at YDS was itself inspirational. The beauty of the architecture of the Quadrangle lifted my spirits—the fall foliage, the snow in winter, the greening trees and shrubbery in the spring. I had loved the architecture at Berkeley College, but it was set down in the city with traffic going by. YDS, on the hill two miles away, had a different feel, which I internalized.

My first year was one of growth—sporadic—but maturing. I had been on the mountaintop when I decided to come to YDS and when I first arrived. I was slowly—not dramatically—descending to ground level, but not into a dark valley.

One change I remember distinctly.

All through college days I had gone to Scarsdale for vacations and had felt wonderfully at home there in the luxury of their place at 75 Morris Lane, with a private tennis court, etc. And I had enjoyed being in Scarsdale, one of the exclusive suburbs of New York City. During my first year at YDS, I began to grow uncomfortable with the wealth in that community. My relationship with the McCains did not change. But I remember saying the night before Thanksgiving that I would like to go to the community worship service, and when we got there I was oppressed by the sermon that seemed to say, "Since we are so rich and comfortable and powerful as individuals and as a nation, we are clearly those on whom God is smiling." Enough of the social conscience at YDS was rubbing off on me to make me squirm through that.

My Finances at YDS

Reflections on how I felt, financially, at Yale need to be in two clear sections—one at Yale College and the other at Yale Divinity School. In the former, I had been in an environment where money was significant, a number of colleagues had a lot of it, and being sophisticated in style and dress was important. I bought into that—especially the last observation. I definitely felt "nearly poor" there, not at the bottom of the financial scale, but not far from it.

The atmosphere at Yale Divinity School was a dramatic change. The values were different. That's why we were at seminary. Also, coming from Yale College I was in the "in" group, and it was assumed I had some sophistication and the correct wardrobe. The student body was made up of very, very bright people from colleges and universities from all over the country, many of them quite unsophisticated. I don't know the percentage of people who were on scholarships, but I am sure it was very high, and most had some denominational support. Also, part of the curriculum was having to do field work for at least two years, and for most people that meant going to some church to work with youth and children, and on rare occasion to preach. I did not have to do that because being secretary to Uncle Ken was considered a learning experience sufficient to qualify as field work. I was paid by the hour for taking dictation and typing it up, but I did not type his books! The unspoken, but real, purpose for having a student secretary was to have a companion in his late years (he turned 65 I think the year I graduated from YDS). But that gave me the spending money I needed. My parents paid the tuition and room and board not covered by my scholarship, and I had (reluctantly) accepted a gift from All Souls Church.

Since all the students were struggling financially and I was not dating anyone with any regularity, I felt very "comfortable" financially during the first two years. I did have a couple of dates with Thirza Jones, whom I had met through the Charles McCains. I invited her up once to the Divinity School, and then she invited me to join her mother and brother for a weekend at the Plaza Hotel in New York. The amount of money they were spending let me know Thirza was out of my league, then and forever. So that relationship fizzled out.

I got a leave of absence from YDS for the academic year 1951-52 to take Clinical Pastoral Education, at that time considered the best way to train as a counselor for either the pastorate or as an institutional chaplain. I was also wanting some way of stopping as Uncle Ken's secretary without "rejecting" him. I am sure Daddy paid the tuition for the three quarters I took. I have no idea how much it cost, but it was not high, for we interns were put to work. In exchange, we were given our meals, and during the two quarters I was in Kansas, also our housing. When I went to New York and Bellevue Hospital, we got meals when we were in the hospital, but had to provide our own housing. I rented a room at Biblical Seminary, but I had to pay bus and subway fare, and everything in New York was expensive. I also began to date Ann Williamson that spring and spent some money on that—although we did things inexpensively. I remember taking her to the Met to hear *Madame Butterfly*. It was standing room only, and we stood through the whole opera. But I felt comfortable enough to do a few things like that and enjoyed being in New York for three months.

That summer I served the church at Cotton Plant. I was paid something—enough certainly to cover my travel and out-of-hand expenses. I was given the use of Art's car, for he was in Morocco at this time. That summer, Ann and I began to date seriously and were together in Little Rock, Scott, or Monticello most of my days off (Mondays). Again, I was not rich, but I certainly felt comfortable financially.

When I returned to YDS for 1952-53, I was terribly excited about getting back. That summer I had asked Daddy if he was in a position to let me go without a scholarship. I had come to know the financial plight of some students (especially Marnie) and the way they were barely getting by. My conscience bothered me for us to be taking help they needed. Daddy agreed. That meant that I did not have to do any field work, either, thus freeing me up for weekends more than I'd been since college. I had Ann up to YDS several times, and I went to New York—and was comfortable enough financially to do that. Ann and I became engaged in March and started plans for the wedding. I got the Fulbright Scholarship, so that meant going to Scotland for a year. There were funds enough to make all that possible, and I was reasonably relaxed about finances—knowing we had to watch our dollars carefully.

Summer of 1950

I had known since Christmas that there was a place for me, full time, on the staff at Second Presbyterian Church in Little Rock. It felt good, all spring, to be confident where I would be and what I would do. Some classmates were going off to serve small churches. I knew I was not ready for that. It suited me just fine to work with high school young people, college-age students, and young adults.

On the train over from Memphis to Little Rock in June, there was a young man about my age dressed in a blue seercord suit, like mine. I wondered who he was and where he was going. It turned out later to be Herb Miller, who was going to have a job similar to mine with Bill Oglesby at Pulaski Heights Presbyterian Church, where Lamar Williamson had been the summer before. I don't think we spoke on the train. But we were together a good bit during the summer, for I would have him down on his day off when we would play tennis and golf and swim.

This summer I was a "known" at Second Church and warmly welcomed back by staff and congregation, and the corps of people with whom I had worked the previous summer. But being full time, I had new duties. I was involved in Vacation Church School—something we had never had at All Souls, so it was new for me. I was "volunteered" to be a counselor at a junior high camp at Ferncliff. I had been there only once, years before, when Ann and some of the Scott girls stayed there for a week. But then it had been a private summer place. Now it was owned by the Synod.

The cabins were pretty rustic—screens to keep out the mosquitoes and one light bulb from the middle of the ceiling. There was running cold water in a latrine up the hill for brushing teeth, shaving, and showering (if I could make myself). But there were no flush commodes. I was so repelled by them I got constipated. Ferncliff was run by "Uncle Hugh" Patterson, a very conservative man with Presbyterian connections but who had become a Methodist or Baptist at Ferndale. I remember before the first supper he told all the counselors to come sit, one at a table, and the Pioneers (the campers) were to wait. I went in and picked my table. He came up to me and said, "Pioneers are to wait out there." I was then 22 years old, almost 23, but looked like a junior high student!

There were double-decker wooden beds in the cabins. Most of the boys in my cabin were from East Arkansas. Two of them, Eldridge Douglass and Bucky Currier, were from Cotton Plant (where two years later I would see them again as the summer pastor of their church). The first afternoon, during rest time, they were swapping every dirty joke that had ever been told to junior highs in the Delta. That night when we had "devotions," I told them I did not think dirty jokes were why they had come to camp and suggested they clean up their humor. The next afternoon there were no dirty jokes, but I could hear the sound of dice being rolled as they shot craps. That night I did not suggest they cut out the gambling, for I feared what they might move on to in order to fill the vacuum!

That summer, I was an assistant to a more experienced counselor in the study/Bible group we had two or three times a day. I was working hard to keep my head above water all week. I think this was the year when on a stormy night Elizabeth Plowman, from Second Church, claimed she was sick and had to go home. So I drove her back to town in the pouring rain. The closer we got to home, the better she felt. She was just homesick.

It is interesting that not only did I run into Eldridge and Bucky during my summer in Cotton Plant, but by the time I returned to Grace Church in 1994, Eldridge was an elder there. Earlier, when I was pastor at Grace, Libby Plowman was our church musician for two or three years—and an excellent one. The Presbyterian Church in Arkansas was a small world in which lines crossed and recrossed.

I was named manager of the Second Church Junior Age boys' softball team. A couple of the Flakes were on it, and David Nash. I remember trying to get Bob Moore involved, but his mother (later Miss Lena Belle Young) was so protective of him (after Dr. Moore's death) that she would not let him play. Mrs. Norvell Plowman was a big supporter of the team, and really coached them. The miracle was that our team won the championship of that level in the church league. We had a celebration picnic at Rob-Bell. It was not until then, when the boys tried to get me to play, that they discovered I did not know how to play softball! (I had studied Administration and Supervision of Religious Education—on how to get others to do it.)

It was while we were at Ferncliff in July 1950 that word came North Korea had invaded South Korea and American troops were being sent. I remember Dick Hardie's strong reaction. He had just got Westover Hills going. As a member of the Naval Reserve, he wondered if he would be called up and would have to leave this newly planted congregation. No one had expected another war so shortly after the end of World War II.

In the summer of 1950 we continued our "deputation team" program, going to small churches without pastors. The young adults became really quite good at it. Some of the events I described for the summer of 1949 might have taken place in 1950, for the two summers blur together in my mind. One of the most active of this group was Martin Wilkinson, who preached often at the Woodson Church. He was talking about possibly going into the ministry. He and Adrian Williamson had rooms in the home of some lady in the upper Heights in Little Rock. Adrian warned me once about Martin going into the ministry, for Martin had told him he was going into it for the money. Adrian was shocked, and so was I. I could not stop him, but I never forgot the warning. And years later, when Martin was at some church in the bootheel of Missouri, and also Stated Clerk of that Presbytery, he absconded with the funds so the Presbytery was left broke. He was sent to a psychiatric hospital, his wife divorced him, and I think he was finally de-frocked from the ministry. Another person who came to that group was Richard Knott, whom I had known at East Side and LRHS. He eventually graduated from college, went to Austin Seminary, was a pastor in South Louisiana when I was there, and is now a member of Arkansas Presbytery. He has become very conservative—so much so that the Jonesboro Church, where he was interim pastor, asked him to leave. Elizabeth Plowman went to Mary Baldwin College, then got her master's at the School of Sacred Music, Union Theological Seminary, New York.

That summer Dr. Adams asked me to preach at First Presbyterian Church one Sunday when he was away. I was scared to death and went to early communion at Christ Episcopal Church beforehand to gather some courage. I don't remember what I preached on, but I do recall I chose as the opening hymn "A Mighty Fortress," and some of the people there complained that they had never heard it before!

I think I was also invited to preach at Second Church my last Sunday on the job.

Toward the end of the summer, I told Dr. Boggs I would like to become a Presbyterian and join Second Church. I was still uncertain in what denomination I would wind up, but I was feeling more and more comfortable in the Presbyterian church. After the bishop's rejection the previous Christmas, I was pretty turned off by the Episcopalians. While I was attracted by what I had seen of Lutheran worship at Rock Island at Christmas, that was a Germanic world in which I did not feel at home.

At the end of the summer of 1950, I left with a feeling that I had done a good job. I had established friendships not only with the college/young adult group and with some of the younger boys and girls, but also with some of the adults who remained friends until they began dying off in the 1990s. That is certainly the seedbed for the financial support the Frank Lyon family gave to the start of Grace Church, and is partly responsible for her support of The Oasis.

I remember one episode quite vividly. The college/young adult group had been off on some kind of event. It could have been a party or picnic, but I think it was one of the deputation trips to a church. A young woman/student who had recently moved to Little Rock from one of the smaller towns in the state had started visiting our group. She did not know many people, but had agreed to go on this trip. After we had returned to Second, she was to be picked up by the family or friends with whom she was living. All the others had piled in their cars to go home, so this girl and I were the only ones left. We were standing out on the sidewalk, and it was obvious she was not comfortable being left alone with me. As the last car drove off, they lowered their windows and Emmelou

Mallory called out, "Don't worry. He's harmless!" That really boosted my self image!

I had also had some fun during the summer, commuting back to Scott every night and spending my off day there with all the comforts I had enjoyed before—often asking Herb Miller to share them with me. I did not date much. Many of the girls who had been friends in high school had either married or moved away. I do remember going over the list of possibilities and finally calling Marguerite (Greet) Rice and taking her out once. But I think I discovered she was getting serious with someone else and did not pursue it. I did not date any of the girls in the group at Second Church. In these days, it is called "sexual harassment" for a person in a position of power or influence to make any kind of approach to a woman in his jurisdiction. That had not been thought of in my day. I don't know if it was inhibition, or fear of the consequences if we broke up, or some kind on innate wisdom—but I never wanted to date girls at 301 at the Divinity School, or anyone in one of my church groups, or anyone on the staff with me in Atlanta or Baton Rouge. I was comfortable being friends, but not dating. The one deviation on that was dating Marguerite Schneck *after* I left Grace Church and would come back on vacations or visits. Even then I never kissed her. I must have realized that any physical touch on my part starts me moving farther and faster than I intended to go. So I did not pursue that. Soon afterward our relationship played out, although we remain friends.

It was a great summer and enriched me, and made me ready to go back to YDS much more certain that I was headed toward the pastoral ministry.

At the end of the summer, I told Dr. Boggs I was ready to join the Presbyterian Church. It was still an open-ended question for me whether I would remain a Presbyterian. But this was a working hypothesis. The Session of Second received me as a member before I returned to New Haven.

Lizzie Nowden Bonner

In some ways Lizzie Nowden Bonner does not fit logically at this point in my life story, but she belongs somewhere, and I don't know where else to put her. I'm inserting her here because it was in the summers of 1949 and 1950, when I was living at Scott but working at Second Presbyterian Church in Little Rock, that I was around her for the most extended periods once she became the family cook.

In my early memories, Lizzie played no major role. She was a Nowden, the "first family" of the blacks on our plantation. Her mother was Coochie, who "straightened hair" on the front porch of her house, which was on the south side of the road leading from the store to our house. Evidently, there had been a Mr. Nowden at some point, but I have no memory of him. I learned through Scott Connections (a local history group I helped organize in the 1990s) that the Nowdens came up to Scott from Grady or Gould, in the southeastern part of the state. There were several Nowdens on the place—Lizzie, Tom Cat (Fred), Ben, Ore, and perhaps more. All were intelligent and hard working.

Lizzie Nowden Bonner, our cook at Scott from 1948 to 1969.

Lizzie was an active member in St. Phillip Baptist Church that was located on the north side of what is now called Lower Steele Bend Road, next to the Crittenden farm (past the Richardson's place.) Most of the black people on our place went to Mt. Moriah. I don't know why Lizzie went there.

As a child, I was aware of Lizzie as the wife of Epps Bonner (one of the best tractor drivers), and the mother of many children. Mary was her oldest and much older than the rest, then came Lillian, Elnora, Sonny, J. C., and some more. I think she would occasionally come up to help Marie, then Hattie, when we had a really big party, or when the house was full of houseguests.

Then when Ann and Hoyt were getting married, Lizzie was hired on a full-time basis to help Hattie. Right after the wedding,

Hattie quit, and Lizzie became the full-time cook. She was a very different personality. Whereas Hattie had been trim, fast, cool, and distant, Lizzie was on the heavy side (not really fat), "down home" in her dress (she normally wore house slippers around the kitchen), slower, warm, loving, always smiling. I was in college and divinity school by this time, so was around very little. But when I came home, I always felt a warm welcome. It troubled me that she, who had always called me Don, now called me Mr. Don. But I could not stop her.

How she managed to turn out the quantities of food she did for all our company, I do not know. But she was always (on the surface, at least) pleasant and cheerful. I am sure that was not always the whole story. When I did an interview with Elnora Bonner Calhoun through Scott Connections, she talked about working in the fields and leaving at 11:00 so she could go home to cook the noon meal. I asked in surprise, "You mean you had to work and also cook?" to which she replied, "My mama was cooking for you and your family." She also commented that I had lived in the "white" house while they lived in a "brown" one. (I always thought of weathered cypress as being "gray.")

At some time (I am not sure when) Epps left Lizzie and remarried. He then went to work for Miss Teetie Alexander as her driver and man-around-the-house.

There are many family stories about Lizzie. She was devoted to Daddy. She would try to get him to eat more—"Mr. Campbell, this is just a little piece of (whatever-it-was)." And he would bark, "That's too much, Lizzie." She was an excellent cook. One of her specialties was scrambled eggs—which were always "soft" because she cooked them very slowly over low heat.

When Lizzie thought we were having special company, she would wear bright pink hair curlers in her hair.

One of my favorite stories has to do with her efforts to get running water and a bathroom in her house. One day, she was in the kitchen and said to Mother, "Miz Campbell, I wish you would ask Mr. Campbell is he going to give me a bathroom." Mother replied, "Lizzie, he's right across that wall [a three-quarter height divider in the old kitchen] in the breakfast room. Ask him yourself." Lizzie's response was, "No'm, I wants to hear what he has to say, but I don't want to hear him say it." She did not get her bathroom at that time.

Lizzie welcomed warmly the spouses the three of us brought into the family. She was especially crazy about Hoyt. And as grandchildren came, she took them in, and they dearly loved her.

When Mother and Daddy decided to move from the big house to Mother's "little retirement home" (3,000 square feet), she designed a room and bath up over the garage for Lizzie—except Lizzie refused to live there. So she moved to an old tenant house on the old rock road, which had been the main road before the paving of the cut-through. It did not have a bathroom. Finally, Daddy had one put in for her! One Sunday when I guess all eight of us adults, plus grandchildren, were there, she announced that after dinner she wanted us to come down to see her bathroom. So we all paraded down, went into the bathroom, and flushed the toilet. She beamed with pleasure.

My mother, Margaret Campbell, during my years at Yale.

When my parents moved into Presbyterian Village in 1969, Lizzie moved to the Shorter College public housing, where she had a small first-floor apartment (with bathroom). She and Mother would talk on the phone, and Mother would go see her and take presents at Christmas and birthdays, etc. And all three of us siblings and our families would go, too, for she was important to us all. I was in town when she died, but I think I was going to have to leave before the funeral. I remember buying a large ham for the three of us to take over to her family and seeing some of them there.

Returning to YDS in 1950

Returning to YDS for my second year filled me with as much, if not more, anticipation as when I approached the previous fall. I don't think there was much anxiety about going into a new school in 1949, but now I was returning to familiar territory. I knew two-thirds of the student body. I knew something about the professors—which ones I liked and which ones I wanted to avoid. I think I had decided the previous spring which courses I was going to take, and I had both Bainton's church history and Schubert's introduction to New Testament behind me. Ruth Puckett, the director of christian education at Second Presbyterian, had given me some wise advice about how to avoid the Introduction to Christian Education course and go to second level immediately. I did not have hanging over me the knowledge that I had not learned shorthand as I was supposed to do. I was never good at it, but I could get by with my level, and Uncle Ken evidently was willing to put up with it. Also, I was not wondering what my relationship with him would be like. I looked forward to being in his cell group again, knowing a number of people who would be carry-overs from the previous year.

In Stuart House, Norvin Hein continued on as my next-door neighbor. George Lindbeck was replaced by Carl Nelson, who was a bit strange. He had a photographic memory, and his hobby was memorizing the census reports since 1790. He could tell you the population of any town in the U.S. at 10-year intervals, and also railroad time-tables! But at least he was friendly and more outgoing than George had been. I think Richey Hogg's room had been turned into an office for some new faculty member. But by this time, I knew enough people that I did not have a sense of being isolated.

On top of my own class of 1952, the new class of 1953 was arriving. Bardwell Smith was among them. We had been friends at Berkeley College, but not really close. However, as soon as he got to YDS, we became much better friends. He was married and lived off campus, but would eat most of his noon meals in the refectory. Also, in my last semester at the College I had heard his mother, Gert Behanna, tell her story and it had made a tremendous impact on me. We would talk about her and her new ministry. Bob Raines was in this new class. He had been captain of the Yale football team, but I had not known him before. But our Yale connection drew us together. Harry Smith, a Presbyterian from the University of Texas, soon became a friend; and Alvord Beardslee, an "artsy" type who lived in the house next to Stuart. I think this was the year Jack Gessell, a graduate student, appeared — or at least when I became aware of him. Also, Bev Asbury was one of the new students I liked.

I guess John Fesperman had moved full time to the School of Music, for John Eigenbrodt, who was in '52, became the organist and did an outstanding job. And Jim Borden, '52, became director of the all-male choir. Toward the end of the year, they made a record of their outstanding music. One piece that I especially loved was a Russian version of the Nicene Creed, with Clay Erickson, '53, as the tenor soloist. The chapel services that second year really fed me. Also, some of the students got a mid-week communion service going in the prayer chapel in the basement, and the Presbyterian chaplain downtown had communion early on Sunday mornings every third week. So I was receiving communion at least once a week, every third week twice, and when Battell served communion, or Marquand, it could be four times. The sacrament was becoming more and more meaningful for me by the second year as my interest in liturgy was growing. (I guess this was also the year Betty Carpenter Batchelder, a great social activist, asked me to be a member of the worship committee that she chaired.)

My ties with the downtown Yale campus were getting weaker. I guess Mr. Hemingway must have retired after my first year at YDS, and they had moved to a small house on Lincoln Street where they operated on a simpler scale, without all the servants. I visited them there, and they seemed to welcome my friendship — not just as a Berkeley student, but as a friend. I remember that fall being there on a Sunday. They invited me to stay for supper. She was trying to open a can of soup with an old fashioned opener. She did not know about the grinding kind, so I gave them one as a gift — perhaps for Christmas.

I guess the previous summer Ellie Hutchins had also married Dean Wohlenberg, dean of the School of Engineering. That was the end of another tie with downtown. I did go see them a couple of time in their new home.

I guess it was in my second year when I began having people come to my room for tea. The visit from someone from overseas (perhaps it was the Moderator of the Church of Scotland) was the cause for my inviting Dean Liston Pope to come. It was against the rules to have a hot plate in our rooms, but he sat right next to it and said nothing. My guess is that this was a rule violated more often than observed. But I was increasingly feeling that my room was my home.

At the start of this school year, I was very happy—about as happy as I had ever been in my life. I had a sense of direction. I was associating with people, students, and faculty, most of whom I liked—and even those I didn't like, I realized were people of quality. My courses the second year were more exciting and challenging than some had been the first year—except I did miss Davie Napier in Old Testament. The setting at YDS was one of beauty. Homesickness had long left me. I felt New Haven was "home" in many ways, although I still had a sense of calling to return to Arkansas eventually.

Early Memories of Marnie Smith

I do not remember Marnie in our first year at YDS. I know I knew her then, and I am sure we were friends—as I was with most of the people in our class, and with the women who lived at "301," the women's dormitory—but I do not remember her that year. She and Bobbie Hall were roommates, and I certainly knew Bobbie, for we were among the few Presbyterians. Marnie talks about my bringing some pecans down to "301" and asking her to make a pecan pie. That could have been in the first, or the second, year.

I think it was in my second year that we really got close. She was having real psychological problems and was coming to Albert Outler once a week for counseling. His office was on the floor where my room was located, and she would stop in to visit while waiting to see him. She would also frequently stop afterward. There were many tears. She suffered from anxiety and often had trouble breathing. She would come to my room and stretch out on the bed, trying to breathe. We ate many meals together and saw a lot of each other—but I never had a date with her. I remember wondering if there were possibilities, but I was put off by her extra weight. I remember wondering how Mother would regard her, and that weight issue would come to mind.

I invited Thirza Jones up for one weekend, and she stayed with Marnie at 301. When Thirza was to go back, there was some problem with the trains, so I borrowed Norvin Hein's car to take Thirza back to New York and—I can't believe this—invited Marnie to go with us. On the way back we would be passing near Scarsdale, and I told Marnie I would like to drop by to speak to Aunt Marion and Uncle Arthur. Marnie about died, for she was not properly dressed. She really did almost die when she learned Uncle Arthur was president of Chase Bank. And she never let me forget that.

Marnie graduated from YDS in June 1952. We evidently kept up a correspondence, for she invited me to stop on my way back to Yale in the fall of 1952 to visit her and stay with her family in their home in one of the suburbs of Philadelphia. Marnie had a job as director of Christian education (DCE) at an Episcopal church nearby. I spent one night there. I remember having a pleasant visit. Her mother was charming. Marnie said her mother "took me over," I had no romantic feelings for Marnie at this time—just very good friends.

From then until 1971, we stayed in touch through Christmas letters, and perhaps occasional other notes. I got married, went to Scotland, then to Crossett and Little Rock. Marnie said it was the letter I wrote at the time of my divorce which "got to her," for she said she had never heard such pain described.

Second Year Courses

In the fall term, according to my records, here are the courses I took:
- Exegesis of the Greek NT—Galatians, Erick Dinkler
- Introduction to Pastoral Counseling, Rice
- Sermon Making, Luccock
- World Wide Work of the Church, Latourette
- Methods of Religious Education, Paul Vieth
- Administration & Supervision of Religious Education, Paul Vieth

Greek Exegesis of Galations, my course with Erick Dinkler, proved to be one of the most exciting courses I had at YDS. Many of the others in the class were graduate students, for so few at YDS had taken Greek. He taught us how to use the critical notes at the bottom of each page in Nestle—and so much about the comparative value of various codices and papyri. But he also made the content of the Epistle come alive. He was one of the deepest spirits and sharpest minds on the YDS campus.

The only course I ever took from Uncle Ken was World Wide Church. He had dictated many exam questions to me before. This time he had someone else type them out, but I knew what they would be. I made 100 on that exam! I had not taken his courses because I had heard he was dull and I did not want to disturb our relationship. To my surprise, I found him quite interesting. And his reading list was one of the most stimulating I was ever given. He was convinced that the best way to understand a culture is to read a good novel set in it. I read *Brothers Karamozov* to get a feel for the Orthodox Church in Russia, and *Cry, The Beloved Country* to understand South Africa. There were other novels, but these two stand out in my memory. I think we also read some biographies and autobiographies of missionaries.

Most people took a course on philosophy in the fall, in preparation for Systematic Theology. But since I had taken Epistemology at Yale College, I decided to pass on that.

Mr. Rice, an Episcopal priest, was chaplain at St. Luke's Hospital, New York. I think he came up once a week for an extended period — both fall and winter terms. I was developing an increasing interest in pastoral counseling, so took both terms. He was interesting and helpful, but not one of my key professors — except that his course was what planted in my mind the idea of taking a year of Clinical Pastoral Education.

Halford Luccock was nationally famous as a preacher. I have never heard anyone like him. He violated every rule of homiletics. His voice was high and cracked. When he was preaching at the YDS chapel, he would look out the clear windows at something none of the rest of us could see. He must have had a problem with wax in his ears, for he would stick his finger in them often. He would always start with something funny and would keep going in that vein until about mid-point in the sermon. I remember once when he was preaching at Battell Chapel, people were almost rolling in the aisles. Then when all our defenses were down, he would suddenly turn on the congregation with a prophetic or a gospel jab. He was extremely effective. But those students who tried to mimic him were miserable failures.

For all his skills at preaching, I thought he was the poorest of the four teachers of preaching at Yale — Luccock, MacLennan, Shroeder, and Muehl. Muehl was the best, for he would cut up a sermon as a surgeon cuts with a scalpel, yet usually in good spirit and a lot of humor. Schroeder, who was Master of Calhoun College, and only part-time at YDS, was a worldly man, and I always wondered how much faith he really had. But because he was ruthless in his criticisms, he was a good teacher. I think he filled in for Luccock in my last year. The one value I got from Luccock, other than enjoying him as a person, was the question he asked at the end of each student sermon: "So what?" He convinced me that every sermon should include a second-person challenge to those who listen.

Religious Education had a terrible reputation at Yale (and most other seminaries) as being unbelievably dull. The introduction course was mostly lecture. By the end of that, those who could vowed never to take another RE course. I had talked with Ruth Puckett about this both summers I worked with her. I had come to see the value of religious education in a local church by watching her. She advised me to see if I absolutely had to take Introduction in order to go on to advanced courses. If I could avoid it, I should go directly into second- and third-year courses. I examined the catalog and found it was not a requirement, so my first RE course was Methods of Religious Education, taught by Paul Vieth. He was not highly regarded by YDS students, although he was nationally known in his field. He was no lecturer. But in a seminar I came to value his insights, and to value him as a humble human being. Ruth's advice was excellent, and I came out with a high regard for the educational work of a congregation.

The record does not show I took public speaking in my second year, but my memory is that I took everything Bill Muehl offered. He was helpful, and he was such a delight to be with.

In the winter term:
- Systematic Theology, Outler
- Christianity and Politics, Underwood
- Sermon Making, Luccock
- Introduction to Pastoral Counseling, Rice
- Materials of Religious Education, Vieth
- Presbyterian Polity, Knight

I continued the Pastoral Counseling course from Rice.

With Vieth I moved from Methods to "Materials of Religious Education." Sara Little, on leave from Presbyterian School of

Christian Education in Richmond, was working on her Ph.D. As the only two Presbyterians in the class, Sara and I worked together when we were assigned to do an analysis of our denomination's curriculum. She later became a very distinguished professor at PSCE, I think in doctrine. That was funny, because that winter I would keep raising theological questions about something in our literature, and she was much more interested in methods. We kept in touch for years, and used to laugh about that. Ruth Puckett's advice again proved to be valuable.

In the winter term, I took a course on Presbyterian Polity. I was still not certain about the denomination in which I would wind up, but the assumption was Presbyterian. Our teacher, Bino Knight, was the executive of the Synod of New England. He taught the Presbyterian Church, USA (Northern) book, for that is what he knew. There were some PCUS (Southern) students in the class, and we had the PCUS *Book of Church Order* to supplement, correct, challenge the other. The responsibility was on our shoulders. As a result of this, I came out of YDS knowing more about the Southern book than those who had gone to PCUS seminaries, and once I got ordained, I was considered to be an ecclesiastical lawyer in my work at Presbytery, and also in teaching it to my officers.

I started a two-term course "Christianity and Politics" under Ken Underwood. This area of social concern was one of Yale's strong points. The leader of it was Liston Pope, who was made Dean in 1949. I had a good relationship with him. I was still very conservative and knew I would be fighting his point of view and that of anyone in this department. Ken Underwood was a young professor — very bright, very liberal — who seemed to be driven to read or do something every second of the day. (He died young. I wonder if he had a hunch this would be true.) Many students found him a very exciting professor. I did not — probably because I was resisting and battling most of what he had to say. But what he taught must have soaked in more than I realized, because when I got to Arkansas, I became chair of Presbytery's, then Synod's, Council on Christian Action. And much of that came from what I learned (while rejecting) at YDS.

When we came back from Christmas, I began what was probably (unless it was Napier's Old Testament) the most formative course in my YDS career, Systematic Theology. Albert Outler, a

Methodist who the next year moved to Southern Methodist University, was a brilliant teacher. I knew from Uncle Ken that Outler never felt secure in his role at YDS, compared to Robert Calhoun and Richard Niebuhr, and that was one of the reasons he moved to SMU. He was a master in Latin, and later was one of the Protestant official observers at Vatican II. He had a "hesitating" style of lecturing and would "wrestle" with an issue as though he had never thought it through before. (That was clear when, some years later, he was brought in to Austin Presbyterian Seminary to fill in for a lecturer who was ill. He was covering the same subjects — and still was "wrestling" with the same issues.) Students in most seminaries considered Systematic Theology deadly dull, and it turned most of them off to a love for theologizing. It was quite the opposite with Outler. People would pour out of class and move on to the refectory, arguing with each other over various fine points of theology. Later on Harry Adams wrote a layman's book on theology, and it was clearly Outler's course outline. And the theological parts of my Adult Communicant Class, which I taught so many times, followed the same outline. He taught me how to "think about God," and I still do love to do it. I find systematic theology much more stimulating than either historical or Biblical Theology.

The records do not show, but I think I may have audited one of Bill Muehl's courses.

In the spring term:
- Systematic Theology, Outler
- Christianity and Politics, Underwood
- Exegesis of Hebrews in English, Young
- (Napier on Deuteronomy canceled)(not on record)
- Weekday and Vacation Church School, Vieth
- Sermon making, Muehl (audited?)

I continued Underwood's "Christianity and Politics," fighting him much of the way. The record does not show it, but I think I also took another of Muehl's courses. Somewhere along the way, I know I had him for a course on preaching, for I found him the most helpful of the four in homiletics.

I took an English exegesis course on the "Letter to the Hebrews" taught by Franklin Young. I knew nothing about this epistle. It was helpful, but I did not get really excited by it. I remember I wanted to do my exegesis paper on one topic (I think it was on faith), and he made me write on another — I think it was on the nature of Christ. And that was much richer.

The dominant course for me that spring was Systematic Theology. One of our assignments was to read the "definitive" writing for our particular denomination. This meant I was to read John Calvin's *Institutes*. It was the longest of the various texts and at first I groaned. But as I read it, I found myself fascinated by it. Calvin was to me much more alive and warm and exciting than the Westminster documents. I found many in Presbyterian seminaries had never read the whole *Institutes*, but just excerpts from it. I am glad I had that discipline.

The other demanding part of Systematic was to write, as the term paper, my own credo. Interestingly, as one of my political science papers at Yale College, I had to write "Myself as the last speaker," in which I was to put on paper my political ideology. Now I was to write out my theology. When the term came to an end, I still had not finished it and had to complete it in Larned, Kansas, at the psychiatric hospital where I was taking my first unit of Clinical Pastoral Education. Our room was just around the corner from the room where the people who had been given insulin-shock treatment were recovering, and as they did so, groaned and moaned by the hour. I used to kid and say the reason my credo deals with sin at such length is I was egged on by those groans. That assignment did a great deal to help me sort out exactly what, at that point, I did believe, and it was a great help to me when I got ready for ordination.

Ruth Puckett had so convinced me of the importance of education in the life of a congregation that I also took a half-unit course from Vieth on "Administration and Supervision of Religious Education" — the role of the pastor in the educational program. This was an area most pastors did not like and tended to neglect or slough off onto a director of christian education or layperson. I had expected this course to deal mostly with Vacation Church School, which I knew about from working two summers at Second Pres. The surprise was to stumble into the history of Presbyterian involvement in weekday schools. I was concerned about "Americanism" that was being taught almost as a religion in public schools, with the flag taking the place of the cross. Such weekday church schools were unknown to me in Arkansas, but the prep schools in New England were mostly church related. I got very excited about this as a possible form of ministry in the future. This was in 1952. The *Brown vs. Board of Education* Supreme Court decision in 1954, and the consequent creation of white-flight schools under the label "Christian schools," completely destroyed any interest on my part in church schools as an alternative to public schools — and I think many churches are going to have to answer to God for the way they have capitalized on this to expand their educational schools.

I may have taken another full course, but the record does not show it.

My second year at YDS was a wonderful one academically. I did not make brilliant grades, but I had decided when I came up the hill I was not as interested in grades as I was in learning.

Under Care of Presbytery

I am hazy about the following, but I do not find a "paper trail" to correct me.

I think I violated every rule in the book of the Presbyterian Church, US in my candidacy. That is ironic since in the 1970s I was "Mr. *Book of Church Order*" in the candidacy process.

I did not join Second Presbyterian Church until the end of August or first of September 1950, after having been on the staff there for two summers. My memory is that I "came under care of Presbytery," i.e., accepted as a candidate for ordination, during the Christmas break 1950. I do not know if at that time there was (as there is now) a required passage of time between a person's becoming a member of a church and the Session recommending that person for candidacy. If so, it was waived. Dr. Boggs was the "bishop" of Washburn Presbytery. Whatever he supported passed. (Dr. Boggs used to say he had talked "to some of the fellows" about what was coming up before Presbytery, and when they had agreed, it went through smoothly.) There were only about 19 churches and 27 ministers in the Presbytery. Most of the churches were in the Fort Smith and Little Rock areas, with a few in between. The only member of Second Church who had ever been ordained was James Fogarty, Jr. — and he had been reared elsewhere and was a member only because his father was on the staff of Synod. So Dr. Boggs was very eager to smooth the way for my candidacy.

I had completed one year at Yale Divinity School before I joined Second, and had done one semester in my second year before I came before Presbytery. Somehow, I had won a dispensation from taking Greek and Hebrew, because Yale did not require them for a bachelor of divinity, and actually discouraged people from taking them unless they were going to specialize in Bible. Then, having received a waiver, I had decided to take Greek in my first year and had taken a Greek Exegesis course under Erik Dinkler. I guess permission to go to a non-Presbyterian seminary was also an *ex post facto* approval since I was almost halfway through.

I remember there was a called meeting of Presbytery at First Presbyterian Church, North Little Rock. I guess Dick Nolan, the pastor, must have been moderator. There were only a handful of people present on a very cold morning. No one had turned on the heat in the church, and we almost froze to death standing around a gas heater. Lyndon Jackson from Morrilton was chair of the candidates committee who recommended Presbytery take me under care. The other person coming was Jim Mosley from Batesville whose father was professor of Bible at Arkansas College. I do not remember ever meeting with the candidates committee. As far as that goes, I have only a dim memory of meeting with the Session at Second Church. It was about as loose and casual a procedure as was possible.

At that point, I "thought" I was going into the Presbyterian ministry, but was not absolutely certain. The other two possibilities were the Episcopal and Lutheran churches. The following spring, my retreat at Holy Cross Monastery pretty well shut the door to the Episcopal ministry so far as I was concerned.

I went back to Yale as a candidate for the ministry in the PCUS. I was to take a polity course on Presbyterians under a PCUSA minister. I was well aware that I was going to be an "outsider," and if I was going to be able to function in the PCUS, I was going to have to learn the polity and theology on my own, so I buckled down to it. In systematic theology the next two terms, I read, carefully, Calvin's *Institutes*. And I started learning the *Book of Church Order*.

As immersed as I later became in the Presbyterian world, I started off in a most inauspicious way.

Trip to Buffalo

During my second year at YDS, realizing my days in the Northeast were limited, I invited myself to go to Buffalo to visit the Howard McCains for part of my spring vacation. We had always been much closer to the Arthur McCains than to the Howard McCains, although earlier in life Mother and Uncle Howard had been much closer than she had been to Uncle Arthur. The difference was their two wives. Aunt Marion was strong on family and made more than her share of overtures. Also, her family lived in Little Rock, so they often came for visits. Aunt Jane was a much more reserved person. Her wealthy family was from St. Louis. While Uncle Howard wrote Main letters (always in green ink), I can remember their visiting in Scott only two or three times.

I took the train up. The country was covered with snow (as it usually is in Buffalo). Charles was already at Washington and Lee University, but David was in high school. Uncle Howard was general manager of the largest department store in Buffalo, but they lived in a suburb, Synder. When Main used to go north for two months each summer, she would report on party after party when she was in Scarsdale, but when she went to Buffalo, they would sit home day after day and night after night. That was pretty much the way I was entertained. And it was entertainment, for I have never known two better conversationalists than Aunt Jane and Uncle Howard. She stayed home most of the time, smoking and reading—widely—and drinking from the cocktail hour on. Uncle Howard was at work all day and did not read as much, but could talk about anything—as he smoked and drank. I was charmed by them, and by David who was just about as good at talking as a teenager can be. I remember we spent a lot of time watching TV, for this was when the Senator McCarthy hearings about alleged communists were in full swing, and we were all frightened about the witch hunt going on. Out of this visit, I established bonds with Aunt Jane and David, which later extended to Charles. Uncle Howard died of a heart attack on a bus on his way to work about a year later. I am so glad I went up there. As a result, the following year I went by Washington and Lee to see Charles and David. When Aunt Jane moved to St. Louis and I was traveling for the General Assembly, I would call her from the airport and sometimes would stop to spend the night with her. She had no church connection, so when she died, they asked me to have the service. Later, David and Eleanor asked me to help in Rhoda's wedding. When both sons moved to Big Canoe, north of Atlanta, I saw more of them.

I had another cousin in Buffalo whom I had never met — on the Campbell side. He was Cousin Duncan MacLeod, the son of Grandfather Campbell's sister, Aunt Jennie MacLeod. There was another brother, Colin, on the East Coast. The two of them had no contact with each other because they made a fortune from parachutes, and somehow there was a dispute about how the money should be divided. Uncle Gordon had always been close to the Colin MacLeods, and I think some of them had visited Little Rock. There was less tie with Duncan. Uncle Howard got in touch with him, and Cousin Duncan invited me for lunch at "the" men's club downtown. I remember little else about that visit.

Looking back on it, the "intuition" to go to Buffalo that spring was not "by chance." It was my last visit with Uncle Howard, the only one adult-to-adult. It established a relationship with Aunt Jane, Charles, and David that has been important to me through the years.

Holy Cross Monastery

On my way back from Buffalo, still during spring break, I stopped at Holy Cross Monastery. It is located across the Hudson River from Poughkeepsie, New York.

During my second year at YDS, I had grown more and more interested in liturgy and the life of prayer. Kelly Clark was also moving in that direction. A monk from Holy Cross (Episcopal Benedictines) had been invited to speak at some gathering at YDS. Some of us were quite impressed by him. I don't know whose idea it was, but four of us decided to spend Holy Week at their monastery — Kelly Clark (Congregationalist from Battell Chapel), Pete Lawson (Episcopalian), Bob Bailey (Methodist), and I (Presbyterian) agreed to meet there. I guess it was on Palm Sunday afternoon, or the next day. When we arrived, the other three had agreed that it was going to be a "silent retreat," which meant no talking at any time except responses in the worship services. I was not prepared for this, but went along.

This monastery was small in numbers. Most of the monks were elderly (by my standards at the time), but there were a few young ones as novitiates. At that time, there was a lot of diversity in the Episcopal Church from low to high. These people were at the tip of the highest peak of high church Episcopalians. They were more high church than Roman Catholics.

Each of us was assigned a cell. There were no clocks. We were awakened by a monk who would knock on the door and say, "The Lord be with you." We were supposed to wake up saying, "And also with you." There was a story about one guest who responded to "The Lord be with you" by stammering, "Wait till I get my pants on."

We ate with the monks. They ate in silence most meals, but when they were in the kitchen preparing for and washing up after meals, they talked to each other. But we were "on silence," so we had to communicate with them, and with each other, by pointing and gestures. At first this drove me crazy, but as the week wore on, I adjusted to it.

We spent much of the day at the seven monastical services, plus mass. But we also had time alone for private prayer, and for reading from the monastery library. I really welcomed the time for prayer because I was trying to make some major decisions—about my denomination, about plans for the following year. I do remember one book I read on "Scrupulosity." This was guidance for a priest hearing confessions, and what to do with someone who confessed, walked out the door, then remembered another sin so came back, and on and on. I had never before been aware of the sin of scrupulosity!

That week made the denominational decision for me. I could see that the real vitality of the Episcopal Church was in its high church wing. I found that I could not chant and I was highly allergic to incense. They burned incense like it was going out of style. When a monk would start down the aisle with the incense pot smoking, I would grab a handkerchief to cover my nose and eyes. Even so, I had a headache most of that week. They also chanted everything that could be chanted—even the Bible readings. And I can't chant. I knew I would never make it in high church services.

They did everything in Holy Week one day ahead of when it should be—Maundy Thursday was on Wednesday, Good Friday on Thursday, and Easter on Saturday. I never did find the rationale for that. I had heard that on Good Friday they brought the big crucifix down from the wall, laid it on a pillow on the floor, and people were to come forward for the "Adoration of the crucifix" by prostrating themselves on the floor and kissing the bottom of the cross. Bob Bailey, a staunch Methodist, and I had declared back at YDS that we were never going to do that. But as the service progressed, I got caught up in the movement of the drama and found myself getting out of my seat and moving forward. As I prostrated myself, I looked out of the corner of my eye, and there was Bob Bailey doing the very same thing!

We were planning to leave right after lunch on Saturday to get to other obligations, but because they "anticipated" we were able to be there for Easter mass. They really "put the big pot in the little one" for that. It was so high church that even the monks were confused about who was to do what and when. All week long, there had been no lectern in the church. Instead, one monk would hold the Bible open and another would read (chant) the passages for the day. That was true in Easter mass, too. One monk went over to the celebrant with the big Bible open. The celebrant chanted, "Let us pray." The monk holding the Bible chanted back in Gregorian style, "You're not supposed to be praying now but reading the BI-ble." Whereupon the celebrant did not miss a beat but chanted, "The Holy Gospel...." I thought I would fall off my chair laughing – silently.

That was a great experience, my first real retreat, though we had no director. I did realize that week I was not cut out to be an Episcopalian.

Art and Florence in New York

Art was working for Morrison-Knudsen, one of the major construction firms doing work all over the world. He was located in Louisville when they married in November 1949. After that, they moved to eastern Washington State, Pasco, relocating a railroad on the Columbia River. There, Florence had, I think, a stillborn child, and another who lived only a few hours.

At the completion of that job, Art was "invited" to go to Africa, unspecified nation, for a secret job. Once they got to New York, they learned their destination was Morocco, and everyone in Africa knew they were building five air bases to counter the Russians.

This was after the Chinese had crossed the Yalu River in Korea, and it appeared World War III might be starting. They lived in a hotel in Brooklyn with Art's office in Manhattan. Having no idea how long they would be there because of difficulty with visas, they did not unpack. When Florence finally decided to get settled, they received word they were leaving the next day! In the meantime, Art was acquiring supplies and equipment that would be needed on a job when he had no idea what that job was! I remember his talking about buying 5,000 long-handled shovels, wondering if they would ever be used. How glad I am to have had the time with them in New York before their departure. They wound up staying in Morocco for three years.

During this time, I went to New York at least once to see them, maybe twice, and they came up to New Haven to see me, since out of working hours, Art had nothing to do. One time, I remember Uncle Ken invited them for Sunday lunch at the Graduate Club. In those pre-Vatican II days, Florence would not have been caught dead in a Protestant church, or the University chapel, so they must have arrived about lunchtime. That afternoon as we sat in my room at the Divinity School I, the typical Type-A person, was using the time to darn some socks with holes in them, using a light-bulb as the "darning egg." Florence could not get over anyone darning socks! She had never seen it done, whereas it was a normal part of our household routine at Scott. This was just one of the many "tacit contract" differences between the two families.

I had met Florence in the fall of 1949, before the wedding, and they must have visited Scott in 1950 on their way to Washington State. But this was my first change to get to know her at any depth. And we hit it off.

At the end of my spring break in 1951, after going to Buffalo and then Holy Cross Monastery, I came down to New York City and stayed with the Charles McCains. On Easter Saturday night, I remember Art, Florence, and I had tickets to see the black musical "Green Pastures." I had heard about it for years, but had never read or seen it. The cast was excellent, the music moving. Having just come from a week of silence at the monastery, I found it a profound religious experience.

That Easter, I went to an early outdoor worship service in East Harlem, put on by the East Harlem Protestant Parish, then went to a later service at fashionable Brick Presbyterian Church on Park Avenue. I remember we had Easter dinner at the McCain apartment on Gracie Square. Cousins Charlie and Frances had gone down to be with Grace, so Aunt Grace Walker was the hostess. She and Art and Florence hit it off. She and I had become good friends on previous visits.

What religious gyrations I went through that Holy Week.

Thirza Jones

I have mentioned Thirza Jones elsewhere. I met her when the Charles McCains asked me to come down to New York one weekend to squire her around. Of the women I met through them, Thirza was the one I enjoyed most. She was attractive, but not a raving beauty. She was intelligent, but not brilliant. While obviously wealthy, wealth did not seem to be especially important to her. I was drawn to Thirza, but had no erotic feelings for her.

Some time after visiting YDS one weekend, she wrote that her mother was coming to New York for a weekend. She was coming down from her college and her brother was coming up from Princeton, and her mother would like for me to join them at the Plaza Hotel where they would be staying. We were to go to a Broadway play. They knew either the writer or one of the actors. Her brother had, I think, an interest in drama. The Plaza was one of the top, though smaller, of the New York hotels. I knew that it was very expensive. I think we had dinner at the Plaza on Saturday night. (The Joneses were obviously well known to the staff, for that is where they always stayed when in New York.) Then we took a taxi to the play, and I think afterward went somewhere, but it was not the Persian Room. The next day, we had breakfast (I don't think we went to church) and then lunch at some expensive place, then we all caught our trains back home.

I liked Mrs. Jones. She seemed down to earth, and not impressed by money. I do not remember Thirza's brother's name, but I found him pleasant. And I enjoyed Thirza. But when I went back to YDS, I realized Thirza was used to a level of society, and to spending money on a level I could never match. As nice as she was, I could not imagine her ever being a pastor's wife. I knew I should not pursue this relationship further.

We did exchange Christmas cards and notes for many years, even after she married someone in Minneapolis. I would hear about her occasionally from the Charles McCains. Somewhere along the way she moved or I misplaced her address, so we have lost contact. But I do remember her as someone I liked to date, even though she did not stimulate me romantically (no one else did in those days). I was in no position to think about marriage, and if I had been, I could not see her fitting into the kind of life I proposed to have.

In the journal keeping world, this would be one of those times when I could pursue the question of "What would my life have been like if I had, at this juncture, taken the other route?" My hunch is that it would not have been happy. Her parents would not have wanted her to live on a young minister's salary. They would have subsidized her, and I would have felt like a "kept" man. They would have pushed me to go the "tall steeple" route, and probably in the North. I am glad I had the sense to end this.

Second Year Friends

By the second year at YDS, while one "knew" everyone on campus, my circle of good friends had grown a little more definable.

Marnie Smith, because of using me as a "way station," was becoming a major friend, although we never "dated." I did not want to "date" anyone at YDS—partly because that would be so public, partly because I thought it would be too painful if we parted. But we definitely became close friends.

Bob Bailey was a good friend, a Methodist from Minnesota. He put more into our friendship than I did. He was not exciting, but was solid and steady.

By the second year, Norvin Hein and I had become friends, even though he was on the faculty. We would go to church together at times, and he let me use his car that Thirza Jones weekend. Norvin was serious, and shy.

I liked Kelly Clark. We were in the same cell group, and some of the same classes. He was about as sophisticated a person as I ever knew. He was the one whose grandfather had been a "leather baron" in the 19th Century. Kelly was so rich, and so sure of himself, that he often wore clothes that his father had used when he was in college. I especially remember a wool jacket that came straight out of the 1920s. Kelly often had whiskers during the day, then would appear at supper cleanly shaved. He was used to "dressing for dinner" and kept that up.

Alvord Beardslee lived in the house next to Stuart. He was quite artistic and did some paintings. I remember one he did one of Jesus on the cross, without the loincloth and his genitals clearly showing. That was considered somewhat shocking in those days. Al was an anglophile and always referred to the British royal family as "cousins."

I guess it was through Al that I got to know Jack Gessell so well. Jack was a graduate student in theology, an Episcopalian. He had been a conscientious objector during World War II. He told about his time as an aide in the psychiatric hospital in Williamsburg, Virginia, and some more time in a CO camp in Vermont or New Hampshire where one of the other men was a large, powerful black man from New York who would get tormented by the people in the town where they lived. This man was a follower of Father Divine. His anger would build up, and he would want to strike back at his tormentors. When he was about to explode, he would telephone Father Divine who would talk to him, and the anger would all go away. Jack and I got so we would take walks together after supper, especially in the spring when the mountain laurel and rhododendron were in bloom. We have kept in touch, annually, through the years. I visited him once in Franklin, Virginia, where he was rector of a church attended by one of Mother's Randolph Macon friends. He later became a professor at the seminary of the University of the South, Sewanee, Tennessee.

Another graduate student who became a good friend was Harriet Taylor. She had taught religion at Miss Willard's girls prep school and was back to get her Ph.D. in New Testament. (She never did get it.) She was middle-aged, not attractive, but a lot of fun. She came from Cape Cod, as I remember.

George Chauncey remained a good friend, after our 1949 trip to Rock Island for the Interseminary Conference. But I did not see as much of him that second year, for he got a job as a resident counselor on Freshman Campus downtown. He was around only for classes. I did go down to his room there a few times, but there was a bonding between us that has never gone away. George had a couple of pastorates and then became the Washington lobbyist for the Presbyterian Church, U.S.

I also felt close to Bill Jones that second year, but he also lived off campus, for he was married.

Bard Smith and I grew closer with the passing of years. I would say he was one of my best friends at YDS, and we have stayed in touch—partly because of his mother, Gert Behanna, but also because we simply like each other. He is about as clean-cut a person as I know, and totally unspoiled by the wealth in which he grew up. He taught at Carlton College, Northfield, Minnesota, and became dean. He got his Ph.D. in Christian Ethics under Richard Niebuhr, but has moved into a study of Buddhism and Japanese life.

Gregor Thompson was around that second year. Although she was part of the social ethics and very intellectual group, because of our common Southern heritage we did enjoy each other. I used to call her "Magnolia Blossom," for despite her Louisiana accent she was about as far as one could get from the Southern belle stereotype. It still blows my mind that she was a sorority girl (Chi Omega) at LSU. She was a remarkable artist, and after getting her B.D. went on for a doctorate in art and taught on the university level. She also did freelance art work. She designed the emblem of the Presbyterian Church (USA). At the end of my second year, she married a man named Goethals, the grandson of the man who built the Panama Canal. I did not know him. I don't know where they met. I do remember going to their wedding in Dwight Chapel. It turns out he was gay and they got a divorce. She returned home in Monroe, Louisiana, for awhile and came up to stay with us in Crossett once when Uncle Ken was down for a series of services. We stayed in touch through the years until she died in 2008.

Betty Carpenter was a good friend that year, and through her, I got to know Bob Batchelder. I guess they had started dating by then. I was still very conservative, politically, and they were at the other extreme, but we had mutual respect. I have stayed in touch with them through the years and stayed at their home in New Hampshire in October 2002.

Harry Smith and I became friends, although again, we were on opposite ends of the political spectrum. He was always fun as well as bright. Little did we know he would marry my distant cousin (one I had never heard of at that time) Anne Hebert. He became president of Austin College, Sherman, Texas. Because of our Presbyterian connection, we stayed in touch until his death.

Dean Lewis and I became good friends that second year. A rebellious Southern Baptist who had gone to William Jewell College, Dean was exploring all the options in this new environment. He was an excellent student. In our conversations, he was without inhibitions on theology, politics, and sex. Somewhere along the way, he became a Northern Presbyterian, and through that we have maintained ties through the years. He was the social action man in the Northern Presbyterian Church for years, then went to Ghost Ranch as program director, then established the Cuba Connection.

Bobby Hall was another Presbyterian. Her parents had been in the Salvation Army when she was a child, but then became Presbyterians. She was a very good student, and an early feminist who was determined to be ordained, although that was not yet legal in the Presbyterian Church. I used to kid her about becoming the first Presbyterian minister who had never been baptized (because the Salvation Army does not do that). She later became an Episcopalian and taught New Testament at General Theological Seminary, New York, and then the Episcopal Seminary in Alexandria, Virginia. We have not stayed in touch.

Uncle Ken was a friend, as well as employer and mentor—in many ways, my best friend and the one with whom I spent the most time.

Thoughts of Taking a Year Off

As I began the third term of my second year at YDS, I began thinking about taking a year off before completing my degree. There were several factors at work. I realized I would be only 24 when I was seeking a call, and I looked more like 17. With the exception of the spring at the University of Arkansas, I had been at Yale for six years, and if I stayed, that would be seven in an ivory tower, Ivy League environment—pretty esoteric. I was aware that I had led a sheltered life before Yale, and these six years had not been too different as far as "ordinary" people would see them. I was increasingly interested in the pastoral aspect of parish ministry, and YDS was not strong in this area. For two years I had been

Uncle Ken's secretary and companion. In the eyes of the YDS community, I was identified with him. While I had friends all over the Quadrangle, it was as an outsider and not part of the rough-and-tumble of life in one of the other houses. I was wanting to get out from under Uncle Ken, and I did not know how I could do that without hurting him.

I talked to John Oliver Nelson, Director of Field Work, about wanting to "get my hands dirty" — but not about wanting to get out from under Uncle Ken, for he was a gossip. I shall never forget our conversation. He was independently wealthy from Gulf Oil and a graduate of Princeton University before getting his BD (at Yale, I think). I went into his office in my usual attire: gray flannel slacks, a tweedy jacket, white shirt, and blue tie — which was not one of my best. I had not "dressed" for him. He said, "Indeed you do need to get away from Yale. Just look at you. Your blue tie is too blue, and your white shirt is too white." I said nothing but I thought, "You are a great one to be talking. Just look at you — your mustache is too well trimmed, your gray hair is too well cut, your knit tie and your handsome jacket are too Princeton."

I talked about working as an orderly at the Institute for Human Relations (the psychiatric hospital for Yale Medical School) or taking a half load and serving as a counselor for Yale freshmen on the Old Campus, as George Chauncey was doing. We also talked about my taking three quarters of training from the Council for Clinical Pastoral Education, an ecumenical group all over the country. They took in many students and pastors for one term, but they also took a smaller number for three to five terms to train them to be certified chaplains. I was not interested in the chaplaincy, but the idea of getting training in a variety of institutions in various parts of the country did appeal to me. Then, having served two summers in a large church in a city, I thought I would like to spend one quarter of my year in a very small church in a small community, to see if I could still relate to people like that, especially if that could be in Arkansas, for I still had a strong sense of call to return to my home state.

I began filling out the papers and learning just what openings might exist. I knew I wanted experience with patients in a psychiatric hospital, in some kind of prison setting, and in a general hospital setting. I was somewhat late in sending in my application, so some programs were already full. I remember thinking I would like to go to the federal prison at Chillicothe, Ohio. Why, I do not remember, except I think I had heard it was a good program. Also, St. Elizabeth Hospital in Washington, DC, was said to have an excellent program, and the idea of living in Washington excited me. But both of those were full.

As I remember, I had all three quarters lined up before I left Yale in the spring—in the summer, at Larned State Hospital, Larned, Kansas (psychiatric); Topeka Boys Industrial School, Topeka, Kansas (prison); the general hospital section of Bellevue Hospital, New York.

As I got into this plan for a year, I told Uncle Ken I felt the need for this extra training, and he seemed to be comfortable with that—and got to work lining up Rudy Everest from Yale College to replace me. Rudy had been in the prayer group I formed in the fall of 1948, and I was delighted to see him come.

I need to add that Daddy and Mother were very supportive of this plan. When I first talked about going into the ministry, Daddy was opposed. But once I made the decision, he told me he would finance whatever education I needed and wanted—and did, most generously. And they paid for each of these quarters of CPE.

End of School, 1951

As I try to recall the end of term that second year at YDS, it was a time of nostalgia. The class ahead of me—with people like Bob Batchelder and George Todd and John Turnbull—were about to graduate. I did not know that I would be able to get back to the YDS campus during the ensuing year, and if not, then my own class would be gone. I was leaving a town I had come to like and a university I loved. While I wanted to get out from under Uncle Ken's dominance of my life, I also cherished it and knew I would miss him. I had come to be very close to Jack Gessell, who was about to leave to be ordained an Episcopal minister (at that time at YDS we did not talk about their being priests, although they may have so regarded themselves) and was going to serve in Franklin, Virginia, where one of Mother's college friends lived.

I knew I was coming back to YDS after a year, so somehow managed to store a lot of my things and furniture. Perhaps I lent the latter to Rudy Everest, who would be moving into my room in Stuart House.

As I remember, I took the train to Washington, then one to Franklin, Virginia, to see Jack Gessell in his parish, and perhaps spent the night with Mother's friend. I am quite vague about that. Then I took another train to Lexington, Virginia, to visit Charles and David McCain at Washington and Lee. After one night in their fraternity house, I took a train to Louisville, stayed with Florence's family, and picked up the car Art and Florence had left when they went to French Morocco. I then drove it to Arkansas so I would have transportation to Larned, Kansas, for my first quarter of CPE.

On the way to Larned, I remember spending the night in Wichita, Kansas. I had contacted Aunt Harriet McCain (widow of one of Mother's half-brothers) and her son, Bob. I think I went out to their house in the evening and the next morning had breakfast with Bob. That is the only time I ever saw her. She had been close to Main and Mother after Uncle John's death—I think had lived with Main and Grandfather McCain for some time. But Bob lost his job with the Associated Press in Memphis after he wrote a story with an error in it. Main was in her final illness, and we had a nurse living with us. Aunt Harriet wrote Mother, asking if she could come visit. Daddy said "the help" would quit if we kept piling more work on them. Mother wrote back that she might come for a day (or some such), but they could not have her for longer. I don't think she ever contacted Mother from that time on. So I did not know what kind of reception I would receive. However, they were very nice, and for a few years I did send Christmas cards.

I also stopped to see them going to or from my second CPE unit, in Topeka. I met Bob, but did not see her. Soon after that, letters were returned. Uncle Arthur tried many ways to find what had happened to them. They simply disappeared without a trace.

Intern Year

Larned State Hospital

I drove away from Scott in Art's car, headed for Larned, Kansas. When I received word that was where I would be sent for my first quarter of Clinical Pastoral Education, I had never set foot in Kansas before. People at Yale sympathized with me, saying Kansas was the dullest, ugliest state in the Union, especially in the summer when it was hot and dry and the wind blew constantly. I had no idea where Larned was located. I found it was in the west-central part of the state. It was a very small town. About 20 miles away was a larger town, Great Bend, that happened to be located on the Arkansas River — only in Kansas it was pronounced the ar-KAN-sas river.

The eastern part of Kansas through which I passed had a few hills and a good many trees. The farther west I drove, the trees were fewer in number, and hills gave way to rolling farmland covered with more wheat fields than I had ever imagined to exist. When I first arrived, the wheat was still green, not yet ready for harvest. In most years, rain would be scarce from this time on, the green countryside would start turning brown, the heat would be intense, and dust would begin to blow. This was the center of the "dust bowl" of the 1930s. But 1951 was the year of the "big flood" in Kansas. It rained and rained and rained. The Arkansas River flooded at Great Bend. The Missouri River flooded Topeka and Kansas City — I think probably the highest level of flooding ever recorded. Lawrence, where the University of Kansas is located, was flooded. I don't know which river it is on, but in the winter term (coming or going) I spent a night in a motel there and the water stains were six to seven feet high on the walls.

The good side effect of those rains and flooding was that Kansas was absolutely beautiful that year! Wildflower seeds that had not germinated for decades bloomed with all that rain, and Kansas turned into a flower garden. There were especially lots of sunflowers. Apparently the sunflower (Kansas state flower) came from Mexico. As wagons came back from Mexico, the wheels would be coated with mud, and that mud had sunflower seeds in it. As the mud dried, it would fall off and leave the seed to sprout. Some of that must have fallen in Texas and Oklahoma, but Kansas was the major recipient. Also, the wheat on those rolling plains was beautiful—when it was green, but especially as it turned golden and was waiting to be harvested. With the wind blowing, the wheat field looked like waves of green or yellow. My memory of the state is radically different from the accounts people had given me ahead of time.

Larned was the western most psychiatric hospital in the Kansas system. The exposé *Snake Pit* had been written a few years before about the shocking conditions in psychiatric hospitals, using the hospital in Topeka as the example. This had rocked people all over the country, but especially in Kansas. A reform program was started. The Menningers of the Menninger Foundation in Topeka offered to take over. We went to Topeka to see what was happening there in that state hospital, but we had to delay our trip a few weeks because our scheduled date was at the height of the flood. The facilities were still antiquated (worse than those at Larned), but the staffing was outstanding. Bill Oglesby, then working on his Ph.D. in counseling, was in CPE there, and we had some visits. His ward was experimenting with trying to get some "old schizophrenics," who had been hospitalized for 20 to 30 years, back into the world. One doctor was prescribing quantities of love. While walking through a ward with Bill, I heard some haggard old woman call out to him and hold up her arms. He said, "Excuse me." He walked over to a rocking chair (the main form of therapy up to then), took her in his lap, hugged and rocked her, then gently put her down. In that same ward, if someone "acted out," instead of locking him/her up, he/she was locked *outside* the ward in the hall or yard. These people were so institutionalized, the staff knew they would not run away, for this was all the world they knew. So they would knock, then beat, on the door begging to be let back in. The severity of their punishment was measured in how long it would be before they could get back in. I was amazed at this treatment.

While I'm on the subject of Topeka, I need to tell about the flies. I have said that our visit was delayed because of the flood. When the waters receded, along the river and all over North Topeka there was a layer of mud about a foot deep. As it dried, the stench was terrible, and flies were hatched by the millions. In Kansas, unlike Arkansas, normally window screens are not needed, so none were on most of the hospital windows. When we would eat at the hospital, if I bowed for a moment of silent prayer, I had to keep waving my hand over the food as long as my eyes were closed, or flies would settle all over the plate, glass, and food. All the time we ate, one hand was waving off the insects.

There were three of us in the CPE program that summer at Larned — Tom Mull, an Episcopal theological student from Pittsburgh who was just starting seminary, and Charles (Chuck) Hall, the Methodist pastor in WaKeeny, Kansas, (where my grandfather had been the Presbyterian pastor in the early 1880s) who later became the head of the Council on Clinical Pastoral Training, and me. We lived in a small suite in the headquarters building of the hospital, and the place where pre-frontal lobotomies and insulin shock treatments were done. It seems to me Chuck had a small bedroom, and Tom and I shared one. The three of us got along very well. Chuck was gone most weekends so he could return to WaKeeny, except for those times when he had to lead chapel services.

The chaplain/supervisor was named Gordon Chambers. He was — technically — a Presbyterian, but only "skin deep," judging by his theology and worship services. He had a wife, whose name I have blanked on, who was what my children later would describe as "plastic" — lots of make up, dyed hair, and phony from the bottom up. (At least that was the judgment of the three of us after only a couple of weeks.) And she controlled Gordon completely. Perhaps he would have been OK, but she wanted all of his time and attention, so he put in the bare minimum as either chaplain or supervisor. It seemed to us Gordon Chambers was not interested in the patients or in us. He was out to do as little work as possible and to have as pleasant a life as he could. He gave us very little in the way of instruction or guidance. We three soon disliked him, and as the quarter wore on came to disregard and scorn him. The following fall he was kicked out of the Council and not allowed to have any more students.

The reforms at Topeka State Hospital had not yet reached Larned. The superintendent, Dr. Naramore, was a good and kind man, but out of date on psychiatry. He had probably been "grandfathered in" from the time when a general practitioner who was good with people could call himself a psychiatrist. He was also operating with a very limited budget and staff. There were about 2,200 patients in that hospital. They were very proud because they had just hired their first social worker. One social worker for 2,200 patients!

She was very good at her job, but was completely snowed under. As a result, she encouraged the three of us to do as much social work as we wanted to on the wards to which we were assigned. At the end of the summer, she told me if I ever decided not to complete seminary, I could come out there anytime and she would give me a job.

I think there were five MD's for the 2,200 patients. One of them was an excellent man who from time to time would lose contact with reality and have to switch from being staff to becoming a patient. When he got better, he would go back on the staff. Probably the sharpest doctor was an English surgeon who was very much into the lobotomy business. This was the "coming" procedure at that point in medicine—later repudiated because of the side effects. However, it was effective in calming patients who were violent or who were "old schizophrenics."

I had not completed my "Credo" for Systemic Theology when I left New Haven, and had a deadline of sending it back to finish the course. The first weeks I would work on it every spare moment, at night and on weekends. As I mentioned earlier, our apartment was near the room where people coming out of insulin shock were placed. They moaned and groaned and cried as they were coming out. Being a "dour" Calvinist, this was all I needed to have a very strong section on sin and total depravity!

My assignment was to work in the Criminally Insane building. I managed to postpone my first visit for two or even three weeks. Finally, I could not dodge it any longer. I remember as I prepared for my first visit I left behind my wallet, my keys, and the address and telephone number of my parents in case my roommates needed to contact them! Once I got over that fear and prejudice, I realized how lucky I was, for these were the most intelligent and interesting patients in the whole hospital. Only once did I have anxiety. One of the patients with whom I had an on-going relationship could at times become quite violent. (This was before there were any tranquilizers.) He was isolated in a "quiet" (i.e., padded) cell. A few days earlier in a manic phase, he had torn up his metal cot and shoved it out, in little pieces, through the small window in the door. But he had calmed down, so I went in to see him. He was sitting between the door and me. As we talked, we hit on a subject that agitated him, and I saw a wild look come in his eyes. I said something I thought was soothing, then managed to get out!

At the end of the quarter, as I was preparing to leave, I got very weepy over leaving these people whom I had come to know and care about. I knew there would be no replacement for me. The chaplain would never go there, and the one social worker could not possibly offer much attention to these people.

There was an adjunct section of the Larned Hospital over at Great Bend, mostly for elderly patients and "long-term schizophrenics," so there was little need for security. I was visiting one day with a nice elderly woman who told me she had been put in the hospital by a nephew so he could get all the money off some oil wells on her farm. There have certainly been instances when relatives have put away in a mental hospital someone they found to be a nuisance. Also, there were a lot of oil wells scattered on farms in Kansas at that time, and they produced a lot of revenue. I didn't know this was the case, but it was in the realm of possibility. Then she told me that King George V of Great Britain was her uncle—and I, at last, realized I was in a realm of fantasy. It was not always easy, under hospital conditions, to discern the line of demarcation.

Part of our CPE experience was to lead in worship at the chapel services. Gordon Chambers' wife was the pianist. I don't know where she came from or what her background was, but I think it was not very churchy, because when I wanted as a hymn "O God, Our Help in Ages Past," she said she had never heard of it!

Once a week, the three of us would meet with Gordon to discuss various theories about psychiatric problems. Then once a week, each of us was to have a private conference with him. I am sometimes a slow learner, and I'm sure part of the block was my low regard for Gordon, but it was not until almost the end of the quarter that it began to dawn on me that problems were not just about "them" (i.e., patients) but also about me. I did not trust Gordon enough to open up to him, but by the time I left Larned, I was ready to take a look at my "innards" and to make use of a good supervisor/counselor.

The one great contribution Gordon made to my formation was in my last, required, interview with him before I got in the car and headed back home. He said, "Don, you have disliked me and have been angry with me this whole quarter, but you have never expressed it. How you feel about me is, at this point, irrelevant. But until you are able to tell someone you are mad at—or even hate—

him or her, you will never be able to tell that person that you love him or her." He was right on target. I have quoted him many times since. I was reared to be polite, to be a gentleman, and not to offend others — because I wanted everyone to like me. I have kept a lid on my anger, and therefore have had to work hard at prying that lid off, and also becoming free to express my love.

That, alone, was probably worth three months in Larned, although I did learn other things. And there were other benefits. I was glad to get to know that part of Kansas. I enjoyed my roommates. I felt comfortable with the doctors and social worker. I got over my fear of psychiatric patients. The fact the social worker wanted me to stay on gave me some self-confidence. As fall approached, I missed heading back to New Haven after all these years, but I was also glad I was taking a "breather." Despite Gordon Chambers, it was a good start to a fantastic year.

Credo

I have already indicated I had not finished, by the time I left New Haven for Larned, the term paper for Systematic Theology, which was a "Credo," or statement of my beliefs. I concluded it while at Larned. It was 35 pages long, double-spaced. Most of it restates my affirmation of basic Christian doctrines, e.g., the Trinity, salvation by grace, predestination. But toward the end, I spelled out some convictions that were to get me in trouble with Washburn Presbytery when I was licensed and with Ouachita Presbytery when I was called to the Crossett Church. Please remember this was written before we were aware of sexist language. This is the part that got me in trouble:

> These (baptism and communion) are the two greatest sacraments. They are for all men who can and will receive them. However I think there is a third sacrament. I believe that ordination is a sacrament. I believe that we have evidence in the Gospels that Christ sent His disciples out to minister. Certainly in the Epistles we have examples given of the laying on of hands, the setting aside of certain men for this task. There is the promise of the gift of the Holy Ghost for them, and abundant

evidence that this promise was fulfilled. There is the physical act of the laying on of hands, which I believe to be more than just a sign, but to be rather a "seal." I believe that in the ordination there is a special working of the Holy Spirit. For those who receive Him in faith, there is something present the rest of their lives that had not been present before. For those who in unfaith reject Him or desecrate Him, there is the deeper sin because of the more certain and obvious repudiation.

I am not so certain about my belief that there is a fourth sacrament—marriage. Though our Lord did not marry, and though St. Paul seemed to consider it a poor second to celibacy, there does seem to me to be evidence in the Bible to consider it to have God's blessing and even institution, and at the same time some sort of promise—a promise of a unity which was not before but which will be for the rest of this life. "Have ye not read, that he which made them at the beginning made them male and female, and said, For this cause shall a man leave father and mother, and shall cleave to his wife: and they twain shall be one flesh? Wherefore they are no more twain, but one flesh. What therefore God hath joined together, let not man put asunder" (St. Matthew 19:4-6). I do not know of any seal ordered for it, though the consummation of the marriage in sexual intercourse as the culminating expression of love might be so considered. I do believe that when a man and a woman are married, there is a bond, not just between the two of them but including God, which is not dissolved until death. Such a belief, of course, makes one consider divorce and remarriage in a much more serious light. I believe that our denying the sacramental nature of marriage has been a contributing factor to the divorce rate. But I am not certain enough of my position in regard to marriage to assert as firmly as I do with the previous three that it is a sacrament. It is either that or a "sacramental."

WaKeeny, Kansas

When I met the two other interns in the CPE program at Larned, Kansas, and we introduced ourselves to each other, I was amazed to learn that one of them, Charles (Chuck) Hall, was pastor of First Methodist Church in WaKeeny, Kansas. I told him that is where my father was born, because my grandfather was the Presbyterian pastor there in 1882.

We would often talk about this. He suggested that some Monday, our day off, I drive up there. I asked him to see if he could find anyone in the Presbyterian Church who remembered my grandfather.

One week he came back saying that he had asked the Presbyterian minister, and they had found one old lady who did have childhood memories of Grandfather.

So, one Monday I did drive up there. WaKeeny is a little north and west of Larned. It is said that it was the dead center of the "dust bowl" of the 1930s. In 1951, it was still possible to see dirt that rose like a small hill, then suddenly dropped straight down. They said this was where there had been a barbed wire fence. When a dust storm would come, the dust would pile up against the fence on the windward side only. With the passing of years, the fence poles would have been removed or rotted. All that was left was this peculiar pattern, repeated over and over.

By the 1950s this was rich wheat farming land, especially in 1951 with all the rains and floods.

In his autobiographical reflections, Grandfather said that in WaKeeny he had bought some land to farm, thus supplementing his income. He said it was there he learned that one cannot be a successful farmer and a pastor at the same time.

Chuck did take me by to meet this lady. (I do not remember her name.) She said she did have a faint memory of Grandfather. She was five years old when he left in 1882. She said she also remembered, about the same time, they had their last "Indian scare." Reports came that the Indians were on the warpath and headed for WaKeeny. They all left their farm homes and gathered together in the town of WaKeeny, but the Indians never showed up. It was awesome for me to meet someone who tied together the memories of Grandfather and an Indian scare.

I learned that the name of the town came from two people who founded it—one name began with WA (such as Washington) and the second ended in EENY (such as Tweeny). Each wanted the town named for him. So they compromised.

Grandmother's 90th Birthday

After my quarter at Larned State Hospital and before going on to Topeka, I returned to Arkansas. Grandmother Campbell was about to have her 90th birthday. My parents and the Gordon Campbells had planned a big celebration for her and were driving up to Bloomington, Illinois, to put it on. Since I was around and free, and would be the only grandchild who could go, they invited me to join them.

The five of us drove up together. It was a rare treat to be with the four of them for an extended period—probably the longest ever, and certainly the longest since I was an "adult." And they did treat me as an adult. As always on a cross-country drive, we had a chance for much conversation. They were interested in my CPE and my plans for the future. I remember I talked them into stopping in Osceola, Arkansas, to look at the Presbyterian Church there. I was very much into visiting churches, to see what they looked like, and when alone I would have a period of prayer.

Aunt May Campbell was present. I think she must have already moved from Pontiac to Little Rock, but maybe not. Perhaps she had gone up for a visit in Pontiac and just came down for this occasion. But we have a family picture that includes her.

I guess this was the next-to-last time I ever went to 1501 Olive Street—where Grandmother lived. Ann and I stopped by there after our wedding on our way to Scotland so I could introduce them to each other.

Grandmother had lived in Bloomington for many years—probably since about 1912. She was known in the city, and certainly in First Presbyterian Church where she had taught one Sunday School class and where another class had been named in honor of Grandfather even before he died. But she could not stand the pastor there. She had not liked him before, but the final straw was when she returned from the winter in Arkansas after Grandfather's death. She met the pastor downtown. He spoke to her and then said, "Well, now I won't have to call on you at your home."

On the other hand, the pastor at Second Presbyterian Church, Dr. Martin (who later was elected Moderator of the USA Church), lived right across the street from her. They were very attentive, and even picked her up each Sunday and would drop her at First

Presbyterian Church before going on to their own. Afterward, they would come by and take her back home. Grandmother very much wanted to go to Second, but she was such a good "church-woman" that she felt since she belonged to First, she should not move simply because she did not like the current pastor.

However, she was very clear that she did not want her pastor to give the invocation at the birthday banquet. Instead, she wanted Dr. Martin. She realized this was not "proper" and could be a source of embarrassment for Dr. Martin, but we all agreed that at 90, she should be able to have the person she wanted to pray. And we hoped that her pastor would never know. What we did not count on was the widespread interest in her, for the local newspaper sent a reporter and a photographer. And the next morning on the front page of the local paper was a picture of Grandmother and Dr. Martin! And was she embarrassed.

I remember that gathering as being a very happy one. As I recall, her brother, Dr. Walter Dill Scott (president emeritus of Northwestern University) and his wife were there, and her favorite brother, Dr. John Scott (professor of Greek, emeritus at Northwestern) and his wife came, plus Aunt May and the five of us from Arkansas—plus many neighbors and friends. Soon after that birthday, her health began to deteriorate. If I am not mistaken, she was 94 when she fell down the stairs in her house and lay there for some time before her next-door neighbor, Mrs. Solomon, saw the lights on late at night and checked. Grandmother ended up with a broken hip, and we all assumed that was "the end" of her, but granddaughter Edith Coles, an RN whom Grandmother and Grandfather had put through nursing school, came down from Canada and nursed her—making her to do the exercises prescribed and forcing her to walk. It put a real strain on their relationship, but she did walk again. Then when she was about 98, she fell again, and this time she never fully recovered.

Grandmother, whose two children died as children, took on her stepchildren and their families as her own—and for us, she was the "real" grandmother, for we never knew our father's birth mother. When she would spend the winters with us at Scott, we looked forward to her coming.

Boys Industrial School

After returning from the Bloomington trip, I drove up toward Kansas. When I reached Topeka itself, which is on low hills, it was not badly damaged from the recent flood there, but when I crossed over to North Topeka, I realized how that city had been almost wiped out. And as I drove out to the Boys Industrial School (BIS) campus, I could see marks on the sides of buildings that had been ruined, and mud still covering large areas.

BIS took care of boys who had been remanded by the courts. They ranged in age from about eight to 18, and had been sent to BIS for a variety of reasons. Some had acted out so badly that their parents turned them over to a juvenile court. Some were orphans or neglected children. Some were in for crimes — mostly minor ones, I think. They lived in five "cottages" divided by age, except for one that was for blacks. (Kansas, although a "northern" state, was the site of some bloody battles prior to the Civil War over whether it was to be "slave" or "free." This was three years before the Supreme Court decision *Brown vs. Board of Education*, brought because of segregation in the Topeka schools.) BIS was "integrated" in classes and all activities except at night when it became segregated.

BIS had benefited from the Kansas reform that followed the publication of *Snake Pit*. When Karl Menninger offered to help bring Topeka State Hospital out of the dark ages, he also had an interest in BIS. Menninger residents were consultants for BIS, and we got to sit in on some of their staff meetings. The staff at BIS was a major leap ahead of that at Larned. There were social workers, psychologists, counselors, and schoolteachers who seemed to know what they were doing. And even the aides were a cut above those I had known at Larned.

For me, the decisive change was the chaplain/supervisor. Chuck Gerkin was top-flight. Of the three I worked with, he was by all odds the best. He later became a professor of pastoral counseling at Candler School of Theology, Emory University, in Atlanta. His wife, Mary, was equally superior to Mrs. Gordon Chambers. I liked both of them and felt immediately they were genuine. They were very open about their trauma the previous summer during the flood. Their home had been destroyed. Nobody had expected a flood in the middle of Kansas, so people didn't even talk about flood insurance. Chuck said he was about ready to go to a high building and jump out because he was financially ruined. Then his insurance agent called and said, "Congratulations. You are one of five people in Topeka with flood insurance!"

They were also very open in talking about their relationship with each other. Once I asked him something about church history. He said he knew very little church history because he took it the year after they got married, and the class was at eight in the morning—and he usually was busy doing other things and rarely made it to class. Another time when the three of us were driving to some event, Chuck must have said something about hoping someday they would live in Florida. Mary said, "The only thing you like about Florida is that penis like thing which hangs down when you look at a map of the state." This was a kind of openness that was new to me—embarrassing at times, but also liberating.

Since I was the only intern that fall, I had a big, barny single room on the top floor of the building where aides, cooks, and lower level employees of BIS lived. Having lived with two other interns the previous summer, I missed their companionship. On the other hand, it was nice to have some privacy. I did not have bathroom privacy, however. All of us on that floor shared one bath—and it was a communal one, just one tub, one commode. There was no shower, so I had to use the tub. It had a "ring" around it that made me think twice about whether I wanted to get in it. I stood it for a while, then went out on a day off, bought a sponge and Dutch Cleanser, and scrubbed it down to the enamel. Some others in the floor commented on how nice it was, but I don't think anyone shared in keeping it clean. However, I did from then on.

As I remember, there was a staff dining room where we ate our noon meal, but for breakfast and supper I would eat with the boys. One of my assignments was to get to know them and to build up a relationship with as many as I could. So most nights after supper when they were locked in their houses, I would go over to play pool or basketball. I would rotate around, trying to go to each house one night a week. I had never played pool before in my life, and they loved beating me. I never had been good at basketball, but of all the "contact" sports, this was the only one I liked at all. So I could do pretty well, at least with the younger ones.

Having had my "racial conversion" only three years before, it was a real step for me to be living so closely with the black boys. I wanted to, and think I did a fairly good job. But I had to work at overcoming life-long behavior patterns. I thought I knew how to understand "black talk," having heard it all my life on the plantation. When I was in the black cottage, I would be playing pool or basketball with the boys, communicating openly with them. Then all at once, I realized I did not know a thing they were saying. I wondered what was wrong with me, and first thought it was just a bad night. But it kept on happening—not all the time, but just sporadically. I finally went to one of the social workers, a black man who worked with the boys from this house, and asked him if I was crazy or what. He said, "No. They have just decided they wanted to talk about something and did not want you to hear what they were saying, so they began to use 'black talk.' When they are ready for you to be included, they'll begin talking so you can understand." I tried to analyze what they did. They continued to use English words and sentences, but the inflections and the cadence were changed from those we use in "standard English" so that it became gibberish to me. I have remembered that through all these years and would still like to know exactly what they did.

The boys were all in academic school during the day, unless they had a specific appointment for counseling with someone on the staff. And I was considered staff. I went to all staff meetings and could contribute if I had something to share. I had a small office and could make appointments with individual boys.

I shared in leading the chapel services. I'll never forget the first time I was to preach. Just before I stepped out into the make-shift chancel, Chuck said, "I did warn you, didn't I, never to use the word 'Father' when referring to God? Almost all these boys have had bad experiences with their fathers, and if you use that term about God, it will turn them off." Well, to have the word "father" taken out of the sermon I'd been working on and had written out, as well as out of all the prayers, was a blow! I never realized how integral it had been in our liturgies until I suddenly had to find substitutes while preaching and praying. It was a learning experience.

I was given certain boys to work with on a one-on-one basis. I can't recall how I got them. Perhaps they were referred by Chuck or one of the social workers. I know I met several times with several of them. But the one who meant most to me was a black boy named Nate. I can't recall Nate's last name. I think he came from Kansas City. He was totally blind, but navigated the campus skillfully. His way of "seeing" was through touch. Since he had his hands extended all the time as he was moving around, they were always dirty. And when Nate was talking to any individual, he would feel that person's face and hands and clothes. It was always easy to tell with whom Nate had had a recent conversation because they would have smudge marks on their clothes (white shirts just asked for finger marks) and also on their faces. Nate was not in for any breaking of the law. I guess in the frustration of blindness he had become uncontrollable at home, and the juvenile court had taken him out of the home and put him at BIS.

Nate comes to my mind every Christmas. He is the first person I ever heard sing the spiritual "Go, Tell It On the Mountain." Nate would sing it any time, anywhere, as the Christmas season approached. I left just before Christmas to return to Arkansas. Saying goodbye to Nate was perhaps the most painful part of leaving. As I drove away from BIS I found myself trying to cry. I did not know I could get so attached to a group of people in such a short time.

One of the people on the staff who impressed me most was the psychologist. She could run an IQ test, or some standard psychological test, on a boy and with that information diagnose his problems with remarkable insight. This always had to be checked against other staff members, house parents, and the Menninger resident consultant. But I came to trust her skills. Unfortunately, I do not recall her name.

It is hard for me to remember what a daily schedule was like. I was supposed to do a certain amount of reading in preparation for discussions with Chuck. I had appointments with individual boys. I went to staff meetings at BIS, and then would go to other presentations across the river in Topeka, including Topeka State Hospital, and the children's part of Menninger. Chuck was good about keeping me posted on the learning opportunities in the area. At least once a week, I would have a private supervisory session with Chuck in which we would talk about the school, about my reflections on what was going on with the boys in general, and about specific boys with whom I had built up a counseling relationship, and I was free to talk about insights I had gained about myself.

This was new for me. I had not respected or trusted Gordon Chambers enough to let him "inside" me. My trust for Chuck Gerkin was a quantum leap ahead.

Since I was going to be in Topeka for three months, and didn't know a soul other than those at BIS and Tom Klink at the state hospital, I decided I needed to meet some other people. Most Sundays I had to be at BIS for chapel on Sunday mornings, but I was free some Sundays and went to First Presbyterian Church. I also began going to their young adult group on Sunday nights. I remember they had a couple of parties that I attended. There was one girl in the group I liked and who seemed to respond to me. I think I had one or two dates with her, but I did not encourage that relationship to develop, knowing that I would be leaving in December and would not return.

The food at BIS was OK, but certainly was dull. I had one day off a week. After doing my laundry and other necessary chores, I would often go to Topeka to shop, to see more about the city, and to treat myself to a good dinner. There was one restaurant that I especially enjoyed and often returned to. I remember the bread was usually some kind of cinnamon roll. I found Topeka to be a charming city and quite lovely, with rolling hills and lots of trees that turned colors in the autumn. One house that especially fascinated me was where Alf Landon lived. I think he was still alive. It was a Southern Colonial type with big white columns and a spacious lawn. He was roundly defeated for president by F. D. Roosevelt in 1936. If I am not mistaken, Daddy said that election was the one time he voted for a Democrat for President because he thought Landon's farm policy was a disaster. I think Landon carried only one or two states.

Washburn University was located in Topeka. I think it was a Congregationalist college, but I am not sure. Somehow I met one of the professors there who had earned his Ph.D. at Yale Divinity School. It was he who told me a story about Reinhold Niebuhr and the Beecher Lectures. Reinhold had graduated from Eden Seminary and gone to YDS to get his Ph.D. But he and the then-dean, Dean Brown, had not only a clash but apparently a battle. I have no idea whether it was due to personality differences or theology. Anyway, Reinhold Niebuhr left after one year with a "terminal Master's Degree" and never did get a Ph.D., although he taught for decades at Union Seminary, New York.

After he became famous he was invited to give the Beecher Lectures at YDS, the most distinguished theological lecture series in the USA at that time. There was a custom at YDS when someone came to give a series of lectures that a faculty member would introduce the speaker—again—before each lecture. Before the second or third lecture, Dean Brown (emeritus for many years at that point) was asked to do that honor. He got up and said, "Every generation of theologians has its shibboleth. In my generation it was 'Mesopotamia.' If one could bring that into a talk, it suggested great scholarship based on archaeology and a knowledge of ancient languages. Times change, and shibboleths change. It seems in our time they are 'bourgeois' and 'proletariat.'" And he sat down.

The Washburn professor said he was a graduate student at YDS at the time. As Reinhold Niebuhr began his next lecture, about the second sentence he said something about the bourgeoisie. There was a hush across the chapel. A sentence or two later he referred to the proletariat. There was a titter in the audience. A couple of sentences later he spoke about a bourgeois approach—and the place exploded in laughter.

When that died down, Mr. Niebuhr said, "Dean Brown has taught me a lesson. I did not realize how frequently I use those terms." For the rest of the lecture he would be going at his normal fast pace of speaking, then would suddenly halt, so he could think up a synonym. Then he would go on, and again a pause.

That night graduate students were called in on an emergency basis, given the texts of the remain lectures, and were told to find alternate ways of saying something without using one of "those words." The Washburn professor was one of those graduate students.

By the time I returned to Arkansas for Christmas, I had spent six months in Kansas, a state I'd never seen before. I came to love the state, both the wheat fields around Larned and the hills of Topeka. I still have a warm spot for it.

Chuck Gerkin at Boys Industrial School

While much at Larned State Hospital had been good, my relationship with my supervisor, Gordon Chambers, was terrible. I did not trust him as far as I could throw him. However, right at the end of that first quarter it did finally dawn on me that in discussing the psyche we were not only talking about "them" but also "me." But I would never have laid bare my soul with Gordon.

When I arrived at the Boys Industrial School, with Chuck Gerkin as supervisor, I decided I could trust him and began with my usual thoroughness to delve into the hidden depths of who I was/am. We would meet once a week for a counseling session. I am not sure where I started—probably with my anger toward Gordon and with the one insight I gained from him: that until I was able to express my anger and other negative feelings, I would never be free to express my love and other warm emotions. This was revolutionary for one who had been brought up to believe that it was a sin to be angry (especially if the anger was directed at a lady), and that in dealing with "inferiors" (i.e., in those days, blacks), to express anger was to lower oneself to the level of the cause of the anger and therefore to become vulnerable to a counter attack.

As I began talking to Chuck about my unacceptable thoughts and feelings, I suddenly became aware that I was not being attracted to girls in a romantic sense as many of my contemporaries were. That was followed by a lightning bolt of wondering if I might be a homosexual. I had had no such experiences, except the one episode of mutual masturbation in my senior year in high school. There had been none in college or the first two years at YDS. In those days homosexuality was considered both a sin and a serious illness, from which recovery was difficult. Once I faced up to this as a possibility of who I was, I went into shock, and I guess near panic.

Just as we got to this point in my counseling relationship with Chuck, he had to leave town for about 10 days to attend the annual meeting of the Council on Clinical Pastoral Training. He told me to "put the lid" on this. There was nothing else he could do, for there was no fallback counselor available. I guess he did not consider it as explosive as I felt it was. So on a conscious level, I did shut down my inner exploration.

I am sure it was not a coincidence that soon after Chuck left I developed a cold that got worse and worse, so I stayed in bed for several days, getting up only to eat. I was sick in body and soul, and experienced real depression. I felt I was standing on the edge of a bottomless pit.

When Chuck returned from his meeting (reporting that Gordon Chambers had lost his accreditation as a CPE supervisor), I think he suggested that we "cool it." We never did explore this possibility further, although I found him very helpful as a counselor in other areas of my life.

That second quarter of CPE was the most fruitful of the three, largely because of Chuck as supervisor and counselor. I wish I had pushed him harder to follow up. Perhaps he felt my ego was too fragile to move ahead with less than two months left in my time in Topeka. Or perhaps he did not feel qualified to handle it. I'll never know why. But this issue had been brought out from under the table and laid out for me to acknowledge and deal with.

George Chauncey at Christmas

After our trip to the Interseminary Conference at Rock Island, Illinois, during the Christmas vacation in 1949, George Chauncey and I became very close friends. He was having a terrible struggle with the Southern Baptist Church. Bill Jones was about to leave the Presbyterian Church to become an Episcopalian along with his wife. He was talking to George about making the same move. But I was encouraging him to take a look at the Presbyterian Church, US.

I guess it was in the spring of 1951 that I wrote Roy Davis, the Executive of the Synod of Arkansas, to see if there was a church where George could be a summer supply and get a "feel" for what the Presbyterian Church was like. George had gone to Southwestern in Memphis, a Presbyterian College, so he knew something about its theology and documents. But he had never been a part of a Presbyterian congregation. Roy Davis had been on the staff at Southwestern during George's college days and knew him. The Presbyterian church at Helena was vacant, and Roy recommended George, whom they called for the summer. It seems to me Walter Johnson was the summer supply at West Helena that year, but I'm not sure. He went there as pastor after graduation, but I think he may have spent a summer there earlier. I know Walter and George became close friends. Whether Walter was around that summer or not, George had a very good experience in the Helena Church and proceeded to take the necessary steps to become a candidate for the ministry in the Presbyterian Church, US.

In 1951-52, he was in his last year at YDS, and he was moving toward marriage with Barbee Davis, but he had no "network" to help him find a call to a church. I invited him to come over to Arkansas for two or three days during Christmas break, and I would drive him around to various towns where there were vacant churches and introduce him to any people I knew in them. I know one of the towns we visited was Des Arc where we spent the night with Laura and Shuford Nichols in their luxurious home. We may have gone to Lonoke, which the following summer called Bill Fogleman. I know we went to McGehee and perhaps Dermott, and then came through Monticello.

As we were driving toward Monticello, I told him I wanted us to drop by to see the Adrian Williamsons, cousins of mine. It is hard for me to believe I did it, but I think I told him I wanted him to meet the woman I would probably marry — Ann Williamson! At that point, I had never had a date with Ann, or thought of her in any way other than a cousin whom I enjoyed and thought attractive. When we arrived at "The Hill," the only member of the family around that day was Margaret, five years her junior and a student at Agnes Scott College. I remember we visited with her back in the library of their house, then headed on back to Scott.

The following summer George did not get a call from any of the Arkansas churches, so far as I know, but did accept one from the Presbyterian church at Brownsville, Tennessee. Two years later in 1954 when Ann and I were returning from Scotland, the Monticello church was looking for a pastor, and I strongly recommended they visit with George. He was miserable in Brownsville and quickly accepted the Monticello call. At the same time, I was being called to Crossett. He and I were examined by Ouachita Presbytery on the same day in October 1954. I'll write about that later, but fortunately the called meeting was held in Monticello. I probably would not have been received had the whole Williamson clan not been sitting on the front row!

Bellevue Hospital, January-March of 1952

Bellevue Hospital in New York City, unlike the other two places where I took Clinical Pastoral Education, did not provide housing or meals except when we were on duty. This meant that I had to find some place to live. I must have done some correspondence in advance, for I do not remember having to find temporary housing. I got a room at what was then called Biblical Theological Seminary (later changed to New York Theological Seminary). As the name would imply, it was a very conservative school. I never got to know any of the students. It was located on East 49th, as I remember, between Second and Third Avenues. The "el," or elevated trains, ran down Third Avenue, making a lot of noise. But I was far enough away so they did not bother me. The whole seminary was in one building—perhaps six or seven floors high. I had a private room. I am almost sure I did not have a private bath, but there must have been so few people living on my floor that I rarely if ever met any of them in the shower. There were no dining facilities at Biblical, or if so, I did not have access to them.

I did not take a car to New York, so depended on the bus or subway to get around. Bellevue was located on First Avenue, at about 14th Street (as I recall). I could walk over to First and 49th (one way streets) and catch a bus that let me off right in front of the hospital, then catch another one back at night. This was very easy and convenient. There were some small stores in the Seminary neighborhood. I could buy food to get me over weekends, and I found a Chinese laundry to take care of my clothes. There was also a branch bank where I could cash checks after opening an account. There was a problem in that the bank was closed on Saturday and Sunday. And getting a check cashed in New York City, other than at your bank, was almost impossible.

One weekend I had forgotten to cash a check on Friday. I was to preach at Bellevue on Sunday morning, then go out to Scarsdale for the rest of Sunday and all day Monday, but I would not arrive on Sunday until after lunch. I tried a couple of places, such as the laundry where I traded, but no luck on getting cash. I realized I had enough to pay my bus fare to Bellevue, then from there to Grand Central Station, and then enough to buy a one-way ticket to Scarsdale, with something like 27 cents left over. I had skipped lunch at the hospital so I could catch my train. I was hungry, and I remember going into the lunch counter at Grand Central, putting my 27 cents on the counter, and saying, "This is all the money I have. What can you give me for that?" It was not much—even in those days—perhaps a donut. When I got to Scarsdale and told them my tale of woe, Edith, the McCain's cook, insisted on warming up a meal "for the Rev."

Bellevue is the big charity hospital for Manhattan. It is famous for its psychiatric unit, but I was there to get training in general hospital work. I have never seen a "caste system" such as the one that operated in the dining rooms at Bellevue. Staff doctors ate in a paneled dining room. Residents ate in the big room, but in a sectioned off part; interns and registered nurses in another; orderlies, aides in another; and assorted others in still another section. They did not know what to do with chaplain interns. In the morning, for breakfast, we were allowed to eat with the residents — who usually sat at a table for their specialty, e.g., one for surgery, one for ophthalmology, etc. At noon, when things were more crowded, we were put in with the nurses. At night, we were to sit at the table with the ambulance drivers. On weekends, when the head chaplains stayed home, we took turns being "Protestant Chaplain In Charge" for a day. On that day, we were to eat all three meals in the paneled dining room reserved for the staff physicians. It was so absurd that I found it amusing.

The Protestant chaplaincy program at Bellevue was entrusted to the Episcopal Church. The head of that, and the general supervisor of the CPE program, was named Tom Morris. He was a very large, tall man. Under him was a very nice, older Episcopal priest whom I liked but did not get to know well. He was a brother-in-law or some such of one of the Episcopal bishops. Then there was a man named Dick Powers who was in training to become a CPE supervisor. There were about eight to 10 of us in the CPE program that winter, compared with three at Larned and one at Topeka. After being an "only child" in Topeka, I was glad to have some companionship. I liked most of the others. I think all were men except one woman. I do not remember the names of any of them, but the one I liked best was a black minister. There was also one man who was confined to a wheel chair, pushed by his wife much of the time. He had a "chauffeur's leg" to handle his urine output, but from time to time it became full and we would have to take him to the rest room to let him drain it into a urinal. Most of these people already lived in New York or thereabouts, and the rest of us were scattered. So it was "on the job" fellowship and not like Larned. I know one man was pastor of a Reformed Church of America congregation out on Long Island, for he invited me out there to preach one Sunday when he had to hold services at Bellevue.

We were not to work in psychiatry, unless there was emergency surgery there. There was a rule in Bellevue that no one, under any circumstances, could be given a general anesthetic until he or she had first been seen by a chaplain. So all day, whoever was in the office would get frantic calls to go see someone in obstetrics or surgery or the emergency room who had to be operated on right then. Under those circumstances we would simply appear, say, "I'm the Protestant chaplain" and have a one sentence prayer as the orderlies were moving the gurney toward the operating room.

I remember one Saturday when I was the only Protestant chaplain around, I got a call from psychiatry saying they needed me for a pre-surgery. Rarely did psychiatry have any surgery, especially emergency. The name of the patient was Celestial Light. She was a follower of Father Divine, and they all take new names when they are baptized. (Anyone who was not Roman Catholic or Jewish was categorized "Protestant," even if they were Muslims, Father Divine, Buddhists, etc.) It turned out Celestial Light had an abscess on her behind and needed to have it lanced!

Another memorable emergency call was to a surgery ward. As I got off the elevator, I saw the Roman Catholic chaplain coming out of the ward and preparing to get on the elevator. When I reached the man's bedside and introduced myself, he exploded and said, "God damn it. Get out of here! I am an atheist, and I just sent the Catholic chaplain packing." I left, and as I was waiting for my elevator, I saw the Jewish chaplain getting off. I knew where he was heading—and I can only imagine the kind of reception he received! Evidently, the person in the office decided if he claimed he had no religion, he was going to be exposed to the others, equally.

Perhaps the best story I have from the Bellevue experience is about my first funeral. As noted above, when head chaplains would take off for the weekend, they would leave a chaplain intern in charge for that hospital of some 2,000 beds. Before my first Saturday, Tom Morris told me it was not likely that I would have a funeral, but it was possible. (At this point, I was not ordained and had completed only two years of seminary and had never had a funeral.) He said, "If you have one, you can use the *Book of Common Prayer* over there, and here is a metal gismo we fill with sand from the banks of the River Jordan. At the end of the service we make a sign of the cross with this sand on the casket. Good luck." I nodded and assumed I would be safe.

The next morning shortly after I arrived, I received word that I was needed to conduct a funeral in the Mourners' Room in the Morgue. It seemed that the woman to be buried had been dead for about three weeks, but the service had been postponed because her husband, also a patient at Bellevue, had been desperately ill from having both legs amputated and could not attend, but he was now better. When I asked how she had died, they said it was probably suicide. All the family were gathered, and would I come over immediately for the funeral?

While at the hospital, the "garb" for chaplain interns was a short white jacket. I had come to Bellevue that morning wearing gray flannel slacks and a tweedy sport coat, for I was going out to Scarsdale for the weekend, leaving right after work. I did not think either the white coat or the tweed jacket seemed appropriate for a funeral. I saw in the closet Tom Morris' black cassock. He weighed 250-300 pounds, and I weighed about 130; he was over six feet tall, and I was 5'10". But off I went with it draped over my shoulder, along with the gismo full of sand and the Prayer Book. I was no expert on Episcopal canon law, but I had heard that a suicide could not (at that time) receive a Prayer Book funeral.

When I arrived at the Mourners' Room, I found the family were all Finnish. I could locate only one person who spoke English—a cousin. I wanted to be delicate in my inquiry, so I asked, "How did she become dead?" She said they were not sure. She had swallowed a bottle of iodine, but she also had double pneumonia. I decided to give her the benefit of the doubt and proceeded to open the Prayer Book. Then I looked for the casket. It was nowhere to be found! We looked in this room and that. Finally, someone remembered the funeral home man had said he had a friend who worked down in the basement, and he thought he would go have a smoke while he was waiting for me. So he was called to come up. It turned out he had taken the casket with him. In New York, one does not leave anything lying around lest it be stolen! In the meantime, I had put on Tom's huge cassock, winding it around me two or three times, with lots of it trailing on the floor.

When the freight elevator, clanking and grinding, reached our floor and the door opened, there was the casket—open—with the deceased reclining on some pillows, almost half-sitting, with a pleasant smile on her face. When this was rolled into the Mourners' Room, there was a gasp, then a flood of grief and emotion. The husband had not seen her for three weeks. All of them were talking in Finnish. I stepped back to allow them a chance to express their grief. When that subsided, I said to the funeral home man, "Please close the casket." He looked distressed and obviously did not want to do that. I said, "Please close the casket. There will be no funeral until the casket is closed." So he pulled down the lid until it suddenly would go no farther. It had hit her nose! I indicated he should try again. This time he began taking out pillows and other stuffing, and again lowered the lid. But her body was rigid in its position, without the pillows. He pulled and he tugged, but it would not close. The family were all watching. Finally I said, "Just lay it gently on her, and we'll proceed."

So I began reading the Prayer Book service, and did quite well until we got to the Lord's Prayer. When the only two voices were mine and the cousin who could speak English, I realized the rest of the family had not understood a word I had been reading.

Then came time to make the sign on the cross on the casket, per Tom Morris's instructions. I moved over to the casket and in a dramatic gesture made a large cross with the sand. Then it dawned on me that I had made it over her feet! So I moved to the other end, so I could do the same over her head. Only half way through, I ran out of sand! But I kept on as though I had plenty.

As soon as I pronounced the benediction, being utterly embarrassed at the way I had flubbed the whole affair, I rushed to the Morgue office and took off Tom's cassock. Then it dawned on me that perhaps I should go speak to the family, even though my Finnish was zilch. So I walked back into the Mourners' Room. They saw me, then huddled over in one corner. Finally someone emerged from the huddle with a 10 dollar bill in her hand. It struck me that they, from the Old Country pattern, thought I had come to be paid. I shook my head vigorously, waved my hands in protest, and they withdrew with their money. At that point, all of them departed in a rush.

As I was about to leave myself, I noticed off in one corner was a man in a wheel chair. It was the widower, left by all his family! An orderly had brought him down from his ward, and I presumed eventually would take him back. But in a big hospital, one never knows how long that will be. So wanting to continue being "helpful," I decided I would take him back to his ward. I rang for the freight elevator. When it arrived, we rolled in and I punched a button I thought was for his floor. But when the door opened, we were in the embalming room of the Morgue! At that point, I pushed his wheelchair toward one of the workers and pled, "You take him back to where he belongs," and fled.

Another of my Bellevue stories has to do with an Episcopal confirmation service. As I noted earlier, the chaplaincy program at this hospital was run by Episcopalians. There were a good many Puerto Ricans in that part of New York. Many of them had left the Roman Catholic Church of their ancestors. If they had replaced that religion with any other, it was usually Pentecostal or fundamentalist Protestant. Some of these people would be at Bellevue for extended periods of time, during which they had been touched by the care of the chaplains. As a result, several of them had decided they wanted to be confirmed in the Episcopal Church. Located very near Bellevue was an Anglican Benedictine convent—very, very high church. Some of those nuns, who had worked with these Puerto Ricans, came to their confirmation. One of the auxiliary bishops came down for the laying on of hands in a very formal service. But the chaplains had told the Puerto Ricans they could choose the hymns they wanted for the occasion. They were not exactly the hymns one would expect to hear at St. Thomas or St. Bartholomew, but were very evangelical. One of them, the title of which I can't at the moment recall, had in the chorus "Jesus, Jesus, Jesus, sweetest name I know, Keeps me singing as I go." At that point in history, high church people genuflected every time the name Jesus was mentioned. I looked over during the hymn, and there the nuns were bobbing up and down as fast as they could go, trying to get in three genuflections at a time. They looked like life buoys bobbing up and down on a stormy ocean. I had to muffle my laughter in a handkerchief.

My Psyche in New York

In Larned, I had finally learned that CPE was not just about "them" but also "me." At the Boys Industrial School, with Chuck Gerkin, I decided to delve into the mysteries of my psyche, for I did trust Chuck. When I went to Bellevue, in the anonymity of New York, I decided this was the best opportunity I would ever have to explore who I was. I was disappointed not to have Tom Morris as my personal counselor, but was assigned to Dick Powers. He was closer to my age than Tom. I decided to give him a try. If he could not handle it/me, Tom was there as a backup. So from the very start I brought up the issue of possible homosexuality.

After the first night when I took Ann Williamson to a play and enjoyed her company so much, I reported that—and then the subsequent, and more frequent, ways in which we got together. I told him I thought Ann was waiting for me to at least hold her hand, and perhaps kiss her, but I had inhibitions dating back to Mother's scolding Art for putting his arm around Marjorie Shook. Mother had expressed such disgust, I assumed it was evil. As many dates as I had in high school, during college, and the first two years of Divinity School, I had kissed a girl only once. Now I was feeling I "ought" to show some affection, which I was feeling, for Ann. Finally one cold night as we were walking back from the subway to James House, I held her hand, and kissed her as I told her goodnight. I remember, as I walked back to the subway, almost floating on air—not because I was in love, but because I had "broken the sound barrier" and had expressed my feelings physically. I could hardly wait to tell Dick Powers about this at our next meeting.

Ann and I were having a wonderful time, and I realized I was more attracted to her than I ever had been to any girl before. I would report to Dick after each date. He would encourage me to feel my way along.

Between my counseling and my relationship with Ann, this three-month period was a turning point in my psychological growth. I guess I was going through what most boys/men experience in adolescence as they experiment with their growing sexuality—only I was about six years behind schedule. By the end of the quarter, I had pretty well convinced myself that I was heterosexual, and I looked forward to dating Ann when she came back to Arkansas for the summer. I still had some inhibitions, dating back to Mother's injunctions, but I was expressing affection physically for the first time.

Living in New York

This was the only time I ever lived in New York. By this point in my life, I had visited there many times, but never before as a "resident"—even if for only three months. It was quite a different experience.

While I was expected to be at Bellevue from 8:00 or 9:00 a.m. to 5:00 p.m., once I got off in the evening I was free—and I was free on weekends when I was not "on call." I was rather strategically located. The cross-town bus could take me to Fifth and Park Avenues, and to Broadway near the theater district and Times Square. I was not far from Grand Central where I could catch trains to Scarsdale and New Haven, or the subway shuttle connecting with the subway that went up to the Union Seminary-Columbia University-St. John the Divine area.

Often I went out to Scarsdale on weekends, or on Sunday afternoon when I had finished my work at Bellevue and would have Monday off. After seven years in New Haven, the Arthur McCains had become my second home. Uncle Arthur was then president of Chase National Bank (the second largest and one of two most prominent in the USA). They lived at 75 Morris Lane in a large and beautiful home with a private tennis court in the back yard. At that time, Scarsdale was one of the most exclusive suburbs in the New York area.

By this time, I had also come to know well, and feel close to, the Charles McCains. He was Mother's first cousin. They had a third or fourth floor condominium at 10 Gracie Square looking out over East River. (This was a "very good" address. Boris Karloff, the actor, lived there, as did the conductor of the New York Philharmonic, who was married to one of the Vanderbilts.) When ships would pass by, we would be about on the level of the crew on the decks.

At this point only Cousins Charlie and Frances McCain, and her mother, Aunt Grace Walker, lived there. They had a cook and a maid and a chauffeur, and Cousin Frances had a masseuse come in twice a week. By this time, Cousin Charlie's health was deteriorating, so they had a male nurse every day. There was also a footman at the door, available to call a cab when people were leaving. He also had to approve someone before taking him up in the elevator to the proper floor. This was luxury beyond what I had seen in Scarsdale. But no one could have been kinder or more gracious to me.

During these three months, I did go back to YDS at least once, perhaps twice, to visit friends, especially those in my original class of 1952 who would be graduating in June. I saw Uncle Ken at that time also. I think he offered me the job as secretary again, but I was ready with an answer and declined without its destroying our relationship. I felt good about my being firm on this decision that I had made the previous year.

I did take advantage of my three months in New York to do lots of things. I went to the theater several times. One play I remember was *Lost Under the Stars*, the musical version of *Cry, The Beloved Country* by Alan Paton. That may have been the year Ann and I went to see *Porgy and Bess*, because we especially wanted to hear Leontine Price sing the lead role. We had splurged to get tickets and were deeply disappointed that on our night she was not singing. She and her partner rotated the role to avoid ruining their voices. (It was not until years later in Atlanta that I finally got to hear her in person.) I also went to the Metropolitan Opera, sitting way up in the top balcony, and I went to the Metropolitan Museum of Art and the Modern Art Museum. I did not do the touristy things, for I'd been to most of them before.

It was during these three months that Mother and Daddy flew to French Morocco to visit Art and Florence. That trip turned out to be a turning point in their relationship. My parents had been so opposed to the marriage (as had hers). I am sure Mother was behind this effort to "reach out" to Florence. And she more than matched their effort. She filled their days with short trips and expeditions, and they began to love her.

From there, they went to Europe, visiting Spain, France, and Belgium before going to London. In Belgium, Daddy came down with a chest infection that turned into pneumonia. He was quite sick, but they were in a hospital with a foreign language. The doctor there permitted them to fly to London where he was confined to his bed in a hotel.

During their trip, King George VI of Great Britain had died. The new Queen Elizabeth II was in Kenya when she got the word. She hurried back, but it took a while for all the heads of state from around the world to gather for the funeral in Westminster Abbey.

One morning, Mother left Daddy's room with just enough money to buy the morning paper. In the lobby people told her the funeral procession was about to come down the street in front of their hotel. When they asked if she was going to watch she said no, but the English could not believe she would pass up such a possibility, so she decided she would go out to the sidewalk. She was a small woman, 5'2" at her peak, and could not see over the heads of those in front of her, but she noticed a boy selling cardboard boxes people could buy to stand on. The cost was exactly what she had in her pocket for the newspaper, so she bought one. She weighed only 120 pounds, so she planned to stand on the box. A nice gentleman next to her offered to help her up and let her hang on to him. He also had a newspaper that listed the order in which the dignitaries would pass on their way to Westminster Abbey. He read them out to her as they appeared, so she got a world-class view of the event the rest of us were having described on the radio.

As soon as the English doctor would release Daddy, they secured a bed on a flight from London to New York. (In those days, by combining two rows of seats, a bed could be made—similar to a berth on a train—and was curtained off for privacy.) He made the trip well. I know I went to some kind of family gathering on their return. I don't remember if they went to Scarsdale for further recovery, or if they stayed at a hotel in New York and the gathering was at 10 Gracie Square. But I did see them, briefly, before they flew on to Arkansas.

Another of the riches of being in New York was attending church as often as possible at Madison Avenue Presbyterian Church where George Buttrick was pastor. He was one of the greatest preachers in the country at that time—both profound in his theology and Biblical insight, and in his ability to communicate. I had heard him once a year at Battell Chapel at Yale, but I enjoyed the experience of going most Sundays much better—and not only once, but twice, for they had an evening service also.

Ordinarily, both of his sermons were brilliant. But I found great consolation one Sunday. In the morning he laid a "goose egg." We went back that night, and he laid another one! How comforting to know even George Buttrick had his bad days!

I was very tempted to stay on in New York after my quarter at Bellevue ended. I was digging deep in my counseling relationship with Dick Powers, and I had started dating Ann by then. So I approached Madison Avenue to see if there was any chance they could use me on the staff that summer. (I had planned to have a summer in a small, rural church, but thought this might "do.") I did get an appointment with Buttrick, who took me to a luncheon staff meeting. They said they did not have such a spot budgeted. I thought about doing this on a volunteer basis, getting a job as an orderly at the hospital or washing dishes in a restaurant. But eventually, they decided they were not going to create such a job.

In that staff meeting, I did learn something about how a major New York church operated. I found that most of the ministers did not own a car! They made their pastoral calls on the subway, or more often, calling a cab. They said that was cheaper than paying for storage for a car, not being able to find parking, etc. Also I found that while Mr. Buttrick did very little pastoral work (his emphasis was on preaching, and he had many appointments around the country, such as at Yale), he felt it was essential that he have some such exposure to people if his preaching was going to be relevant. So he blocked off a small segment of Manhattan in the northwest, around Columbia University. Perhaps that is where he lived. They had very few members in that part of the city, but enough so that he was brought in on illness, divorces, deaths, etc. I was struck by the healthiness of this way of dealing with the isolation which often comes to "tall steeple" ministers.

One of the major events of that three months was the beginning of my "new" relationship with Ann Williamson, my second cousin, whom I had known all my life. She had attended the Presbyterian School for Christian Education in Richmond for a year—and hated it. She had transferred to Union Theological Seminary in New York, where with one more year she could earn her Masters degree in Christian Education. She was drawn there because of Dr. Lewis Sherrill, a Southern Presbyterian then head of the CE department at Union. The women at Union lived in a building called the James House. Once she got to Union, she took the minimum of Christian Education, and instead concentrated on theology and church history. Union was at its zenith at that time. (Yale and Union were the two "biggies" in the seminary world of that period). She had Paul Tillich for church history, Reinhold Niebuhr for theology, Muhlenberg for Old Testament. She ate it up.

Dating Ann Williamson

Soon after I arrived in New York, I called Ann and made arrangements for us to go to a play on Broadway. I think I did this on a "cousin" basis. I took the subway up to the Columbia area and walked to her residence for women at Union, called James House. I was not allowed to go in beyond the entrance hall. I do not remember what play we saw, but I know I enjoyed it, and she seemed to as well. After I brought her back and returned to the Biblical Seminary where I was living, I had a great feeling of having a wonderful time and knew I wanted to see her again. I do not remember the details, but I think I called again within a week and made arrangements for some other activity together.

The Arthur McCains had us both out to Scarsdale one weekend. They did not realize we had started dating, and it was a bit awkward as I recall. In fact, I am not sure when I realized I was seeing Ann as a date and not as a favorite cousin.

I remember the first time I kissed Ann. We had been out to some event and were walking back to James House on a cold winter night. As we approached the door, I kissed her for the first time, and she made it into a French kiss — my first experience with that. I found it very stimulating sexually. As I mentioned earlier, I had been talking with Dick Powers, my direct supervisor at Bellevue, about my questions about my sexual identity. I reported to him this new development with Ann and would talk to him each week about the developments between us. I began to be certain I was heterosexually oriented and relaxed about my fears.

Ann was to graduate from Union in the spring. She knew she did not want to get a job as a Director of Christian Education at a Presbyterian Church, but wanted to come back to New York the next fall for some kind of secular job. However, she did intend to go back to Arkansas for the summer of 1952. I knew Dr. Boggs at Second Presbyterian Church in Little Rock was looking for help in the field of Christian Education at this point, so I contacted him, and he hired Ann just for the summer. That suited me fine, for I was looking for a church in Arkansas, and I knew we would be able to be together.

By the time I left Bellevue to return to Arkansas in the spring of 1952, it was clear that I was dating Ann. I had no idea where it would lead, but I knew I wanted to see her during the summer. This is the first time I felt I "had a girl."

Looking for a Job in Arkansas

Once I arrived back in Arkansas, I picked up my pursuit of a call to a small church in a small town or in the country where I would be on my own, and where I could get a taste of a very different kind of church life from what I had observed at Second Pres. I had talked to Dr. Boggs and Roy Davis, the Synod Executive, about this when I was home at Christmas, and both said they would be on the lookout. I told Roy I wanted to go to some church that was in such desperate need that nothing I could do would damage it—for I realized that I was not the "normal Southern Presbyterian" theological student. I was high church in liturgy, concerned with social issues, and liberal in my theology. None of those fit in with the mind-set of small-church Presbyterians in Arkansas, and I knew I could trigger an explosion.

Roy Davis had two churches in mind. One was at Bassett, right on the Mississippi River between West Memphis and Osceola. I had never heard of it before. The other was at Cotton Plant, which I had not heard of either, although I did know Des Arc just to the west, and Brinkley just to the south. Roy wrote to both, but things in Arkansas move slowly, especially when dealing with a small church that does not have regular Session meetings. So I waited, and waited, and waited. I began to wonder if God really did want me to do this.

As I waited, however, I was having a delightful time being back home. It was always a pleasant place, with wonderful food, lots of friends around, and some free time. It gave Daddy and me a chance to be together more than we had been in a long time—only this time it was adult to adult. I had begun losing my fear of him during college, and especially after he told me he would finance whatever education I needed to go into the ministry. During these weeks, we began to draw closer—or at least that was my perception. We rode around the plantation a good bit, watching land being prepared and then planted for crops. He took me on a trip up to Jonesboro and then over to the cattle ranch he and Mr. Edgar Dean had bought and were developing. (This was with the money from selling the farm at Caraway that had been bought with the money Mother inherited from Main.) Mother never did trust Mr. Dean, but Daddy did. Mother probably encouraged me to go so I would at least know where the land was and would have laid eyes on it in case there was some dispute in the future.

Other than the spring I was at Fayetteville, this was the first time I had been in Arkansas (and certainly on the plantation) for an extended period since my senior year in high school in 1945. It gave me a chance to see the revolution that had taken place in farming methods and crops in the previous seven years. At this point, Daddy was 70 years old but looked and acted much younger, even after having come through that bout with pneumonia when he was in Europe. It also gave me my first chance to see how a plantation operated after my "conversion" on race in 1949. Economically and politically, however, I was still a conservative Republican, along with Daddy. That must have been when he invited me to go with him to the state Republican convention. The one thing I remember about that was the small number of black people there as delegates. I told him I thought the Republicans were making a serious mistake by not reaching out to blacks — that they had been excluded from the Democratic Party for so long in primaries that they were "ripe for picking." He rejected my idea, saying they did not want to get labeled as the Black Republicans, as the GOP had been during Reconstruction. I do not remember who was nominated for what. It did not matter in those days, for Republicans never got elected to anything on a local level. The only interest was in the national ticket. As usual, Daddy was a strong supporter of Senator Robert Taft of Ohio, the more conservative of those seeking the nomination.

It was a great time, but I was certainly ready to move on.

Finally, word came that Cotton Plant might be interested. I drove over for an interview, and they invited me to come. I was excited, and scared.

Cotton Plant, Arkansas

I have had many interesting experiences in my ministry. Cotton Plant is one of those at the top of the list.

Cotton Plant, population about 1,500 (probably 600 whites and 900 blacks), was a "Delta" town, but not where the soil was as rich as in the river bottoms of the Arkansas, White, and Mississippi rivers. It was "whitish" rather than the darker brown of real Delta. It was near the rice country, but I do not believe any rice was grown there my summer. There were plantations, often called farms, but the pattern was quite different from that at Scott. The owners, typical of most of the Delta, lived in town and went out to look after their farms. I assume more of the farm labor lived on the farms, but I am not sure, for I was not taken out to see them — as a minister at Scott would have been.

There was the Southwest Veneer Mill in Cotton Plant, the source of jobs for blacks and blue-collared whites, and some managerial officials — locally owned by the Bush family. They took hardwood trees, grown in the Delta, soaked them in water for a long time, then put them on a roller that spun them around at a great speed, and a razor-sharp blade would shave off a very thin layer of walnut or oak or gum that would then be shipped off to go on top of plywood for use in furniture or wood paneling. It was hard, hot, dirty work. But that and farming formed the only economic base.

At one time, the Missouri and North Arkansas Railroad had come through Cotton Plant on its way from Joplin, Missouri, to Helena and the Mississippi River. That had given both the veneer mill and the farms immediate rail access, but it was closed in 1946. I did not talk much that summer about having written my senior thesis on the demise of this railroad, for there were still hard feelings about being let down.

There had been a Cotton Plant boarding school for blacks, run by the Presbyterian Church, USA (Northern), but it had closed before I arrived. However, the buildings were still standing. This had been an outstanding school when public schools for blacks were held in rundown buildings with poorly trained teachers and used textbooks. A new school for blacks had been built there, as in many places in the South, in a desperate attempt to make "separate" also "equal," for everyone knew that doctrine was going to be tested in the near future. Cases had gone to the Supreme Court, but no decision had come down yet. I learned later that some of the leaders in the black community in Arkansas were graduates of that school, and I think there is still an alumni association.

Cotton Plant was one of a few towns in Arkansas that, despite its small size, had two Presbyterian Churches. First Presbyterian, where I was to work, was PCUS (Southern). Westminster, adjunct to the school, was PCUSA (Northern). After the Civil War, some of the denominations from the North sent missionaries to the old Confederacy to educate the illiterate former slaves. The Congregationalists were especially active in this work east of the Mississippi. I do not know when the Northern Church came to Cotton Plant, but I think it was sometime later. Such schools were widely scattered, so children came from quite a distance, and thus housing had to be provided. I have since learned that a similar school, Haygood Academy, a Colored Methodist Episcopal Church, was established in 1882 in Washington, Arkansas (started by a former slave, and possible grandson, of my great-great uncle, Samuel Williamson.)

The two Presbyterian Churches apparently never had any contact with each other. In Brinkley, a dozen miles to the south, there had been two Presbyterian Churches (both white), but some years before I arrived, they had merged to become a PCUSA congregation. However, even in the PCUSA there were separate black Presbyteries. One of the women from Westminster, Cotton Plant, said she had gone to the PCUSA General Assembly, and there was a commissioner from Brinkley who greeted her in a friendly way, pretending they were colleagues, then when he came back acted as though he had never known her because she was black.

There was one main street in Cotton Plant, running east and west, that was also the highway leading to Des Arc on the west and McCrory on the east and north. There were about two or three streets parallel to Main on both the north and south sides. On the north were the larger houses for whites, and way to the north a new development called the James Addition for blacks. On the south were smaller houses for whites and then the "quarter" where the rest of the blacks lived—whatever their income. Most of these houses were little more than shacks, although Louise Held, who belonged to First Presbyterian, was building on to her house. She would build only when she had the cash to pay for the materials, which she and her husband worked with. As a result, the house was "in process" and remained that way for years, but I understand eventually she got a degree, was the town librarian, and completed the house.

Along Main Street, there were stores on both sides. I don't remember them all, but I know there was Sol Nathan clothing store (very nice clothes). There were three drug stores (one owned by a Presbyterian who did not come to church, but his son, Bucky Currier, did) and two doctors' offices, one with a dispensary for post-surgical patients. Often in a small town, each doctor would be a "silent partner" in a drug store and a funeral home, shuttling all his patients to them, and frequently the town would divide into camps, some loyal to one doctor and some to the other. There were also six grocery stores, one (greasy spoon) restaurant right downtown with another one just a bit farther out, a John Deere store for farm supplies, a barber shop with four chairs and four barbers, and the Leader store (which had everything from groceries to hardware). I think there were several filling stations, a branch bank from Forrest City, and several liquor stores (one owned by a Presbyterian who never came to church). To the west there were some nice residences and the yellow brick First Presbyterian Church.

On the north side of Main, there were some very nice, comfortable houses, but only two or three large ones. One, owned by Miss Margaret Carter and her sister, Mrs. Marie Cheshire (both active Presbyterians), was the typical kind with large white columns. Miss Carter evidently had a good bit of wealth, for she took trips overseas often. Another substantial house was owned by the Roy McGregors. (There were several Presbyterian McGregor families in town, some of the rest being Methodists I think.) He was a financial supporter, but his wife "Miss Minnie" was a powerhouse in the church, and their children, John and Sally, were very active in children's events. There were also some houses that once had been nice, but which the owners could not keep up, especially one owned by "Miss Kate" McGregor, a lovely widow who was one of the matriarchs of First Presbyterian Church. TV had just come to Memphis, and it was possible to pick it up in Cotton Plant, only with a lot of "snow" on the screen. Most people did not have sets, but one of our members, Mrs. McLeod, did and would let people come to her house to watch. In those early days, one of the main fetures on TV was wrestling matches. Mrs. McLeod loved to watch those and knew all the "holds" used and would demonstrate them if asked.

There was no place for people (white or black) in Cotton Plant to swim (something that was so much a part of the life at Scott).

The nearest swimming pool was in Forrest City, about 40 miles away. There were "bar pits" on some of the farms, dug to get fill dirt to build up the roadbed for highways. Water would drain into these from the fields — and snakes abounded in them. Some of the kids would go out to swim in these, but I never did.

Cotton Plant was isolated. There was no movie theater in town, and I don't think Brinkley had one, either. I know I never went. Forrest City to the east was larger, but if people were going that far, they usually went on to Memphis. The other alternative was drive to Little Rock. Cotton Plant and Brinkley were pretty much at the "watershed" between the two. I did not realize until I went to Cotton Plant how much the proximity of Little Rock had shaped our lives at Scott in giving us access to shopping, medical care, better schools, entertainment, and cultural events.

Shortly before I arrived, a terrible tornado had hit just west of Cotton Plant, destroying much property and killing several people. It was the talk of the town when I arrived — such as how a piece of oat straw had been driven through a wood fence post, sticking out on both sides of the wood, but had not broken. Almost everyone had a story to tell about what he or she was doing the day of the storm.

The telephone system had a woman operator who connected calls — and who everyone knew listened in on conversations. When someone would ask to be connected to Mrs. Boone (for instance) the operator would often say, "She is not home. I saw her walking toward the drug store." The telephone office was in Mrs. Tarpley's home, I think.

One Presbyterian family who lived on their farm out from town were Mr. "Nig" and Ms. Eleanor Mathis. He got his nickname from having dark skin. She was active in the church, but he rarely came. Their sister-in-law was "Miss Mabel" Mathis, a widow. She was one of my favorite people, for she was lively and full of fun. One of her idiosyncracies was that when she was listening to you and agreed with you, she would say, "You told the truth that time," as though you never had before, and might not again.

I had lived near Keo and England and Lonoke, but I had never had any real contact with any of them because our world outside Scott was oriented to Little Rock, so this was my first exposure to really small town life.

One of the big events in Arkansas during the summer of 1952 was the Democratic primary for a nominee for governor. (At that point, the nomination of a Democrat was tantamount to election.) Governor Sid McMath had come in as a reform governor. After World War II, he had been district attorney in Hot Springs and had closed down the illegal gambling and mixed drinks there. I had been all for him when he was first elected, but there were accusations (which seemed to be substantiated) that his administration was corrupt, especially with Highway Department funds. There were stories of fire insurance policies being taken out for concrete bridges and roads being paved to the front steps of some members of the Highway Commission.

Francis Cherry, a judge and Presbyterian elder from Jonesboro, was running against him on the corruption issue. Mother had known Mrs. Cherry quite well from her days in Jonesboro, but knew him only slightly. They were considered "nice people." The Harvey Haleys had recommended Sid McMath when he first appeared on the scene, but his wife had killed his father (for self protection), and then the scandals in my mind took away the "nice" qualification. (This is interesting, for in later years Sid married Betty Ruth Dortch Russell, and we became friends.) There were several "old hand" politicians seeking the nomination, for McMath was trying for a third term, something no one had at that time won since the days of Jeff Davis at the turn of the century. Cherry was toward the back of the line in the polls, but then he started a new method, a "talkathon," some consultant had sold him on. He got on the radio and answered phone calls that came in. It seems to me he was on something like 12 hours a day. He was able to reach more parts of the state, and more individuals, this way than would have been possible in the traditional stump speeches. He was intelligent and forthright in his responses, and I became enthusiastic about him. I remember going back to my room at Mrs. Boone's house in the middle of the day (it was terribly hot), turning on the fan, and stretching out on the bed and listening to the radio for extended periods of time. To everyone's amazement, Cherry defeated McMath and got the Democratic nomination and then was elected. He won the reputation of being the most honest governor we had had for a long time. I remember Governor and Mrs. Cherry came to church at Second Presbyterian the morning of my ordination. They thought I was to be ordained that morning and were so sorry to find I would be ordained that night when they would not be able to be there, but it certainly was a gesture of family friendship. Years later in 1973 when I took the children up the East Coast, we went to Williamsburg, and Mrs. Cherry, then a widow and a guide at Williamsburg, took us on a special guided tour of the Governor's Mansion. Cherry was defeated for re-election (I was in Scotland then) because he was tied in with Arkansas Power and Light and people blamed Cherry when the company raised its rates just before the primary. Also, in a tight race with the then un-known Orval Faubus, in the McCarthy era, he accused Faubus of having gone to a Communist college in west Arkansas. This is a digression, but it was a lively part of my summer in Cotton Plant. I was still very conservative, but it does show that early on I was deeply concerned about politics.

Ministry in Cotton Plant, Arkansas

I do not have a clear memory of my interview in Cotton Plant that resulted in their asking me to serve there and my accepting, but I am sure I met with the Session, which consisted of three men. Mr. James Roy, the clerk of Session, and Mr. Ben White, the superintendent of the Sunday School, really decided things. There were also three deacons, one of whom was Mr. Eldridge Douglass, Sr. At that time, women could not be officers, but they "ran" the church. The leaders of the Women of the Church were the real powerhouses, but they would not have been in on the interview. In that discussion, we talked about where I could live. Someone suggested that Mrs. Stella Boone, a widow and a member of the church, had an extra room and I could probably rent it, but she did not provide meals. As I recall, we worked it out that I could keep in her refrigerator what I needed to make breakfast and lunch/supper, but I would eat my main meal in one of the two restaurants in town.

My ministry in Cotton Plant got off to a very shaky start. I drove over from Scott on a Saturday. About five or 10 miles east of Brinkley on Highway 70 in the middle of the Cache River swamp, my (Art's) car broke down. In those days, fortunately, people did pick up folks who were stranded on the side of the road. Some man in a pick-up took me in to Brinkley to the Chevrolet dealer, who went out to get my car. Someone in the shop lived in Cotton Plant, so after work he took me there and dropped me at the home of Mrs. Boone. I went to one of the "greasy spoon" restaurants for supper, then later in the middle of the night, I developed a bad case of diarrhea and vomiting. Whether it was the greasy spoon food, Cotton Plant water, the heat, or the anxiety of having a borrowed car break down, I do not know, but the next morning, my first to be the summer minister and with all the folks turned out to check me out, I was as limp as a dishrag. During the first part of the service I held on to the pulpit, but when it came to the sermon, I told them I had been sick and reminded them that when Jesus went to the synagogue, the Gospel says he read from the scroll then "sat down and preached to them." I told them I was going to do likewise. Fortunately, I had a sermon I had used before so was able to operate from my notes. Some, at the end of the summer, said that was the best sermon I preached there!

"Sister Boone," as she was often called, had been a widow for many years, and was clearly living on a limited income—less than she had once known. She had one grown, adopted daughter who was married to the editor of the paper in Clarendon, some 30 or 40 miles away. Mrs. Boone supplemented her income by being the Cotton Plant correspondent for one of the Little Rock newspapers—not that there was that much news coming out of Cotton Plant, but she had reported the recent tornado, and she sent in obituary notices of white people who died. Her house was nice, but simple, a bit rundown. The living room had some nice pieces of furniture in it, but she never used it and kept it closed off most of the time. When I would go in there and sit down, clothes moths would fly up from the velvet upholstered chairs. I once had a young peoples meeting there, and the air was full of moths. In those days most homes did not have air conditioning, and throughout that hot summer, it was noticeably absent. I finally brought over from Scott an oscillating electric fan for my bedroom, where I not only slept but also spent my free time.

Mrs. Boone and I had a very pleasant relationship. She was completely supportive of me and my ministry. She gave me no critical observations—certainly not negative, but not positive either. Mrs. Boone and her next door neighbor took the Apostle Paul seriously and had decided they, too, needed "a little wine for their stomachs" — just a tablespoon each night before turning in. It would have been totally unacceptable for those ladies to go to the liquor store to buy their wine — even though the owner was a nominal Presbyterian. They had a black man (who probably mowed their grass) make the purchases for them, but one time, the bottle ran dry, and he was nowhere around. They decided their reputations would be tarnished if they went down to buy the wine, but that mine would not! So down I went to Main Street for everyone to see (for everything that happened in town was seen by everybody). At that time, I was a tee-totaller and was just about as nervous about going into that "den of iniquity" as they were. But even then, I found this hilarious for me to be the "front guy" for two widow ladies, hiding their drinking habits.

After having worked in a church of some 1,200 members, I wanted to experience one where I could know everyone and become a part of their lives. Cotton Plant had 35 members who lived in town. I was in and out of their homes about once a week, if not more. Attendance averaged about 32 that summer! If someone was not present on Sunday and had not told me he/she was going to be out of town, I was on the doorstep Tuesday. I think they decided it was easier to go to church!

The Cotton Plant church building had been constructed in the early 1920s to replace an older structure. A minister who was a refugee from Armenia, due to the genocide by Turkey, was their pastor. He was a product of Presbyterian missions in Armenia, and I think his father had worked for the mission, so he was fluent in English. I do not remember his name. But apparently he was a very good preacher, had an evangelistic outreach into the community, and dreamed big. At the height of his ministry, I think the church had something like 250 members, and they built for that — or built for what they thought someday would be 250. It was a yellow brick semi-Gothic structure with a double flight of stairs leading from the sidewalk to the sanctuary, which was also semi-Gothic. It was pulpit centered, with the choir sitting behind "in the lap of God." They had no organ, but a pretty good pianist, Mrs. Cleve Walker, who also led the choir of some five to eight people.

I was already "high church" by this point. I don't know if I had the sense to ask the Session's permission. (I probably didn't, but they were so desperate for someone to serve them on a regular basis they let me violate all kinds of what I later learned are "tacit contracts.") I pushed the pulpit to one side of the raised platform, found a table and a stand on the other side to hold the Bible, and located a small, square table in one of the back rooms that I put in the middle, down on the floor level, to serve as a communion table (although, of course, I could not celebrate the sacrament, not being ordained). I think I got some retired minister to come one Sunday for communion.

I had asked for a church in such trouble nothing I could do would hurt it. Cotton Plant was ideal. They were so desperate, they let me do anything I wanted to. They had never had an Every Member Canvass, and never asked anyone to pledge. I pushed them hard on this. I invited Roy Davis, the Synod Executive, to come over to a church supper to talk to them about stewardship — and urged him to be forceful. He told them if they did not have a canvass and collect pledges, Presbytery would seize the church and nail the door shut. (Of course, he did not have the power to close the church, but they did not know it.) They were furious with him. But they did make pledges!

I came in all revved up to go full speed, knowing that I had only from mid-May until the end of August to try to resuscitate this dying church. I visited and visited and visited. I found this was very easy for me to do, and they seemed to like it. I organized a "youth group." Eldridge Douglass, Bucky Currier, and Mary Lou Whiteside were regulars, and Nancy Lee Cheshire, home from college, came occasionally. We met every week, and sometimes did on other occasions, although both boys (high school age) were working during the summer. I remember one Sunday there was going to be some kind of Presbytery youth event at Forrest City in the evening. There was a swimming pool in Forrest City, but none around Cotton Plant. So I took them over there early and we swam — to the shock and dismay of the Forrest City pastor, Henry Acklin (a good friend of mine) who thought we were violating the Sabbath.

I had known Eldridge Douglass from some years earlier when he was in my cabin at Camp Ferncliff — I think the first year I was a counselor, in 1949. By this point, I think Eldridge was finishing the 11th grade. A week or so after I arrived, he told me the junior-senior prom was coming up and suggested that I attend. It would give me visibility among the young people in town. It was a formal dance. I was going back to Scott each week on my day off, so I brought my summer tuxedo back with me. When I arrived in that formal garb (all the boys were also wearing tuxedos and the girls long dresses) at a *dance*, some heads turned, for "ministers didn't go to sinful places like that" (according to the Baptists). And when I asked one of the young single teachers to dance and we got out on the floor, I could feel eyes fixed on us. The next morning, everyone in town had heard what the young Presbyterian minister did.

The Session and Board of Deacons met once a quarter, for that was required by the *Book of Church Order*, but rarely any other time short of a dire emergency, such as a leak in the roof. Most decisions were made informally out in the church yard or by phone during the week. The women would decide what needed to be done, then tell their husbands to approve it. The treasurer, a woman, would tell them whether or not their could afford it. I pushed them to have monthly meetings. They were not used to an agenda, but I would tell them issues I wanted dealt with.

I was trying to get the few young people involved, both on Sunday night and on Sunday morning in a Sunday School class. The room where they could meet had not been used for years. It was rundown and most unattractive. I proposed that the young people and I paint it. This called for action on the part of both boards, to let it be done and to provide the funds to buy a couple of gallons of paint. The young people and I spent many hours cleaning and painting the room—finishing about the time I left. And I don't think it was ever used again.

Preaching was never my long suit. I would put off writing a sermon as long as I could—sitting up Saturday night. This was the start of a habit that I never broke as long as I was in the pastorate. It would often be 2:00 or 3:00 a.m. when I would leave the church to return to Mrs. Boone's house, then drag myself out of bed in the morning. But the worst time was when I went to Memphis to be an usher in George and Barbee Davis Chauncey's wedding. I had gone over on Friday for the rehearsal, then the wedding was Saturday about sundown. I believe the church was a garden one in the home of her parents—he was Congressman from Memphis for years, and it was a big social event. Then there was a reception. I decided I needed to get back to Cotton Plant, for while I had been thinking about my sermon for the next morning, I had not started writing it. I said goodbye and started driving. After about 20 minutes, I looked in my rear-view mirror and noticed that the glow of the lights of Memphis were behind me instead of ahead. I had turned in the wrong direction and was headed east instead of west! So I had to wheel around, make up that 20 minutes, and drive through Memphis, then about 85 miles to Cotton Plant, arriving in my tuxedo about 2:00 or 3:00 a.m. I finally finished my sermon at 6:15 a.m., took a half hour nap, showered, and went to church! That afternoon, I collapsed until time for youth group.

Mr. and Mrs. James Roy (Pearl) were the real pillars of the church. They had a small, but nice, house right on Main Street, as I recall. Her garden was spectacular. She specialized in day lilies of all varieties. He was the bookkeeper for the veneer mill. I was welcome at their house any time. One day, I remember going over to talk to Mrs. Roy about something. When I arrived, she was in the middle of washing her Venetian blinds in the bathtub. She said I was welcome to come back to the bathroom and visit while she completed the job, so I sat on the closed commode, and she knelt on the floor of the bathroom, sloshing the blinds in the water. I have forgotten what we were talking about. I think she was expressing disapproval of something that I thought was all right. For years she told the story that I sat in her bathroom on the toilet and told her she was a self-righteous Pharisee! But she loved it.

The Roys had only one son. They were proud of him and talked about him a lot. He was a lawyer. During World War II, he had been an FBI agent in Latin America, but was now practicing in Blytheville and had married Elsijane Trimble, also a lawyer. I never met her that summer, but knew of her. Her father was the Federal Judge, and her brother, Walls, had married Margaret Spenser in Fayetteville the spring I was there. I think Jim may have come down once during that summer. (I will record later how both James and Elsijane became part of my life in later segments.)

I also always had a warm welcome at the Douglass home. They were so pleased there was a minister who was interested in the young people, and especially so because Eldridge and I hit it off. Mrs. Douglass was an Episcopalian. She participated fully in the life of the Presbyterian Church, but had no intention of switching over. Mr. Douglass had been an engineer with the state highway department. Apparently, the high point of his professional career was building the Highway 70 bridge across the White River at DeValls

Bluff. He talked about it many times. He also had a small farm west of Cotton Plant. I guess that was the bulk of their income.

Miss Margaret Carter and her sister, Mrs. Marie Cheshire, who lived in the big house, were more formal. I was certainly welcomed there, but I would not have gone without being invited or phoning ahead, whereas I could drop in any time with most of the members. I remember Miss Carter took a cruise up to Nova Scotia that summer, and we talked about my family connections there (although at that point, I knew little about them).

Mr. and Mrs. James McCain where also in the church. (He had the Ford dealership, which had been in Cotton Plant, but he had moved it to Brinkley.) He was rather quiet, but she was a very strong personality. She was very interested in politics. She had run the women's section of the campaign for Senator Fulbright (although she was much more conservative than he). In one of my visits with them, as we talked about my future, I said that when I graduated from YDS I would like to spend a year in Scotland. She said I should apply for a Fulbright Scholarship. I protested I was not a good enough student to win one of those, but she insisted I try. She said she would write to Senator Fulbright and give me a glowing recommendation. I think we corresponded about that once or twice the following year. Without her planting the seed, and giving me encouragement, I am sure I would never have thought of applying for a Fulbright—which I received some eight months later!

The Roy McGregor home was always welcoming. The power in that family, and one in the church, was "Miss Minnie," his wife. She was behind whatever moved. They had two children, John and Sally, who were not old enough to be in the youth group, but were in Sunday School.

Miss Kate McGregor's daughter, Alice, was home that summer. Alice's husband was in the Army and was away—I guess in Korea. Alice was "young" by that congregation's standards and interesting. She worked for one of the doctors and was his assistant when he did surgery—though she had no training.

There was a Mrs. Davis who ran a "hotel" or boarding house. She had Presbyterian roots, although she never came to church that summer, and I don't think ever had. But I called on her, and we discovered that she was the grandmother of Donna Davis, one of my friends in high school. That was the bond we needed. One time when I went to call, she gave me 10 dollars—a significant gift in those days. I declined it, saying I could not accept a gift for visiting her and suggesting that we give it to the church. At the end of the summer, she told me she was so embarrassed when a few weeks later she found that I was a planter's son and was not the impoverished student she imagined.

That summer, Ann Williamson was working at Second Presbyterian Church. She roomed with Sarah McKee, an Agnes Scott classmate, who was Director of Christian Education at Pulaski Heights Presbyterian Church. Sarah was seriously dating a man named Wade Burnside from Newellton, Louisiana—whose family owned a large plantation there. We double dated some, and I invited Wade to stay with me at Scott at least once when he came up to visit. I liked him then, and still do. They later married and settled in Fayetteville where he was a pediatrician, and I still run into them at Presbytery meetings.

My day off was Mondays. Almost every Sunday night, after youth group, I would go either to Little Rock and have a date with Ann or invite her to come down to Scott (since she was a cousin, this was normal), or I would go to Monticello and we would be together there. It was becoming clear that we were "dating," but there was no talk beyond that. Toward the end of the summer, after people in Cotton Plant had been so gracious to me, I felt I must respond to them someway. I decided to have a watermelon party for the congregation in Cotton Plant. I invited Ann and my parents to come over. Laura and Shuford Nichols, hearing about this, invited us to have lunch at their home in Des Arc, then we came to Cotton Plant in time to set up for the watermelon cutting.

The race question always lurked just beneath the surface. I had had my "conversion" three years before, but I walked around it gingerly that summer. I remember once we had a potluck dinner for the congregation, and afterward a hymn sing. Their repertoire of hymns was so limited, I was trying to get them to learn some new ones. One I picked was "In Christ There Is No East Or West." I thought long and hard about this, and especially the third stanza. One member I thought might blow her stack was Mrs. McCain. Should I say, "Let's sing stanzas one, two, and four" (as was frequently done in small churches), or risk singing, "Join hands, then brothers of the faith, Whate'er your race may be! Who serves my Father as a son Is surely kin to me." I am sure they had never sung that, or anything like it, before. I wondered if the roof would fly off, or I'd be called before the Session. But no one said anything that night, or later. Looking back, it is incredible that this was considered a daring step to take! But that was the ethos of the Delta in 1952. "Don't talk about it, and the problem will go away." There was a state-run training school for blacks over in Fargo, not too far away. This was mostly for delinquent children, I think. They got by on almost no money. I did convince the women to collect clothes and food and books, and then got them to go with me to deliver them. In the South in those days, there was a lot of "compassion" on the part of whites for blacks, but "justice" was another matter — and never even discussed.

I think my contribution to the Cotton Plant church was primarily in my pastoral work. I really got close to the people. When I returned to Little Rock 10 years later to organize Grace Church, anyone with Cotton Plant roots came there. Anna McGregor Greenway told me that her mother and her sister, Alice, gave her no option about where she was to go to church — and she was just glad I was located out in west Little Rock, for she would have had to go to Grace whatever the location. I also think I helped them get some organization. I don't feel my preaching had much impact, but somehow I did instill in them some hope and vision, and gave them the courage to try something new.

Early in the summer, I went to Brinkley to meet the minister of the Northern Presbyterian Church there, Carl Murray. Brinkley was the "big" town of about 5,000. He and I played tennis together and got to be friends. His church was struggling to pay him a salary. As the summer drew to a close, it was clear Cotton Plant was not going to be able to afford, or attract, a minister for their church alone. At one point, they had been linked with Des Arc, but they did not want to get back into that. I explored with Carl the possibility of his serving both Brinkley and Cotton Plant. He liked the idea. I brought it up with Synod and Presbytery, and they did, too. So for some years the two churches were linked, though of different denominations. I think I was able to postpone the death of the Cotton Plant church for a few years. As population continued to dwindle in Cotton Plant, eventually they merged into one congregation, meeting in Brinkley. Now Brinkley is so small, it is yoked with Stuttgart, I think.

When I called to get help on names as I was writing about Cotton Plant, Eldridge Douglass, Anna McGregor Greenway, and Cleo Mattox all said that I made a lasting impression on that congregation, and on the town. I know Cotton Plant had a profound impact on me. I was convinced, after that summer, I wanted to be a pastor—not an associate in a large church. I felt that although my views on race were not those of the Delta, I wanted to have my ministry there because I could "talk the talk" of those folks. That summer gave me a self-confidence when I returned to YDS for my last year. Each quarter of that intern year was valuable, but the time in Cotton Plant may have been the most formative of all.

When I returned to Yale, Bill Emerson, one of my friends from Little Rock who was by then an instructor in the history department, said he got invited to dinner parties all winter in New Haven just so he could tell the story about his friend who had spent the summer in Cotton Plant, Arkansas.

Dating Ann in Summer of 1952

I remember that summer's dating as being a lot of fun. I had Monday off, so as soon as I finished working with the young people on Sunday, I would head out for Scott or Monticello. I'd have all day Monday, spend the night, and then drive back to Cotton Plant early Tuesday morning. I don't think I saw myself as "going steady" with Ann, for I remember going by to see Frances Craig one night. She was there as a Sunday School Extension Worker with the Synod. But certainly, Ann was my main attraction. We dated in Little Rock some. Often she would come out to Scott and spend the day and/or night. Mother and her father were first cousins, and very close, and we had grown up having a good relationship with all the Williamsons, especially the Adrian Williamsons. She and Mother had a warm relationship at that time. I don't know how much our parents were aware of our growing closeness, but my guess is they were quite cognizant and encouraging. The Williamsons on some of those times would also invite me down to Monticello, as they had done in previous years. It was always a pleasure to be on "The Hill." The house was lovely, with a private tennis court and fishpond. Annie Mae was a great cook, and they would often invite couples for dinner. If the Dunklins came from Pine Bluff, we would play tennis before dinner. Jim and Bobby Hurley from Warren came over, plus Margaret's friends — Trish Trotter, Patty McClendon, and Judy Norris (the Congressman's daughter), and Ann's friend, Barbara Pomeroy.

I cannot remember how much physical expression I was giving to my growing attraction to Ann. I think we did some hugging and kissing, but it was pretty light. There was very little time we had alone, with all the family and partying.

That summer Ann was working on getting a job in New York. One of Cousin Emmy Vaughn's sons was in middle management at the United Nations. Through him, Ann got a job as a receptionist before she left for New York. Through one of Charlotte Williamson's relatives, she found a room at a women's residence for her first weeks in New York. So by the end of the summer, her plans for New York were firm.

I was going to be leaving for my last year at YDS in New Haven, an hour and a half away from New York by train. I was excited about returning to YDS, and Mrs. McCain of Cotton Plant had planted in my mind the possibility of applying for a Fulbright scholarship. I very much wanted to go to Scotland to study and was increasingly interested in liturgy after having been responsible for planning worship services every Sunday in the same church all summer. Ann and I talked about getting together in both New York and New Haven.

As I think back, I am not sure how far our relationship had progressed by the end of August. There is no question we were dating. I was not dating anyone else by then. I knew she was special, and I had begun to wonder if she might be "it." But I had my eye on a year in Scotland, and I was not thinking of marriage for two or three years. I think by then, we were doing a lot of kissing, including French kissing. I was sexually aroused, but we were not doing any heavy petting at this point. I still had a lot of inhibitions, drilled in since childhood, about not taking advantage of a lady. As I have written elsewhere, Mother had reared me to be a "gentleman," not a "man." That was so obvious that I think any mother would have been comfortable if I took her daughter out on a date.

The summer was a happy one, both at work, and in my social life. I was moving along in my delayed adolescence — probably to where most boys of my age were as college freshmen. Ann was pretty (not as pretty as she became after marriage), a bit heavy but not fat, intellectually stimulating (my equal if not more), and socially "proper." Everything was in line for this to develop as we both headed East.

End of Intern Year, Return to Yale Campus

Trip to New Haven, 1952

Looking back from my perspective at 75, I think it is ironic — or prophetic? — that after dating Ann during the summer, and picking up again in the fall, when I got my train ticket to return to New Haven, I scheduled a stop in Philadelphia in response to an invitation from Marnie Smith to spend a night in her parents' home in one of the suburbs (Wyncote?). She had found a job as DCE (with preaching rights) in an Episcopal church not far from her family home, where she was living. She and I had never dated at YDS, but were very, very good friends. I had thought some about dating her, but her weight was a real problem with me. And while I would never have put it into words, I remember thinking that Mother would not find her quite "proper," whereas Ann met Mother's standards in every way.

I was not stopping at Marnie's as a date, but as a good friend. We would not be seeing each other, now that she was working and I was returning to YDS. I considered it just a friendly visit. I don't know what she had in mind.

I do not remember her father well, but I found her mother to be charming. In later years, Marnie told me how angry she got at her mother for "taking me over." I knew nothing of the Smith situation at that time. I was aware that Marnie got no financial backing from her family, and that she barely scraped by at YDS. (I did not know then that she was so broke at one point, she was about to have to drop out of school until Uncle Ken lent her some money — with the stipulation that she not pay him back, but that she give an equal amount to someone else in need when she was able.) I guess I did know that Mr. Smith, who had been a salesman for Armour or one of the other big meat packers, lost his job during World War II because the meat shortage abolished any need for salesmen to sell something that did not exist. I don't know that I was then aware that Mrs. Smith had come from great wealth. She covered her lack of finances by putting on airs and surrounding herself with antiques. This, of course, fit right into the impoverished Southern gentility I had known all my life. And I guess since I knew all the things to say and how to act, Mrs. Smith responded to me.

I did not have a lot of time alone with Marnie because of this. But certainly there were, from my perspective, no "dating" or romantic overtones to that visit. I don't know about Marnie, but I don't think there were for her, either.

As I remember, I don't think I went out to Scarsdale on that trip to New Haven. I was so eager to get back, I went straight through.

Returning to YDS, 1952

I really was excited about getting back to YDS after having been gone a year. There was some sadness in that most of the people in my entering class of 1952 had graduated and moved on, although a few were there for graduate work. I had learned so much in my year away, both in CPE and at Cotton Plant, that I was seeking for answers about questions I had not before known existed. I had a lot more self-confidence. For the first time I would not be living in Stuart House and would not be Uncle Ken's secretary. This gave me a lot more freedom.

I had corresponded ahead of time with Kelly Clark and Pete Lawson about the three of us sharing a suite, and they had agreed. I was looking forward to that. I guess it was not until I arrived on campus that I learned Kelly had decided he wanted a private room. He was the glue that would have held the three of us together, so Pete decided he would get a single room also. I guess they had decided this before I was told, for they got rooms and there was no single room on campus for me. This was an unpleasant jolt. So I had to scrounge, by asking two people with a suite to let me move in. As I have found so often in my life, what looks like a setback can be a real blessing.

This suite was occupied by two first-year students, one of whom was a Yale College graduate. I knew about him, but did not know him—Jim Blanning. His roommate, whom he did not know, was Ross Snyder. I went to them and asked if they would take me on. Jim said yes, and said since he had the larger back bedroom, I could have the upper bunk there. The three of us could not have been less alike! Jim was from the "second tier" of social life at Yale

College—not part of the inner circle, but he knew them all and had contacts with them. He was attractive, outgoing, and cheerful, but not top flight intellectually. Theology was not Jim's long suit. If he had any, I would say it was "mild liberalism." After college he had gone to the University of Michigan Law School, then decided to come to YDS. He kept many contacts with the College. His father was pastor of a large United Church of Christ (Congregational) congregation in Benton Harbor, Michigan. Jim had a good voice and sang in the YDS choir.

The other roommate was Ross Snyder, Jr. His father was a professor of Christian Education in Chicago and had written several books and was respected in his field, but was on the left side of Christian Education circles. If Jim Blanning was "mild liberalism," Ross was "strong liberalism," on the left side of the spectrum of the UCC, which sometime was not too far from conservative Unitarianism. His mother was very high in the volunteer side of the UCC Church and was widely respected in women's circles. I don't think I ever met either of his parents, but Ross talked about them a great deal. If Jim was socially suave, Ross was on the naive, if not "rough," edge. I am not sure where he went to college, but I think it was one of the Quaker ones—perhaps Haverford. Clothes meant nothing to him, nor did neatness. His bedroom was always a mess. He had a voice that was even better than Jim's—a tenor, I think. It was ironic that I, who could not sing, was in a room with two members of the select choir. If Jim was not intellectual, Ross was very much a thinker—always a bit out of step with the general run at YDS. He was not as skeptical as Dean Ferm, but fell not too far short.

What an unlikely trio we were! Yet we got along very well. There were other people on campus whose company I enjoyed more. We did not all three eat together every meal, as some roommates did. But it was comfortable. And it was a welcome change from the semi-monastic atmosphere of Stuart House. There was some of the rough and tumble dormitory life, not unlike that at Berkeley College. Next door to us were two people. One was the son of a very tall-steeple UCC minister in Massachusetts, and with him was an Episcopalian whose father was a wholesale liquor dealer in North Carolina. He had a constant supply of liquor, and the two of them had many parties. Neither Ross nor I drank, and Jim's social life was elsewhere. We had pleasant relationships with our neighbors, but not close. They did have a telephone that we were allowed to use for local calls, and that was a great help.

I really don't remember many others in our house, nor the name of the house. I do know Jim and I had a balcony, just outside our bedroom, so we could store things there when the weather was cool.

I wondered what my relationship with Uncle Ken would be, now that I was no longer his secretary. I did not sense any strain. His secretary that year was Bob Johnson, who had been at Yale College but I had not known him there. He and I became very good friends. I think he found it helpful to have someone who had been in that role before with whom he could discuss issues. Rudy Everest, who had followed me as secretary, had moved down to Freshman Campus where he was a counselor. But he was on campus for classes, and the three of us had a fellowship.

I am jumping ahead, but I remember later in the year there was an ice storm that knocked out all the electricity at YDS. This meant even Uncle Ken could not do his usual writing at night. The electricity came on downtown before it did on our hill. We learned that the Lincoln Theater was open, so Bob and I talked Uncle Ken into going to a movie—something he rarely did. The movie showing was "The Four Poster." All the action centered around people getting into and out of and on top of the bed. It was, by the standards of those days (not now), risqué. We had not realized that when we enticed Uncle Ken into going with us. When we got to some of the sexier scenes, Bob and I roared in laughter, partly at the script, but mostly at the fact we had the Puritan Uncle Ken there. I can still see Bob shielding his face from Uncle Ken and doubling up in laughter.

When I was planning to return to YDS, I told Daddy I would like to go without a scholarship. I could tell that he was making a good bit of money on the plantation. I had also become aware, especially through Marnie, that other YDS students were barely getting by, so I could not in good conscience ask for a scholarship. Daddy, good on his promise to get me whatever education I needed, agreed. Every scholarship student had to do some work, but I was now free. I had met my fieldwork requirements with two years as Uncle Ken's secretary and with three quarters of CPE and a summer at Cotton Plant. So for the first time in my Yale career, I was free from all obligations except my studies. It was a good feeling. I had time for some social life. Since weekends were free, I was able to go to New York to visit the Charles McCains and Ann. Sometime in that year, the Arthur McCains moved to Memphis. I am not sure when, but I had a real sense of loss. I had no "second home" in Scarsdale anymore. I had spent every Thanksgiving with them from 1946 on. Fortunately, my relationship with the Charles McCains had grown strong enough for me to be able to invite myself down there. Also, on at least one weekend — perhaps two or more — I invited Ann to come up to New Haven.

Bard Smith, who had come to YDS during my second year, was now in my class as a senior. We had seen a good bit of each other during his first year, but were much closer after I returned. I liked, respected, and admired him, and he apparently liked me. He and Nancy and some of the other married couples at YDS had a social life that I had not been part of before. But once I started bringing Ann up, we would get invited to some of the parties. Once Kelly and Pris Potter got married, they were in it; also Bob and Peggy Raines. I think by then Rick Mapes had married Maryann. Jim Blanning was getting serious with Jean McClure (the most attractive girl on campus), and they would come.

This year of 1952-53, Bard Smith's mother, Gert Behanna, moved to New Haven to write her story, which was printed as *The Late Liz*. She was invited to some of these parties, also. I had been fascinated by her since I first heard her in 1948 and sought out chances to visit with her. She was as vibrant as I recalled. I had talked about her to my roommates. Ross's religious life was pretty cerebral. Jim's seemed to be more "inherited" and the professionally and socially acceptable thing to hold. So I told them I would like for them to have dinner with me and Gert in the refectory. They agreed they would. Then I invited Gert. To my surprise, she agreed. They were not turned on by her, and I think she felt they were pretty superficial in their faith. It went nowhere from there. But I did continue to see Gert until graduation time.

As I think back on my return to the campus, I missed some of my friends from the Class of 1952, but picked up with the Class of 1953 and the two classes younger. There was no stratification of students by classes that I was aware of. Also, we mixed freely with graduate students who lived on the Quadrangle. However, many of them were married, and that did make a difference in how much we saw of them. Bev Asbury and I became good friends that last year;

Harry Smith; Bard Smith, of course; Harriet Taylor was still around; Alvord Beardslee; Bob Johnson; Rudy Everest; Kelly Clark; Gregor Thompson was in and out until she got married in the spring.

A graduate student from Scotland arrived on campus that fall – Robin Barbour. He was married and had a baby, so lived off campus. But I heard he was a graduate of St. Mary's College, University of St. Andrews. Since I was thinking about going there if I got a Fulbright, I looked him up. We hit it off immediately. When he would eat lunch in the refectory, I would often sit with him. As we began to get acquainted, he asked about my background. When I told him my father was a cotton planter, he said his father had been a farmer, too. Thinking of Robert Burns, I assumed he had about 10 acres of poor land up in the Highlands and asked no more. I think I may have been in Dinkler's course on Early Christian Art with Robin, but I know the Dinklers had a party and invited both of us. That was probably the first time I met Margaret, and liked her. She and I must have been together some more. I knew that Freeland, their little boy, was an albino. Perhaps I learned it when Robin expressed concern about driving him across the desert as they headed for California. As he asked about the best way to make that trip, I told him about the Paynes in Knoxville and the Arthur McCains in Memphis. I got my parents to invite them to visit at Scott. Ann had also come to know the Barbours, so the Adrian Williamsons invited them to come down to Monticello. The result of all this was it became a family-to-family friendship, with repercussions that have echoed down through more than a half-century.

When I returned to New Haven, I looked up Ellie Hutchins Wohlenberg. After I graduated from college she married Dean Wohlenberg, who was a widower. I think I met him once, although I had seen him in processionals for years. He died the year I was gone, I think, leaving her a widow. The Assistant Dean, Grant Robley, had been her mainstay during Wohlenberg's final illness and death. A year or two later, Ellie and Grant married, but I think that last year, Ellie was alone. I saw her from time to time, inviting her for dinner at YDS. After Ann and I got engaged, I took Ann to her house for them to meet each other. I was conscious that Ellie did not rave with enthusiasm. She said nothing negative that day, of course, nor later when just the two of us talked. I asked her many years later if she was surprised when we were divorced. She said, "It was obvious to me that day you two were not in love with each other. But it was certainly not my business to say anything. I wouldn't have, even if you had asked me." She was a wise woman.

I also looked up the Hemingways, or at least Mrs. Hemingway. I can't remember if he had died by the time I got back. They were living quietly in a small house, on Lincoln Street, I think. They had pretty well used up their financial resources running the Masters' House at Berkeley

I also looked up Mr. and Mrs. Bill Beasley, Sue and Tap Hornors' friends. The Hornors had introduced us in 1945. After the Hornors went back to Arkansas, I stayed in touch with the Beasleys, seeing them once or twice a year. He had "made it big" in real estate. They lived out in one of the suburbs in a lovely, though not lavish, home. They were really the only "townies" I ever got to know in New Haven. It was a pleasant relationship. I even would call them in the 1970s when I would visit students at YDS.

My relationship with faculty that last year was changing. Most of them were just faculty, and I was just a student. But I did have a personal relationship with Uncle Ken, of course; Norvin Hein was a friend; Bill Muehl and I had a relationship which was somewhere between student and young friend; I had a bit of that with Davie Napier; George Lindbeck was on the faculty by then, but I had known him from Stuart House days; Dave and and Mrs. MacLennan were also friendly, as were the Dinklers.

As I think back on that last year at YDS, my memories are pleasant. I remember feeling, after having taken that year out, that for the first time in my life I was "where I ought to be." Up until then, I had always felt a bit young and immature, and was having to push myself to measure up. But after the internship, I relaxed and felt I was in the right niche. It was a wonderful, secure sense of belonging. I was ready to move on to ordination, but I did want still one more year of graduate work.

I did not set a brilliant academic record that last year — nor had I in any year. I was certainly in good standing, probably in the upper quarter of the class. But I had deliberately decided that I was not going to push for grades, as I had at Yale College. The Phi Beta Kappa key and graduating with high orations had met those needs. I wanted to study to learn and equip myself for ministry. And I think I did that.

By this time, I was firmly a Presbyterian—if they would take me. And that was no foregone conclusion. If that was not my slot, then I would look to the Episcopal or Lutheran Church. I knew that I was yearning for liturgy. But I felt if I went to the Episcopal Church, it would be to "take from" their tradition. If I went to the Presbyterians, I felt I could "bring" something and add to the tradition. The thing that held me off about the Lutherans was their Germanic/Scandinavian background. That would be alien to me, and I was not sure how I would fit in. Also, my foreign language was French, not German, and I would have a hard time not knowing that. So I began working in early fall on what steps would be necessary for me to get an answer from the Presbyterians.

One thing that happened in the spring of that last year was the accession of Queen Elizabeth II. This was news around the world, and the coronation was a spectacular event. Al Beardslee was especially caught up in this. I remember there was a television set in the snack section of the refectory where we gathered to watch.

Another big event during the fall of 1952 was the Presidential election. While I had changed my views on race, I was still quite conservative. The YDS campus was wildly liberal and very supportive of Adlai Stevenson. I found him fascinating as a person and was stimulated by the fact the Stevensons came from Bloomington, Illinois, and Grandmother knew them. (When Adlai was getting serious about the Borden heiress, his sister called up Grandmother one day. Miss Stevenson said she knew Grandmother's brother was the president of Northwestern University. She wondered if Grandmother would ask Dr. Scott what he knew about the Borden family. Were they "suitable" for Adlai to marry into?) I also was leery about electing a general as President. I knew enough history to remember that usually generals did not make good presidents. But I finally voted for Eisenhower. I think there were only three of us on the YDS campus who did—Uncle Ken, Paul Vieth, and I. And it was the last time I ever voted for a Republican for President! I remember the morning after the election when I went into the refectory for breakfast, there was a dish of aspirins where we had to sign our meal slips. The sign said "Last act of the Welfare State" and was signed "Liston Pope, Dean."

Third Year Courses

The period 1951-52 had been a time of tremendous growth for me. The four experiences of my intern year equipped me to return for my last year at YDS not only a little more mature, but with questions I would never otherwise have known to ask, and with an eagerness to get ready for the parish ministry. When I arrived on campus I had pretty strong feelings about the courses I wanted to take. I was more interested in Bible than before. I had received a waiver on Hebrew from Presbytery, but decided I wanted to have some exposure to the language. I could not take a full year of it because of other requirements (especially Niebuhr's two-term course on Christian Ethics), but I did have one vacant spot in the fall. I did not need the credit to graduate, which was good, for there was no credit for only one term of Hebrew. I signed up for the course. I was told I could not take only one term. I appealed and was again turned down by the faculty. I went over them and asked for an interview with Dean Pope, explaining to him that I did not need the credit, but did want to know something about the language since all my Presbyterian colleagues would know it. He finally gave me permission. It was hard, but I am so glad I took it, and I still think it was a wise decision. I learned the fundamentals of the alphabet and the difference among the tenses of the verbs so I could understand the commentaries. And I learned something about the "philosophy" of Hebrew and how it differs from Greek. It is more concrete, less philosophical; more earthy, less speculative. It was well worth the effort. In fact, I think for most theological students who are not going into graduate work, a course on "The Philosophy of the Hebrew Language" would be more beneficial instead of requiring all Presbyterians to spend a whole year on the language alone. Most of them never use it once they are in the parish.

According to the records I have (and I think there are some inaccuracies) I took:

Fall
    Elementary Hebrew (one term only) — Marvin Pope
    Theology of the Creeds — Claude Welch
    Comparative Religions (Hinduism) — Norvin Hein
    Personality and Religious Experience — Hartshorne

Practice in Preaching—Luccock
Public Worship—MacLennan
Audit: Protestant Theology since Schleiermacher—Richard Neibuhr

I had been so turned on by Outler's Systematic Theology that I wanted to take some more theology, but did not want Calhoun's History of Doctrine because it had a reputation of being terribly demanding. (Instead, I bought a copy of the notes on his course and have used them through the years.) With my emphasis on liturgy, I was also interested in the various creeds. I found Welch's course demanding, for there were some graduate students in it, including Mike McGiffert. It was partly lecture, but part seminar. The first paper I had to write, and share with the class, was The Cappadocian Fathers. I remember in my oral presentation I began with, "I do not understand why anyone would spend his life working on the Doctrine of the Trinity." I remember smiles and simpers went around the table. I wondered what I had said. The next week Mr. Welch's new book was published—*In This Name*—*the doctrine of the Trinity*! I am glad I took the course, for it gave me an understanding of early doctrine. But it was not as exciting as Systematic had been.

Comparative Religions had never been of great interest for me, but I was not interested in more philosophy so I took it. I had postponed it until Mr. Archer retired and Norvin Hein took his place. Norvin had been my next-door neighbor in Stuart House his first year on the faculty (my second year), and I used to hear him typing his lectures until about 6:00 a.m. He would dash to the shower just in time to make his 8:00 a.m. class, then collapse. We had become friends. Norvin was solid, but not exciting. And while Hinduism was his specialty, I did not find it very relevant.

Because of my CPE work, I thought I would like to go deeper into the interrelationship between personality and faith. Hugh Hartshorne had a national reputation in the field as one of the pioneers, but he was past his prime. I think the most helpful thing I got out of that course was reading William James' *Varieties of Religious Experience*.

I had Hal Luccock in Practice Preaching. He was delightful, but his comments on student sermons were mostly affirming, with little help. I remember he commented one day that no one should ever feel compelled to preach on the Song of Solomon. That challenged me, and I did preach a sermon—not a very good one—on some text in that book. The most helpful part of Luccock's instruction was that at the end of every student sermon he would ask "So what?" He was convinced every sermon should be intended to motivate those who heard it to respond in some way. Preaching did not excite me then any more than it did during most of my ministry. I had shocked Donald Miller at Union, Richmond, when Walter Johnson quoted me as saying "Preaching is a necessary evil in the pastorate."

That fall term I took the first half of David MacLennan's course on Public Worship. This was where I could get excited. While he had "blithered" in his preaching courses, I found him quite helpful in Worship. I was still trying to decide if I was going to be a Presbyterian, Lutheran, or Episcopalian. I was seeking a liturgy that would be acceptable to a Presbyterian congregation, but would also meet my needs for structure and the "numinous." I guess it was out of this class that I formulated my Fulbright proposal to study Church of Scotland liturgics.

That fall I audited Richard Niebuhr's "Protestant Theology since Schleirmacher." He was regarded as the "saint" and the "guru" of the YDS campus. I admired what I had seen of him and was planning to take his Christian Ethics courses the next two terms. I wanted a chance to sit under him on pure theology without having to write papers and do all the reading. So I audited his course. It was good, but not as stimulating as Systematics had been.

Winter
    Exegesis of I Corinthians (English)—Dinkler
    Christian Ethics—Richard Niebuhr
    Comparative Religion—Norvin Hein
    Public Worship—David MacLennan
    Seminar for Advanced Students (Theology and Christian Education)—Randolph Crump Miller and Paul Vieth
    Audit: Christian Communication—Bill Muehl

Dinkler was excellent in his presentation of I Corinthians, but I found it not as profound as the Greek exegesis of Galatians. For one thing, we did not deal with the critical text that I had found so fascinating. It confirmed my appreciation of working with the original language.

During the winter, I continued my Comparative Religion course, and I think we got partway into Islam. Solid but not exciting.

I also continued MacLennan's course on Public Worship, and my interest grew, and along with it my participation in Communion. We had a student-sponsored communion on Wednesday mornings in the little prayer chapel in the basement. Presbyterians had communion at Dwight Hall every three weeks. Battell Chapel had communion each first Sunday, and at Marquand, we had communion once a term. This sacrament became a part of my life, made richer as I began to understand the structure of the service.

The seminar with Randolph Crump Miller was, in my memory, called "Theology and Christian Education." When a second full professor in Religious Education was being chosen, I had read Miller's *The Clue to Christian Education* and had found it much deeper than most Religious Education writing, and I was turned on by it. I was one of those who went to Dean Pope and urged that Miller be considered. How disappointed I was when he arrived! He was self-important and arrogant—and more superficial than his book had been. The chief thing I learned from the course was watching Paul Vieth, who had been "the" CE man, quietly step aside and allow Miller to take the spotlight. I never saw Vieth show any jealousy or anger. It was a wonderful lesson in humility and made my respect for him go way up. It was interesting to take specific Christian doctrines and relate them to the educational process. Miller brought in people from theology and Bible for specific seminars. I think Paul Schubert was involved, for that must have been the context in which I sat close enough to him to hear his off-the-cuff mutterings about a text. These were so much richer than his lectures. And that must have been where he got the impression I was a New Testament scholar. One of my frustrations was with Dean Ferm, who had started with me in 1949. Perhaps he was a graduate student by then. Every time we would get started on a topic, such as Incarnation or Atonement or Resurrection, Dean would say, "Now, let's start back and consider, Is there a God?" It was not an exciting class, but was helpful in making me consider how one communicates aspects of the faith that lay people might consider esoteric.

The big new course for that semester was Richard Niebuhr's Christian Ethics. I had been waiting for this. It was his specialty and his reputation was enormous. His office was in Stuart House, and I had admired him as I saw him come and go. I also, after my intern year, was seeking answers on some ethical issues—especially, since I was dating Ann, on sex and marriage. I was deeply disappointed that he did not deal with specific ethical issues, but took a much broader approach—of how one is ethical, not pat answers to specific problems. It was certainly the right approach, but one that did not turn me on. My most specific memory of his class that winter term did not even involve him. Ann and I had been dating, and I was wavering about the tempo of the relationship, and also hoping to get a Fulbright. I wanted to go to Scotland alone and then to pick up our relationship when I returned. Ann was not interested in this. One day I picked up my mail just before Niebuhr's class. In it was a letter from Ann saying, essentially, "get on or get off." My head was spinning. I was not listening to Niebuhr, but trying to decide what to do.

That term, I could not take another "credit" course with Bill Muehl, so audited him. That was just as helpful as taking it.

Spring
    Exegesis of II Isaiah (English)—Davie Napier
    Early Christian Art—Erich Dinkler
    Christian Ethics—Richard Niebuhr
    Town and Country Church—Becker
    Christian Communication—Muehl
    Audit: Seminar for Advanced Students—R. C. Miller, et al.

I took my last course with Davie Napier—on II Isaiah. I found him inspiring, whatever he did, and was sorry I could not take the Deuteronomy course. I am sure II Isaiah was good, but for the life of me I can't remember it—although II Isaiah has certainly been important in my ministry. His reading the text was, by itself, a religious experience. He truly made the Old Testament come alive. While I did not have any outside personal relationship with him, strangely enough, we re-established ties after I saw him in Little Rock where he was speaking, and we had a warm reunion at my 50th Class reunion. When I called for some kind of class protest to the Bush invasion of Iraq, he really got behind that and was most helpful in writing it.

I continued Niebuhr's Christian Ethics — solid, but still he did not turn me on as a teacher as he did many other students. As a man, however, he was profound. The man was truly humble in the best sense of the word. It also showed in his preaching. He was not the dynamo of power his brother Reinhold displayed annually when he preached at Battell. It was rather a matter of deep water flowing smoothly. He was the "saint" on the YDS campus.

I took Dinkler's course on Early Christian Art — which really was Mrs. Dinkler's field. I think he offered it so she would be able to share and to show the slides she had collected from all over. It was good, but not as exciting as his exegesis. He, like Niebuhr, had come out of his time of darkness (Russian prison camp) refined by fire. During that term, I was invited to a party at their home. Robin and Margaret Barbour were there, along with others. The level of conversation was very high, above my head. They got to talking about words for colors and were discussing words used in classical Greek, i.e., there was no word for "blue" but rather said "the color of the water reflecting the sky on a clear day." I felt I did establish some personal relationship with the Dinklers, for we exchanged letters for years.

I took Becker's "Town and Country Church" because of my experience in Cotton Plant the previous summer. I realized I was ill equipped to live in a small town, or be pastor of a small church. The only experience in that was at All Souls, and that was not a pattern I wanted to follow. I did not find this course especially helpful, however. It was more about sociology than about small-church life.

In my final term, I switched Muehl from "audit" to "credit" because I wanted to take every course he offered.

That last term, I continued the Advanced Seminar (or Theology and Christian Education) under Randolph C. Miller — only this time as an audit. Perhaps this was when Paul Schubert sat in with us. He had been so dull as a lecturer. But in a seminar, when he made off-the-cuff comments on a text, he was very insightful and stimulating.

Some YDS Professors Who Made an Impression on Me

Dean Luther Weigle

Luther Weigle was for many years Dean of Yale Divinity School. He was also named by the Federal (later, National) Council of Churches to chair the committee to produce the Revised Standard Version of the Bible. The New Testament was published in 1946, the Old Testament in 1952, and the translation committee normally held its working meetings on the Yale Divinity School campus. To celebrate the completion of this monumental task, Dean Weigle (by then retired) was asked to give a series of lectures on the significance of this new translation. I attended those — at least some of them. I remember in one he said in his opinion the most significant single change from King James to RSV was in Romans 8:28. The King James said "all things work for good." The RSV said, "in all things God works for good." Dean Weigle contended it makes all the difference in the world what is the subject of the verb. Is it "things" that work for good or "God" who works for good?

Through the years I found it very helpful, pastorally, when working with someone who has suffered a blow (death, illness, accident, humiliation) to be free of having to say, "This is going to be good for you." That is cruel. It is profound good news to be able to say, "Even in this, God can work for your good."

When the New Revised Standard Version came out in 1989, I was dismayed that the main text reverts to "all things," although the footnote says some manuscripts have "in all things God works for good." I have asked several New Testament scholars why the reversion, but have not found anyone yet who can give me a clear answer. When I read that passage today, I use the footnote version!

I have another story about Dean Weigle and the RSV. His office, after retirement, was in Stuart House in Sterling Divinity Quadrangle. Most of the rooms were used as faculty offices, but because I was Uncle Ken Latourette's secretary, and he had his apartment there, I lived in Stuart.

Dean Weigle's secretary at the time was Leonora Hernlein. As I would come and go from my room to class, I would often see

Leonora coming back from the mailroom with small boxes, along with letters and publications. This happened so often that I stopped her one day and asked what in the world the boxes were. She said "Ashes." I asked, "Ashes of what?" She jolted me with "Ashes of the RSV." There were protests by fundamentalists all over the country, but especially in the South, over the RSV because in Isaiah 7:14 the RSV reads "a young woman shall conceive" instead of "a virgin shall conceive." Leonora said the opponents would gather for a "Bible burning" and then mail the ashes to Dean Weigle to show their disapproval and contempt.

Richard Niebuhr

One of the towering figures on the campus at YDS in its "golden era" was Richard Niebuhr, professor of Christian Ethics, and brother of the more famous Reinhold Niebuhr who taught at Union Theological Seminary in New York, the other outstanding seminary at that time. People at Yale all thought Richard was the greater theologian of the two, but there was no question that Richard was the more saintly.

Uncle Ken Latourette told me Richard Niebuhr was always a towering intellect, but he did not have that special quality about him until he had a nervous breakdown and then recovered from it. There was a gentleness and humility that made him stand out among the giants who peopled the campus. I took only one course from him, and was not that turned on by him as an instructor, but for most students at YDS in those days, he was the "premier" professor. However, I was impressed by him as a person.

There is a wonderful story illustrating the qualities that made him unique. It seems he had a graduate student who was working on his Ph.D. under Niebuhr, but this man was also having serious marital problems. He had a regular weekly appointment for counseling. One week, things were going very well at home. The student showed up at the appointed hour, stuck his head in the door and said, "Mr. Niebuhr, things are going well, and I don't have anything troubling me this week. I know you are busy, so I'll waive my hour with you." Mr. Niebuhr always wore his glasses on the end of his nose. He looked up over his glasses and asked, "Bill, you have no problems this week you need to discuss?"

"No, sir" was the reply. Then Mr. Niebuhr said, "Why don't you come then and let me tell you about mine?"

William Muehl

Bill Muehl was the instructor of public speaking at Yale who became a professor of preaching. He had no theological training at all, being a graduate of the University of Michigan Law School. He was an Episcopal layman and an authorized lay preacher. Politically, he was perhaps the most liberal person on the YDS faculty, when I was probably the most conservative student.

As I mentioned elsewhere, my first contact with him was in the required public speaking class. Each one of us had to get up and speak for two minutes on anything, so he could hear our voices. When I sat down, he said, "Mr. Campbell, where are you from?" When I told him Arkansas, he asked, "Where did you go to college?" When I told him Yale College, he looked shocked and said, "You've been gone four years, and you still sound like that?"

I took every course he offered, for I came to like him very much. Finally, in my last year, he said, "Don, sometime if you can't lick 'em, jine 'em. Let's capitalize on your accent."

He also told me, in senior year, that he rarely encouraged anyone to read sermons, but he said my writing style and my speaking style were identical, and that if anyone could get away with it, I could. Because of the prejudice in southern Presbyterian circles against read sermons, during my time in Crossett and my first years at Grace, I would write out my sermons, then make detailed outlines from which I would preach. Then in the '60s, I went to a meeting where someone read the account given by a woman in Florida about what it was like to be desperately poor and the mother of a child. I was overwhelmed by it. Mother's Day was coming up, and I always hated that holiday, for usually it was pure sentimentality. I decided on this Mother's Day I would read "Being a Poor Mother." There was a tremendous response. I decided if I could communicate that well while reading something someone else wrote, I would try it with my own manuscripts. It went over very well, and I was much more relaxed—for when I would look at an outline, I would sometimes wonder what a given phrase meant.

But back to Bill. Next to Bill's office was a small classroom used for speech. One day when I went by, Bill was sitting on a small stack of cushions in the bottom of his chair. I asked what they were. He said they were prostate cushions. Then he explained that the Revised Standard Version of the Bible was translated at YDS because the chair of the committee was Luther Weigle, the former dean. They would meet over weekends and would have their sessions in Bill's speech class room around tables. Bill said most of these old men (for they were all men, and all getting up in years) had prostate problems, so they would ask to have a cushion. Then they would go off and leave them behind. So he "liberated" them and was bouncing up and down in his chair.

Bill was a powerful preacher. I remember one sermon he preached on "The Tart with the Golden Heart." He said the image in the past used to be the almost perfect person with one fatal flaw, an Achilles heel; but now we assume everyone is fallen, and celebrate one or two virtues that shine. There was another sermon in which he used as an illustration of the depravity of human nature a story about a woman who had put her child's hand in a fire and held it there. The child was rescued, but the hand was deformed for life — and I can still see him hanging out of the pulpit with his hand and fingers distorted as though deeply scarred.

It was strange that we would bond, coming from two such different backgrounds, but we did, and would occasionally exchange letters.

Kenneth Scott Latourette

No listing of outstanding Divinity School faculty of that era could omit Mr. Latourette. But I have written so much about him I'll not add more here.

Erick Dinkler

Erick Dinkler was a distinguished New Testament scholar in Germany before World War II, I believe at Heidelberg University. He had studied under all the great German Biblical scholars. A Lutheran minister, he was not a part of the Confessing Church led by Bonhoeffer, but I think was never a part of the Nazi party. He was drafted into the German army, I think as a chaplain, but I am not sure of that.

After Germany's invasion of Russia, he was on Germany's Eastern Front, I guess after the Germans began to fall back. He was in a foxhole with another German soldier, who was a Roman Catholic. It was apparent they were about to be captured by the Russians. His hole-mate evidently knew he was a Lutheran pastor. He asked Dinkler if he would give him, a Catholic, communion. Dinkler did, having only muddy water from the bottom of the foxhole for wine, and the German counterpart of C ration biscuits for bread. The other soldier died — either in battle or later in prison. Some years later, Mr. Dinkler asked a Roman Catholic bishop if this had been "valid" communion for the soldier. He said it had been. (This was long before Vatican II.)

Once captured, he was sent to a Russian prisoner of war camp for German soldiers. The war ended in 1945, but he was retained as a prisoner. I don't know how many other German soldiers were also kept. He was not released until 1948, by which time his health had pretty well been broken. He perhaps would never have been freed had it not been for the persistence of his wife — Erica von Schubert Dinkler. She came from a very prominent family and was herself a highly regarded scholar in early Christian art. She kept on, year after year, appealing through church and academic and ecumenical circles to have the Russians release him. Eventually, it paid off.

After a period of hospitalization and recuperation in Germany, the Dinklers arrived at Yale in the fall of 1949. He was still weak and emaciated looking. One of the profound experiences of my first year at YDS was his sermon preached at the Christmas service in Marquand Chapel just before we left at the end of the first term. His English was spoken with a heavy German accent. He told us that one of the Christmases when he was in prison (perhaps his first), the Russians allowed the Germans (for whom Christmas is very important) to have a Christmas gathering, with someone speaking — but there could be no mention of Jesus or God. Dinkler was chosen by the prisoners to lead it. So he "preached" the Gospel in figurative language, about darkness and lights and candles. The Communist guards, who had received no religious education, did not understand and thought this was a fairy tale. But the Germans,

Protestant and Catholic, all knew exactly what he was talking about and found spiritual strength. Then he preached to us the sermon he had used in prison. I can't reconstruct that sermon, but it made a powerful impression on me.

I only saw him around campus my first year, but the first term of my second — even though I had taken only one year of baby-Greek — I took his seminar on Galatians. I had been so turned off by Paul Schubert's Introduction to the New Testament in first year that I learned very little. But under Dinkler, I was set on fire — primarily by his insight into Paul's writing, and the meaning of the epistle, but also by his use of the footnotes at the bottom of each page of the Nestle text, and his explanation of why one text was chosen over another variant.

When I returned from my intern year, I managed to have Dinkler for two more courses. I took exegesis of I Corinthians with the English text. It was very good, but not as rich as the Greek exegesis. Then my last semester, I took "Early Christian Art." This was Mrs. Dinkler's field, but he was also interested. With three semesters under Mr. Dinkler in small seminar-size classes, I got to know him fairly well. I have written elsewhere about being invited to a party at their home my last term.

I am not sure when the Dinklers returned to Germany — sometime after my graduation and Fulbright. I had them on my Christmas card list, and we exchanged letters every year or so. She wrote me after his death, and to my dismay, sent me pictures of him lying in his casket. Apparently this is a German tradition, but it was new to me. Then she and I exchanged letters, spasmodically, for years until I received a card edged in black. I could not read the German, but was able to figure out she had died — I think on New Year's day, probably around the year 2000.

Theirs is a story that should not be forgotten.

Dating Ann in Fall of 1952

Back to the fall of 1952. Ann and I had dated all that summer, and it was clear that our relationship was progressing. How far it would go, and at what pace, I did not know. I'm not sure I was ready to say I was "in love" with Ann (I'm not sure I have ever been able to say that about anyone), but I did love her, found her fascinating, and enjoyed exploring further than I had ever gone before in showing my feelings by kissing and light petting.

Ann, one of Frances McCains' friends who was looking for a roommate, and a couple of girls from the UN rented an apartment with a kitchen, living room, and two bedrooms in a respectable neighborhood in midtown Manhatten. That turned out to be a happy relationship for all concerned. Each of the girls was dating someone, with the potential of a serious relationship. We men would run into each other from time to time. In those days, people did not sleep in with girl friends, or even fiancees.

Before I went down to New York, I invited Ann to come up to New Haven for a weekend. I think it may have been for a Yale football game. (I thought Ann would like to go to at least one Ivy League game.) I got one of my girl friends at 301 (women's dorm) to put her up for the weekend. One afternoon, I invited Bob Patterson to come over for tea. Bob was a graduate of Union Seminary in Richmond. The year Ann was at PSCE, they had dated some. When he came to YDS for graduate work, Ann had asked me to look him up and introduce him around. That must have been 1950-51. I got Uncle Ken to invite him to be part of our cell group. Bob and I had become friends, so I thought he and Ann would like to see each other. I can't remember whether it was that afternoon, as he was leaving the room, or whether he wrote her a letter after she went back to NYC, but he asked her for a date. She told him she and I were dating. He was very embarrassed that he did not realize it, and apologized to me (although he did not need to).

I do not remember when I next went to New York, or how often. The Arthur McCains had moved to Memphis, but the Charles McCains had said I could stay with them. When they found out I was dating Ann, I think they invited her over for dinner and a visit. And immediately, Cousin Frances started pushing me to move "before you lose that lovely girl."

I went down to New York for Thanksgiving. In the past I had always gone to Scarsdale, but that was out since the Arthur McCains had moved. The Charles McCains had gone to have Thanksgiving with either Chuck or Bill, and they were out of town, but Aunt Grace invited me to stay in their apartment, and I did. I was going to have Thanksgiving with Ann. I had assumed that some of her roommates would be there, but it turned out each one of them had plans out of town, so Ann and I had the apartment to ourselves. I had talked about our going out for Thanksgiving dinner, but Ann said she wanted to cook the meal. Since there were only two of us, she bought the smallest turkey she could find. I think it weighed less than two pounds and looked like a Cornish hen. That morning she put it in the oven, and then we went to service at Madison Avenue Presbyterian Church, thinking that the turkey would be ready to eat when we returned. But it wasn't. I have no idea on what temperature she set the oven, but we kept checking it all afternoon. It was not finally done until after five in the afternoon!

In the meantime, we talked (we seemed to have endless things to discuss, including intellectually stimulating topics such as theology) and loved. Finally, we sat down to a full Thanksgiving dinner. I think that meal was what really "tipped the scales" for me. We were together for the whole Thanksgiving weekend, just the two of us at her apartment and at the McCains with Aunt Grace. When I left on Sunday afternoon, I knew that I was really serious about Ann. We shared the same background and customs, and I found her fun, intelligent, highly educated, and sexually exciting. I went home at a different place in our relationship than I had been when I came down.

She did not say where she was, but by her actions it was clear to me that she was responding to me as I did to her.

She found living in New York, not in school, stimulating. She liked her work at the UN and found friends there in addition to her roommates. I was liking YDS. We were both at places in our lives that were good.

Christmas and Ann in 1952

I do not have a lot of specific memories about the Christmas vacation in 1952 except I recall it as being a very happy one. Ann, Hoyt, Margaret, and Sally Payne came over and were the centerpiece of the festivities at Scott. By this time, there were a number of young couples living at, or connected with, Scott—Buddy and Martha Craig, Mary Carolyn and Jim Mayo, Carolyn and Marvin Thaxton, Mimi and Bill Dortch, Robert and Mary Jane Dortch, Jim and Juanita Winn, Pud and Claude Westphale, Walter and Janice Estes. Art and Florence were living in French Morocco, so were not present. Grandmother was in too frail health to come down for the winter. We were still living in the "big house," and it was full for sleeping, and the dining room was always full. There were a lot of parties. By this time, my Little Rock connections had become somewhat distant, and most of my social life revolved around Scott friends.

Ann Williamson came up for at least one party, if not more. She was at her charming best and was well received. I also went down to Monticello once or twice. Margaret Williamson was home from Boston, and Adrian breezed in from Little Rock. There were a lot of dinners there, too. As I recall, the Dunklins came down from Pine Bluff and the Hurleys over from Warren. I was beginning to feel as at home in Monticello as I did at Scott, and I was certainly warmly welcomed on "The Hill" and by all the Williamson friends. I know I went down on New Year's Eve, the day after I was licensed by Washburn Presbytery.

Sally Payne, Lizzie Bonner, Mary Ann Payne, Mary Crittenden, and Margaret Payne when the Paynes visited the plantation in Scott in 1956.

I remember especially the New Year's Eve dance at the Monticello Country Club. While dancing with Ann, I was feeling more and more drawn to her. When midnight came and people began kissing, our kisses were more than mere protocol, and when we went back to The Hill, they continued.

The next day, the McClendons had a New Year's Day luncheon, with the traditional ham and black-eyed peas. They said Charles Scott May was coming down from Pine Bluff. I had heard about him and about the way he knew the genealogy of everyone who was anyone in Arkansas. They claimed, "He will know all about you." I said, "I have never met him and have heard of him only recently. I'll bet he won't." Shortly, Charlie Scott arrived. As soon as we were introduced, he said, "Oh yes, you are kin to the Gordon Campbells. Your aunt was a Robinson and is a good friend of Mildred Saunders. And you and Ann are cousins." Everyone roared with laughter.

I said goodbye to Ann and drove back to Scott. I knew the Gordon Campbells were going to come down to Scott for lunch and to listen to football games. I really wanted to see them before returning to Yale, for they were very important to me. As I drove the two-hour trip back to Scott, I can still see the light brown or beige "broom" grass that flourished on the pastures and uncultivated land between Monticello and Pine Bluff, and somewhat less on the road through England to Scott. I watched it as I thought and prayed about my relationship with Ann. I was beginning to feel that I was in love with her and might want to get married. But I was waiting to hear about the Fulbright Scholarship. If I got that, it paid for only one person. I yearned to go to Scotland for a year, and if I got married, I did not

Ann Williamson and me at Christmas in 1952.

see how I could do that. Should I "cool it" and hope she would still be around when I got back? Was I willing to give up my dream of going to Scotland? Was I ready to be ordained and take on a church in the summer of 1953? Was I mature enough to get married? Would she have me if I asked? Could I support her? Yet my guts and my heart were pushing me on. My affections for her were a quantum leap beyond what I had felt for any other girl I had ever known. She was the "perfect wife" for a minister — well educated, very bright (and more, trained in Christian Education), pretty in the face if a bit overweight, and Presbyterian to her fingertips, and she was from the right kind of family (even more than "right" since we were from the same family), with all the social graces. She was just the kind of girl Mother would want me to marry. But "Do I dare, and do I dare ..." as J. Alfred Prufrock asked himself. My mind was in a swirl all the way home. As I approached Scott, I came to the conclusion that I wanted to forge ahead, but I hoped we could postpone the wedding until I returned from Scotland.

When I arrived at Scott, the Gordon Campbells were still there. They asked if I had had a good time in Monticello, and how the people were there. I replied in a polite, superficial way — and revealed nothing of the turmoil I had been experiencing for the last two hours. Why? In our family, we did not share deep emotions — or at least, I did not. I felt this was something private between Ann and me. She did not know what I'd been thinking, and I didn't know what her thoughts were when I left Monticello. But New Year's Day 1953 was a turning point in our relationship.

Presbyterian Progress

Simultaneously with my developing love life, I was having to take steps to make possible my ordination after graduation from YDS.

After serving the Cotton Plant church, I was feeling more and more identification with the Presbyterian Church — although it was still tentative. For one thing, I was not at all sure the Presbyterians would take me, with some of my ideas about worship, the sacraments, and my theology.

One advantage of going to an interdenominational school, where Presbyterians were a minority and where the one small polity course was taught by the PCUSA minister, was that I had to buckle down and learn on my own about the Southern Presbyterian Church if that was where I wanted to minister — and I felt a strong call to return to Arkansas, where the PCUS was the dominant form of Presbyterianism.

I identified at Yale with the Presbyterians, both at YDS, and with the Presbyterians downtown. Every three weeks on Sunday morning, we met at Dwight Hall for a light breakfast and then a Presbyterian communion service before I would go to Battell Chapel. This came to mean a great deal to me.

I was also involved in getting a weekly Wednesday morning communion service started in the little prayer chapel down in the basement of the YDS chapel. We had various ordained persons on campus celebrate. One was from the Dutch Reformed Church in South Africa. I especially liked the way he celebrated.

I had turned in my application for a Fulbright Scholarship and had requested going to the University of St. Andrews (rather than Edinburgh) because I wanted to study Church of Scotland liturgics. A former Moderator of the Church of Scotland had told me during my second year at YDS that if I was interested in liturgy, St. Andrews was the place to go. Early in the fall of 1952, I had met Robin Barbour, who encouraged me and who gave me the name of W. R. Forrester as the professor at St. Andrews who taught liturgy. I had corresponded with him. I was really excited about going. Daddy had said he would send me if I did not get the Fulbright, but I would feel much better if I did not have to depend on him financially for another year.

Because my beliefs were, I realized, not the standard Southern Presbyterian ones, I was concerned I might not be ordained. I did not want to graduate, come up for ordination, and be turned down, and at that late stage have to find another denomination (Episcopal or Lutheran) and begin their whole candidacy process (although I did not really know what that might be). In digging into the *Book of Church Order*, I discovered, to my surprise, that whereas to be examined for ordination, one had to have completed a BD degree, this was not a requirement for being licensed. And if Presbytery approved someone for licensure, the only areas to be tested to move on to ordination were minimal—I think just a statement of faith. It seemed that the licensing procedure was almost never used any more, and in fact it was dropped from the *Book of Church Order* shortly thereafter. But it was still in effect in 1952!

I wrote Dr. Boggs, asking if Washburn Presbytery would examine me to license me to preach when I came home for Christmas. That way, if they turned me down, I would have four or five months to look for another denominational home. I guess Washburn Presbytery had not licensed anyone for as far back as anyone could remember, but it was a legal request, and since Dr. Boggs was the "bishop" of the Presbytery, he could push almost anything through. I wrote him that I liked the Presbyterian system of a "collegiate bishopric" instead of a monarchical one, but I was not sure that a group would take their task seriously.

Dr. Boggs checked with "the fellows," and they agreed they would have a called meeting during the Christmas break. He also passed along to them my request that they give me a "serious" examination, because I really wanted to know if they thought I could fit in the Presbyterian Church.

So during the fall, I wrote out the necessary papers—statement of faith, Greek exegesis, sermon to preach, and I don't know what else was required. At that time, the whole candidacy process in the PCUS was pretty lax, and Washburn Presbytery more so than most others. I faced the Christmas test with anticipation, and with anxiety.

Christmas Church Life in 1952

I sought out Dr. Boggs as soon as I returned to Arkansas, working over the details of the pending examination.

I was asked to conduct the Christmas worship service for the Woodson Presbyterian Church—one of the small ones we had supplied with deputation groups during my two summers at Second. They were without a minister and desperately wanted to have a Christmas worship service on the Sunday before. Woodson was a small community on some land near the Arkansas River that was rich and grew cotton, but most of it was second growth pine woods, and some people worked in Little Rock. It was a low income and low educational level community, for both whites and blacks, but there were two or three families determined to maintain a Presbyterian Church there.

I had written out my sermon (probably for a preaching class at YDS), but instead of reading it, I had a full outline from which I would preach. I had been there many times before and knew the setup of the sanctuary. However when I arrived, I found that a couple of nights before, they had had a "Christmas party" and had used the pulpit to support the Santa Claus House, and they did not want to take that house down. So the only thing I had on which to put my notes was a coffee table. Being tied very closely to those notes, and not having telescopic vision, I had to squat down every two or three sentences to remind myself what I wanted to say, then I would stand up and preach them, then squat again. This went on the whole sermon.

The only person in the congregation who could play the piano was the wife of one of the men, only she was a Seventh Day Adventist and did not know any of the Christmas carols. So our Christmas music was "The Old Rugged Cross," "My Faith Looks Up to Thee," and "There's a Church in the Valley by the Wildwood" — or some such combination.

On Christmas Eve, I had a strong desire to drive in from Scott to the service at Trinity Episcopal Cathedral. I had gone there in 1948 with Jim Boyes and had returned every year since. It was a time and place for soul searching and rededication for me — and was especially important that year.

On December 30, 1952, the called meeting of Presbytery was held at Second Presbyterian Church. The Presbytery was small, and many ministers and elders were out of town. I don't think there were more than 15 or 20 people present. As I have already written, I had told Dr. Boggs I wanted a *thorough* examination because (1) I wanted to see if a Presbytery would take this major responsibility seriously and (2) I wanted them to know all about me, to decide if this was where I belonged, and if not, to tell me ahead of time so I could make other plans. The word had gone out, and they did indeed give me a thorough examination. This was the only item on the agenda. They spent about four hours questioning me.

At one point T. B. Hay asked if I was a dispensationalist. I said I did not know what one was, but I didn't think so. (I had never heard the word at YDS). He said I had better find out what it meant, for it was a problem in the South.

I just about got turned down because when they asked if I believed there were only two Sacraments, I said I believed there were two — but I could find no scriptural basis for saying there are "only two." I said foot washing met all the requirements. And Calvin in the *Institutes* had written that ordination and confirmation might be sacraments. This threw the brothers into consternation. They had never heard such heresy! They came very close to rejecting me.

On theology, they asked many questions. When they finished, I told them there were a couple of points on which they had not examined me, and they might want to know where I stood. I said I did not agree that praying for the dead was a sin, as the Westminster Confession stated. I said that if I was praying for someone in India and that person died, but I did not find out for several months, I did not think my prayers after his demise were a sin. I told them the Communion of Saints meant a great deal to me, and I thought the blessed dead prayed for me. This, too, threw them into a state of confusion. They tried to persuade me, but I did not budge.

I have forgotten the other heresy I told them they should know about.

When they dismissed me in order to vote, I left the room deeply impressed by the seriousness with which they had examined me. I knew that if they would take me, I really wanted to be a Presbyterian. I was thrilled by the thoroughness of that examination. I had found that the episcopal responsibility could be handled collegially as well as by one person at the top.

After some time, Dr. Boggs came out and told me that they had voted to license me. They would take me — although they had some doubts. I got several lectures or sermons from some of the ministers, chiefly from Dr. Paisley, charging me to re-think my views.

But it was a great day. And the licensing took place that afternoon.

I was on my way to becoming a Presbyterian minister — through my knowledge of the *Book of Church Order*.

Winter of 1953

There was a lot going on in my head, heart, and gut the last six months I was at YDS. I had finally made the decision that I was going to be a Presbyterian, and the Presbytery, despite some reservations, had decided to take me. So that issue was settled.

Fairly soon after Christmas, I learned that I had been awarded a Fulbright, so it was settled that I would go to the University of St. Andrews in Scotland to study liturgics. This was a hope fulfilled. I was going to New York, or Ann was coming up, about every other weekend by this time. When in New York, I would stay with the Charles McCains. They had invited Ann over for dinner at least once, probably more, and liked and approved of her. Their children, Bill and Grace, were already married, and Chuck was engaged to Connie Vanderbilt Davis. I got very positive "vibes" from Mother and Daddy and the Paynes, plus my student friends at YDS all liked her. One or two of Ann's roommates were also dating seriously and talking about getting married. It was contagious.

My next trip to New York was in the middle of February. I spent Friday night with the McCains, all day Saturday and Saturday night and Sunday morning with Ann. Saturday night, I took a deep breath and finally asked her to marry me. To my surprise, she said she needed time to think about it. Sunday morning at breakfast, Cousin Frances really gave me a hard time about pussyfooting around. She warned I was going to lose Ann. I just listened. I did not feel I could—nor did I want to—tell her that I had proposed the night before. That was private until Ann made up her mind.

When I returned to Yale, I continued to be in a state of turmoil, but again did not feel I could tell anyone that I had actually popped the question. Nor did I tell my parents. I was (still am, but less so) a private person—and Ann was (and is) so in spades.

I went back to New York the middle of March. Perhaps it was spring break, for it seems to me I had more than just a weekend. Again, Cousin Frances was on my back about when I was going to propose to that lovely girl. The first night I was there—I remember it was March 15, then the deadline for paying income tax—Ann said "yes." The first call we made was to her parents, who were delighted. Then I called my parents, who were equally pleased. The next morning, I told Cousin Frances—that I'd been waiting for a month for an answer, and she had said "yes." She was ecstatic.

Until March, it had not been settled whether I would go to Scotland alone or with Ann. I really wanted to go alone. I did not see how we could afford two people, and I really wanted the freedom to live in a dorm and travel. But Ann made it clear that if I went alone, she was out of the picture for good. So from the middle of February, and definitely from the middle of March, it was clear that we were getting married and she would go. Somewhere about this time, we had a conversation in which each of us spoke the truth—but the other refused to "hear" it. How powerful are the heart and mind to discount what we do not want to believe. Ann told me she did not want to marry a minister. I told her my first calling was to the ministry, and she would play second fiddle to that. We were heading for trouble as soon as we agreed to marry. What a tragedy we did not have some counselor to make us face up to these two statements.

When I returned to Yale, all my student friends cheered me on. I had joined the groundswell of marriage! When Ann came up, we were immediately included in all the "couple parties," and Ann was liked by all of them.

There was romance in the air at YDS that winter and spring. It was very hard in those days for a single man to get a call as pastor of a church. He could get a job as an assistant pastor or a youth worker, but people had doubts about single men as pastors. So there was a lot of professional pressure on senior students to latch onto someone. Also, people who could not afford to get married while in school now saw a salary in the near offing. Kelly Clark married Pris that year. Jim Blanning proposed to Jean McClure and got married right at the end of school — with Ross and me as ushers at their wedding in Marquand Chapel. I can't remember all the others, but it seemed as though a new engagement was announced every week. I have no doubt this was a real impetus for me. Looking back on it, I know that I loved Ann, but I was not "in love" with/infatuated by her — I was "in love" with love and marriage. I suppose in many ways we were an "arranged marriage" in a society that did not understand or respect such.

The first time Ann came up after we were engaged, I took her to meet Ellie Wohlenberg. As I mentioned elsewhere, I was puzzled by Ellie's tepid response. It was polite, and she said all the right things, but I knew her well enough to know she was not enthusiastic.

The other significant person who expressed mild pleasure was Uncle Ken. It was not that he, a bachelor, could not become enthusiastic about someone getting married. I had seen him beam over other engagements. I was very much aware of his near-silence. I did not want to hear why, so did not ask him, but the question lurked in the back of my mind.

So, here were the two "adults" at Yale who knew me best, and to whom I was closest, being almost silent in their congratulations.

My friendships on the YDS campus were shifting. When I had returned in the fall many of my best friends during my first two years had graduated. Even though we were very different from each other, Jim and Ross and I had come to be good friends. Robin Barbour and I were seeing more of each other and were getting close, and I had met Margaret. Also, I was growing closer to Bard Smith — and Gert Behanna through him. I was feeling very much the need for pre-marital counseling, for I knew I was not ready to get into a married relationship. Ann was not open to this at all. In

June, I asked Bard if he would do some pre-marital counseling with me. We did not find time for this until the morning of our graduation when we had breakfast together and a couple of hours of visiting. I do not remember anything he said. He did not give me any sex instructions. I knew his marriage was not the best in the world, but did not realize how shaky it was. But that one conversation was the sum total of pre-marital counseling I got, other than talking to Dr. John Price about some of the physical aspects of sex. Bard and I have remained good friends through the years, and I suppose part of that is because of the role he tried to play. And I am sure one of the reasons I emphasized pre-marital counseling during my ministry was a realization of what it could have done for us. It might have led to a break-up, either before or after engagement, or it might have exposed some of the trouble areas for us to discuss when we did not feel "trapped," or it might have given us some tools to use when troubles arose, as they do in every marriage. All I know is, I wish I'd had some.

I was very conscious, as the year wore on, that I was coming to the end of my time at Yale. When I graduated from the college, I knew I would be returning to YDS. At the end of my second year, when I took off for my internship, I knew I would be back. But this was really going to bring to an end an era of my life. I had arrived in 1945 so homesick, so young, so naive, and feeling like a fish out of water. It was now eight years later. Instead of being 17, I was 25. I had become an "Ivy Leaguer" in my dress, in my outlook on the world. I had deepened immeasurably in my faith. I had found that I could have deep friendships with men, and I had found that I loved a woman who had agreed to marry me. While not setting a brilliant record at YDS, I was leaving Yale with a more than acceptable record. I had broadened my outlook on life. It was time for me to leave Yale and move on. I had a sense of "well done," but I also realized that I would miss Yale, and especially YDS, and many friends I had made through eight years.

Graduation in 1953 was not as exciting as it had been in 1949. Ann was in Arkansas. Mother and Daddy did not come up for it, nor did I expect them to. I think I had two tickets I could give out. I'm not sure to whom I gave them. Perhaps I gave one to Dagoberto Weisbach. I know he was there when I took the train. He was then in North Carolina in graduate school, and I think came up for graduation. I may have given the other ticket to Ellie Wohlenberg or to Mrs. Beasley. I did not graduate with honors, but I was one of the representatives of the class at the big ceremony before Dean Pope gave out our diplomas back at YDS.

Engagement in Spring of 1953

Several couples at YDS had no engagement ring, but just a wide gold band for a wedding ring. I suggested this—but it went over like a lead balloon with Ann. Then I proposed that I give her a pearl. That is what Bard's wife, Nancy, wore and I thought it was "different" and good looking. That also was not acceptable. Ann wanted a diamond. I had no money and would have had to buy a microscopic one. Then Mother and Daddy said they would like to buy the ring as an engagement gift. Ann and I looked at jewelry stores in New York, although we knew we would not buy it there. My folks had access to some kind of discount jewelry catalog. I knew—and still know—nothing about diamonds and could have cared less, for jewelry means nothing to me. I don't remember the size of her diamond. I think it was something like a half carat and it cost about $250—which was a good bit of money in those days. I don't remember when the ring arrived and I put it on her finger. I suppose we waited until June 21 when the announcement was in the paper, but I am not sure.

We talked about what we wanted in the way of silver and china. I remember saying that I would like our china to be very plain—just a gold band around the edge—and that I would like our silver also to be plain. What I liked best was "Old Maryland" that had no pattern at all. Art and Florence had "Old Maryland Engraved," which was the most expensive pattern because each piece required hand engraving. But "Old Maryland" by itself was not out of sight. I thought Ann was in agreement with me, but when she got back to Arkansas and went shopping with her mother, she wound up getting the King Richard pattern that is almost as elaborate as Francis I. And the china she picked had a pattern of brown with pink and blue all over it. She asked me what I thought of it, and I said, "Whatever you like." When, since our divorce, I have eaten at Ann's house, we use that silver and china, and it certainly brings back memories. At my house, I have

Buckingham china (a gold band) and Wedgewood silver, which has a design but it is simpler.

During those weeks, we talked about wedding plans. We both agreed that we wanted excellent music. Father's secretary for many years was Mrs. Arnold. Her daughter, Eloise, had an excellent voice and had sung in the Robert Shaw Chorale. Her son, Corliss, was at Union Seminary in the School of Sacred Music. We hoped we could get them to do the music, and we found they were both going to be in Monticello in August. Once when Ann was visiting at YDS, we got an appointment with John Eichenbrodt, the YDS organist, and went over his suggestions for music. Neither of us wanted the Wagner processional, so he suggested what was then called Purcell's "Tune and Trumpet Air" (now attributed to Clark and called "The Prince of Denmark March"). I wanted to avoid the Mendelssohn recessional also, but Ann liked it, and I agreed. John also suggested "Sheep May Safely Grace" and "Jesu, Joy of Man's Desiring" and Handel's "Water Music." It was a most productive session with John.

Ann Williamson and me in 1953.

I remember one crisis in our relationship that spring. Ann was up for the weekend, and we went to a movie at the Lincoln Theater. The name was "I Confess." It was about a priest to whom a criminal had made his confession. Someone had been murdered, and an innocent man was on trial. The priest was the one person who could save him. He was struggling with his conscience, but felt obliged to honor the silence of the confessional. Afterward, as we walked home, I said that I could identify with the priest's dilemma, for I knew as a pastor I would hear confidences that I could not ever share. Ann said she certainly expected me to share things with her. I said there were going to be things I could not. We got into a real row over this.

In my last year at YDS I had come to be good friends with Bev Asbury. He knew I was going to New York. One time he asked me if Ann could get him a date with some of her friends there, for he did not have a girl friend. Ann came up with a woman who worked with her at the UN. It seems she was an heiress of some gold mines in Canada! I don't think Bev knew this when we planned our trip, but Ann told me only at the last minute. I remember I got a room for Bev and me at the Biblical Seminary. (I did not feel comfortable bringing someone with me to the McCains' apartment.) We did go out together — perhaps to dinner and a play. (It is interesting that many years later when Bev was chaplain at Vanderbilt University, his daughter and Sarah attended Camp Sequoia at the same time and knew each other.)

Once we got engaged, we knew that we would need to get married during the summer so we could leave in September. Ann, who had been working as an information person at the United Nations, resigned her job so she could go home to start getting ready for the wedding. I'm not sure just when she did that. I know she was not around when I graduated in early June, and I remember after she left I felt a real void in my life, with no one to date and no reason to go to New York.

On her way back to Arkansas Ann took the Southerner train that stopped in Knoxville. When Ann Payne greeted her and kissed her, she said, "Thank you! Thank you! Thank you! We thought Don would never get married."

Ordination, Marriage, and My Fulbright Year

Our Engagement Announcement

It is significant that I have much clearer memories about my ordination to the ministry on June 21, 1953, than I do about the announcement in the paper that same day that Ann and I were going to be married.

The public announcement of the engagement was an anticlimax. The time when my heart beat fast was on March 15 when I came to New York to find out what answer Ann was going to give to my proposal in mid-February. I thought she was going to say "yes," but I was not sure, for we had laid out some differences between us. But it seemed "right."

By the time Ann returned from New York in May, and I from New Haven in June, everyone who knew us at all well was aware we were planning to marry. The date had been set, for in those days engagement announcements always gave the date of the wedding. There was no big "engagement party," as took place in the East then, and now in the South at places. Without a "secret" to announce, such seemed ridiculous.

There had been quiet "conversations" with the society editors of the two Little Rock papers, and of course the *Advanced Monticellonian* made big news of the engagement of the elder daughter of one of the most prominent families, and leading lawyer, in the town. I, personally, did not think Ann's engagement picture did her justice. It was not nearly as good as her wedding pictures later in the summer.

I don't remember whether Ann was at Second Church that Sunday morning or if she remained in Monticello with her parents and came up in the afternoon. It seems to me I preached that morning at Second, but I am not sure. I know I had a part in the service. I do not remember standing at the church door with Ann, which I think I would have done had she been present.

Once her picture appeared in the paper, things were in motion, and nothing short of a disaster could stop them. I do not have any memory of feeling "trapped." I was in love with love and wanted to get married. It was what the script called for. Our wedding, next to the Tripplet-Fullerton one, was the social wedding of the summer in Arkansas. Cousin Frances had determined to come to it, and to force all her family to come along, too. I am sure there were many objections, but she was hell-bent on having a McCain family reunion in Arkansas before Cousin Charlie got too feeble to make the trip. He was very close to that condition as it was. Our wedding was the focal point. Everything seemed to be shaping up.

Getting Ordained

Once I returned from Yale after graduation, things moved at a fast pace. Our engagement was announced in the paper on June 21, but plans for the wedding were already getting firmed up. Since my "major" examination by Presbytery had taken place at Christmas, I had only a *pro forma* examination for ordination, whereas others (I think David Davies) had the full examination. That was the first (and probably the last) time this Presbytery had ever licensed someone prior to graduation.

I was being ordained to do graduate work in Scotland (PCUS still allowed this, although there were many who wanted to abolish this provision, and soon afterward did), but I needed income for the summer, and also I wanted some kind of ministry to do. I guess Roy Davis was still the Synod Executive. He told me there was a place where I could be of service in Hot Springs. While the PCUS (Southern) and PCUSA (Northern) denominations were still separate (although both were looking toward a vote for union in 1954), they did have a lot of communication between the two. Coy Lee was the executive of the PCUSA Presbytery in the northwest corner of Arkansas. Most of their churches were in that region, with only a scattering of PCUS. Most of "our" churches were in the other three quarters of the state, with only a scattering of PCUSA. Roy and Coy had worked out a "horse trade" — that Orange Street Church in Hot Springs would become PCUS, and some church in the northwest about the same size numerically would become PCUSA. This was made possible because the pastor of Orange Street had just moved. They needed someone to be the "caretaker" and "transition minister" as the change was being made. Roy thought I could fill in there while Orange Street started looking for a PCUS minister. Since I wanted to work only until the end, or middle, of August, that fit my schedule well. I went over for a visit, and the Session voted to invite me. So, I had work to do.

Then I needed to work out the details of my ordination service. This was a high point for me, and I wanted it done well. I had asked Uncle Ken Latourette, my spiritual father, to come down to preach the sermon, and Presbytery had agreed. (Dr. Boggs was there to make sure I got my way on each point!) Then Uncle Ken had emergency surgery. It was not life-threatening, but he was not in any condition to make that long trip. I was terribly disappointed, but I did want some kind of Yale representation in the service.

There were two people who started out with me at YDS in the fall of 1949. George Chauncey was a PCUS minister in Brownsville, Tennessee. We were very close friends, and I had been in his wedding. Also, Dean Lewis was a PCUSA minister serving the church at Springdale, Arkansas. He and I were also good friends and had talked much about love and marriage. I did not know which one to ask to preach. I thought Dean would probably be the more brilliant preacher — if he prepared, but I had an idea he would possibly write his sermon the afternoon of the service as they drove down to Little Rock. I knew George would be solid and that what he had to say would be good, if not brilliant. So I chose George, and am glad I did.

(While Dean had been ordained in 1952, he still did not have a degree from YDS. Yale gave him permission to leave campus because he had a call and he was getting married, and because he would earn the one more credit required for graduation by completing his term paper in Richard Niebuhr's course. Dean promised he would right away, in 1952. He kept promising and not delivering. It became a real "thing" at YDS. I understand even the saintly Richard Niebuhr wanted to spit every time Dean's name came up. This went on for something like five or six years. Finally, Yale said they would give him a degree if he went to Eden Seminary in St. Louis for a term in residence.)

The night of the ordination, June 21, 1953, Emmett and Frances Whipple (he was son of Cousin Lizette Whipple, a cousin on the McCain side) had a dinner party for Ann and me, my parents, and hers, I think. They lived on what was then called Hayes Street (now

University) in the "upper Heights." They were at the very end of the paved street, just before the descent of that hill. There was not even a walking trail from that point to the intersection of Hayes (University) and Markham, and even at that intersection, both were two lanes, and gravel.

As I write in 2003, it is hard to realize how much Little Rock has changed. University Avenue went on to become the "main street" of the city and is now fighting to survive commercially because the population has moved even farther west. The memory of that dinner party at the Whipples helps date the world into which I was ordained—compact city, segregated schools (*Brown vs. Board of Education* would not be handed down for 11 more months), no black participation in political life.

George preached on the footwashing in the upper room—on the role of minister as servant. (Until I wrote that out, I never connected that text with my concept that footwashing could be another sacrament. I wonder if he knew about that debate?) It was an outstanding sermon. I asked Dean to read the Scripture lessons—II Corinthians 5:14-21 and John 13:1-17. I did not trust Mrs. Mathis' selection of organ or choir music, so I asked for two Bach pieces for the prelude. And so she would not pick some florid anthem, I requested the choir sing the "Gloria In Excelsis" (which I had come to know and love at the Interseminary Conference in 1949 which George and I attended) and "Of the Father's Love Begotten." Some in the choir suggested I was turning Episcopalian!

Dr. Boggs was chairman of the ordaining commission, and "presided" at the service. I asked to have on the commission T. B. Hay (pastor at Pulaski Heights Church), who had pressed me on dispensationalism at my December examination, and Dr. Henry Paisley (retired), who had expressed dismay at my idea there might be more than two sacraments, and also my idea of praying for the dead. Both had wound up voting to license me. I do not remember why I chose them, except I knew I did not want R. D. Adams from First Church. It may have been my "political" instinct (dating back to my campaigns at East Side Junior High) to try to win over and make friends with the adversary! I have used it many times since.

One elder from Washburn Presbytery was necessary to make a quorum. I asked Gaston Williamson, my second cousin and an elder at Second Church. I had also pushed the Presbytery to invite people from other denominations to come share in the laying on of hands as "visiting brothers" — Uncle Ken (former President of the Northern Baptist Convention); Mike Carozza (Southern Baptist, and pastor of All Souls Church, Scott); James Workman (pastor of First Methodist, North Little Rock and a Yale Divinity graduate, and a good friend of Uncle Ken's); Franklin Henderson, PCUSA, pastor of Allison Presbyterian Church, Little Rock (this was a black congregation, and he was one of the two people who had led to my conversion on race in 1949); and Alvin Hodges, rector of Christ Episcopal Church, Little Rock. (Bishop Mitchell would allow him to come to the service, but would not allow him to join in the laying on of hands lest somehow the "Episcopal juice" somehow get through to me!). Adrian Williamson, Sr. (Ann's father) and Uncle Lamar Williamson were also invited to sit as visiting brothers and share in the laying on of hands.

Dr. Boggs had gone the "second mile" by having his Session invite Frank Henderson's congregation to come for the service. That was the first time that black congregation had ever been invited to worship in a white church! Until the 1990s when Frank Henderson died, he loved to tell people that when such things were not done, he was invited to share in my ordination and his people were invited to come to the service. It obviously was a real breakthrough for him and them. When I went to Allison about 2001, one of the older women there told me she was present at my ordination — and asked if I ever got my robe (which was delayed in delivery.)

My family and Ann's were all present that night. Many people came from All Souls, for I was the first person reared in that congregation who had ever gone into the ministry. Many people from Second Church came (although Presbyterians are noted for being allergic to the "night air"). Dr. Boggs was so pleased about all this. I was the first person from Second Church who had ever been ordained to the ministry (other than James Fogertie, who did not really come from Second, but was passing through because his father was on the Synod staff at the time). Also, I had worked there for two summers and Ann for one. I think a few people came over from Orange Street Church.

Another one of my quirks was that I wanted us to celebrate communion at this service. It was not normal in the Southern Church, but the sacrament had come to be very important to me. I even asked for permission to be the celebrant — as soon as the "hands" were taken off me. I still think the symbolism is powerful, to begin one's ministry this way. Presbytery's commission, under Dr. Bogg's firm hand, agreed. So, still sweating from the heat on that summer night, intensified by the gathering of ministers and elders circling around to lay on hands, I moved to the communion table and began serving for the first time in my life—using the service in the 1946 *Book of Common Worship*. It was moving to have my future father-in-law and uncle and Gaston laying on hands. It was even more so for me to serve them the bread and wine, and then send them out to serve others. I could not ask Uncle Gordon Campbell to partake, for he was an ordained deacon, but not an elder. And I could not ask Daddy, for he was a member of All Souls Church, but not an elder.

The hymns I picked for that night were:

"All People That on Earth Do Dwell," "In Christ There Is No East or West" (with the third stanza about "join hands, then, brothers of the faith, whate'er your race may be"—with Allison Church in mind and memories of singing that in Cotton Plant), "O God of Bethel," and "Ye Servants of God, Your Master Proclaim."

In my opinion, it was well planned and carried out perfectly. My memory of it is one of the high points in my life. Of all those who played official roles that night, so far as I know, the only two still living are George Chauncey (with whom I talked this morning by phone) and Dean Lewis.

So, June 21, 1953, when I was 25 years old, I was a fully ordained minister in Washburn Presbytery, Synod of Arkansas, Presbyterian Church in the United States.

My parents invited Ann, the Chaunceys and Lewises to come spend the night at Scott. I remember when we got down to the house, the six of us sat on the front porch of the "big house," reminiscing about things since 1949 when we met and wondering what the future would hold for us all.

I have warm, deep, rich feelings about my ordination, and am grateful for the ministry that began that night.

Ann in Summer of 1953

There was a lot going on at the beginning of the summer—the public announcement of our engagement, my ordination, my moving to Hot Springs and serving Orange Street Church. In

Monticello, Ann and Cousin Catherine were working full time at planning the wedding. This was going to be a "big one," made bigger by Cousin Frances McCain's decision to celebrate it by having a reunion of the McCain clan. So plans had to be made for that, too.

On Sunday nights, Mondays, and Tuesdays, Ann and I would get together. Most of the time I would drive, after Sunday night activities, to Monticello. It must have been between 100 and 150 miles one way. I recall I would have to fight sleepiness on the way. The roads were two lane and went through lots of small towns. I came to know them well.

When we were together, there were social events. The Williamsons were great entertainers, and "The Hill" with its tennis court was a place people loved to visit. So friends were in and out of there, and also the Lamar Williamson clan, especially Cousin Charlotte, were involved. I also came to know better the McClendons, Pomeroys, Prices, Davises, and Trotters, some of the family friends in Monticello. I had known Ann's parents all my life and had always called them "cousin." We talked about what I was going to call them after the wedding. I was determined not to follow my sister's way of hedging between "Mr. Payne" and "Ga-ga," so in advance, I proposed Father and Mother Catherine. Ann was going to use Mother Campbell and Daddy for my parents.

Despite all the social aspects of the visits, Ann and I would get some time alone after her parents went up to bed. We did heavy petting on the sofa in the living room at The Hill.

Both of us, from our counseling training, wanted to get help on our sex life. We both had read everything we could find. I had picked up at Yale a book *Ideal Marriage* by van de Velde that was supposed to be the most explicit and helpful book of its type. We made an appointment with Dr. Johnny Price, their family physician and also a family friend, to talk about the sexual aspects of marriage. He said he had never counseled a couple who wanted more knowledge and help than we did, and he was sure we would be successful in our sexual life. I left with more confidence.

I did not get negative "vibes" that summer. I don't remember our having any serious clashes. It was a summer of fun, of stimulating petting, of support from family and friends, and of anticipation of a year in Scotland.

Fullerton Wedding

In the summer of 1953, "the" big wedding in Arkansas was that of Fufa Triplett of Pine Bluff to Sam Fullerton of Warren. Our wedding was "number two" — a lot of attention to it, but nothing like that given the Triplett-Fullerton wedding. Sam was heir to a lumber fortune. Fufa's father was a prominent lawyer in Pine Bluff, with a lot of money from land. Her mother had the fascinating name of Vashti. Fufa had been to Miss Porter's Finishing School in Farmington, Connecticut. Sam had been to some prep school in the East, then the University of Arkansas. Her crystal was Steuben, and everything else was costly and from Dallas. They had a champagne fountain at the wedding reception.

I was not invited, for I did not know either of them. I was surprised Ann was not, although I think Margaret Williamson was. But Ann's father had been Mr. Fullerton's attorney, so they were invited to ours. The first time I ever met them was when they came down our receiving line.

Ann and I seemed so perfectly matched — both from similar backgrounds, and both bright, well educated, theologically trained. Fufa and Sam were both spoiled children. I think he was 21 and she was 18. They had everything money could buy. They seemed to be all "fluff," and her nickname backed that up. Even though I did not know them, I remember thinking that the chances of that marriage lasting were slim. On July 31, 2003, however, I went to the fiftieth anniversary of their marriage! Ann and I have been divorced 34 years, our marriage lasting 16.

I have come to know Fufa and Sam partly through Gert Behanna. They found Gert inspiring. When I was at The Oasis, we worked together to get the 16mm movie of Gert's "pitch" made into a VCR. Also, once I moved back to Little Rock, Fufa would call to ask me to be the supply preacher whenever their church was without a pastor (which was often). I was invited once to do some conflict management with one of the pastors. Both Fufa and Sam have been elders in that church and are pillars there.

This certainly is a reminder that "God sees not as man sees." Our predictions of which marriages will be strong and which fragile are certainly unreliable.

Orange Street Church, Hot Springs, Arkansas

I think I went to the Orange Street Presbyterian Church in Hot Springs on June 1, even though I was not ordained until the 21st. I know I left after the service on August 24, the Sunday before the wedding. If I did not start until June 24, then I was there just two months. This was a church of maybe 150 members, a "stunted" congregation. I would guess that the building had been erected around 1915 or so. It was a one-story, red brick church with a couple of white columns in the front. There were two floors in the back where some educational rooms had been added. It had been kept up pretty well, so did not have a rundown appearance. It stood in the boarding house section of Hot Springs, hemmed in by apartment buildings. It was overshadowed by First Presbyterian Church, which had lots of members and influence, and all the money it could want because of the Brown family. There was a small corps of hard-working, committed members who pretty well ran the Orange Street Church. The congregation was made up of folks who worked in the nursing or bathhouse industries, some merchants of small shops, a masseur, a real estate agent, some teachers and retired persons, a middle management person at a wholesale grocery chain. They were not poor, but none of them was rich. No one was a person of influence in the community. No one was in the "social circle" of Hot Springs. It was very different from Second Presbyterian, Little Rock (which was the "silk stocking" crowd) and Cotton Plant (which, though smaller, included members from plantation owners to a day laborer in the veneer mill). The Orange Street members were intelligent, but my guess is few of them, other than teachers, had college degrees—perhaps one or two years in college. But they were far from being ignorant. And they had had some good pastors, especially the one whose departure had opened up the way for me to come as an interim. He had been called to a larger church in "Northern church" territory—perhaps Oklahoma. I was grateful that he had left an order of worship that might not have been ideal in my mind, but was one with which I could operate with comfort. They also had an organist who could play decently any hymn I wanted to pick. They paid their bills on time and were not in financial distress. Walt Smalley was the "Uncle Charlie" of the congregation, without whose consent nothing could be done. But there were a couple of other powerhouses. The finances were as limited as the size of their property. As they worked on the budget, I expressed amazement that the budget was about twice the size of anticipated pledges. When I asked how that could be, they said it was due to the horse-racing season. Being the only Northern Presbyterian Church in town, they got a lot of visitors from the north during racing season. They said people would win at the racetrack, then put in enough "guilt money" during those six weeks to equal the pledges for the whole of the year!

I lived in the manse, which sat next to the home of Walt and Fern Smalley. They had no children and took on the pastor and his family as their own. This, I gathered, had been the pattern during a number of pastorates and was especially so of my predecessor. So they took me on as soon as I moved in. They lent me equipment that I needed that summer. They invited me over for some meals. There were a few others in the congregation who also invited me for meals or visits in their homes. But they were not, on the whole, people who were in the habit of entertaining.

I did a lot of routine calling, since that was the aspect of ministry I liked the most. I am sure I called on every home in the church at least once, if they were in town, and probably made the rounds twice. I don't recall friction with anyone in the church, but I did not get my roots down as I had in Cotton Plant.

With our wedding looming, I arranged a deal to work long hours five days a week and to have Monday and Tuesday off. Even though I was at Orange Street only a few weeks, and for only five days of those weeks, I did feel I made some real ties. However, I did not maintain any of them over the years. I would say that of all my short- and long-term ministries, this was probably the most superficial and left the least impression. There were no negatives to my time there, just no major accomplishments. But I was there only as a "transfer" processor, and I guess that worked.

Hot Springs depressed me. There were so many old people, just sitting and waiting to die, and so many sick and crippled people who had come for the baths. Others have found Hot Springs to be a fun place to visit, but most of that attraction was on the lakes around Hot Springs. The gambling had been closed down (or at least I thought it was), the horses raced only in the spring, and I did not have money to eat at the expensive restaurants in town.

There is one "pastoral" experience I need to record. There were many transients in Hot Springs and other people left destitute after gambling losses, so each church had a fund for the pastor to distribute, but no coordination among churches that I knew of. One day, a man appeared at the door of the study, asking for money for gas and for food for his wife and four children who were hungry. I asked him some questions. When I inquired what was "home," he said Lexington, Virginia. I had been in Lexington some 15 months before, so I asked some questions about the name of the hotel there, and something about the colleges in town (Washington and Lee and Virginia Military Institute). His answers were all correct, so I assumed he was probably on the level. I gave him some money, I think, or some other kind of help and walked out to the car to make sure there was a woman and four children. There were. About 10 days later, a woman appeared at my door asking for help. They needed money for gas and for food for her four children who were hungry. I asked her where she was headed and where she came from. When she said Lexington, Virginia, I thought this was very, very strange, so I suggested I walk out with her so I could see the children. There in the car sat the man who had come in to me, the same car, the same four children. Evidently, they had hit up so many churches they had forgotten they had been to this one before! I did not give help this time. And it certainly made me wary about people who were "passing through."

A few years after I left, there was a church fight at First Church. Mr. W. C. Brown and his sister, Miss Jean, the wealthiest people in Hot Springs, moved from First to Orange Street. Other strong leaders also made the move. All at once, the future of Orange Street brightened. It was not long before they bought land out near one of the lakes and moved — and when they did, "Orange Street" was not an appropriate name. They changed to Westminster and put their past behind them. Very soon it was stronger than First Church.

Wedding Rehearsal

The rehearsal for our wedding went very smoothly. Lamar Williamson, our mutual cousin, was in charge and did a fine job. Following the rehearsal, the Lamar Williamson, Sr., children and their spouses gave a beautiful dinner at the Monticello Country Club.

As Ann and I were leaving the rehearsal for the dinner, we had to go to the church office to meet with Lamar to sign some kind of paper. As we did so, he said, "Ann, as I have told you before, I don't think you two should get married. You are both perfectionists, and that spells trouble." I was astounded and so caught off guard I said nothing at the moment. As we drove out to the dinner, I asked, "What in the world did Lamar mean by that? I think we need to follow up." Ann replied, "You can ask him if you want to, but I won't. It's none of his business."

And I backed down. Had I sought him out, and had I seen the wisdom of what he was saying, would I have had the guts to cancel the wedding? I doubt it. Mother used to tell a story about when she was a teenager and was to be in a wedding in Pine Bluff. On the afternoon of the wedding, the bride's mother called all the bridesmaids down to the living room and read a letter from the groom saying that he "had storms in his bosom" and was not going to be married, and was taking a train out of town. That is what I call courage! His name was mud. Would I have risked anger and scorn from all these friends and relatives who had come from great distances? I fear not. I never discussed this again with Ann, but I never forgot it.

When Ann and I divorced 16 years later, I wrote to Lamar, who was then a missionary in Congo, to tell him and Ruthmary of what was happening. In that letter I reminded him of the warning he gave us that night. He wrote back saying he had not forgotten either, and had felt guilty ever since. He said either he should have said nothing or else refused to perform the ceremony if he felt that strongly. I have tried to assuage him of his sense of guilt, for as I have indicated above, I doubt I would have had the courage to do anything about it.

Wedding

August 29, 1953, was the hottest day of a hot summer. This was before churches and homes had central air conditioning. First Presbyterian Church had sold their old building in preparation for erecting a new sanctuary. They had bought the old country hospital and were using what had been the cafeteria as their place of worship. It was not a lovely room to say the least, but the florist had done everything possible to make it attractive. I looked up the society page write-up that was in the family scrapbook, and it says there were banks of laurel and huckleberry greenery, interspersed with candelabra holding pink tapers. There were arrangements of pink stock and chrysanthemums in the center, behind the kneeling bench.

One side note had to do with the typical Southern summer wedding custom. People who gathered would speculate on how many of the candles would melt before the service was over. Some always did. Several did during our wedding, especially on the groom's side. Daddy jumped up for two or three that had fallen down on the canvas runners, stamping them out before they caught fire.

Ann and me on our wedding day, August 29, 1953.

Ann and me with our parents (Arthur and Margaret Campbell on the left, and Catherine and Adrian Williamson on the right) on our wedding day, August 29, 1953.

The write-up describes Ann's dress as being made of lace and tulle, with a cathedral train, a floor length veil of illusion, coming down from a Juliet cap. (I have never mastered all the terms society writers use.) It was a lovely dress, but not ostentatious and certainly not satin in that hot weather. Her bouquet was white orchids and stephanotis. The bridesmaids wore waltz-length pink nylon net, and their flowers were Fuji chrysanthemums and ivy.

Margaret Williamson was maid of honor, and Sara Campbell Harris (no relative, but Ann's best friend from college) was matron of honor. The other attendants were Sarah Tucker (both Sarahs were Agnes Scott friends) and three cousins—Frances McCain, and Lillian and Leila Riggs. My best man was Hoyt N. Payne, Jr., my brother-in-law (Art was in French Morocco), and my attendants were my cousins Adrian Williamson, Jr. (Ann's brother), Arthur McCain, and Gordon Vineyard, as well as Bill Dunklin (married to

Ethel Smart, Ann's cousin, who was too pregnant to be in the wedding) and Buddy Craig, my best friend from Scott.

With Corliss Arnold as organist and Eloise Arnold as soloist, the music was first class. The electronic organ was limited, but Corliss got out of it all that was possible. I remember Eloise singing "Sheep May Safely Graze" and "If Thou Be Near." The music just prior to the processional was "Jesu, Joy of Man's Desiring." (I still love that piece of music, but every time I hear it, I remember standing in the side room with Hoyt, both scared and excited.) As I mentioned elsewhere, the processional was what was then known as Purcell's "Tune and Trumpet Air" (now usually called Clark's "Prince of Denmark March"). This was a break from tradition, and many people thought it was something from Scotland, since we were going there. Eloise also sang "O Perfect Love" after we knelt for prayer at the end of the service. Against my wishes, we recessed to Mendelssohn's "Wedding March."

Lamar Williamson, Jr., Ann's first cousin and my second cousin, performed the ceremony. He had a rich voice and a real involvement with each of us, plus many of the people who packed the room. He did a fine job, though I kept wondering what he had meant after the rehearsal the night before.

On the morning of the wedding, I had asked that we have communion for the wedding party and immediate family. George Faison was pastor of First Presbyterian. Since we had not asked him to share in the ceremony, we asked him to have the communion service, and that meant a great deal to me. At that service, I learned that my sister, Ann, was sick. She was also pregnant, with her third baby—Mary Ann. At first they were not sure of the illness, but Dr. Price said she had the mumps! As a result, neither of my siblings was at the wedding. (Neither Ann nor I got to Art's wedding, but all of us had been at hers.) Margaret and Sally Payne were very small children—too small to be flower girls. Mother and Daddy had brought Lizzie and Epps down from Scott to look after them. Having never had mumps, and fearful of the consequences if they "fell," I kept my distance when we came out of the church on our way to the reception. Ann was there in the car, with her girls, waving to us and crying.

The church was completely full I am sure, although I do not remember counting. There were many people from Monticello, for the Williamsons were an old and prominent family in the community, and pillars of the Presbyterian Church. They and the Campbells were also known around the state, and both sides had relatives galore in the state, so there were lots of people from Warren, Pine Bluff, Scott, Little Rock, and Memphis. Cousin Frances McCain, who felt she had proprietary interest in our marriage because she had urged me to move ahead in my dating, had rounded up McCain cousins from all around for a reunion in conjunction with the wedding. Someone commented that Cousin Frances, in her elegant New York long dress, walked down the aisle with sweat coming through the back of the dress! Fortunately, she never knew. One of the cousins-in-law was Connie Vanderbilt Davis McCain (Chuck's wife). She was Mrs. Cornelius Vanderbilt's favorite granddaughter. Her grandmother had given her as a wedding present the Vanderbilt jewels. Everyone was wondering if she would wear them. Mother had the nerve to ask, and her reply was, "Heavens, no. They are in the lock box. We couldn't afford the insurance to take them out."

As I think back on it, the wedding (despite the heat) really was beautiful, both in appearance and in sound.

We have a picture taken of us just as we were leaving the sanctuary, and the clock shows 7:30. It had started at 7:00.

I have forgotten who drove us out to The Hill where the reception was held in the backyard, which was a garden. Mother Catherine was quite a gardener, so it was always lovely, but that night it had been turned into fairyland. I don't remember what all was done, but there were flowers and candles, and the concrete block picnic table had been covered with white cloths and was the serving table. The write-up of the wedding lists 33 women and girls who were assisting!

In those days, the bride and groom, parents, and female attendants stood in the receiving line. It took a long time. I remember meeting Fufa and Sam Fullerton for the first time in that line. I was touched by the people who had driven long distances to be present—Dr. and Mrs. Boggs and the Andrew Fribergs from Little Rock, the whole Campbell clan, etc.

As I have written earlier, this was a very hot day. As darkness fell, it became a little cooler and a breeze set in. Toward the end of the reception, there was some summer lightning in the west. Later that night, I am told, there was a real thunderstorm which, a few hours earlier, would have ruined that carefully planned reception.

Honeymoon and After

After the reception Ann and I went upstairs to separate rooms to change into our traveling clothes. My ushers and I had worn summer tuxedos—white jackets, tux pants, and black bow ties. I put on my blue seercord suit. The write-up says that Ann wore a brown Italian silk linen (whatever that is) dress.

Hoyt drove us from The Hill to a place in downtown Monticello where he had hidden our car. In those days, friends and ushers liked to paint up the get-away car and tie tin cans, etc., to them to attract attention. Careful Hoyt had found a place behind a filling station, and I guess paid the attendant to protect it. We got away from The Hill all right. When we arrived to pick up our car, there was Dr. Marion Boggs' calling card under the windshield wiper! Of all people to find it, there was no one I'd rather have. He later told me when they drove into town, he wanted to get gas for the return trip. While there, he told the attendant they were down for the Williamson wedding and casually asked, "Do you know where the get-away car is?" The man had said, "Right back there."

Since our car had not been painted up, we were able to leave immediately for Greenville, Mississippi. We were going to Biloxi, but that was too far away for a night drive, so I had made reservations at the Greenville Hotel. (It was said the Mississippi Delta ran from the lobby of the Peabody in Memphis to the lobby of the Hotel Greenville.) Having heard horror stories of ushers who found out where their "friend" was going and called in a cancellation, I had insisted the hotel send me a written confirmation. It's a good thing I had, for when we arrived, the person at the desk had no record of our coming and said because of some big event in town every room in the hotel and other motels was taken. At this point, I had presence of mind enough to ask for the manager and showed my written confirmation. They found they did have one room on a floor that was being remodeled, but the air conditioning had not been on and it would be warm. Rather than drive on, we took it.

When we got there, not only was the room hot, but there were cracks in the ceiling. Obviously, this was one of the rooms that needed to be worked on, but we were exhausted. I have often suggested to couples with whom I have done premarital counseling, that if they have not already been living together or have not had a lot of intercourse before marriage, they might be wise to agree ahead of time not to try for the first time when both are stressed out. We were both shy and embarrassed. We had done a lot of playing with each other, but this was different. We were both virgins. Our first lovemaking was a fiasco. I felt I was a failure.

We went down for breakfast, and then to worship at First Presbyterian Church. I have forgotten who was pastor there, but it was some well-known Presbyterian minister of whom Ann had heard. That afternoon, we drove on down to the Gulf Coast, where I had never been before, but Ann had. She was the one who had preferred that as the place for our honeymoon. We stayed in a nice motel that was separated from the beach by the highway, but there was a pedestrian overpass. We ate in the restaurants that were plentiful along the beach, and I remember Ann talked me into trying flounder — my first taste of that fish. The sand there is nice, but not white like at Panama Beach. The water was not crystal clear, but far better than Old River. I think one day we rented a little Sunfish sailboat that let us run up and down the beach. Another day, we went down to the home of Jefferson Davis, which has been turned into a museum, and one day I think we went over to the Edgewater Beach Hotel, the big one at Gulfport. We went by the Presbyterian Church and happened to run into the pastor, who introduced himself as Maynard Miller. (Later that year, he was called to Orange Street Church in Hot Springs where I had served that summer.) We continued to be frustrated in our sexual adjustment, each of us feeling guilty. I don't know if we stayed two or three days, but I (and I think Ann) was more than ready to leave when the end of our reservation came. We were to leave on September 11 and had a lot to do back home about wedding presents and packing for Scotland. Our ship sailed from New York on September 17.

We had received an enormous number of beautiful wedding gifts — all of our good china, good silver, a dozen silver goblets, a silver service, serving pieces, and every piece ever made in our everyday pottery. The jewelry store in Monticello did not carry either our china or silver, but did the pottery — so we got everything in the catalog. We also got 17 silver compotes. I understand at every wedding, there is one item that seems to be "it" for that season. Cousin Lizette Whipple said when she got married, it was cut-glass water pitchers, but ours was silver compotes. Mother Catherine was a bit nervous about our returning anything, but we insisted we could not use them all, and we could use the credit to fill in what we missed. One night we had all 17 of them gathered on the display table in the back bedroom, trying to decide which ones to keep. Just then the doorbell rang. It was the Pomeroys who had come to see the gifts. They had given us the largest, nicest, and most expensive of the silver compotes. But there it sat, with 16 others gathered around it. It was difficult to explain.

But we did assemble duplicates and boxed them up so we could take them to Stifft's and Cave's, the two big jewelry stores in Little Rock. They were very gracious about exchanging and giving us credit. If I am not mistaken, they even gave us some cash refunds so we could have money to buy things in Europe.

Then we went out to Scott to see my family and friends. We were sleeping in the double bed on the sleeping porch, with no one else on that second floor, so we had privacy. At long last, we were successful sexually.

I think we may have gone back to Monticello one more time, to take items that we had gained in exchanges, then came back to Scott in preparation for leaving on the train on September 11.

We took a Pullman from Little Rock to St. Louis, and then changed to a train that was going to Chicago, but we stopped for one night in Bloomington, Illinois. Grandmother Campbell had not been able to come to the wedding, and I don't think she had ever met Ann. She was getting up in years, and I wanted Ann to be sure to meet her. We spent the night in her home, then the next day caught the train to Chicago. I don't think we did anything there except make our connection to New York. We were still traveling by Pullman. We had a compartment, rather than an upper and lower berth, because we were wanting to have privacy.

Crossing the Atlantic

I am a bit vague, but I think when we arrived in New York we went to 10 Gracie Square and spent the night with the Charles McCains. The day our ship, the *USS United States*, the world's largest liner, was pulling out, they had their chauffeur drive us and our baggage down to the pier, and gave Ann a corsage and other *bon voyage* gifts. Some telegrams came to us on the ship—as was the custom in those days.

Ann had told me ahead of time that she tended to get seasick. I had never been on an ocean before, or abroad. She had when she went over one summer to do field work at the Waldensian camp, Agape, in the Italian Alps. In preparation, we had stored up on Dramamine, the new medicine designed to avert, or at least ameliorate, seasickness.

I think we boarded ship in the late morning, for we soon had lunch. Ann started getting seasick before we pulled out of New York harbor—it seemed to me she was getting sick before they cast off the ropes from the pier. And she was seasick practically the whole way over, sometimes more so, sometimes less.

The Fulbright people had arranged our travel, and there were many Fulbright recipients on board. When we gathered, there was one man whose face I recognized. He had been in Freshman English with me at Yale College. We had both continued through Yale, but I never saw him again—although I found he lived in Calhoun College, which is on the same block with Berkeley College and next to it! I don't know if he remembered my name, or I his, or if we both had to ask—though both of us recognized faces. He was Bill Kelly, married to Lynn. I can't remember where he went to seminary—perhaps Hartford, or it could have been Drew. I think he had been student pastor at Ohio State in Columbus, Ohio, for a year, and that is where he met Lynn, whose father was pastor of the big Methodist Church. The four of us hit it off immediately, spent a lot of time together on the voyage over, and remained friends for years. They were going to Edinburgh, and we arranged for them to meet the Barbours. Another couple on board were John and Billie Maguire, also going to Edinburgh. He had just finished college and was starting theology, and was going to live in the home of John Baillie, the principal of New College. John later went to YDS, where I introduced him to Uncle Ken. (John became president of one of the New York State University campuses, on Long Island; was elected president of Union Theological Seminary in New York—and resigned after one day; then was president of Claremont Theological community in California.)

We were assigned tables in the dining room. We introduced ourselves to the couple seated at our table, but I do not remember their names. They came from Virginia City, Nevada. I knew nothing about the place. They told us there were more bars than people in Virginia City. They asked about us, and I told them I was a minister. I asked them what church they belonged to, and they looked at each other blankly. She said she had once been a Roman Catholic, but didn't believe that any more. She said to him, "What denomination do you belong to?" His reply was, "I think my mother was a Christian Scientist and my father was a Methodist, but I am not sure." Introduction to the secular world! We had to share the table for the whole crossing. We made polite conversation, but we had little in common with each other, and never were together other than at meals. That was too bad, for friendships can be formed at mealtimes.

There were three "classes" on the USS United States—first class, second, and third. Regular Fulbright students were in third class. Our cabin was nice and clean (the ship was almost new), but below the waterline, so we could hear the water passing all the time—except when the ship rolled. Then there would be silence, until the ship rolled back the other way. (I will comment later on how often this happened.) Professors on Fulbrights were in second class. Professor Paul Schubert, who taught New Testament at YDS, and his wife were on a Fulbright sabbatical, and that's where they were. We were allowed up there once, on his invitation. Billy Graham was on board this same voyage. He was in first class. We never saw him. I think he preached on Sunday, but only to first-class passengers. I believe we were in the middle of a hurricane on Sunday, and very few went to our service.

We were traveling in mid-September, the height of the hurricane season. We thought it was wonderful to be on the largest ship afloat—that it would be so safe, especially if we hit a hurricane. It seems our assumption was wrong. During a hurricane, a very large ship can get hit by two huge waves at the same time, so it rolls more than ever! We went through not one, but two, hurricanes on our way over. Ann was deathly nauseated for about three of the five days we were on board. Actually, I think the USS was trying to set a record for speed from New York to Southampton. It came very close, and would have done so if we had not had the two hurricanes. Strangely enough, even though I had always had a queasy stomach, I never once got nauseated on that trip and never missed a meal. The thing that almost upset me was the smell as I would walk down the halls, for people were vomiting all over the place, and the ventilation system was not capable of clearing the air quickly. Even members of the crew were getting seasick. I remember once, when the waves were huge and breaking over the deck of the ship, I went to the one place where we could open the door and step out—just to get a breath of fresh air that did not smell like vomit.

On the night of the "gala dinner," when people were supposed to dress up and there was live music and decorations, not 10 percent of the people showed up in the dining hall—but I was there, big as life. I think I was the only one of the four at our table. As waiters would come out of the kitchen with a load of food and dishes, they would often lose their balance, and there would be the crash of broken china. There was much talk from the crew (those who were still walking) that this really was not normal, that they had rarely seen a crossing as rough as this.

Finally, we did emerge from the storm, but the seas were still high. When we could get outside, the sky was clear, the weather cold enough to want a wool coat, and the seas were green in the surging waves. Ann was finally able to get out of her berth. I remember how excited we were when we saw land to the north (the tip of Ireland) and then began to see land in England, until we finally docked in the morning at Southampton.

I don't remember any tension between Ann and me on that trip—just misery for Ann, and therefore little communication of any kind. She did not want company most of the time. I'm not sure what I did other than eat. They not only served breakfast, lunch, and dinner, but tea in the afternoon and supper just before bedtime. I suppose I must have spent a good bit of time with Bill and Lynn Kelly, for by the time we reached England, we were good friends. There were many other people with Fulbrights, some going to Great Britain and others to various spots in Europe. I must have had superficial visits with a number of them, for I remember they were a very bright group—from all over the United States.

London in 1953

When we arrived in Southampton, we had no trouble with customs, for the Fulbright people were there to meet us and shepherd us through. We took a train up to London. That was my first jolt about tea/coffee. I had been a tea drinker ever since I started Yale College (because the coffee was so bad), and I had been looking forward so to a cup of real English tea. People came through the cars serving refreshment, so I asked for tea. They said they had none! They were serving coffee only. (I learned later that most places serve tea only at tea time.)

I do not remember the hotel in which we were lodged, but this, too, had been arranged by the Fulbright committee. It was OK and was centrally located. I guess it was that first night, or perhaps the second, that the U.S. Ambassador, Winthrop Aldrich, and his wife gave a reception at the ambassador's home for all the Fulbright people — students and professors. Having been interested in diplomacy at one point, I was excited to see what an ambassador's home — especially the one at the Court of St. James — would look like. I was also interested in meeting Mr. Aldrich, for he had been chairman of the board at Chase Bank when Uncle Arthur was elected president, and it was because Uncle Arthur refused to do something Aldrich wanted that he got demoted to vice-chairman, which really meant "look for another job." At our wedding, I had told Uncle Arthur and Aunt Marion that a reception was on the schedule, and they politely said to convey their greetings. So when we were going through the line, I came first to Mrs. Aldrich and told her my connection with the McCains. She turned to Mr. Aldrich and passed on word to him, and he was more than perfunctorily pleasant in asking about them.

Another person in the receiving line was the chancellor of the University of London, who chaired the British Fulbright committee. As a routine way of greeting people, she asked me where I was going. I told her St. Andrews. She asked what I was going to study. When I told her "Church of Scotland liturgics," she responded, "Oh, I remember reading your application form. I was so interested in it because I did not know the Church of Scotland had a liturgy!"

We had two or three days to see the tourist sights of London, as I recall — the Tower of London, Buckingham Palace, the changing of the guard, perhaps one of the museums. I was fascinated by London and liked it from the moment I arrived. It did not seem to me to be a huge city so much as a series of towns or small cities, for there were no skyscrapers. Ann had been there before, so I was the gawking tourist and was much helped by her knowledge on how to get around, pay for things, etc. (I think in Southampton I had paid the baggage man something like 10 pounds, instead five shillings at most. He probably retired the next day.)

Ann had a friend from her work at the United Nations who was back in London and who invited us to come out for tea at her parents' beautiful apartment. As we walked from the subway to her house, we passed several Rolls Royces. I had never seen one outside movies.

My memory of London at the end of September 1953 is lovely. The sky was clear. Some leaves had begun to turn. It was crisp. It was everything I had hoped London would be. We were off to a wonderful, wonderful adventure! I believe we left London on September 29, exactly one month after our wedding.

London to Edinburgh

Since we had become good friends with Bill and Lynn Kelly during the Atlantic crossing and we were both going to Edinburgh, we decided it would be fun to travel together. We caught the train and watched the countryside through England. I remember we kept seeing wagons and carts loaded with very large brownish things. We could not figure out what they were. The Kellys were as ignorant as we, and there was no one in our compartment to ask. (We later learned, after eating some, that they were turnips and would become part of our diet—stringy and unpleasant. Some they fed to horses and cows, and some they served to people.) It really was picturesque as we watched the harvesting in the neat fields, which were so much better kept than American fields, I thought.

We decided we wanted to see Yorkminister, so we got off the train at York and spent the night. I really was captivated by that beautiful cathedral. We went to sung evensong, which was lovely. Walking through this old medieval town, I saw in the window of a butcher shop a pastry with a sign "meat pie." Having read about these so often in books, I was excited about eating one, so bought it. I guess the others did not taste it. That night I got very sick—vomiting and diarrhea. I continued with an upset stomach for about a week or two.

On arriving in Edinburgh, the Kellys went to the apartment where they were to live for the year, and we to the Barbour apartment, where Robin and Margaret had invited us to stay.

I want to digress now to tell more about the Kellys. Throughout the year, we would see them when we came down to stay with the Barbours, and they came up to St. Andrews on two or three occasions. During the year, Lynn was diagnosed with cancer. I don't remember where, but it was serious. She had an operation that was successful—in one of Edinburgh's excellent hospitals. Her illness was what finally tipped the scale for me in deciding not to go on for a Ph.D. in liturgics and teach, but to go into a pastorate. She made me realize we do not have an unlimited amount of time on earth, and I asked myself what God would want me to do with my years. It was a wake-up call. While I was fascinated by liturgics, I did not feel that was the living water for which people were thirsting.

Lynn recovered well. Ann and I were planning to go to the Continent for the summer after school was out at St. Andrews. We found Bill and Lynn planned to do the same. When Dave McAlpin offered me the use of his car for two weeks, if I would deliver it to the dealer in Paris for him, we invited the Kellys to go with us. It was a glorious trip.

We drove back to Paris and delivered the car without having wrecked it. The Kellys were headed back home, and we were to spend the rest of the summer on the Continent, so we parted.

We kept up with them. Lynn's cancer returned, and they had a long battle until she died. Bill was chaplain at the University of Connecticut when I went to the Yale School of Alcohol Studies in the summer of 1956, and I went up for dinner. I think he had remarried. We kept occasional contact. In the late 1980s, I went out to San Francisco for some kind of meeting and got in contact with Bill. He drove up and we spent the evening together, but his current wife did not come. It was a happy time of reunion. He told me Ann had made contact with him the year she spent at San Anselmo. That friendship was deep, like mine with the Barbours, but had not remained alive until 2009 when Bill and I reestablished telephone contact.

Back to the Barbours. They had been so overwhelmed by the hospitality of the Campbells and Williamsons in Arkansas earlier that summer that they were determined to welcome us. Robin at the time was chaplain to foreign students at the University of Edinburgh.

Once, as we came into the apartment, I saw hanging on a coat rack a tam. I thought I would like one and asked Robin where I could buy one. It is the only time I have ever seen Robin wrap himself in his aristocratic heritage. He said, "You can't. Only members of the Duke of Atholl's army can wear them." It seems the Duke of Atholl is the only nobleman in all of the United Kingdom who is still allowed to have his own army. (I never did find out why.) It is an army of 60 people. They are the lesser nobility and the gentry in the neighborhood of Blair Atholl, and Fincastle is just over the hill, so Robin was a member of the army.

The Barbours showed us around Edinburgh as much as was possible. I think we stayed for only one night. They made us promise to come back for a longer visit. It certainly was good to know they were nearby, because we knew no one at St. Andrews.

Robin Barbours, 1953-54

Now I want to digress again, this time about the Robin Barbours. I have written elsewhere about looking up Robin when he arrived at YDS because I had heard he was from St. Andrews and I was applying there for my Fulbright. I liked him immediately, and we began to see each other at lunch and around the campus. As that school year was drawing to a close, I found that Robin, Margaret, and their son, Freeland, were driving to the West Coast and were going the southern route. I got my parents to invite them to stay at Scott for a few days. Then the Adrian Williamsons invited them down to Monticello, and Adrian, Jr., flew Robin's sister, Caroline, down in a plane — a real thrill for her.

While they were at Scott, their little son, Freeland, who is an albino, would not only cry but scream, and nothing seemed to stop him. In the middle of one night, Mother had a brainstorm. She went to their room, knocked, and said, "I think he is thirsty. He is not used to this heat, nor are you." They got him a bottle of water, and he immediately stopped crying and went to sleep. Margaret thought Mother was an angel. And it is good she diagnosed it, for they were driving across the desert country, and it could have become serious. As a result of this, the Barbours and our families bonded.

When Ann and I arrived in Scotland, they introduced us to his cousin, Miss Cunningham, who lived in St.Andrews and who was lovely to us throughout the year. I am sure Robin also sent a note to Donald Baillie to look out for us.

Not too many weeks had passed when they invited us to join them at Fincastle, the family home. At this point Robin and family occupied Fincastle, which had been built in the 19th century, before Bonskeid — the really big mansion the Barbours had had to sell for income tax in the 1920s and that had been turned into a YMCA hostel. The Honorable Mrs. Barbour (so titled because her father was a Lord) lived in Old Fincastle, which was built in 1647 and had the name Stuart over the door. We went down to meet her. She was getting a bit frail by then. We had dinner at Fincastle that Friday night and toured the country on Saturday. We saw Killiecrankie, a famous battleground where some Scottish hero escaped the English by jumping from one bank, across the stream, and landing on the other side — a distance that was amazing. The English could not follow him. We also went to Queen's View, just down the road from their house, overlooking a loch with the mountains in the distance. (Supposedly, Queen Victoria had been visiting the Duke of Atholl and had gone on a carriage ride. When the carriage crested a hill, with this view laid out before them, the Queen called for the horse to halt so she could take in the beauty.) I remember we also went to Pitlockry, the beginning of the highlands, and looked in a shop Robin's sister-in-law ran.

On Saturday night, there was a party on the Fincastle farm that included a talent show where the tenants on the farm got up to sing or play or dance. I think one or two of the Barbours did something. Then began the Scottish dancing. I remember we were ready to go home, but Mrs. Barbour said to Caroline, Robin's sister, "Now you can't leave until you have danced with all the men on the place."

The next day we went to church at Tenandry, the wee church almost on the grounds of Fincastle Farm. I believe Robin preached that day — the first time I'd ever heard him preach. After that, we were invited for lunch at the home of General and Lady Drew. We had fresh salmon for lunch — fish the General had caught the day

The "Queen's View" of Loch Tummel, Perthshire, Scotland.

before from his own stream. I remember I had to get instructions from some Scots in St. Andrews on how an envelope should be addressed to them.

I am not sure how many times that year we went to Edinburgh to stay with the Barbours for a weekend—at least two or three times. We introduced them to the Kellys there. I remember one weekend we went to church at St. George's West, where Alexander Whyte had preached (the great preacher of the Free Church in the 19th century, and about whom Robin's father had written the definitive biography), then after lunch we went to a club in New Town (beautiful Georgian architecture). We had them up to St. Andrews at least once, if not twice. Or they may have stayed with Miss Cunningham, to whom they were very close.

Toward the end of the year, Robin told me we were going to be invited to the Queen's Garden Party at Holyrood Palace—through the Barbours' knowledge of the inner circles. We were really looking forward to that, then she got pregnant, and the party was canceled.

The Barbours were the Scots whom we came to know best in 1953-54—and have remained good friends ever since.

South Street No. 17

Now back to our trip from Edinburgh to St. Andrews. We took the train to Cupar Junction and there changed to the little train that ran to St. Andrews. How exciting it was as we could see the towers across the fields on that lovely early fall morning.

Mrs. Gertrude Hardie, who was the secretary for St. Mary's College (the theological school of St. Andrews University), met us at the train station. She was the one with whom I had been corresponding about finding a place to live. Her son's wife, Sally Pat, had been Grace McCain Durrell's roommate at Vassar. Sally Pat had asked her to make a special effort on our behalf. Mrs. Hardie was a small, cheery woman with blue eyes that sparkled, and we wound up becoming good friends. She was also secretary to Professor W. R. Forrester, the man under whom I was to study liturgics. I guess she really was secretary to the whole faculty (of some six or seven). She found us a taxi that hauled our baggage—and us—to 17 South Street. I was elated at arriving at St. Andrews, a dream now being fulfilled.

The house was one block west of the ruins of St. Andrews Cathedral, and just across South Street from St. Leonard's School, one of the most prestigious girls' schools in Great Britain, certainly in Scotland. That is where the Queen Mother Elizabeth had attended. The girls wore uniforms—brown wool in the winter, dark green something when the weather was warmer. They wore what I called "pudding bowl" hats at all times, even when going out for sports. They had broad brims and round crowns, with a ribbon hanging down the back. They were just like the illustrations in English children's books.

The house had been built in the late 18th century. It was what is called a "row house," completely separate from neighbors, but with the sidewalls adjoining the houses on either side. At one point this had obviously been a rather grand house. There were four floors. The first floor was the dining room, library, and kitchen. The second and third floors were bedrooms, except for some kind of large living room on the second floor. The fourth floor was for the servants. And that was where Ann and I lived. Our apartment consisted of a narrow livingroom that ran from the front to the back of the house, one bedroom overlooking South Street, a bathroom, and a hall connecting all three rooms and also serving as our kitchen.

One great advantage of 17 South Street was its proximity to St. Mary's College—about two blocks and easy to walk. It was also in easy walking distance of all the small shops in town, and of the major churches and all the University buildings.

In the kitchen we had a small oven, without any insulation on the top, so when we were baking, we could put a pot on top of the oven and bring it to a boil. We had a tiny gas stove where we could put two other small pots. There was no refrigerator, but there was a cupboard (common in Scotland at that time) that was open to the outdoors in the back to let in cool air. I don't think there was a screen on the back. Most of the year, it was cool enough to "hold" food for several hours, but it required shopping every day so things would not spoil.

The house at 17 South Street in St. Andrews, Scotland, where we lived on the fourth floor. The dormer window was in our bedroom.

The bedroom was a nice size, perhaps 14x14. We had a double bed and a small dresser, but there was no closet. In post-war Britain, most men owned one suit—or at most two—and most women would have two or three dresses. Our floor had been designed for maids, who would have worn only uniforms, but we arrived with Ann's trousseau and our typical American supply of clothes to last a year. We decided we had to do something to hang them on. So somewhere I got a long wooden pole, supported by three or four other poles, and hung our clothes on it. There was no door or curtain to hide them. That was not needed when just the two of us were using the apartment, but when we had company, the only place for people to lay their coats was on our double bed — which meant all the guests saw all our American wardrobe on display. Without exception, the Scots who came would say, "Oh, how many clothes you have!" — not in envy, but admiringly.

The living room had a skylight on the south end (the one next to South Street) but no window. At the east end, there was a small dormer with windows that looked out over part of St. Andrews Harbor and across the way to Angus, with the Angus hills in the distance. The living/dining room was where we lived, and it was a pleasant room. It was made cheery by the fact that the side walls were painted *orange*. In the living room we had a couple of "easy chairs" and a table; in the dining area we had a table and I think four straight chairs.

The house at 17 South Street was a "winner" of a place to live because it was one of five houses in all of St. Andrews that had central heating. That was important, because in 1953 coal was still rationed, continuing since World War II days. However, coke was not rationed, and a furnace could burn coke. So we had an unlimited supply, as long as we were willing to pay for it. The "furnace," however, was located in the kitchen on the first floor. It was about the size of an oil drum turned on end, and it had to be stoked every 45 minutes or it would go out. When that happened, a new fire had to be started by means of a gas "torch" that we lit and stuck inside until the coke caught on fire.

There were three men living in the house. We rotated furnace duty, a week at a time. In February, Joe Elkins got tuberculosis and had to go to the hospital in Edinburgh, so for the remainder of the year, two of us took turns. This meant the last thing I would do at night would be to come down from the fourth floor and bank the coke, in the hope there would still be some burning embers when I returned the very first thing the next morning. Sometimes there were, but most often there were not, so I would have to start from scratch. Then all day, during classes and at night, there would be the run to the furnace to keep it going.

However, no one complained for there were two great benefits. First of all, we could keep the house as warm as we wanted it — and were willing to pay for (and no one ever objected). Most married students living in other houses (even the McAlpins who were both of the Rockefeller family and very wealthy) froze to death most of the winter, so the Americans always loved to come to our house. The second big advantage was that with a furnace we had an unlimited amount of hot water! In homes heated by a fireplace with a rationed amount of coal, the water was heated by a tank in the back of the fireplace, and they were fortunate if in a day of fireplace fire they could get enough hot water to wash dishes and one person get a bath. The McAlpins used to come to parties and spend the whole evening arguing over whose turn it was to get a bath that night!

In the back of the house was a "garden," in Scottish terms. We would have called it a backyard, fenced in on one side by the house and on the other three sides by high stone walls. We could look out of our dining room window and see our garden, which was rather bare, and those of our neighbors, who had lovely flowerbeds.

There was quite a story behind 17 South Street. Originally, it was a fine home, but through the centuries it had run down. Finally it had turned into a house of ill repute, to the great dismay of the neighbors. Joe Elkins had come a year before we did and had lived in the dormitory. He did not like that. Being an enterprising Texan bachelor, he decided to do something about his living conditions. I do not know how he found that the lease of the bawdy house had expired, but somehow he got the owner to let him lease it for a year, with the right to sublet. He had spent the whole summer fixing it up. It was absolutely filthy when he started, but he threw out, scraped out, repaired, and painted all summer long. The neighbors at first were concerned about what a bachelor student would do with such a large house. Was he going to run his own whorehouse? But as they got to know Joe (who was very friendly), they began to take interest, and by the time we arrived, they were pleased to death that the house had been "redeemed" and the neighborhood improved.

Joe had made many, many trips to the paint store during the summer and had come to know the proprietor well. One day, he went in and said he wanted some orange paint. That is not a color most Scots would use, so it was amazing the man had some in stock. He sold it to Joe, and as Joe was walking out the door, the proprietor asked what he was going to do with it. When he said, "paint a living room," the man tried to take it back! All the neighbors were distraught at the idea of an orange room. It sounded pretty bad to me at first, but in actuality it was not a violent orange, and in a room with only one skylight and one small window facing north, it helped create a warm feel to the room.

There were three "families" living in the house. Joe had rented the first floor and most of the second to Bob and Margaret Bender (an Episcopal priest and his wife) and her mother, Mrs. Black. They came from Ohio. The Benders seemed "old" to me at the time — probably in their late 40s or early 50s. They were very pleasant people, and we got along with them beautifully. But we did not have a lot in common, except the house — and the fact that I went into their kitchen often to stoke the furnace that was located there. Bob Bender wore his clerical collar all the time. I don't think I ever saw him without it, even at night when he was reading in the living room. One of the amusing, and repeated, events of the year was when, as he read, he would hear the doorbell ring late in the evening. He would go, in his clerical collar, to the door. There would stand a confused and embarrassed young man who thought 17 South Street was still providing the services of the previous years. His eyes would get big as he found Mr. Bender standing there and asking, "What may I do for you?" The young man would stutter, "Oh, I must have the wrong address" and retreat in confusion.

Ann and me at 17 South Street in St. Andrews in April 1954.

The other occupant was our landlord, Joe Elkins. He had all of the third floor, the big room on the second floor, and use of the kitchen on the first floor. Joe was from a small town in Texas and was a graduate of Perkins School of Theology, SMU. His father had been killed in a plane crash in Arkansas, with his father piloting it. It took weeks before his body was found. Joe was the only child. His mother came over for a visit at the end of the year.

Joe was absolutely delightful—always laughing and full of stories and jokes. He bought a little dog that he named "Moses," to the dismay of the Old Testament professor. He was working on his Ph.D. in philosophy and theology. It was typical in Scottish universities for a Ph.D. candidate to write about some obscure divine in the 17th or 18th century—and Joe had found one. We used to laugh about the way the theology of the church had been revolutionized by the work of this dull divine. Joe became probably our best friend in St. Andrews, with much visiting back and forth between the fourth and third floors.

Number 17 South Street was a delightful place to live—both for its physical comfort and for our relationship with the other occupants, especially Joe. When I have gone back to St. Andrews in subsequent years, I have felt a strong pull to see it from the outside, but I never had the nerve to ask if I might go in. What I really would like to have done was to go up to the fourth floor, but that would have been invading privacy.

Start up at St. Mary's

Soon after we got unpacked, St. Mary's, the theological college of the University of St. Andrews, opened for the fall. When all the students were gathered together, Principal Duncan asked for all the Americans to stand. It seemed like two thirds of those present rose. I was aghast. I had deliberately decided not to go to New College, Edinburgh, for that was the Mecca toward which most American Presbyterians headed. I wanted to be with Scots and thought St. Andrews would meet my needs. Apparently, several other Americans had the same thought in 1953. We were far more than they had ever before had from America. Others were as shocked as I. We outnumbered the Scots in enrollment. There were only five or six Scots in each of the three classes working toward the basic theological degree, but the positive side was that we had a sizable American community with enough variety for people to find kindred spirits.

The faculty at St. Mary's was small. I think there were five or six full-time professors. Principal George Duncan was also professor of New Testament. He had made his name by writing the commentary on Galatians for the Moffatt Series. It was a good commentary. I took his course on Galatians, although I had had one from Eric Dinkler at Yale. The Principal had gone to sleep at the switch intellectually after writing that one book and mostly read from his notes. I somehow, before the year was out, managed to stop going — on the plea of needing more time for reading liturgics.

Professor Baxter taught church history. He seemed to be quite competent, and knew his field, but he was arrogant and conceited, and most of us who did not have to work under him for a degree avoided him. I know I did — although his home was on the route from St. Mary's to 17 South Street, and I passed it at least twice a day. The only time he seemed human was at the Christmas party when he sang some kind of song about immigrants to Great Britain with a chorus about "and then there were the Portuguese."

Professor Edgar Dickie was in philosophy. I guess at some point he had been a competent scholar, and had written something, but by the time I arrived, he seemed "burned out," and "blithered" when he lectured. I went to one or two of his lectures and stopped.

There was a "lecturer" in Hebrew who was younger than the rest of the faculty. I guess he also held a post in the main university, for he was not around much. He seemed to be quite competent in his limited language field of Hebrew language. I don't think he was the one who taught Old Testament, however. Come to think of it, I don't know who did.

There was a semi-retired man from Canada whose name I forget. He was there to help Donald Baillie, I guess, and took over after Baillie got sick. I liked him as a person, but had little academic contact other than sitting in lectures with him. He was not a part of the permanent faculty and was on the periphery.

Professor William R. Forrester (Willie — behind his back) was the person under whom I was supposed to study liturgics. He was able to refer me to some basic books to read, but soon after I got there, I found he did not know a whole lot more about liturgy than I did. This is not surprising, for he was the *whole* "practical theology" department! He was responsible for teaching liturgy, preaching, Christian education, pastoral counseling, church administration, ethics, social ethics, polity, and perhaps a few more areas! He had been a distinguished local church minister many years before, I guess, and was a great storyteller of the blow-hard style. The students laughed at him behind his back and never took him seriously. His greatest asset was his wife, who was brilliant and charming and a real driving force in the college and community. She was a first cousin of Donald Baillie. He also had a son, Duncan, an undergraduate in the university who sometimes came around St. Mary's and was delightful. (Duncan later became Principal of New College, Edinburgh.)

Professor Donald Baillie held the chair of theology. I knew about him from having read *God Was In Christ*, a first-rate work on Christology. His brother, John, was better known for being Principal at New College, Edinburgh, and the author of several standard theological works, plus *The Diary of Private Prayer* that I had read and that enlarged my concept of intercessory prayer. (The Edinburgh students jokingly said that Donald must have written the *Diary*, for John never prayed that much in his life!) Donald was a bachelor, an ascetically handsome man with gray hair, a scholar, a magnificent teacher, and a saint. I shall write more about him elsewhere. I was struck by him when I saw him that first day. When I soon discovered how weak Forrester was, I signed up for every course Baillie offered, and Ann went to many of his lectures, too. It was Baillie who made that year outstanding academically.

Right at the start, perhaps it was that first day, people told us that we should go to the fall graduation ceremony. I was not interested in that, for I had been to many graduations before, but I guess it was the Americans who had been there a year or so who kept insisting that we really should not miss this one. It was necessary to wear a crimson St. Andrews undergraduate robe to get in, so somehow we borrowed two for Ann and me. It was a beautiful sight as we gathered out on the university grounds, with the faculty in their various robes and hoods (many with Continental degrees or ones from Oxford or Cambridge wore brightly colored robes), the graduate students in black robes, St. Mary's students in black robes with a purple cross on the facing, and the undergraduates in their red robes.

The way the crimson robes were worn revealed which of the four classes the student was in. During the Middle Ages, Scotland and England were enemies, and Scotland was much more influenced by the French than the English. So instead of having freshmen, sophomores, juniors, and seniors, they had begeants, semis, tertians, and quads. Begeants wore their robes right up close to the neck. Semis would let the color of the robe slip down a bit, to the top of the shoulders. Tertians would wear them on the shoulders, dipping part way down the back. Quads let their robes hang from the elbows in front, and drooping down almost to the ground in the back. Throughout St. Andrews, no one was permitted in class without wearing a robe. The red ones were quite warm, so students used them instead of coats, and it was general custom to wear those everywhere they went. One of the American theological students was married to a woman who was working on her undergraduate degree. We never saw her without her robe, even at parties. It was toward the end of the academic year that we discovered she was eight months pregnant, for she did not "show" when wrapped up in that robe! The red robes gave a great deal of "color" to the town of St. Andrews.

So the robes added to the scene. Also the vines on the stone walls (it looked like Virginia creeper to me) were beginning to turn to autumn shades. The grass was green. It happened to be a clear day with blue skies. All of this was lovely to behold. But what, I wondered, made this different from any American graduation, except that most of ours take place in the spring?

Then we marched into the big university hall. As soon as the students were seated, the faculty processed in—and the students began to chant, "Here come the animals, two by two, the lion, the tiger, and the kangaroo...." This was before the cultural revolutions of the 1960s, so in the 1950s such disrespect on the part of an American student body would have been unheard of. Then as things proceeded, students pulled out from under their robes rolls of toilet paper, and began throwing them up to the balcony and onto the stage where the faculty were seated. Then "noise makers" were produced and either twirled around or blown to make raucous sounds. When the graduation address began, both toilet paper throwing and noise making were supplemented by boos and yells and any other distraction an inventive student body could create. The "game" was to drown out the speaker (some dignitary who had been invited in) so he eventually would give up and sit down. No police were called in. No effort was made by the administration to stop this near riot. Everyone knew in advance this was going to happen—including the faculty and administration. It was part of the academic world in Scotland that we in American had never heard of! It did make an impression on all us Americans, and when we get together we still talk about it.

Health Care in Scotland

Because I had a stomach upset from eating the meat pie in York, we asked the Barbours when we spent the night with them if they could recommend a doctor in St. Andrews. We were going to be on National Health, so we had to be registered. They gave us the name of the doctor they had used when they were there. (Looking back, I should have questioned this choice, for he is the one who recommended treating Freeland's albinism by feeding him baby liver.)

So, on almost the first day we were in St. Andrews, I looked up this man (whose name I have managed to forget), told him my complaint, and asked for some medicine to calm my GI tract. His reply was, "The only thing wrong with you is the American public health system. You are not used to germs. You'll get adjusted to them." Then I was dismissed.

Fortunately for me, I had very little need to go to this man during the year. Unfortunately, Ann had to use him a great deal. Soon after we arrived in St. Andrews, she developed vaginitis. When she went to our doctor, he suggested as a cure that she should pour salt in a tub of hot water and sit in it! This was a problem off and on most of the year. Perhaps this is often a problem for newlywed women.

Also, once winter set in, Ann came down with colds that resulted in sore throats and chest infections. I guess it was the flu. When she finally would recover, within a few weeks she would come down with it again. I do not remember what medicines the doctor prescribed, but they were not effective.

When our landlord, Joe Elkins, came down with "galloping consumption" (the most virulent form of tuberculosis), we went to our family doctor to ask what kind of precautions we ought to take. His prescription was, "Well, you might air the bed linens." I kid you not!

I guess it was at this point Ann declared she would not return to this man. She had talked to some of the women who were a part of the American student community, and some of them had found a woman doctor whom they liked. Ann transferred her registration to this woman who really was a help. I think she gave her something for her vaginitis, too. With some reluctance, I transferred to her—just hoping I would not have a physical examination, especially one for hernia. And I didn't.

On the other hand, after Joe Elkins' diagnosis, he was sent down to Edinburgh to a hospital that specialized in tuberculosis. There, he was treated by specialists and got the best possible care. He was still in the hospital when we left Scotland, and he remained a patient for many months before being completely cured. He said the facility and care could not have been better. And it cost him not a penny. On being released, he returned to St. Andrews and finished his Ph.D.

My Finances—Fulbright Year

Our year in Scotland was unique in many ways. It was the first year of our marriage. We were adjusting to each other, and to sharing income and outgo with another for the first time in our lives. It was the first year I had not been supported by my parents, or Ann to a large extent by hers. It was the first time either of us had lived abroad for more than a few weeks (for me the first time ever). Scotland was still recovering from World War II.

My Fulbright scholarship paid my tuition, my travel to and from where I was studying, and 50 pounds a month to live on. At that time a pound was worth about $2.82. It would have been very difficult for a couple to live on about $140 a month in the US, even at that time. (According to www.eh.net, $1.00 in 1954 = $6.86 in 2003, hence $140 = $960 in 2003 prices.) But prices were very low in Scotland, and the selection of things to buy was even lower. Also, all the people with whom we associated were graduate students, just getting by without a Fulbright. The only exceptions were David and Joan McAlpin, who were fabulously wealthy, but other than having a car and running home for Christmas, did everything they could not to flaunt their wealth.

Ann was not signed up to take courses, although she did from time to time sit in on Donald Baillie's. Her big job was writing thank-you notes for wedding presents, but other than that it was to "run" our little apartment, which meant cooking most of our meals. When we did go out to eat in St. Andrews, it would cost 2/6, or about 28 cents. We did watch our expenditures carefully, but we entertained a great deal—having people in for tea or for dinner. I never remember feeling that we could not afford to have them in. When Ann got sick, she did not have the energy to entertain at times, but it was not for lack of money.

As a matter of fact, we saved enough from our monthly allotment to be able to travel a little bit in Scotland and down to England for Christmas, with a little left over to travel to Italy in the spring. On top of the monthly income, we had $1,000 from my parents that Mother said was a delayed trip to Europe they had offered me when I was in college and I deferred until I knew more of what I wanted to see. (A remarkably wise decision on my part.) And I think we had some wedding money left over.

So we traveled in France, Germany, Low Countries, and Switzerland for about two months in the summer, going on a bus tour of Germany, and then spending two-and-a-half weeks at Bossey, Switzerland. I had also paid for Ann's passage back on the ship and train ticket to Little Rock. By the time the Bossey event was over, we were running short of energy and also money, so we economized by settling in a pension (a boarding house) in Geneva while waiting for our ship to leave.

Other than those last two-and-a-half weeks in Geneva, I do not remember being stressed financially other than doing things economically. It was a remarkable year—disturbed by conflicts in our relationship, but as far as visiting Europe, it was a great success. It was the last time for many years when I did not feel "poor."

Snow in Angus

As I have mentioned elsewhere, there were two windows in our fourth-floor apartment in St. Andrews. The one in the bedroom let us look out over South Street and St. Leonard's Girls School, the exclusive school the Queen Mother had attended. The other, a dormer type, was in the dining area of our living room. From it on a clear day, we could see the part of the North Sea that led into the Firth of Tay. On the far side of this inlet lay Angus with hills in the distance that in the winter were often white with snow. One of the attractions of St. Andrews is its mild climate. The Gulf Stream goes up the west coast of the British Isles, around the north of Scotland, and a final tongue of it laps into St. Andrews harbor. This makes it attractive for tourists, especially golfers. As a result, rarely did we have snow that stuck. But Angus did.

I have a warm memory of sitting at our dining table for a leisurely lunch (it must have been on a Sunday, for on weekdays at noon I was usually in a rush) and enjoying the picture of the sea in the foreground and the white-clad hills that were quite distant but on that clear day seemed only a few miles away. There was much in this first year of marriage that was good, and this memory brings me joy. Writing these memoirs has brought to the surface the many hours of happiness we enjoyed, such as this leisurely meal with beauty laid out before us, and the rare experiences we shared in Scotland and on the Continent.

Thanksgiving in St. Andrews

The year we were in Scotland, Professor Paul Tillich was giving the Gifford Lectures — the most distinguished series for theologians in Scotland, and one of the most prestigious theological lectureships around the world. He delivered most of his addresses in Aberdeen, but he was coming to St. Andrews for one or two.

One of the Americans realized Tillich would be speaking in St. Andrews just a couple of days before the American Thanksgiving Day, and suggested to our group that we put on a Thanksgiving dinner in his honor. We all thought it was a great idea. He was contacted and agreed to come. Then there were the questions: Where? What would we serve? Who would sit where? The women got together and decided all of these.

The largest house in our American circle was 17 South Street, so it was agreed we should have it in the drawing room on the first floor, where the Beckers lived. There was no turkey to be had in St. Andrews, but it was decided a goose would do. (I did not ask because I did not want to know, but I feared it was one of those that had been hanging in the poultry shop with feathers on, without refrigeration, since we arrived in September.) Other dishes were assigned to various couples, and we combined china and eating utensils, for no one had enough — same with linens.

Ann had studied under Tillich at Union Seminary, New York, so it was decided she should sit at the head table. I guess she must have sat on one side of him, because I found myself sitting next to him on the other side. Why Dave and Joan McAlpin were not given this assignment I do not know, for Dave was at Union for three years, and his father was on the Board. However, all I know is I sat next to Paul Tillich.

I had heard Tillich preach at Battell Chapel almost every year since I went to Yale and had read one or two of his books, but I certainly was no Tillich student, or fan. He had a very heavy German accent. (Eric Dinkler said the longer Tillich was in the U.S. the heavier his accent became!) It was not always easy to cut through the accent to realize what English word he was saying. Mr. Tillich was a philosophical theologian who dealt in abstract ideas and who had developed his own theological vocabulary.

So there I sat, throughout the meal, trying to hold up my responsibility by making dinner conversation with someone who was not given to "small talk."

I knew from Ann that he talked a lot about counseling and the theological basis for this. At that time, one of the leading pastoral counselors in the U.S. was Carl Rogers from Chicago, who developed the "non-directive" approach. So during one lull in the conversation, I asked, "Mr. Tillich, how do you think your theology fits in with, or challenges, the writings of Carl Rogers?" I expected him to take off on a 15-minute lecture. His reply was, "Never heard of him."

I sat in silence a while. Then I tried again. "Mr. Tillich, who do you think will be the outstanding theologians of the next generation — comparable to you, Barth, Brunner, the Niebuhrs?" His reply was, "There aren't going to be any." This time I refused to drop the ball, so I came back with "Why?" He said, "They are all writing too soon. This 'publish or perish' approach of the universities is making people write before they have something to say. I don't think anyone should write a book until he is at least 50." After that I gave up. (I checked later and found he had published several books before he was 50.)

But the party was a great success. All the people who didn't sit next to Paul Tillich had a wonderful time.

Donald Baillie

I had read, and been impressed by, Donald Baillie's *God Was In Christ* when I took systematic theology at YDS. He was the "big" name at St. Andrews, but I went over there to study liturgics. I thought I might sit in on one of his classes, but that was all. However, when I arrived and found how superficial was W. R. Forrester's knowledge of liturgy, I began attending all of the courses Baillie offered. I took his systematic theology course, one on sacraments (later turned into a book published posthumously), his course on the Westminster Confession, and a course on Barth. Ann went to a good many of his lectures, for she was as fascinated by him as I was.

He read his lectures, which were handwritten — and beautifully put together. He was a rather small and thin man, with sharp features and a head of almost white hair. One of my treasured memories is of the prayers with which he opened each class. How I wish someone had recorded or written them down, for they were as outstanding as his lectures. I especially recall how on Friday he would always begin with, "O Lord, we who are weary come to you...." He was a scholar, a teacher, and a saint. His presence at St. Andrews was comparable to that of Richard Niebuhr at YDS. He was also good at dealing with questions from students — except for one man, Donald Rennie, who somehow had a way of getting under Baillie's skin. He is the only person who made Baillie turn abrupt and sometimes harsh in his responses. I never knew why the "chemistry" between them was so negative.

The only area in which I disagreed with Baillie, and I voiced this through questions all year long, was the fact that I thought his emphasis on the necessity of *understanding* the Gospel left no hope for those incapable of grasping concepts. Having had three quarters of CPE during which I had worked with people whose mentality or emotional illness or sociological background kept them from ever being about to grasp some abstract truths, I would say, "But what does this say to, or do for, someone whose IQ is in the moron level, or some boy whose only experience of a father has been a man who was a drunkard and who beat him regularly?" I was never satisfied with his answers. And, kind as he was, I think he wished I would quit asking them.

I had learned much from Albert Outler in systematic theology at YDS. What a treat it was to cover the various doctrines of the faith again under the guidance of another great teacher, and probably a better scholar. Donald Baillie had no advanced degree (other than honorary) as was typical of many scholars in the British Isles in those days. After seminary, he had been a pastor/scholar who read and wrote, and then was called to teach at St. Andrews, the smallest of the four Scottish universities, and smallest Divinity Faculty. I am sure he had offers to go elsewhere, but apparently felt a commitment to remain.

Perhaps one of his ties was Mrs. William Forrester, who was his cousin. She was much more intelligent and forward-looking than her professor husband. She and Donald were real "soul mates." Donald was a bachelor, and I think she filled the role of mother and sister and spouse for him. Baillie lived in a rather large house out in the nice residential section of St. Andrews, with a housekeeper. He would have students out for tea (although I don't think I ever heard of anyone being invited for dinner). His housekeeper made the best shortbread I ever ate. Ann and I were invited more than most, I think, because we had him to our apartment several times — perhaps first for tea, then dinner on more than one occasion. He was very impressed by Ann's cooking, and especially how colorful her meals were. She was a charming hostess. When he came as a guest, he always brought a bouquet of flowers.

All year long, Baillie would cough a good bit in class. The doctor had him taking physical therapy for what he thought was some kind of pulled muscle in his chest. The physical therapist's office was in a building just two or three doors down from 17 South Street. Several times during the year when Ann was sick and he missed seeing her in class, he would appear at the head of the stairs leading to our apartment, knock, and inquire about Ann, whom he liked, and present her with a bouquet of flowers. I especially recall in the spring he would bring daffodils. I was impressed at the time by his thoughtfulness, and his readiness to climb three flights of stairs. I really was overwhelmed when, the next fall, we learned that he had died of tuberculosis! He had been misdiagnosed (by the same doctor we had?) that whole year. In addition, he had been coughing TB germs over all his classes. Joe Elkins, who had come down with TB, was writing his dissertation under Baillie. I wonder if there was any connection.

I have mentioned Baillie's opening prayers in class, but I also need to record my memory of daily chapel. This was held every weekday morning in St. Salvator's Chapel, the main one of the University. Leadership was by one of the divinity faculty. I made it part of my daily routine to attend chapel. (It became one of the friction points with Ann.) Normally there would be only 20 to 30 people present, and often the services (no sermon) were deadly. But when Baillie would take leadership on Monday, the service was vital. Word would spread around the campus quickly, so on Tuesday there would be a doubling of attendance. Attendance would grow every day that week so that by Friday it was hard to find a seat. Then the next Monday, when it was someone else's turn to preside, attendance would drop back down to the hard core again.

In Scotland, as distinct from American Presbyterianism, a minister who is not pastor can be a member of a local congregation and can be elected to serve on the Session. Baillie went to Martyrs' Church and was on the Session there. He was much in demand around Scotland as a preacher so was often gone on Sunday. But when in town, he was there faithfully. From time to time in class, he would recount something that had happened at Session meetings.

Toward the end of the year, Uncle Ken Latourette, with his student secretary Hugh George Anderson, had been to Scandinavia for lectures and then came to Scotland to visit us. The St. Andrews faculty was delighted when they heard this, for he was a world-renowned historian. He and Donald Baillie hit it off perfectly. Uncle Ken was invited to participate in chapel, where he wore his academic robes. One of the pictures I have treasured (I don't know if it survived the fire) was of Uncle Ken and Donald Baillie standing together before the ruins of St. Andrews Cathedral. It is a picture of two of the people who were so instrumental in my formation.

After Baillie's death, the Canadian minister who had sat in on his classes that year pulled together his lectures on the sacraments and published them as a book. I fear my copy of that was among those destroyed. But in reading it, I could mentally see and hear Baillie giving those talks.

While I learned little academically about liturgy in St. Andrews, I got a deeper grounding in systematic theology, and I learned a great deal from Baillie about worship as it came into discussions, especially on the sacraments, and in his leadership in worship both in the classroom and in chapel, and in the few sermons I heard him preach.

On the subject of sermons, I remember one of his devices was to make a point, then as he moved on, to say, "I imagine you are asking..." or "Perhaps you are objecting..." What a saint.

Christmas in 1953

This was going to be our first Christmas as a married couple, and our first one away from our families. It was also going to be the best time for us to go down to England for sightseeing, because we had traveled straight from London to Edinburgh on the train coming up.

One of the student groups at St. Andrews (probably the Student Christian Movement, which was very strong then) organized a retreat for St. Mary students and spouses as soon as the term ended. We went to some retreat facility, but I do not remember the name of it. As I recall, it was quite comfortable. It gave Ann and me a good chance to get to know some of the Scottish students better. It was a great experience for us both.

The "speaker" for the retreat was pastor of a church in the Borders Country on the Tweed River, right above the boundary with England. I believe he was in Berwick-on-Tweed. He was intelligent, sophisticated, and interesting, as well as inspirational. And I was needing some spiritual renewal at that point. Ann and I both liked him, and he seemed to like us very much. When he learned we were going to England by bus, he insisted that we had to come to Melrose to see the Melrose Abbey ruins and then to come by his manse. So when the retreat broke up, we stopped in Edinburgh for a night with the Barbours, and then took a bus to Melrose. In Scotland in December, the sun comes up quite late. We arrived in Melrose about 10:00 a.m., and the sun was just rising—casting a rosy glow over the ruins and tombstones, which sparkled with the morning frost. Ann got some excellent pictures that we later enlarged and framed. I still think Melrose is one of the loveliest sights in Scotland. I believe it was destroyed in the 1400s in the wars when England was trying to subjugate Scotland. It is also said that the Masonic Order started there, by the masons who worked to build the abbey. (I know next to nothing about the Masons, but

I think the York Rite ones are more "Christian" and the Scottish Rite ones tend to be deists—or did.) I feel terrible that I cannot remember the name of this pastor, for he and his wife were so cordial to us in December and again in the spring when Uncle Ken came to visit.

From there we went down to see Durham and Lincoln Cathedrals on our way to Cambridge. Kings College, Cambridge, and Berkeley College, Yale, are sister colleges. (Yale's President Charles Seymour, the first master of Berkeley, had gone to Kings College). The chapel at Kings is one of the architectural masterpieces of England, and the choir was world famous. The Provost of Kings was Sir John Shepard. He had visited Berkeley two or three times while I was there, and I had met him at the Hemingway Sunday afternoon teas and some other places. I guess it was in my senior year I felt I knew him well enough to invite him up to my room for tea. He learned that I

The altar of the bombed out ruins of Coventry Cathedral in England, which Ann and I visited in 1954.

was thinking about going into the ministry, and in the summer of 1948 I received a letter from him inviting me to come to Kings College to "read for my theological tripos." How tempted I was to go! But at that time I was resisting the idea of ministry. If I did go to seminary, it was to find out if I could fit into the American church, and I decided I needed to do that in the U.S. and not in England. So I declined. When he heard that I had applied for a Fulbright, he said that I must come by Kings College and have tea with him.

So I had written ahead. We were to go to Evensong at the chapel, then come to his house for tea. The chapel service, sung by the boys' and men's choir, was ethereal—an experience I shall never forget.

When we went to the Provost's house (one always called him Provost, not Sir John), a maid came to the door to lead us back to his library. I had warned Ann he was a character, but I don't think she believed me. It is said that when he learned he had been named Provost he went away for a long weekend. He had left as a brunette, but came back with snow-white hair. He was short and plump, and the epitome of an English don. He and Queen Elizabeth (George VI's wife) had been great friends for years. She would often drive up to Cambridge just to visit with him. He came in to the entranceway, short and plump, with a cutaway coat over dark pants and a walking stick in his hand. When I introduced Ann to him, he grabbed her hand with the intention of kissing it. She wasn't sure what was happening and had a reflex action—and she almost hit him in the nose. The conversation at tea was a bit stiff, but I was so glad we went—I wanted to see him, to see his quarters, and I wanted Ann to meet him.

We stayed in Cambridge with an American couple whom neither of us knew. He was a graduate of Texas A&M where Colonel Morgan was president. Colonel Morgan had been president of Monticello A&M, and the Morgans were great friends of the Adrian Williamsons. So Colonel (now President) Morgan had written this student to tell him we were coming and ask him to put us up. As I remember, we did not have a great deal in common with them, but both couples got through it.

That night after we went to our room, Ann and I had a real argument. I do not remember what it was about, but our room was next to our hosts' and there was not much soundproofing, so we had to fight in whispers. The next day, we took the train from Cambridge to Oxford. We happened to have a compartment with no other passengers, so we were able to fight more openly. I am not sure of the topic, but it was the most serious dispute we had had since we married. I had never seen my parents have a serious argument and work through it to a reconciliation. The concept of a "fair fight" was not part of my mind-set. I wondered if our marriage was going to be able to make it, and if we were going to be able to continue our trip together. When we arrived in Oxford, we were furious with each other. But when we stepped off the train, we put on our proper faces, for we had come to a house party with people from Yale Divinity School. I later learned in marriage counseling that a bad fight is one that ends before both parties are so emotionally exhausted they are ready to work out reconciliation. Ours was cut short and never really resolved.

Paul Schubert was Professor of New Testament at Yale Divinity School. Mr. Schubert had a Fulbright Scholarship on the professorial level — which meant a lot more money. He and Mrs. Schubert had rented a Gate House of some big estate outside Oxford. They had invited all the YDS students spending the year in England or Scotland to come to their place for a two-to-four-day house party. There must have been 10 to 12 of us. I don't remember who they all were. Canby Jones and his wife were there. They were Quakers. The ones I remember most vividly, because we really clicked with them, were Bob and Peggy Raines. He had gone to Yale College and YDS. He was married and so lived off campus, but when Ann started coming up to New Haven for visits, we were included in the couples parties. Bob had been BMOC (Big Man on Campus) at Yale College — captain of the football team, Phi Beta Kappa — and I think was in Scull and Bones Senior Society. His father was a Methodist bishop. Bob and Peggy were both good looking, attractive, outgoing. At YDS they were so "sweet" and loving that I thought, "This can't be for real." But they acted that way for the whole house party, and I finally decided this was for real. I envied them, for Ann and I were having a rocky time.

While we were there I came down with a cold. The day the group went into town to see all the Oxford Colleges, I stayed in bed. (Looking back on it, I wonder how much of that was my somatic response to the verbal fight Ann and I had had on the train coming from Cambridge to Oxford.) But despite that, my memories of that house party are very positive, and it certainly solidified my friendship with Bob. (Later he and Peggy divorced, but I'll write about that elsewhere.)

From Oxford we went to Rugby for Christmas. Jim Boyes, whom I had come to know my last semester at Yale College, and who had come to Scott for Christmas in 1948, had in the meantime married Diana and had become one of the Masters at Rugby

School, from which he was also a graduate. Rugby is not quite on the level with Eton and Harrow, but is in the next tier of "public schools" in England—and a place where many Scots go. (Robin Barbour, for instance, was a graduate.) The school provided Jim and Diana with a lovely big house that had accommodations for us. Jim rolled out the red carpet for us—determined to be as hospitable to us as my parents had been to him. Diana was much more reserved than Jim, but she was certainly pleasant and cordial. I think they may have had their first daughter by then, but she was quite small.

Some of Jim's family came over once while we were there. I think Diana had little family. She (like Margaret Barbour) had grown up in India where her father was in either the army or civil service. They had a big turkey dinner for Christmas Day, but the thing I remember most was Christmas morning. Jim was a deeply religious man. We went to communion that morning. Diana stayed home, perhaps with the baby. It was still dark as we walked to the church, and the stars were bright in the sky as the bell rang to gather people together. It was a "picture postcard" scene, and I felt great peace that morning. I think we stayed three or four days, and saw that part of England.

Me with Jim Boyes in 1996. He visited us at Christmas in Scott in 1948, and we spent Christmas with him in 1954.

From there we went to the Lake District. Mrs. Hemingway was a member of the Women's Touring Association, a very limited group, and had got Ann into that. It gave a list of bed-and-breakfast homes that were "safe" for "ladies." We got a reservation with two sisters in the Lake District. One of them was a "bell ringer" for her church and was late arriving for dinner because she had to ring the bells. I remember they were both members of the Liberal

Party—the middle road in Britain, the remnant of the old Liberal Party of Lloyd George. They were delightful.

I don't remember what else we saw. We got back to St. Andrews before New Year's Day, which at that time in Scotland was still more important than Christmas.

Winter Activities in 1954

All my sermons and prayers for 1953 were destroyed in my 1998 fire, so I have no record if I supplied any during the fall of 1953 in Scotland. However, I don't think I did. I do find that I preached twice at St. John's Kirk, Cupar, Fife, on January 3, 1954, for the morning and again the evening service. On February 17, I spoke to the Women's Group at Trinity Church (the Town Kirk), St. Andrews, on February 21 to the World Student Christian Federation service at St. Salvator's Chapel, University of St. Andrews (a pulpit from which John Knox had preached), and on April 16 a Good Friday sermon at the Student Christian Movement Cabinet retreat at Strathkinnes, Fife. I think Ann and I did another joint presentation to some women's group—at the end of which they sang "Will ya no cum back again?" (written for Bonnie Prince Charlie when he fled, but now a traditional way to say thank you to a guest speaker). I remember how moving that was.

It must have been in January or early February, before Joe Elkins got sick, that we were asked to entertain Dietrich Ritschl, the grandson of the great German theologian. He was then chaplain to the German students in Edinburgh. He was to speak on a Sunday night to the Student Christian Movement group, then we were to have him for dinner. He was to sleep in one of Joe Elkins' rooms, and we were to have him for breakfast before he returned to Edinburgh. Ann really went all out to prepare an excellent meal for him after his presentation, and I was looking forward to a stimulating theological dialog. When we brought him back to the apartment and Ann began to serve the meal, he said he did not eat after he had given a talk! That was a jolt. Then in our discussion, he was what I described as "the most bull-headed Barthian I have ever met." His grandfather had been one of the groundbreaking liberal German theologians of the 19th century, and I guess he had swung back to the other extreme. He insisted that there was no need to relate the

Bible to people's everyday needs — that the only job of the minister was to Proclaim the Word. There were no shades of gray for him in any area — it was either black or white, and his ideas were always the white ones. I was polite, but it was clear we operated on different wavelengths. Then the next morning Ann had again prepared a rather lavish breakfast, American style. He announced that he did not eat breakfast, only coffee. That was a downer. (Later, when he was about to be brought to Austin Seminary on the faculty, I told people he was a "bull-headed Barthian," and Dick Hardie repeated that to Dietrich. So when he came to Westover Hills, he said he wanted to visit with me and agreed that he had been bull-headed at that point. He returned to Westover several times, and we got to be friends despite our rocky start.)

Another activity that winter was going to meetings concerning the Mau-Mau uprising in Kenya. For Christmas, Margaret Williamson had sent me a copy of Michener's *The Tribe that Lost Its Head*. While fiction, it had striking similarities to the Mau-Mau. This added to my interest, which would probably have been keen anyway. There were a lot of retired Colonial Servants living in St. Andrews, some having been in Kenya. They were hard-liners. The liberals in town were up in arms about the way the Mau-Mau,

Inverary Castle, which Ann and I visited in 1954. Inverary Castle is the seat of the Duke of Argyll who is the head of the Campbell clan in Scotland.

for all their atrocities, were being treated—and even more, about the conditions that had created the climate for the Mau-Mau to flourish. There were civic meetings with much debate, and Ann and I went to them. Although we had no voice, we had strong opinions. And in the process we got to know some of the townspeople, especially the liberals. Mrs. W. R. Forrester was always there, but Willie never came.

I guess it must have been through one of those meetings we got to know a young woman named Fiona MacLeod. We had her up to visit us several times and got to see a side of Scottish life we had not known before. She evidently came from a socially prominent family, but probably without any wealth left. One of my "learnings" in Scotland was that attendance at a university was for those who wanted academic learning—not a prerequisite for a social life. There were many people with the intelligence and finances to go to a university who chose not to do so. Fiona was one of those. She was attractive, intelligent, socially poised. She had a delightful ability to back off from the kind of life in which she had been reared and to look at it with open eyes. I remember her telling how during World War II, and in the austerity following it, she would visit in homes where they still dressed for dinner, the ladies wearing evening dresses that were pretty bare at the shoulders, in unheated rooms where they froze to death. And after dinner, with no servants anymore, they would clear the table and scrape off the crumbs with a silver crumber. I think Fiona was planning to take secretarial training and be a secretary. I wonder what did become of her.

I think it was during the winter that Miss Cunningham invited Ann and me to see a performance of *Little Women* by the students at St. Leonard's School. (Miss Cunningham was on the Board, so could get us tickets that were impossible for the general public to come by.) I will write at more length about this performance and the significance of St. Leonard's School.

During the winter we were more and more appreciative of the small furnace in 17 South Street, which could burn unrationed coke instead of coal. I remember going to tea at the home of Principal and Mrs. Duncan. As she poured tea from a silver pot, I noticed her nails were black from handling coal that had to be put on the grate.

A luxury greater than heat was the hot water we got from our furnace. Our bathroom was tiny, and since it was just under the roof, part of the ceiling was slanted and had a skylight to let in some light. While I much preferred showers, we had a tub and I was grateful for it. We had a commode in the bathroom but no sink, so we had to brush our teeth in the kitchen sink. And speaking of toilets, the toilet paper in Scotland in 1953-54 was like wax paper! Terrible. As the year wore on, some of the Americans found one place in St. Andrews where "real" toilet paper could be purchased, and we all made a dash for it. Our budget was limited, but that was one luxury Ann and I agreed had to be worked in.

Willie Forrester told a story about when Jack Lewis came to St. Andrews to study, only a year or two after World War II. He brought with him a huge carton of toilet paper. Forrester thought this was ridiculous. He asked, "Did he think we were barbarians?" (The silent response from all Americans was "In that respect, yes.")

Perhaps it started in the fall, but certainly by winter, one of the most fun things in St. Andrews was to go to an auction that was held every other week. The mansions and estates in Great Britain were breaking up, so there was a huge supply of furniture, china, and silver up for sale. St. Andrews was a regional center for that, I gather. Our funds were so limited there was little we could afford to buy, although we did get a few things we needed for our apartment, and a few other things we bought with wedding money to take back home. There were gorgeous pieces of furniture for sale — and the larger they were, the lower the price. People were moving into small apartments and could no longer use dining tables that could seat 30 or chests of drawers and chairs that called for large rooms. The American community would usually gather there in the afternoons on auction day to look and admire.

Church Life in Scotland

I had so looked forward to experiencing church life in Scotland, having heard about it for years. It was the Mecca for Presbyterians. I had read Ian MacLaren's *Beside the Bonnie Briar Bush* that presented a picture of 19th century Scottish church life, seen through rose-colored glasses.

I was in for a rude shock. The Church of Scotland was in bad shape, partly because of World War II, with facilities in semi-disrepair and a severe shortage of clergy, but even more, by a serious drop in attendance. During the war, people had been dislocated, many worked on Sundays, and the habit of church attendance had been lost, especially among the "working classes" — and there were such class distinctions.

When we arrived in St. Andrews, we visited various churches. The first week we went to Trinity Church, which was the Town Kirk. It was a large and handsome structure, stone with good architecture. It had come from the Old Kirk tradition and was fairly liturgical. But the minister was deadly. I think his name was Dr. Ware. He had been there for many years. His associate was equally deadly, and he had some kind of "right of succession" so he had no intention of leaving. They were examples of one of the sicknesses of the Church of Scotland, of the near impossibility of getting rid of a pastor who was killing a congregation. We may have gone back there one more time, but we quickly scratched it off our list.

There was a church "out west" called West Park Church that, I think, had come from the United Presbyterian tradition before the 1909 merger and then the 1929 merger that brought together three traditions into the present Church of Scotland. It was quite "low church" and not at all to my taste in worship. This is the one Mrs. Hardie attended, and she invited us there. (I understand one of my contemporaries at St. Mary's became pastor there in the 1980s, and when Jim Monroe visited, it was a booming, lively church.) We went there maybe once or twice more.

Across from the University was Martyrs' Church. This was from the Free Church tradition and was the one where Donald Baillie was on the Session. I have forgotten the name of the pastor there, but he related pretty well to students and was the "least poor" of the preachers in town. That became our regular place of worship, except when we went to the University Chapel. There was no Christian Education program that we could see. Whereas Trinity and West Park seemed to have no involvement in the community, other than acts of compassion, Martyr's did seem to be aware of the issues of the day. We didn't form any real friendships with members of the congregation, although they were pleasant as we came and went. It was there that I became familiar with the Church of Scotland hymnal — the "Dutch door" version. The metrical psalms were printed on the bottom half of the page, and the melodies were printed on the top half, so the minister would say,

"We will sing Psalm 46 to the tune of XXXX on page 92." Then members of the congregation (who brought their own hymnbooks) would turn to one section for the bottom and another for the top. The pastor and musicians could "mix and match," although generally each psalm was "married" to a particular tune. I can't remember if this was also true of the hymns, but I think not. I learned that the Scots knew only a limited number of tunes, so often several psalms would be "married" to the same tune. It is said that a couple of centuries ago they sang all 150 psalms to five tunes! I came to love the metrical psalms, and also the paraphrases, which were another part of the "Dutch door" section. One of the shocks for me was to find that familiar words that are "married" to one tune in America are "married" to quite a different one in Scotland. The biggest shock was "Nearer My God To Thee." I had grown up knowing that it had been played as the Titanic was sinking, and I "knew" the melody that wafted over those cold waters. Only the British sing it to a different tune, and being a British ship, I'm sure that was the music played by the band.

One of the things that struck us was the way clergy in Scotland always were robed, usually the Geneva gown and tabs, with an academic hood — even in the smallest church. In the U.S., robes were worn in Presbyterian churches in cities, but in small towns and the country in 1953, many ministers wore street clothes. In the U.S., I don't recall any choir in a Presbyterian church, even a small one, that was not robed — sometimes in fanciful ones, pretending-to-be academic — but in Scotland in 1953-54, I don't think I ever saw a choir wearing robes. And the women all wore hats — which were of all shapes and sizes, usually unattractive. If the sermon got too dull, one could study the hats and speculate what they said about the owners.

The other place we attended fairly often was St. Salvator's, the University chapel. The music there was excellent, and the choir. There was a university chaplain, I believe, but the sermon was normally preached by a visitor. Sometimes it was one of the Divinity faculty at St. Andrews. Whenever it was Donald Baillie, Ann and I went — as did anyone connected with St. Mary's who was not otherwise obligated on Sunday mornings. I think the Moderator of the Church of Scotland would preach annually, and other academics. In some ways, it was like Battell Chapel and Yale.

In ancient days, the visiting preacher normally came to St. Andrews by ship, for land travel was so slow and also could be dangerous. The ship would come into the harbor and unload onto the pier that ran out to separate the harbor from the North Sea. In the past, the "townies," who had a lot of resentment toward the Church, had been known to attack the visiting preacher, so the students after church would surround the visiting cleric and escort him back to safety on the boat that had brought him. The danger had long since disappeared, but typical of Scotland, the tradition carried on. In order for students to get into chapel they had to wear their academic robes, and if any faculty went with them, all their regalia. (Wives had to sit in a section behind the students, and partially screened off — and Ann did not like that one bit!) As soon as the service was over, the bulk of students would process through town and down to the pier, especially on a good day. It was one of the most colorful events in St. Andrews, and something we always wanted our guests to see.

At the two services I led on the first Sunday in January at St. John's, Cupar, Fife, I found the sanctuary rather bare. The exterior of the church, with a steeple as I recall, was striking, but the interior did not live up to the outside. And there were only a handful of people present. How much of that was because a student was preaching, how much was because this was "low Sunday" and therefore the pastor had decided it was a good time to be away, and how much it showed the spiritual state of the congregation, I do not know.

We worshipped one Sunday at Tenandry Church, near Fincastle, where Robin preached. This was to a large extent a chapel for Fincastle and nearby farms. It had been built as a "chapel of ease" in the 19th century. Fincastle was in the Blair Atholl Parish (seat of the Duke of Atholl) that was across the hill from Fincastle, but it was a very long walk of several miles for people to get there. As a result, many did not go. In the revival of church life in the 19th century, this church was built for their comfort or convenience.

While on the subject of Fincastle worship, there is a wonderful story about the Barbours and their religious life. I guess it was Robin's grandparents, or it could have been great-grandparents, who figure in the story. At the time of The Disruption in 1843 (when about one third to one half of the ministers at the General

Tenandry Church (built in 1836 near Fincastle, Perthshire, Scotland) where Robin Barbour preached in 1954.

Assembly walked out over the issue of whether lairds were going to continue to have the right to select the pastor of the kirk, or if the congregation could elect their own), many families were split. Those who left formed the Free Church of Scotland. On the whole, they were the intellectual leaders and the strongest spiritually, but in leaving they — and the congregations that went with them — lost their church buildings, their manses, their "glebes" (farmland pastors could cultivate or rent out to supplement their incomes), and their salaries. Families and friendships were split — somewhat like in the border states in America during the Civil War. Children in the schoolyard would divide up and taunt each other. The Old Kirk children would point to the Free Kirk children and chant, "The Free Kirk, the wee Kirk, the church wi' out a steeple," to which the Free Kirk children would respond, "The Old Kirk, the big Kirk, the Kirk wi' out the people."

Well, Mrs. Barbour went with the Free Kirk; Mr. Barbour held with the Church of Scotland. The Free Church people had no church building, and the pastor and his family were in dire straits financially. In the Old Church, little emphasis had been paid to financial support, because the government helped it and there was the glebe. But it was a new day in the Free Church—and every Sunday, great emphasis was placed on the offering. Mrs. Barbour had given generously, but at that point in history, the husband controlled the finances. However, she had a very heavy gold necklace Mr. Barbour had given her, so one Sunday she took it off and placed it in the offering plate as it passed. When she came home from her church and sat down for lunch, Mr. Barbour noticed it was gone and asked its whereabouts. She told him. The next day, he went to the treasurer of the Free Church and bought it back. The following Sunday, the necklace was missing again at Sunday lunch. On Monday he bought it back again. Then on the third Sunday, she gave it again. This time Mr. Barbour decided he had given all he intended to contribute to this schismatic church. The gold necklace disappeared from the Barbour family for good.

The Reverend Alexander Whyte, leader of the Disruption, was an illegitimate child from Edinburgh. I have forgotten how he managed to get an education, but he was brilliant and was a spectacular preacher, known about the world. Somehow he and Mrs. Barbour became very close friends. He would come up to Fincastle

Kilchurn Castle, Loch Awe, Argyllshire, Scotland.

to visit the Barbours when he needed to escape from Edinburgh. I am not sure of the dates, but I think many of those visits took place at Bonskeid, the Victorian mansion the Barbours built and lived in until just after Robin was born. Robin's father grew up in that home and knew Whyte from childhood. He was one of those Victorian/Edwardian gentlemen who lived off his income and was free for scholarly activity. Out of that, he wrote the definitive biography of Whyte. I bought it while in St. Andrews and read it with great interest. Unfortunately, that was one of the books lost in my 1998 fire.

Another place I learned much about the Free Church/ Established Church life was from the Ian MacLaren novels — the first being *Beside the Bonnie Briar Bush*, which Ann had given me while I was at YDS. Willie Forrest put me on to all the others. In those, both types of churches were present in the mythical town, and also the "rabbi," the schoolteacher who had been trained theologically but who could not secure a call to a church and so resorted to teaching. MacLaren was known as part of the "kaleyard" school of writers, people who romanticized Scottish life in the 19th century. You really have to be able to decipher the dialect, but once you do, it is a wonderful world to enter — and a very sentimental one.

The Free Church and the United Presbyterian Church came together in 1909 to form the United Free Church. But some in the Free Church felt they had been "sold out," so refused to merge. They retained the name Free Church, but their popular name was "Wee Frees" because they were few in number. They were found mostly in the Highlands and in small isolated towns. They were the archconservatives. Mrs. Forrester used to mimic them by showing how they prayed with the "holy moan" — much to Professor Willie's embarrassment. I had heard about them, but had never been to one of their services. When Uncle Ken came in the spring and took us on the tour of the Highlands, we spent a Sunday night near Fort William. He said he suspected there would be a Wee Free Church around, so we inquired. Sure enough, they had an evening service that he, Hugh George Anderson, and I attended. (Ann chose not to go.) It was a barren, small building. There were perhaps 15 to 20 people there. They sang without instruments, and the sermon was long and dull, as were the prayers. But there was a teenage boy, very attractive, in the congregation. Somehow we learned that he was about to go off to the university. For years after that, Uncle Ken would say he wondered what had happened to the boy — had he gone back to his people, had he lost his faith in the university, had he loosened up and become part of the Church of Scotland?

In 1929, the United Free Church and the Church of Scotland merged to form one major Presbyterian denomination in Scotland. It was not the Established Church, as the Church of England is in England, so it did not receive a governmental subsidy. But it was the National Church, which meant that every inch of Scotland was in some Church of Scotland parish. The people could elect to belong to other denominations (Anglican and Baptist and Roman Catholic were the major others ones), but anyone in that area had a right to call on the Church of Scotland minister for baptisms, weddings, and funerals.

Also, when the Queen crosses the border between England and Scotland, she ceases to be a member — and head — of the Church of England, and becomes a Presbyterian, a member of Crathie Parish that includes Balmoral. The Scots used to love to point out that the Head of the Church of England was subject to the discipline of the Kirk Session in Crathie! Also, at the annual General Assembly, the Queen or her representative (the Lord High Commissioner) is to be present, but by invitation, not by right. She/he knocks on the door and asks for permission to enter. The Assembly then votes, and she is invited in.

The King/Queen would come to the Assembly spasmodically. When she chose not to (the year we were there she stayed away because she was pregnant), she would name a Commissioner to represent her — or actually, her Prime Minister would. Usually this was a Duke or some other nobleman. While the Assembly was in session, that person and spouse lived in Holyrood Palace and received all the honors and respect that would have been given to the sovereign. Once when the Labor Party was in power, Jimmy Jones, head of one of the labor unions, was named. How was he going to know what to do? More important, how was Mrs. Jones going to know what to do in social settings? So three duchesses invited themselves to tea at Mrs. Jones' home and told her what to do, how to dress, etc.

Eating in St. Andrews

During most of my life, eating has not taken a central place in my consciousness. But it certainly did that year, and even more in Ann's. She had cooked a little bit during the year she was in a New York apartment, but both of us had grown up with full-time cooks in the kitchen. As a child I had learned to make cornbread, but had not tried it since, and that was the sum total of my experience. However, Ann was a quick learner and became an outstanding cook.

I'll begin with shopping. Elsewhere, I described our "kitchen," which was part of the hallway. There was no refrigeration, just a small cabinet that was open on the outside facing north, so most of the time it was cool, but that was all. Also, we had almost no other cabinet space to store things bought in advance. On top of that, Great Britain was just beginning to recover from World War II, and many things were still in short supply. Sugar had just been taken off rationing when we arrived (and as a result, the Scots were wild for sweet things). There were few things in cans. Paper was so scarce that paper sacks were unheard of. Each shopper had one or more net bags in which various purchases were placed.

As a consequence, Ann had to go shopping every day—sometimes twice a day. Milk, for instance, would not keep more than a day. And there was no "supermarket" in St. Andrews where most food needs could be bought in one stop, so shopping meant going into a number of different stores, one after the other. There was the bakery, the green vegetable grocer, the fruit store, the meat market, the fishmonger, a general grocer where one could buy staples and the few canned goods available, the milk and cheese shop, and the poulterer. In Scotland at that time, it was legal to sell wild animals, so there would be deer and rabbits and other game hanging in the window of the meat market—no screens and no refrigeration. The smell was almost overpowering as one walked by, but what has stuck in my mind is the poultry shop with geese and ducks hanging head down. The markings on the deer, but especially on the geese (with feathers still on them), was distinctive enough so an observer could tell when one was sold and replaced by another. Again, the fowl were kept without refrigeration. I swear, one goose hanging there when we arrived in September was still there in May when we left!

Since Ann did most of the shopping, she got to know the stores and the salespersons much better than I. She and the other American wives did a lot of swapping of information and experiences about where what could be found. The clerks in Scotland were extraordinarily courteous and helpful. If you wanted six ounces of something and they had only 12-ounce containers in stock, they would refuse to sell you more than you needed, and would not only tell you where you might look for the correct size, but walk out to the sidewalk and show you where to go. They would also do a lot of visiting with regular customers, and that slowed down the shopping trip. After collecting the day's needs from various stores and putting them in the shopping bag, Ann would then have to walk back to 17 South Street (fortunately, it was in the middle of town) and up three flights of stairs to our fourth-floor apartment. I think she would spend an average of one or more hours a day just shopping. In addition to the time, Ann had to watch the money.

We would have breakfast in the morning before I left for class. Then at St. Mary's, there would be "elevenses" (coffee or tea and a cookie) in the middle of the morning, lunch at 1:00 when I returned home, tea in the late afternoon, dinner or the evening meal around 6:00 to 8:00 p.m., and often "supper" just before bed — perhaps hot chocolate and a cookie. It seemed to me we ate most of the year I was in St. Andrews. Many people gained weight with this kind of schedule, although we did a lot of walking by necessity. However, I lost weight. I weighed about 160 pounds when we married, and I was about 145 when we returned. Looking back on it, that should have told me clearly that our marriage was in trouble from the start, since most men gain weight after marrying.

Because both Ann and I had grown up in homes where entertaining others at meals was the norm, we both fell into this pattern easily. We could get only four (or five at the most) around our small dining table. Those single students who lived in dorms, and ate refectory food, jumped at any invitation to eat — especially the Americans who craved American cooking. Our Scottish friends were eager to see how we entertained. And our American and New Zealand couple friends were also quite ready to accept invitations — as were the few adult St. Andrews residents whom we came to know. All who came were complimentary of Ann's cooking, for she was a good cook. The Scots were also taken by how "colorful" her food was, and how beautiful the table looked. This was without any of our wedding china or silver, of course. But at that time, Scottish food was mostly white or beige in color. As a result, whenever we issued an invitation we knew we would have acceptances.

She was quite a hostess. The standard way to entertain in Scotland was to invite people in for tea in the late afternoon. And that became our pattern, perhaps two or three times a week. People would come up to our apartment, to the room with the orange walls, for tea and refreshment. ("Savories before sweets" was the rule of thumb, which meant cheese or fish or meat dishes before cookies, cakes, or shortbread.) And they would often stay right up to the dinner hour. We loved it. I came back convinced that the most civilized thing the British did in their colonial empire was to introduce the custom of afternoon tea, and I vowed when we returned we were going to continue the practice. (Of course, that lasted only about one week under the pressure of American life.)

When we had people in for dinner, Ann would usually serve fish or meat (usually the former was better), a starch (always potatoes, fixed in a variety of ways — but never chips), two vegetables (one green — maybe a salad, the other another color), then a dessert with coffee. She usually had some flowers on the table. They could be bought cheaply in the market. But that was not unusual, for the Scots also love flowers. At that time we did not serve alcohol, so there would be a glass of water for the Scots and tea or coffee for the Americans. Getting all this ready at the same time was tricky, for our gas burner had only two outlets. Afterward we would have to stack the dirty dishes, for the sink was in the same hall with the stove and oven, and it was the only exit from the apartment. But none of this deterred us. We entertained some of the St. Mary's faculty, Miss Cunningham (the Barbours' cousin), Uncle Ken Latourette, and Hugh George Anderson, his secretary.

In return for our entertaining, we were invited out often, especially for tea. We got into a few Scottish homes in St. Andrews, to the Barbours' both in Edinburgh and at Old Fincastle near Pitlockry, and once into the home of a farmer out from St. Andrews whom the Denzil Browns knew. His accent was so thick that Ann and I could understand very little of what he and his wife said.

There was a St. Mary's luncheon once a week, if I am not mistaken. This was for students and spouses, and we made a point of going. The meal would usually consist of ground beef, two kinds of potatoes (either boiled and fried, or fried and mashed, or mashed and boiled—but always two forms), plus either turnips or Brussels sprouts, as well as coffee or tea and a cookie or shortbread. This would cost "two and six," i.e., two shillings and six pence (written 2/6), which at the rate of exchange at the time was 28 to 30 cents! This was when we got to know the Scottish students better and when we would invite a couple of them to come up for tea.

When I went back to Perth for six months in 1996, the most dramatic change I noticed in Scotland was the food. They had made a quantum leap forward in 40 years.

Friends in St. Andrews

In some ways St. Andrews was a terrible place to start a marriage—mostly because of the lack of trained marriage counselors. However, in other ways, it was ideal. In any place in Arkansas, one, if not both, of us would have had prior relationships in which the other was the "outsider." But in Scotland, the only people we knew ahead of time were the Robin Barbours, and they were acquainted with both of us, although they were closer to me. Essentially, we began together making friends.

The one with whom we spent the most time, and to whom we were closest, was Joe Elkins, our landlord at 17 South Street. He had a great sense of humor, was a good conversationalist, and loved to entertain and be entertained. He would come up to our apartment the moment invited, and we would go down to his quarters. He knew a lot of people in the University and at St. Mary's, and was always having them over to his place. He helped us get settled and introduced us to places for shopping, the auction house, etc. We experienced a real loss when he contracted TB and had to go to Edinburgh for treatment. When Joe returned to the U.S., he visited us in Crossett at least once, perhaps twice. I have kept up with him through spasmodic Christmas cards, and recently talked to him on the phone in New Concord, Ohio, where he was chaplain of Muskingum College and is now retired in poor health.

One person who showed up at St. Mary's that year was David McAlpin. Ann had known him slightly when she was studying at Union Seminary, New York. It turned out he and Joan had married the same day Ann and I did—and they, too, were second cousins! David's family owned the McAlpin Hotel in New York and were descended from the Rockefellers—not the John Rs, but the William Rs, I think. Joan had been Joan Rockefeller before the marriage. They had never known one another until he saw her at a family wedding. There was no doubt they had wealth (which none of the rest of the community did), but they did not display it. They did own a car that they had bought in France before coming to St. Andrews. Dave was quite bright and a serious student. Joan was rather slow mentally, but very sweet. She also had some physical handicap that made it hard for her to walk distances, and that made her suffer terribly from the cold. Dave and I were in many of the same classes and saw each other at school. Ann and Joan were both writing thank-you notes for wedding gifts. They would go to each other's homes, but I think mostly Joan would drive in with Dave and come to our apartment. We must have received 300 to 400 gifts; the McAlpins had received more than that because of their family connections. Ann plugged away, writing in alphabetical order. She said Joan had never heard of most of their donors. She would go down the list and say, "Oh, I know these people. I'll write them." At the end of the year, Joan still had not finished her thank-you notes!

In the spring, we mentioned our plans to go to the Continent. The McAlpins had to get their car back to France and out of Great Britain. They were taking the ship back with his parents and did not want to go to France. Dave asked me if I would deliver it for them if we could have it for a couple of weeks to drive around. What a gift! We had made plans to travel with Bill and Lynn Kelly, and this was a godsend. When we were getting all the papers in order, I still remember my shock when I saw that the liability insurance was for half a million dollars! That's when a half million was REAL MONEY.

When we returned to the U.S., Joan made a real effort to keep in touch by mail, although her notes were almost child-like. When I went to Princeton for the Career Development Center, and then when I began visiting seminaries (including Princeton), I looked them up. We have kept in touch through the years. Joan died and Dave remarried, and I took him and Sally out to dinner last fall when I was in Princeton.

I remember one night in St. Andrews Ann and Joan were out doing something—perhaps an American wives affair. Dave came over, and the two of us were studying in the living room in our apartment. At one point, we put down our books and began talking—one of the few times other people were not around, and the only time we had an intimate conversation. Dave shared the loneliness that comes from being wealthy. I'll never forget that he said when you are rich there are people who seek you out, but you are always scared they are trying to "use" you—so you draw back from them. Then there are people to whom you'd like to be close, but because you are rich and they don't want to seem to be sucking up to you, they pull away. And the result is you are lonely.

We had been in St. Andrews a few weeks when one afternoon at St. Mary's I had a conversation with a New Zealander whom I had only met briefly—Denzil Brown. He had come to study under Donald Baillie and was very interested in the sacraments. Perhaps we were in the same class, but immediately each of us found the other was Presbyterian, very high church, intensely interested in liturgy. I remember going home for dinner that night and telling Ann, excitedly, about Denzil. His wife, Marget, was there, but she was teaching school. Because they were part of the Commonwealth, she could earn money, whereas Americans could not take paying jobs. I think we invited them over for tea the next day or so—and that was the beginning of a friendship that blossomed quickly but, unlike many of such acquaintances, also put down deep roots. They left Scotland during the Christmas break, so we were together only about three months. It seems to me they came through Arkansas on their way back, and I think visited both sets of parents. Out of all that came a friendship that has continued to the present time. While I have never been able to accept their invitation to come to New Zealand, they have been to this country several times. Denzil stayed with us on Brookside Drive, remaining a day longer than expected because a spring snowstorm closed the Memphis airport. Years later, he told me during that visit Ann told him how miserable she was in our marriage, and he knew ahead of time the divorce was coming. I think he visited me in Little Rock after the divorce, and I visited them in California in the 1980s. Their daughter came to New Orleans and I picked her up and took her back to Baton Rouge. Malcolm visited them in New Zealand. We have corresponded through the years. That has perhaps remained the most active friendship formed at St. Andrews.

Brownie and Joyce Ketchum were a couple we enjoyed. They came at least a year before we did. He, too, was working on a Ph.D., perhaps in philosophy. I think he was Methodist, but that did not seem to be a big part of his life. He was heading toward academia, either to teach or be a campus pastor. They were always fun to be around and we enjoyed them. I did not have the depth of friendship with them I developed with the Browns or McAlpins, but we have kept in touch through the years with Christmas letters. And in the fall of 2002 I went by to see them and had lunch. We were able to pick up rather quickly in just a few hours.

Bill and Val Peters where there. Ann had known them at Union Seminary in Richmond. He was at Union and she was at PSCE. We had Southern Presbyterian ties in common. I liked them, but both seemed a bit pedantic to me. We have kept somewhat in touch through the years. At various times he has been in Knoxville, Tennessee, and I have seen them there. I have not been motivated to seek them out, however.

Stan and Nell Barlow were part of the American crowd. We were not especially close to them, as the McAlpins were, but Stan was the life of any party where they were present. One of his contributions to our life was his discovery of the poems of McGonnigal, a wealthy Scot who in the 19th century paid to have published the worst "verse" anyone ever wrote. At parties, Stan would proceed to read us a poem, with great emphasis and bravado. We would all roll on the floor. My copy of the poems was destroyed in the fire. He had a gift (or curse) of being able to mimic anyone, especially professors, and could bring down the house with laughter and applause. He had had one serious encounter when he was at Princeton Seminary and was imitating President John MacKay, when MacKay walked in! We have kept on each other's Christmas list, but that has been the only contact through the years.

Bob and Mary Goodloe were friends. He, too, was working on his doctorate. Both of them were good-looking and attractive. We saw them at parties, and I am sure had them over from time to time, but were not really close. After we returned to this country, they stayed on for his degree. They went to Africa as missionaries for awhile, then he was on the faculty at Hendrix College,

Conway, Arkansas. After we moved to Little Rock and Malcolm was born, I remember they came down to our house on Brookside. When Mary asked the baby's name and Ann said "Malcolm," Mary's face lit up, and she said, "I know where that came from" (Malcolm Duncan, about whom I will write later). Following that, I would run into them from time to time on racial issues and the Arkansas Council of Churches. We were kindred spirits. I think he did not get tenure at Hendrix and moved back to Texas. In the 1990s there was a report in the media about a couple who had been caught in a flash flood in Dallas, and the wife was drowned. It turned out to be Mary and Bob. She had picked him up at work. Their car was flooded, and I believe he told her to stay in the car while he got in the water and went for help, then the current swept her away before his eyes. I remember writing him at the time and getting a reply back. I think he has since remarried, but I have lost touch with them.

Ken and Kathleen Anderson were friends, although not close. He was an Oxford graduate and had been in the British Foreign Service before feeling called to the ministry. They had more of an "English" than "Scottish" air to them. Later they went to Pakistan as missionaries, then came back to England near Cambridge. I have exchanged Christmas cards with them. I think I heard he is in very bad health.

There were several single men at St. Mary's. We would usually invite two at a time to come over for tea. They were always ready to accept an invitation to eat American food and get away from the university dining halls! I can't remember all the names. One was Donald Rennie, the one who could irritate Donald Baillie so easily. He really was rather uncouth in some ways and not attractive socially. But he could be fun when he began to poke fun at the faculty. However, I think he was one of those with the worst BO. This was a real problem in post-war Scotland. Most students owned only one suit, which they had to wear every day. Sometimes they would have it cleaned during the term break, but sometimes they would not. I don't know if they took baths daily, but I suspect some had grown out of the habit of daily showers when coal had been rationed and hot water came from the back of the fireplace. Some probably had never developed that as part of their lives. Sometimes in class, if the room got warm, the odor was overwhelming.

Angus MacLeod was one whom we liked very much. And Duncan Campbell we liked. He was short and often wore a kilt. Later he came to Austin Seminary and I think visited us once in Crossett. He stayed in the U.S. for many years in the Presbyterian ministry, but I think went back to Scotland. We did not maintain ties with him.

Malcolm Duncan (for whom Malcolm Campbell is named, at Ann's insistence) was one of the most handsome men I have ever seen. His hair was a dark auburn. He always wore a kilt. I don't remember ever seeing him dressed any other way. His physique was excellent, and he was good looking in the face. In a kilt, he was a knockout. On top of that he was charming and intelligent. All the women would swoon when he came in a room. After graduation, he went to Pakistan as a missionary. I remember the women said "What a waste of manhood!" I don't know if it was in Pakistan, or before he left the UK, but he got married. We exchanged Christmas letters for years. He would write about the difficulty of being Christians in a Muslim world. At one point I guess Pakistan and India were in one of their wars. He and his wife were in the UK on sabbatical and had planned to return, but because of the war they could not leave on schedule. So they went to Iona for a vacation. (He had always been part of the Iona community.) While there, he went swimming and was pulled out by the tide and drowned. It was a great loss to many people.

There were two single Americans studying at the University, but both took some courses at St. Mary's, for each of them was going into the Episcopal ministry in the U.S.

One of them was Charles Scott May, from Pine Bluff, Arkansas. I had heard of him, but had never met him until New Year's Day 1953 at the McClendon's party. He was a Washington and Lee graduate, was hipped on family connections and the Episcopal Church, and was in many ways a stuffed shirt Southern Episcopalian. But he was also good company, and we enjoyed him. I remember once he said, "If you think I'm bad, you ought to meet my friend Joel Pugh who has no use for anyone who is not a 'white Southern Episcopalian.'" At that time, Charlie or Charlie Scott, as we called him (now he is Scott), was as unreconstructed as I had been at Yale College. He really latched on to our Arkansas connections, for I think he did not find the Scottish students particularly warm. So he, usually with Sam, would come over for tea anytime we suggested it. I have kept in touch with him through the years and often see him when he comes to Arkansas to visit relatives. At one point he was the Associate Rector at Christ Church, Little Rock. He wound up being rector of a large Episcopal Church in Marietta, Georgia—but lived in an apartment in Atlanta. He has never married. He spent all his vacation time in Europe. I invited him in 1996 to join me on my trip to the Highlands of Scotland, but he had an apartment in London and turned me down. He has done as much an about-face as I did on race relations. He has become very leftwing on many issues such as race, homosexuals, etc. He and Joel Pugh (who was dean at Trinity Cathedral, then went to Bruton Parish in Williamsburg) have drifted so far apart that they have no contact anymore.

The other was Sam Hulsey. He came from Texas. Perhaps it was he who went to Washington and Lee—or maybe that is where the two of them met. Sam was what is known as a "cradle Episcopalian," which seems to be a notch higher than a converted one! But he was not offensive about it at all. He was attractive looking, low key, a good conversationalist, socially charming, and a serious student. We saw him and Charlie often, and usually together. At the time I liked Sam better than Charlie, but did not know him as well. After one year in St. Andrews, he came back to seminary (I forget which one, but probably Alexandria) and became an Episcopal minister. Then he was elected Bishop of the Episcopal Diocese around Lubbock, Texas. He has now retired. His wife had Altheimer's for years, then died. He has remarried, I think Scott May told me. Sam and I have exchanged Christmas cards. I would very much like to visit with him again.

In addition to the students and faculty, we had two good town friends. One was Gertrude Hardie, the college secretary who found us our apartment. Her son, Donald, was married to Sally Pat Connally from Atlanta, who had been Grace McCain's roommate at Vassar. Mrs. Hardie did not like Sally Pat, and I gather the feeling was mutual. But despite the Sally Pat connection, we clicked instantly with Mrs. Hardie. She was gray, with pink cheeks and blue eyes that sparkled. She was extremely helpful to us throughout the year. We had her over for tea and dinner, and I think she had us come to her house for tea. When Mother and I visited St.

Andrews in 1975, we took her out to lunch. She and Mother really hit it off. She had retired by then. I exchanged Christmas cards with her for years, but she has now died.

Our other "in town" connection was Miss Anna Cunningham, who was Robin Barbour's cousin. He asked her to look us up, and she did indeed. She was constantly doing kind things for us, not only inviting us to her home. She had never married. She was one of many thousands of women of her generation whose fiancés or future husbands had been killed in the massacres of World War I. She was on the board of St. Leonard's School, right across the street from 17 South Street. Once she invited us to come to see the play *Little Women*, and it was a special treat to be allowed inside St. Leonard's, for many of the nobility sent their daughters there. It was funny to hear the play done with British accents, and instead of going to Washington, Mrs. Alcott had to go to London. When we were preparing to leave for home, Miss Cunningham offered us a trunk that had belonged to her brother who had been in the Colonial Service in India between the World Wars. It had an address in the North-West Frontier Province—next to Afghanistan. She was indeed a lovely, gracious woman—a representative of the best of the Scottish aristocracy. We exchanged Christmas cards for some years until she died.

As I look at this list, I am amazed at how many friends we made and with how many I have maintained some contact. They were an important part of my year in St. Andrews.

My Relationship with Ann in 1953-54

During the academic year at St. Andrews, Ann and I were feeling our way along in building a marriage. In many ways we were very compatible—intellectually, theologically, and on social and political issues. We both liked to entertain and entered into the social life at St. Mary's and with the American community there, and with the Kellys and Barbours in Edinburgh. Ann was a charming hostess, so people liked to come to our apartment and invited us back to their homes. Ann's two major responsibilities were to run the house and to write thank-you notes for our 300 to 400 wedding gifts. She did both faithfully. When free, she would often come audit Donald Baillie's courses and struck up a real friendship with him. I imagine anyone looking at us from the outside would have regarded us as the ideal couple.

In private, things were not going so well. Sexually, I was not able to meet her needs and felt very guilty about that. I did not recognize depression when it came; I did not then know the concept of "tacit contracts," but I found, as similar as our families were, we had totally different ideas of what constituted "companionship" in the evening hours between dinner and bedtime. I thought if each of us was reading and we were in the same room, that was "togetherness." She did not, and resented my studying at night. This is not to say that there was constant friction between us. We had many good times together. When we were with other people, involved in some project, or traveling, we were very congenial. But in our private times, we knew something was amiss.

We talked about the desirability of having a marriage counselor help us, but we knew of no one in St. Andrews to whom we could turn. Our family doctor was incompetent. The pastors in town seemed remote. The only member of the faculty we really respected and trusted was Donald Baillie. But he was a bachelor, and we felt he would not be helpful. I suggested talking to one of the student married couples, such as the Browns or Ketchums, but Ann vetoed that. I do not know if we would have sought out help at this stage if we had been in the United States, but we might have. Instead we let our problems fester.

Spring 1954

One of the big events of the spring was to go to the Continent during the spring break. I had never been there. Ann had, the year she went to Italy on a work camp with the Waldensians in Italy. The Barbours wrote ahead to introduce us to some friends of theirs near Agape, the Waldensian camp. Robin had been stationed there during World War II, and "aristocrat sensing aristocrat" had come to know some of the leading families in the area, especially a German family.

I am not sure I can recall all of our trip, but I know we crossed the English Channel on a ferry. It was rough, but I did not get seasick, and I think Ann did not either. I know we stopped in Paris. We visited with Loretta and Boogey Brown. They were kind, but we were on different wavelengths. We wanted to go to the Moulin Rouge nightclub, because we had been fascinated by the movie with that title. They went with us. When I ordered snails (to see what they were like), I thought they were going to throw up. He was in the military, and we found they had as little contact with the French as possible. Their idea of going out for a meal was to visit the cafeteria connected with the U.S. Embassy. But we had time to go to the Louvre and saw some of the great works of art. I was shocked at how small the "Mona Lisa" painting was. We also went to Notre Dame and Les Invalids and out to Versailles and most of the typical tourist spots. Ann had seen most of them before, so was my guide. I found that my four years of French were useless. I could hardly ask for the men's room. I had always thought I would love France, but was deeply disappointed. The people seemed very cold.

From there we went to Switzerland. Ann had planned our trip, and we stayed in a small hotel in Grundewald. Switzerland, contrary to France, lived up to all my expectations — the valleys were green, but just a small way up the mountains, there was snow. We took a train up the Jungfrau one day — and got in a snowstorm going up. We could see nothing out the windows, or when we reached the platform for viewing, or on the way back down. But it was an eventful day. A woman in our car was alone, and we fell into conversation with her. She turned out to be the wife of an American naval officer. She had lived in Washington and had been a member of the Church of the Savior. I had heard of it, but did not know too much about it. She talked about it all the way up and back down the mountain, and the more she talked, the more excited I became. I got an address from her, wrote for some material, and what I learned shaped my ministry from there on — the idea of having a church composed of a small corps of trained, disciplined members who took their faith seriously and were willing to make sacrifices. I do not remember the woman's name. When I visited Church of the Savior years later, they had some vague memory of her, but that was all. We spent all our time in the German section of Switzerland. I do remember going to the capitol in Berne and seeing how tiny the legislative chamber was.

The train from Switzerland toward Italy went through the Italian section of Switzerland, along Lake Como. It looked exactly like what I thought Italy would be — and turned out to look much more so than

Italy did. We went to Venice, which I loved. The art was "gaudy," but that did not bother me. I saw all those blue skies with pink clouds in paintings that I had thought were phony in reproductions. But in Italy, we often saw sunsets just like that. Venice was dirty and rotten, and helped me realize how corrupt it had been in its hey-day. I was fascinated by the canals and the gondolas.

I guess it was from there we went to Milan and saw the cathedral, then to Turin. From there we had to take a bus to Pinerolo, the town where Robin Barbour's German friends lived. We were invited to tea in an elegant home. Again, Ann was greeted by having her hand kissed by our host. From there we had to take a taxi to get us out to Agape, the Waldensian retreat center Ann had helped build (and hurt her back, so it was never the same again). I think the man she had worked with was there. We could not stay long, for our taxi was waiting for us, but it met a real need for Ann to "revisit the site of the crime." It had been a high point in her spiritual pilgrimage, working there in a World Council of Churches work camp. I had known very little about the Waldensians before—just a name in the church history book. They were an early protest group from the Roman Catholics, prior to Martin Luther. They were persecuted and took refuge up in the valleys of the Alps. They were just one mountain range away from the French border. Looking up at the peaks, you knew that was France.

We then went to Florence—the city Ann fell in love with. The art there is spectacular. I do not remember the names of all the museums—the Uffizi was one. We went up to a monastery on a hill outside Florence to see the Fra Angelico frescos that were beautiful. The David statue was overwhelming. Also, the bronze doors to the Baptistry. I was disappointed in da Vinci's "Last Supper," for it was faded and there was scaffolding as it was being restored. For some reason I did not like Florence as much as I had Venice, despite its art being far superior, but it was an eye-opener for me on Renaissance art.

From there we took a bus to Rome, one that passed through the low mountain towns where there were castles and churches that dated back to 1000 A.D., and even into the 900s. It made me realize how the recovery from the Dark Ages moved north, with such buildings in England Scotland coming 200 to 400 years later. We stopped at Assisi, and I loved both the town and the monastery where Francis started his movement. In fact, I got so excited about taking pictures of the interior that I left our camera behind. When I discovered this later in the day, I got the tour company to call back, and somehow they mailed it to me.

When we arrived in Rome, we were welcomed by Walter Lowrey and his wife, Kjerstin, whom I had never met before. Walter was also on a Fulbright. They had a nice apartment with a bedroom for Ann and me. And they served as our tour guides over Rome. If I am not mistaken, Walter even had a car. Walter is very anti-religious, so he was not interested in some of the things I wanted to see. We took a tour that went out to the catacombs. What struck me most was when the guide pointed to aqueducts still farther from the center of Rome and said the city was that extensive. At the lowest points in the Dark Ages, however, the population of Rome got down to 400, and wolves were roaming in the streets. It made me realize as never before that "empires come and go" — and it is only a matter of time until our Western Civilization will be abolished and superseded, if we don't destroy the whole of civilization. And that insight was in 1954!

While Michelangelo's "David" had impressed me, his "Pieta" in St. Peter's moved me deeply. I had never before been moved by a statue. Fortunately, this was before the vandalism, so we were able to go right up to the statue and get a "feel" for it. I also liked St. Peter's as a whole. I felt most Italian churches were too crowded, the art too much. St. Peter's was the one that was big enough to "take" all that ornate art. I was not that struck by the Sistine Chapel (this was, of course, decades before it was restored to the original colors).

We saw all the tourist spots in Rome. That was fun, because the Lowreys had been there long enough to know what to see and how to get there. And doing it with Kjerstin was especially fun. She is Swedish and speaks English with a heavy Swedish accent (still, in 2003) and evidently also gives that tilt to Italian. But she waves hands and bargains like crazy.

While we were there, Ann became constipated. Kjerstin tried some home remedies that did not work. Nobody knew the Italian word for "laxative." Finally, as we went through the English-Italian dictionary, I saw an Italian word that looked like *cascara*. I remembered when I was a child Mother used to have constipation problems and took cascara every night. So Walter and I went to a pharmacy, pointed to the word, and said, "voila." He gave us a bottle of something that Ann took. Then the dam broke, and she had diarrhea that would not stop. We called the American Embassy to see if they could recommend a doctor who spoke English. They told us there was a British doctor in Rome, so we called him. He came to the apartment. His prescription (I kid you not) was that she was to eat, five times a day, two pounds of Irish potatoes boiled and mashed, with no salt in them but with an uncooked egg mixed in. (We decided the reason he was in Rome was because he had been run out of the UK.) He said the potatoes would absorb the excess liquid. Ann ate part of one such serving, then she ate just a couple of forks of the second and refused. But she sure did dry up—in time for us to take the train back.

We got off the train at Pisa. All I had heard about Pisa was the leaning tower, the Baptistry. Pisa, as I remember, is made of black and white marble in stripes, almost like a zebra. It is less florid that most of the Italian cathedrals, and I liked it very much. It, like Canterbury, is underrated in the tour books.

I can't remember the exact dates of our trip, but it was interesting as we headed back north to see spring recede. I was also struck by the fact that 1,000 feet in altitude often makes more of a change in the vegetation climate than 1,000 horizontal miles does.

Once we returned to St. Andrews, we were much involved in preparing for the visit from Uncle Ken Latourette and Hugh George Anderson, his student secretary. Uncle Ken had been to Sweden for some lectures. Uncle Ken suggested that they stop in Scotland on the way back, and that he rent a car and take the three of us on a 10-day tour of Scotland. Joe Elkins was in the hospital, so rooms on his third floor were available for our guests. Also we could use the big room on the second floor for a party. So we planned an open house for the faculty and students of St. Mary's. I think Uncle Ken was asked to preach the sermon at the University Chapel that morning. And he was invited to come to the General Assembly of the Church of Scotland, both as past president of the American Baptist Convention and as a church historian of worldwide fame. He was invited to a reception at Holyrood Palace by the Queen's Lord High Commissioner. I remember Uncle Ken told one of the faculty that there was no RSVP address and he was not going to be able to attend, for we were leaving right after he was presented to the Assembly. He was told, "Her Majesty does not have RSVP because you do not decline her invitation! If you can't go, you just don't show up, but you don't tell her."

I guess it must have been before our open house that the pastor from Berwick-on-Tweed invited us to come down for lunch with him and his wife. Ann declined in order to cook. But we three men went, and what an experience. His wife, who came from South Africa, had just returned to Scotland and brought with her a refrigerator that made ice, so she put ice in the water glasses for us three Americans. She asked me, "What does it taste like?" for she had never drunk ice water. When I offered her my glass to let her see, she said, "Oh, no."

The pastor knew I planned to return to the U.S. soon, but he asked me that day if I would like to serve a small country parish that had two churches in it. He said the Session was made up of three men — two dukes and a peasant! I declined, for I was eager to get home, but what an experience that would have been.

It was fascinating to go to the General Assembly, which operated with much ceremony. But as soon as Uncle Ken had been presented, we did take off. I do not remember all the places where we went. I know we stopped by Fincastle and saw the Barbours, who had known Uncle Ken at YDS. Since Ann and I had had no car, we had not gone to many parts of Scotland. (I had taken the train up to Aberdeen once to confer with the chaplain, Iain Pitt-Watson, who gave me the idea of a "moveable" anthem — an idea for which I have been grateful for decades. But other than that, we had stayed mainly in St. Andrews.)

On the trip with Uncle Ken, we went through the Highlands when the broom and gorse were in full flower, as was the rhododendron. It was spectacularly beautiful. We drove to Kyle of Lachalch and over to Skye by ferry, but it was too cloudy to see anything. At that time I did not know much about my family history, so we did not look up any of those places. We must have gone to Inverness, for we came down the Great Glen, spending a night at Ft. Williams, where we attended the Wee Free Church. We did not get out to Iona on that trip. We had to take into consideration Uncle Ken's health, and Ann's, so did not push. Hugh George was a great companion. There was always an undercurrent of tension between Ann and

Uncle Ken, although it never came out in the open, but from the time they met, they did not really like each other.

One amusing event took place that spring. While we were in St. Andrews we got by very well with what we could buy in local shops—except for three things, which we wrote home and asked our parents to mail us: black-eyed peas, Crisco, and corn meal. We really hungered for those and could find no substitutes. Well, during the spring at one of the parties for American couples someone told us they had found, on the far side of St. Andrews, a shop that could special order something like corn meal—only they called it "ground maize." Almost the next day, Ann and I walked over there, probably a mile or two away. They did not have any in stock, but said they would order it and could have it within a week. On the appointed day, we walked back. When I asked the price they said one pound, weight-wise, would cost five pounds, money-wise! Our total income for a month was only 50 pounds. We gasped. I said I would take a quarter pound, which was a very small amount in a paper sack. As we walked back we smelled a lovely aroma. We assumed we had passed, without noticing it, a bakery. But the smell kept going with us. Even in St. Andrews there were not that many bakeries. When we reached 17 South Street and walked up our three flights of stairs, the aroma went with us. When we opened the sack we found that my American accent had got us in trouble. We had a quarter-pound of ground *mace*! I don't know that I had ever heard of that spice before, for I did not cook, but Ann knew about it. It is not something a cook uses often, only for a few special dishes. We had enough mace to last us until after the parousia! We brought it back to the U.S. and carried it to Crossett and Little Rock. I think it was one of the spices Ann left behind when we divorced. I may have still had some of it when the 1998 fire destroyed all my herbs and spices. (When I was in Scotland in 1996 and wanted some ground maize, I made sure I hit the "z" very hard—and looked at the contents before I paid for them.)

Another development in May appeared in a very small article in the Scottish papers reporting that the American Supreme Court had handed down the *Brown vs. Board of Education* decision outlawing separate-but-equal segregation in the public schools. We Americans were all delighted by this. Little did I know the impact that would make on my future ministry and life.

As the spring drew to a close, we were saying goodbye to friends—both Americans and Scots. We really did feel we had formed some good friendships (as is evident from the number with whom I have maintained some communication). We had a final tea with Miss Cunningham, who gave us her brother's steamer trunk to carry back some of our acquisitions. We had a final tea with Donald Baillie, and he came to see us off. We began making reservations for a ship at the end of the summer. Fulbright paid my ticket, but I had to pay Ann's, and since our funds were running close, I wrote them asking for the cheapest quarters they had on the *Mauritania*. We did not want a big ship this time, remembering how the *United States* had rolled in hurricanes coming over. I learned that was the wrong way to inquire! I'll report on that later. We found John and Billie Maguire, Fulbrights in Edinburgh, were going to be on the same ship and looked forward to being with them.

Start of Summer in 1954

The curtain rang down on the final scene of our time in St. Andrews the morning we caught the bus on our way to Iona to spend a week. Donald Baillie had told us he would see us off, but the bus was about to depart. Then down the street, walking as fast as he could, came Donald Baillie, with his robe hanging over one arm and in the other a small bouquet of flowers he had brought to Ann. I shall never forget that scene, for it was the last time we ever saw him. He died the following fall from tuberculosis.

I guess we must have gone all the way to Oban by bus, then spent the night there. The next morning we took a small bus across Mull, then a motorboat to Iona. We had made reservations at a farmhouse that was a bed and breakfast for tourists. They had no electricity in the house, so once it was dark, there was nothing to do but go to bed. However, by that time of the year darkness was falling quite late—perhaps 10:00 p.m. We did have running water and a commode! The food was country style, good but simple. We knew a number of people in the Iona Community who were in residence at the time of our visit, so we had an "in" there. We went to all the services and discussion groups that were open to other people. It is a hauntingly beautiful island, and the restored buildings are also great. We had time to wander the whole island at will.

At one end, there are the remains of a marble mine from which the famous Iona green marble was taken. We found some chunks of marble that I put in my suitcase (adding to its already great weight) and then it lugged all over Europe. I got home with several. One large piece I kept on my desk in Crossett and Grace for years, and used it as a paperweight as well as a memento. Somehow in the move to Atlanta, it was lost, and I have missed it. As we walked the beaches, the water around Iona was a beautiful mixture of deep blue and green. I remember sitting on the west side of the island and looking out to sea and thinking that America was over there — and I was getting anxious to get back.

I had read about Iona back at YDS in Sir George MacLeod's *We Shall Rebuild*. The Iona Community was, in my opinion, the most vital part of the Church of Scotland — one of the few bright spots. When traveling around Scotland and going into churches, one could tell immediately if the pastor was a member of Iona. If so, the communion table would be in the center of the sanctuary; there would be a notice in the vestibule about when communion would be celebrated; there would be a notice about healing services; there would be Iona material available for purchase. Robin and Margaret Barbour were members — which meant they followed the discipline of study, prayer, simple living, and giving generously. There were also associate members. Donald Baillie and Mrs. Forrester both were that. It was a rare treat to be able to worship with that community and participate in some of their discussions. It and

Iona, Scotland, 1954.

Church of the Savior in Washington were role models for me as I thought about my future ministry.

I think we must have gone from there to Glasgow and caught a train to London, where we were to pick up Dave McAlpin's car. I know we stayed in a hotel for at least one night, for we went to the theater. Was that when we saw the play about the Dame of Sark, one of the Channel Islands during World War II when the Nazis took it over? I remember it was a delightful play about a stalwart woman who would not be intimidated. The afternoon before, I had gone to the School of Tropical Medicine to get my booster shot for typhoid. There was no serum in St. Andrews, or in Edinburgh, so I was told this was my only source, and I was determined never again to take the full series of three shots. After the theater we went to bed — and in the middle of the night I had the only rigor I've ever experienced — sweats, chills, shaking. We called the desk for the hotel doctor, who came to our room. When he learned we were Americans, we could see him licking his lips and thinking he was going to get a good fee in American dollars — only to watch his face fall when he looked at our documents and saw that we were covered by National Health. He asked what I had been doing, eating, etc. When I told him about going for my typhoid shot, he asked to see the card. He said, "No wonder. Instead of giving you .1cc of serum they have you 1.0cc! You are having a mild case of typhoid fever!" But he said I was not contagious and we could start our trip the next morning, for we had to meet the Kellys.

I ached from head to foot. I don't recall whether I drove or Ann did — probably she did for I was so miserable. On the way to Dover, I remember we stopped at Canterbury, for neither of us had seen it before. Despite my misery, I remember it as one of the most beautiful cathedrals in England. I don't know why it is not on all the tours. I was also eager to see it because of the Thomas à Becket history, and the YDS production of *Murder in the Cathedral*.

We crossed the channel, with our car, in fairly calm seas without even Ann getting seasick. Instead of going to Calais, we must have gone to Antwerp where the Kellys were waiting for us. They had been traveling for awhile before we got there. Lynn was recovering from her surgery for cancer, and that was ever present in our minds.

That was the beginning of two delightful weeks with the Kellys. The four of us got along beautifully. It diverted Ann and me from any of the tensions between us. It was early spring, the weather was perfect, and tourists had not arrived in numbers.

I remember I was not impressed by Brussels, but was taken by Bruges and the beginages there. Ann took some lovely pictures that were almost like Vermeer paintings. I had not really been much aware of the Begins before, a semi-monastic group of women. There were still some of them there in 1954.

We went on to Amsterdam where Bill and Lynn knew an Indonesian student who had been in Edinburgh. I could not get over the wonderful Dutch breakfasts — bread and cheese and various kinds of meat. And the bicycles! There were thousands of them on the street. There were few cars still. At a traffic light, the bicycles would be lined up all across the street, rows and rows deep. I had the feeling if we did not move quickly we could be run over like a herd of buffaloes in a Western movie. We went to the Anne Frank house, for the *Diary of Anne Frank*, had recently been published — the story of the Jewish family hidden by a Dutch family for years until the Gestapo finally found them and shipped them off to concentration camps where they perished.

I remember the Indonesian student took us to an Indonesian restaurant for supper one night. While talking about their food, he told us a real delicacy in Indonesia was baby mice, held by the tail and dipped in butter, then swallowed whole! We did not order that! Also that night as we were walking down the sidewalk, a Dutch man stopped me and said, in English, "You should not be seen walking with that black man." I remember being shocked by his racial prejudice. Obviously he thought he was being helpful, but it gave me my first insight into the Dutch treatment of the East Indies, which they lost to the Japanese during World War II and then had to grant freedom. It also helped me understand for the first time why the Dutch influence in South Africa was so rigid on race.

We loved museums in Amsterdam, especially the Vermeers and the "Dutch ugly" school. On the way out of the city, we stopped at one of the suburbs where there is a Frans Hals museum full of his works of people with pink cheeks.

From there we drove through Luxembourg, mostly to say we had been there, and then down toward Strasbourg where Al Beardslee was on a Fulbright. Just across the Rhine, in Germany, the town was being completely reconstructed and was booming.

Strasbourg, on the French side, was still in a mess. He told us the French would say, "If those Germans would just stop working so hard, we could keep up with them!"

We drove along the Maginot line that was supposed to protect France from Germany, but was made worthless when Hitler invaded Holland and Belgium and did an end run in 1940, making the Maginot irrelevant. I think we by-passed Paris, for the Kellys had been and we were going back later, but none of us had been to the chateaux country along the Loire. With a car, we were free to follow our interests and to see the ones we wanted to. I do not remember all the names, but they were fabulously beautiful and extravagant. I remember thinking that the Loire River reminded me of the Arkansas, with lots of sandbars and not very beautiful.

We drove to Chartres. We could see it, miles away, standing out above the flat plain on which it is built. When we got there, it lived up to expectations. The building was magnificent, but the stained-glass windows (which had been taken down before World War II and then put back up) blew my mind. I was struck by the fact that it, like all the cathedrals, had movable wooden chairs instead of pews so that much of the floor was vacant. What I did not notice was the labyrinth in the floor. (Years later in the 1990s, I read a book about it, and it has now become very much a part of church life here in the U.S., but no one paid it any attention in the 1950s.)

From there we went to Mont St. Michele, the island fortress-cathedral on the coast. I have written elsewhere about our ordering a picnic lunch to take with us that day from our bed-and-breakfast host, and our four college-French attempts to describe what we wanted to eat, including the "ouefs dur" which we hoped meant "hard boiled eggs" — and, fortunately turned out to be.

I guess it was at that point we left the Kellys, perhaps at Cherbourg, to catch their ship back. They were eager to get back to American doctors to follow up on her cancer surgery, and I think Bill had a job lined up. It was the last time we would see Lynn, although we did not know it. And the last time I would see Bill until 1956 when I went to the Yale School for Alcohol Studies and he was at the University of Connecticut. But we kept up with them frequently through Lynn's subsequent illnesses and death, and with Bill for years. I saw him once again in California in the 1980s. He was a great friend, as was Lynn.

From there Ann and I drove to Paris to deliver Dave's car. That was some experience driving into Paris and finding the right address. I guess we spent a few days there. Some of the Paris experiences I attributed to our spring trip might have taken place in June.

Austria-Germany in 1954

The Kellys peeled off to catch their ship home, and we delivered the car to Paris where we stayed a day or two. Before we left Scotland, we had signed up for a British bus tour of Austria and southern Germany. Neither of us had been to either country before and neither of us knew any German, so we thought it would be good to be part of a tour. When Joe Elkins learned of this, he wanted his mother — who had come to Scotland to check on him in the hospital — to go with us. We had never met her, but found her to be delightful. And she was a blessing. We had been with British people for nine months, but they were educated folk. These people, I think all English, were mostly from London — beauticians, small shop owners, bus drivers, etc. Their accents were harsh, their range of interests limited, their conversation dull. We did not find a single person on the tour who interested us, except Mrs. Elkins. And I think she felt the same way, so most of our days we were a trio.

The scenery was beautiful. We were in the Alps on July 4, and it snowed. We went to Salzburg and heard a concert there. We went to Munich and visited one of the major beer gardens. It was the only time I felt uncomfortable being in Germany. The people there, when they heard us speaking English, seemed hostile in their looks.

One of the most memorable events was when we left our bus tour to go to Oberammergau one day to visit an artist Ann's family had gotten to know after the war. It seems that after World War II Ann's father was in Little Rock one day and saw an oil painting on display in the window of Kime's frame shop. The painting caught his eye and tickled his fancy, so he went in and inquired about it. Mr. Kimes said that an American soldier had bought it when he was in Germany and had decided to sell it. He said the artist lived in Oberammergau. I don't know what the price was — a healthy one, but not exorbitant. Father brought it to Monticello and hung it in the living room, and everyone admired it. Father studied the signature and decided it was Ackermann Passig, so, typical of him, he wrote a letter to Painter Ackermann Passig, Oberammergau, Germany, wondering if it would ever reach anyone. In the letter, he explained how he had found the painting and described it in detail. In a few weeks, a letter came from the artist, who said he knew exactly which painting it was from the description. The only discrepancy in the story was that the soldier had not bought it from him but had "liberated" it. That moved Father, with his high moral standards, to send back an immediate reply saying he had no intention of keeping stolen property and wanted to pay for it. And he sent a CARE package or two. The artist replied that he would not accept money, for Mr. Williamson had bought it fairly. But he did say that he had other paintings that he would be willing to sell, if Mr. W. wanted some. Father, as a way of paying for the original, said he would like another. This led to another and another. The house on the Hill began to get full of them. Then the Lamar Williamson clan began buying them. Eventually, even they had to call it quits. But Father kept up a correspondence with Ackermann Passig.

When we were getting married, Father wrote that the wedding was coming up and that we were going to spend a year abroad. A-P said we must come to Oberammergau, because he had a wedding gift for us. We had received many beautiful wedding presents, but we did not have a single picture to put in whatever manse we finally moved to, so we were delighted to pass up whatever the tour was to cover that day. We took a small train and arrived in Oberammergau about noon. We toured the town, and while the Passion Play was not on, we were able to wander through the scenery and stage. Finally the time came for us to go to A-P's for tea. When we arrived, we found he spoke no English, nor did his wife. But soon his son came, and he spoke English fairly well. To make conversation, he asked where we had been during the year. When we said we had been in Paris, he said, "Oh, I remember being in Paris—it was beautiful. It was May 1940." I almost swallowed my cup of tea. That meant he was in the German army when it captured Paris in the blitzkrieg.

Then A-P took us into his gallery. All four walls, from floor to ceiling, were covered with his paintings, all similar in style to those in Monticello. Not knowing which one was going to be given us, we raved about each one whether we liked it or not. We went back into the living room, and A-P said, through his son, that he was so grateful to Mr. Williamson for helping him get back on his feet after the war that he wanted to give Ann a gift. Wondering which painting was to be ours (and how we were going to get it back to the States), we were jolted when he came out with a silk headscarf. He said he had designed this for the Garmish ski festival the year before, but not as many people came as were expected, so he had some left over, and he wanted to give this to Ann for her wedding gift! I hope we were able to disguise our faces! I have never felt such a letdown. Ann graciously thanked him, took off the white silk scarf she was wearing, and put on his. We said goodbye and got on the train. We didn't know whether to laugh or cry. Later that night, Ann was ready to do the latter, for the white scarf she had worn and loved somehow came out of her coat pocket on the trip back. All she had to wear the rest of the summer was the Garmish souvenir!

When we left the bus tour, we headed toward Switzerland for the Theological Students' Conference at Bossey, near Geneva.

Theological Students Conference

I don't remember how we learned about this conference, but it was while we were in Scotland, for we signed up well in advance. The World Council of Churches had a study center in Bossey, a little town on the north bank of Lake Geneva about 20 miles east of Geneva. The Bible study leader was Suzanne de Dietrich, a world-famous teacher. She had grown up as a secular Jew and had been active in the Resistance in France during World War II, although she was almost a gnome in size and posture. At one point she was locked in a boxcar left on a siding, and almost died of hunger and thirst. Somewhere along the way, she found a Bible. She had never known a Christian, and certainly had no contact with the Church except as a part of French culture. But somehow, she was converted just from reading the Bible. And what insight she did have in it! I had never met her, but knew about her reputation.

Chateau de Bossey had been the home of some wealthy person who gave it to the World Council of Churches, which had its international headquarters in Geneva. Ann and I, the first week, were given a room on the second floor that looked out over a wheat field just about ready to be harvested. Beyond that was the blue of Lake Geneva and then Mont Blanc, with its snow-covered top. It was about as beautiful a scene as I can remember. The second week we were moved out of that room, which had been reserved for one of the leaders I think, and were given one on the back. But we could not complain.

The WCC at this time was only six years old, having been officially organized in Amsterdam in 1948 (although the Faith and Order and the Life and Work sections and the International Missionary Council had been functioning prior to World War II). Invitations to this conference went out around the world. As I recall, there were 36 countries represented! I suppose there must have been 100 people, more or less. In many ways, it was the most exciting conference I have ever attended. When we would go in to the dining room and sit down at a table, we would not know in what language the conversation would be held. Often English was used by people for whom it was not the native tongue—unless the people were French. They refused to speak in any language other than French! As a result, they often got left out of gatherings. If the conversation was in German or Spanish, for instance, we were left out. I had never met anyone from some of the countries there. There was a delightful man from Haiti. He spoke French, of course, but also English. And there was another fascinating man from Madagascar. I knew nothing about that island, and he was glad to tell us about it. There must have been about a half-dozen from the U.S. One was a Missouri Synod Lutheran man who had spent a year in Sweden—but was not at all as narrow as so many Missouri Synod people are. He also had a car! There were people from West Germany, but also one or two from behind the Iron Curtain in East Germany.

Ann and me at Chateau de Bossey, Switzerland, in 1954.

The last night we were there, we had a sharing time. I shall never forget a man from the Netherlands saying it had been very difficult for him when he arrived. He said since the Germans were driven out in 1945, he had never spoken to a German, but here he had met some. At first it was hard, but it had been a real spiritual growing time, and he was able now to affirm them as Christian brothers, despite all that the Germans did to the Dutch 1940-45.

The food was also excellent—French and Swiss. I remember we had soup every day, and there would be lots of fresh parsley cut up in it. I never saw parsley used so liberally before. We could not forget Joe Elkin's quote from Ogden Nash, "Parsley is garsely!"

Not only were the meal conversations stimulating, but also Suzanne's Bible studies, the discussion groups on a variety of subjects—with different points of view held by people in the Third World, often contrasting with our assumptions. And the worship services were something I shall never forget. We sang out of *Adoramus Te*, a World Student Christian Federation hymnbook with selections from all over the globe, and the worship services came from *Venite Adoramus*. I especially loved a vesper service from the German Lutheran Church. The closing prayer began, "Abide with us, Lord, for the day is now over. Abide with us...." That book was lost in my fire, and I had not been able to find a copy of the prayer until Lamar Williamson made me one in 2009. I used it often in vesper services in Crossett and at Grace, but all those prayers were lost in the fire, too.

One day, the Missouri Synod Lutheran said he had heard me talking about Taizé. He had found out how to get there and was going to drive over on Sunday. Did I want to go? Is the Pope Catholic? I asked if Ann could go, but he said the car was already full except for one place. She agreed to let me go. It was a day I shall never forget. Taizé was the only Reformed monastery in the world. It had been founded by some Reformed (Presbyterian) French who wanted to be like the worker-priests that had sprung up in France during and after World War II. Taizé is a tiny town about five miles north of Cluny where Bernard of Clairvaux founded in 910 a monastery that really began the rebirth of the Catholic Church in the West. It became a huge monastery later. It is some miles north of Lyon. I had tried all the time I was in Scotland to find out how to get to Taizé. Everyone had heard of it, but no one knew where it was located. In this little obscure town of only 200 or 300, there was a Catholic church where there was no priest and services had not been held in years. The bishop allowed these Taizé brothers to use it for their chapel, with the reservation that mass had to be said there once a year.

The brothers supported themselves in two ways. Half the time they would go away to the working-class part of another city — often the docks of Marseilles, or to Paris; some went into the art world in Paris — anywhere out of the ordinary where the Church was almost totally absent. The ones in residence in Taizé did the housekeeping, but several of them were artists. While there, I bought some things — including two pottery jugs that I carried with me on my return, and which survived the fire and are sitting on top of my bookcase as I write this. I treasure them.

The pottery jugs I brought back from Taizé and still treasure.

Taizé has become world famous now, and there are youth camps numbering in the thousands. And they have recorded music that is used around the world. But we were there in the very early days. We worshipped with them, and while I could not understand the French well enough to comprehend the sermon, I was struck by the special way in which they chanted the psalms. They also wore monks' habits around the grounds.

At the same time, there were three Reformed nunneries for women across the border in Switzerland. I never got to visit them and don't know if they still survive. They were never as well known as Taizé.

On the way over from Bossey to Taizé, we went through some hill country. There were markers and statues from time to time noting one of the Resistance fighters who had been killed. The Dutch student said the underground had been broken by the Gestapo just about this point, but the people in the Netherlands did not know it had been broken. So they kept pouring people down it—American and British pilots who bailed out of bombers, Dutch resistance workers, etc.—right into the Gestapo hands to be tortured and killed. He had told us this before that final night when he shared the experience of associating with German brothers-in-Christ for the first time since 1945.

Being included in the Theological Students Conference was a rare treat and was the high point of our summer. Ann and I both found it to be an enlarging experience.

Geneva Waiting for Our Ship

Reservations were hard to come by on transatlantic ships, so I had made ours months in advance. I miscalculated our financial resources and our energy. We were all fired up during the Theological Students Conference in Bossey. But it ended about two and a half or three weeks before our ship was to leave. We were getting low on money, and while there were many other parts of Europe we had not seen, we were "touristed out."

We inquired at Bossey about accommodations we might get in Geneva. Someone told us about a pension run by a Mme. Psalm. Many people connected with the World Council of Churches stayed with her. Rumor had it that she was part of the underground through which people escaped from Nazi control or Allied representatives entered into Nazi country. That sounded exciting. And they said the facilities were nice and the food good. I had never been to Geneva before, and I think Ann had been only a day or two years before, so we took the train in and got our lodging.

This was a large old home that she had made into a boarding house. Such "nice" places were called "pensions" in Europe. Mme. (she was always addressed as "ma-DAM") purported to speak no English, but we had an idea she understood everything said in that language. She had an interesting collection of people who would gather around the dining table three times a day. They were from various countries and spoke a variety of languages. We could participate when they used English, but the rest of the time we could only listen—including French, at least for me. Ann was better with her French than I was with mine.

The most memorable of the residents was the man Ann and I called "The Colonel." He had a name, but I don't remember what it was. He seemed to us the epitome of what a British Colonial Servant would be. He dressed formally. He pontificated. He was intelligent, well read, and blustering. He would address Mme. Psalm in English. When she acted as though she did not understand, he would repeat himself, only louder. The next repetition would be louder still. Having lived in many parts of the world, one would think he would have picked up some other languages, but the British between the World Wars assumed that all others would speak their tongue. (Very similar to our American attitude now.) He had served in several places, but his last and I gather longest, tenure was in South Africa. I had read Alan Paton's *Cry, The Beloved Country* years before, and then I guess it was in Scotland I read *Too Late The Phalarope*, which I pronounced phala-a-ROPE. He knew the bird and told me the pronunciation was pha-LARE-o-pee. He also told us a lot about the country, although he was a defender of apartheid.

Ann and I walked to see many of the sights in Geneva such as the "jet d'eau" in Lake Geneva and the Reformers' statues. We went to worship at St. Peter's, John Calvin's church. I could not follow much of the service, but was glad I went. Then we went to the small church next door where John Knox had held services for English and Scottish exiles before he returned to Scotland. Ann wanted to go up the Salève, the rock towering above Geneva. The only way to get there was by cable car. I have always had acrophobia and pulled back, but finally agreed to accompany her. I did quite well going up, and we had a wonderful view from the top. On the way down, about halfway, there was a loud "crack," and I knew the cable had broken and we were going to be dashed to death below. But the car kept moving slowly on course. Later we learned that someone had set off a charge of dynamite underneath just as we passed over the spot. I vowed I would never take one of those again!

After we had seen everything there was to see in Geneva, Ann, who had been sick off and on all year, was sick again. Geneva was a medical center, and as a result all the doctors were specialists. So much so that instead of being simply an orthopedic surgeon, one would take only hands—and it was rumored that some were right-hand and others left-hand doctors! We did manage to find her a doctor who could speak English. She had an x-ray, and it was not anything serious.

This was the only time in my life I can remember being bored. Fortunately, the World Council of Churches offices were located within easy walking distance of our pension. We went over there, and I discovered they had a lending library! I think I would have gone crazy if it had not been for those books. One I got was Gunner Myrdal's *An American Dilemma*, his classic study on race relations. I had heard of it, and heard others talk about it, but I had never had time to plow through the tome—hundreds of pages long. Knowing that the 1954 *Brown vs. Board of Education* decision was going to make race relations very important when we returned, I read the whole thing. It was powerful.

On the *Mauritania*

After being holed up in Geneva for two and a half weeks, we went back to Paris for a day or two. After hearing "The Colonel" talk about his days as a civil servant in the British Empire, I was aware that the French empire also was crumbling. These were the days when the French were losing in Vietnam. I think Dien Biem Phu had just fallen. I observed that most of the government buildings in Paris looked "run down at the heel," and I was struck especially by the appearance of the Colonial Office. I remember that our prevailing feeling was eagerness to get on the ship and back to the United States, and on with our life.

I have already commented about my making reservations on the *Mauritania* months in advance. I chose it because we had had such a rough crossing on the *United States*, and we had heard that in rough weather it is better to be on a smaller ship, for it is hit by only one wave at a time whereas larger ships can be broadsided by two. People who had taken the *Mauritania* in the past spoke well of it. And we had to take a British ship, for my passage was being paid for by Fulbright funds—and they were credits the British owed the United States for aid and arms lent them during World War II.

Even though Fulbright paid for my ticket, we were operating on limited funds, and a sea voyage ticket was going to make a big dent. I wrote to Cunard Lines and, in my naiveté, said that I wanted "the cheapest stateroom you have!" I learned the way to ask is to inquire about the range of cabins and rates, and then make a choice. But I learned the hard way, as I often do.

We took the train from Paris to Cherbourg. When we got on the *Mauritania*, we were led to our stateroom. We went down below deck, which I expected since students always went tourist class. Then we went down another level, and I think still one more level. We found ourselves in a part of the ship where we could see the huge pistons going up and down to turn the propeller. When the steward took us *through* the crew's quarters to get to our stateroom, I began to realize my mistake. Ann had to walk through the crew's quarters to get to the ladies' restroom. It was so hot down there that we could not close the door to our stateroom — only pull a cloth cover across it.

Needless to say, we headed toward the lounge as soon as possible and stayed there most of the time during the crossing.

Somehow we had learned that John and Billie Maguire, who had been on a Fulbright in Edinburgh, had booked on the *Mauritania*, also. We had met them I guess at the reception in London at the start of the academic year and had come to know them better through Bill and Lynn Kelly. We had communicated and agreed to meet as soon as the ship pulled out.

I have no specific memory of the relationship between Ann and me on this crossing. That probably means there was no violent explosion or argument. Ann was so excited about getting home and moving on that our relationship was not her primary focus, nor was it mine, although my guess is there was some tension between us, because there usually was. The presence of the Maguires "made" that trip. The four of us got along beautifully. We were able to have fun and talk about other issues and people, and to play bridge and eat, and eat, and eat. John was headed for Yale Divinity School that fall. He was Southern Baptist, and I think had gone to Mercer, but he was one of that group of intelligent Baptists from the South who were rebelling against that denomination's restrictions. We talked a great deal about the *Brown vs. Board of Education* decision and what that would mean for the South. The weather was quite a change from our previous crossing. We hit no bad weather at all going west, even though we were in hurricane season again. Other than living in the bottom of the ship, we found the food and atmosphere of the *Mauritania* pleasant, and liked being on a small ship much better than the huge one. If I am not mistaken, I think there was only one class of passengers on the *Mauritania*. If more, we were not so conscious of the distinction as we had been on the *United States*.

The first few days, we relaxed and enjoyed the cruise. As we got closer to the U.S., I, at least, began to get restless, wanting to move on. I think the others shared the same feeling. I remember the first time the ship got AM radio from the United States. I was jolted by all the advertising! We had lived for nine months on BBC where there was no advertising. We had lived on the Third Program, with classical music and meaty discussions. Here we began to get the junk that filled American radio. This produced a negative reaction in me.

The first time we sighted land, it was the eastern tip of Long Island. Everyone ran to that side of the ship. And then there was the view coming into New York harbor. That was an exciting sight.

However, the moment we disembarked, we hit the New York police. In Britain, the police were polite and went out of their way to be helpful. The New York police seemed to take the stance that people were their "enemy." They were loud and crude. And the taxi drivers were the same! Instead of the black Rolls Royces, there were yellow cabs whose horns seemed to be stuck on "blow."

Our taxi took us directly to Grand Central Station where we got on a Pullman headed for Atlanta. We had a compartment I remember. While we were still stationary in Grand Central, Ann took off her engagement ring to wash up for the night, and in dumping the water down the drain realized the ring had gone down with it. She burst into tears and was beside herself. I remember saying that if it had gone down the drain, it would be on the track beneath us and we could retrieve it, so I called the porter immediately to report what had happened. He was quite calm. He said there was a screen in the system before the water went out. He opened it up—and there was the ring!! I was never generous about tips, but I think this porter got a big one even from me!

We went through Washington to Atlanta, for I distinctly remember Ann's taking me by Agnes Scott to meet Dr. Wallace Alston, her guru in college—first as her professor of philosophy, and then president of the college. He asked me various questions, trying to get to know me. I told him of my interest in liturgy, but said I was aware I could not force it on people, and I assumed in my first church I would wait for people to ask for changes before I made them. I shall always be grateful for his wisdom. He said, "Don, people don't ask for things they don't know exist. If you want to change the worship, just do it and let them come to love it." What a difference that made in my approach. I would have dried up while waiting.

I have no memory of how we got from Atlanta to Arkansas. We must have taken the train to Monroe, Louisiana, where the Williamsons met us. Or we could have gone from Atlanta to Memphis and then over to Little Rock. It is strange that I am blank on all that, and who met us and where.

Living While We Were Waiting

How fortunate we were, on returning from Scotland, to have two homes where we were not only welcomed, but also wanted. And how good that, unlike many newlyweds (or weds for a year but far away), we did not have to get acquainted with in-laws but had known them all our lives as cousins. However, getting to know them as in-laws and learning to use new names — such as Father instead of Cousin Adrian, Mother Catherine instead of Cousin Catherine, Main instead of Cousin Margaret, and Daddy instead of Cousin Arthur — took a little adjustment.

Another thing I began to observe when I was in Monticello was in my relationship with Father. When I was just a cousin, or even when I was a fiancé, Father would ask my opinion on some subject and give it serious consideration. The moment I became a son-in-law, he seemed to disregard my ideas — even as he had always disregarded those of his three highly intelligent children.

I have no idea how we divided the time between Scott and Monticello. We probably were at Scott more because it was nearer the Synod's office and Dr. Boggs, our links to possible calling churches. However, as we entered into conversation with Crossett, the tie was closer to Monticello.

One of our necessary jobs during those weeks was to assemble enough furniture to be able to live in a manse, wherever it was going to be. Tap Hornor came to our rescue. Aunt May Greenbaum Campbell had moved down to Little Rock after her brother died, and the Gordon Campbells took primary responsibility for her. Much of that fell on Tap, who had married Sue Campbell. He was warm and gentle (with everyone except Sue, later on), and Aunt May trusted him. I guess she had made him executor of her estate and probably gave him medical power of attorney — if such existed at that time. For years she had suffered from depression. She had gone to a nursing home — probably before our wedding. However, she had been hospitalized before for depression and had come out of it, so Tap kept her apartment at Rivercliff, with all the furnishings in it. When he learned that we were coming home and would need household goods, he came up with an idea. He doubted that Aunt May would ever get out of the nursing home, so why continue to pay rent on an apartment she could not use? And instead of storing her furnishings, why not let Ann and me "borrow" them so we could set up house? If she was discharged and went to an apartment, we would give them back, and if she didn't, we could buy them from her estate after her death. I think he even set a price — $600, which we could pay out of my part of the estate. He did give the flat silver to Alice Vineyard, but we got everything else. What a relief! We suddenly had a sofa and chairs and twin beds and dressers and a dining table, and kitchen pots and pans, and everyday dishes, and cleaning rags and old quart jars for storage and a broom and mop, etc. We even had a roll of partially used paper towels. (We had learned to keep house in Scotland where paper was very "dear" and was never wasted, so we learned to use cloth rags and towels. When we finally pulled the last paper towel off that rack, we had been in the house in Crossett for one full year!)

There were still things that we needed. We spent some of our "waiting time" shopping around and going through attics and closets. I remember one Saturday afternoon being in the attic in Monticello restoring and refinishing small lamps, etc., while we listened to the Arkansas Razorback football game. Another vivid memory was going to the storage shed behind the big house at Scott and seeing the brass samovar that Mother and Daddy had received as a wedding gift from one of Mother's college friends. Mother thought it was ugly and useless. One of the things we were missing sorely was lamps, so I had a brainstorm. If Mother would give us that samovar, we could have it electrified, find a way to hold up a shade, and make it into the major lamp in our living room. It took a bit of imagination, and convincing an electrician he could do what we wanted, and finding the right kind of shade — but we wound up with a very unusual, and we thought lovely, brass lamp. Only a few years later, imitation samovar lamps were found in all the stores, but we had never seen one at the time of our creation. We got many compliments on it. (At the time of the divorce, Ann told me she would like to have one thing from the house that came from my side of the family — that samovar lamp. I was so depressed that I agreed to that, along with all the silver and china and crystal. Every time I go to Ann's house, I see that lamp, and it brings back memories — happy ones when we were creating it, sad ones when I remember the break-up of our home. But at this point, I am glad she has it.)

We had very little money with which to buy anything, but lots of time to clean up and restore items left in the two attics. By the time we moved to Crossett, we had just about everything we absolutely needed to set up housekeeping.

We had no car, though, and a minister cannot function without a car. I think Daddy pretended he needed a new car and gave us one of their old ones. We had to use it to go interview at churches, as well as to get back and forth between Scott and Monticello, and to be mobile in both those places. Looking back on those months, I am grateful for the generosity of both sets of parents. They housed us and fed us and entertained for us. During those weeks of waiting we were living in the lap of luxury. Each home had a cook and a yardman. Both mothers invited various friends in for dinner. In Monticello we had a private tennis court and a pond stocked with fish. At Scott we had a tennis court at Land's End, a private golf course, and a lake to swim in.

I do not remember during this time any frictions between Ann and my folks — or, rather, Mother. Ann always did like Daddy. Ann had been one of Mother's favorite cousins, and she Ann's. I suppose strains had started before the wedding, and I refused to see them. I remember Ann came up for one of our wedding parties and wore a new dress. After she returned to Monticello, Mother was cleaning up the room and found the price tag for the dress. I think it was something like $400 — a huge amount in those days, and certainly not in a minister's budget. Mother told me — which she should not have done—and there was definite disapproval in her voice. I am sure Ann picked that up, but at least on the surface, there was no friction in those weeks of waiting.

We began to meet the Presbyterian ministers and wives in southeast Arkansas. They were in the habit of gathering every two or three months for dinner. Someone organized such a meeting so Ann and I could get to know all of them. Through this, I met Pete Hendrick, who was pastor at Star City, 25 miles north of Monticello. I liked him and Dot. Bill and Jane McLean were at McGehee. John and Gwen Shell were at Dermott. Jerry and Helen Newbold were at Vera Lloyd Home in Monticello. The Pete McPheeters were at Warren. John and Viola Barton were at Banks & Ingalls. George and Sally Gunn were at Arkadelphia, but I don't think they came to the supper. There was an older man at Lake Village whose wife and children seemed slightly retarded and never quite fit in. But this was the beginning of a support group that made a great difference in our lives.

One of the things we did after coming back, in between weekends when I was visiting prospective congregations, was to drive to Brownsville, Tennessee, where my YDS friend George Chauncey and Barbee were serving the Presbyterian Church. He had been there only about two years, but he was "ahead" of the congregation on liturgy, theology, and race, and was eager to get out of there. Monticello's pastor, George Faison, had just left, so I suggested George's name to Father and Jerry Newbold, and everyone else I could think of in Monticello. They visited George's church in Brownsville and decided to call him, and he accepted! What a difference that was going to make, if I indeed got the call to Crossett.

During those six or seven weeks while all this activity was going on, and even though a number of churches had shown interest in me, I began to lose my self-confidence. What if I never got a call? What would I do? It was unrealistic, for I was a "hot commodity," but I did not realize it.

One of the first things Ann did on returning to Monticello was to see Dr. John Price about her vaginitis. When she reported to him that the St. Andrews doctor had treated her by having her sit in salt baths, he roared with laughter. He gave her an antibiotic that cleared it up quickly. We both knew there were problems in our relationship, but we did not know anyone to whom we felt comfortable turning. We both concentrated on the external developments in life and pushed the communications and sex issues under the rug—or the blanket.

By all outward appearances, our marriage was going beautifully. We were both good looking, had excellent educations, and came from prominent families, and she was trained in church work as was I. When we visited churches, I think we made a good impression. My ideas on race (which she shared) were offensive in the Delta, so those doors were closed. She was as interested in the interviewing process as I, although in those days she was not privy to some of the meetings, for women were still very much "adjuncts." We made it very clear that while she had a degree from Union, New York, a church would hire *me*, not her.

Because we shared in the desire to check out churches and find the right one for us, and because we shared in trying to assemble those things necessary for setting up housekeeping, we were very much on the same wavelength on most points.

Epilogue: The Shifting of Gears

In September 1954, upon arriving back in Arkansas after my year on a Fulbright Scholarship in Scotland and then travel on the Continent for the summer, I had completed a major phase of my life—formal academic training for my professional career and a year of adjustment into marriage. In many ways 1953-54 was an extended honeymoon, for we were living as students under circumstances that we knew were going to be temporary. The years covered in this volume, from junior high school through high school, college, theological seminary, marriage, and graduate school were a time of tremendous change and growth. I have entitled this volume "Formation" because intellectually, emotionally, socially, and spiritually I went through a metamorphosis.

The time had come for me to move on into responsible adulthood. In terms of my profession, if my call was to be the minister of a Presbyterian church, I needed to have that confirmed by a specific congregation prepared to entrust their corporate life, and their individual spiritual lives, to my leadership as their pastor. In terms of our marriage, Ann and I could no longer "play like" we were a couple. The time had come for us in the "real world" to found a home for ourselves and, eventually we hoped, for our children.

The preceding pages have told you the many, and sometimes wandering, steps I took in preparing for the first of these assignments. I was blessed in having some outstanding teachers and mentors to help me on the way. I had been to excellent schools and had studied hard. My spiritual life had come a long way, although I was well aware that I had just started my pilgrimage. I was young—26 years old when I came back from Scotland—inexperienced, green as grass, but filled with enthusiasm.

I was far less well equipped to be a husband or father. I was a "late bloomer" in my romantic relationship with women. Ann was the only person I had ever dated seriously. We were great friends and could converse endlessly on topics of mutual interest. I loved her. Was I "in love" with her? I did not know what the term meant. The only pattern for marriage I'd observed closely was my parents. It was obvious they loved each other, but they were not demonstrative. I had never seen them clash and work through to reconciliation. So when Ann and I had had our verbal conflicts during that first year, I wondered if our marriage could survive. Yet we had made a commitment, and I was determined to keep it, and I believe she was, too.

If I ever publish a third volume of my memoirs, it will relate two stories. The first will be of the parish half of my ordained ministry, as pastor of two churches — the Presbyterian Church of Crossett, Arkansas, and Grace Presbyterian Church of Little Rock, Arkansas. That will cover the years 1954-1973. The second story will be of my role as a husband and father. The husband section will give an account, from my point of view, of our marriage 1954-1973 when it ended in divorce. The father portion will tell of my experiences from 1957 (when Donald was born), through the arrival and growth of Sarah and Malcolm, and end in 1973 when the divorce brought about a dramatic shift in the ways I related to them.

If there ever is a fourth volume, it will tell of my non-parish ministries: in Atlanta as a member of the national staff of the Presbyterian Church, U.S.; as General Pastor of the Presbytery of South Louisiana operating out of Baton Rouge; and as Dean of the Oasis Renewal Center in Little Rock, Arkansas. This would cover the years 1973-1995. It would also tell of my relationship with my three children as a single-and-absentee father through their childhood, adolescence, college, and graduate school years, marriages, and the birth of two of my six grandchildren. It would also tell of my relationship with Marnie Smith.

I do not know that I'll ever complete volumes three and four, and even a fifth volume about my retirement years. But I have wanted you grandchildren to know something about the early years of my life. I have had limited influence on you, but part of each of you comes from me. When you begin to ponder who you are, how you got there, and what you want to do with the remainder of your life, I hope you may find some help in reading this account of the path one of your grandparents followed.

www.ingramcontent.com/pod-product-compliance
Lightning Source LLC
Chambersburg PA
CBHW021912180426
43198CB00034B/128